THE *Crucible*

THE *Crucible*
An Autobiography by Colonel Yay, Filipina American Guerrilla

Yay Panlilio

EDITED BY
Denise Cruz

RUTGERS UNIVERSITY PRESS
NEW BRUNSWICK, NEW JERSEY, AND LONDON

Library of Congress Cataloging-in-Publication Data

Panlilio, Yay, 1913–1978.
    The crucible : an autobiography by Colonel Yay, Filipina American guerrilla / Yay Panlilio ; edited by Denise Cruz.
        p. cm.
    Originally published: New York : Macmillan, 1950, under title The crucible : an autobiography by "Colonel Yay."
    ISBN 978-0-8135-4681-0 (hardcover : alk. paper) — ISBN 978-0-8135-4682-7 (pbk. : alk. paper)
    1. Panlilio, Yay, 1913–1978. 2. World War, 1939–1945—Underground movements—Philippines.
    3. Women guerrillas—Philippines—Biography. 4. Women journalists—Philippines—Biography.
    5. World War, 1939–1945—Personal narratives, Filipino American. 6. World War, 1939–1945—Participation, Female. 7. Filipino Americans—Biography. 8. Irish Americans—Biography. I. Title.
    D802.P5P36 2010
    940.53′599092—dc22
    [B]

2009008507

A British Cataloging-in-Publication record for this book is available from the British Library.

The Crucible: An Autobiography was first published by The Macmillan Company in 1950.

Introduction and scholarly apparatus to this edition copyright © 2010 by Denise Cruz

All rights reserved
No part of this book may be reproduced or utilized in any form or by any means, electronic or mechanical, or by any information storage and retrieval system, without written permission from the publisher. Please contact Rutgers University Press, 100 Joyce Kilmer Avenue, Piscataway, NJ 08854-8099. The only exception to this prohibition is "fair use" as defined by U.S. copyright law.

Text design by Adam B. Bohannon
Visit our Web site: http://rutgerspress.rutgers.edu
Manufactured in the United States of America

Frontispiece: Mrs. Yay Panlilio with children—Edward 9, Curtis 3, and Rae 12. All were with the guerrillas in the Philippines. Courtesy of the Department of Special Collections, Charles E. Young Research Library, UCLA.

CONTENTS

Acknowledgments vii
Introduction ix
A Note on the Text xxix

The Crucible: An Autobiography by Colonel Yay 1

Timeline 317
Glossary 319

ACKNOWLEDGMENTS

Producing this edition of Yay Panlilio's *The Crucible* has been an unforgettable experience. I gratefully acknowledge King-Kok Cheung and Richard Yarborough, whose advice and mentorship guided me through the early stages of this project; Candice Williams, who provided invaluable research assistance; Chris Cotoco, Nilo Cruz, and Nerissa Balce, who assisted with the finer points of Tagalog translation; Karen Inouye and the anonymous reader for Rutgers University Press, who offered insightful suggestions on the introduction; Kat Larson, who created an original artpiece to grace the cover; Waldette Cueto and the staff of the American Historical Collection at Ateneo de Manila University; Simon Elliott and the Department of Special Collections, Charles E. Young Research Library at the University of California, Los Angeles; Richard Kunst and the Humanities Computing Library, for facilitating the scan of the original text; Alison Hack, Carol Bifulco, Jan Bernabe, Muni Cruz, Jordan Blackman, and Sherry Blackman for support during the project's early and final stages; and Yay Panlilio's grandson, Curtis, who shared his memories of his grandmother. Funding to support this project was generously provided by the College Arts and Humanities Institute at Indiana University, Bloomington. Special thanks and recognition must go to my editor, Leslie Mitchner, who saw potential in *The Crucible* and provided the encouragement and guidance that made its republication possible.

INTRODUCTION

On December 8, 1941, Yay Panlilio found her life suddenly and irrevocably changed by the bombing of Pearl Harbor.[1] Panlilio, a *mestiza* Filipina-Irish American woman, had moved from the United States to the Philippines and quickly ensconced herself in the capital city, Manila, as one of its most intrepid journalists.[2] When reports of Pearl Harbor reached Manila, Panlilio was one of a few envoys selected to relay grim news to President Manuel Quezon. The war was on its way to Philippine shores. In a matter of days, she would see her beloved newspaper, the *Philippines Herald*, razed to the ground, American and Filipino troops deployed to Bataan and Corregidor in the north to defend the islands, and Manila in turmoil. Panlilio surveyed the growing chaos surrounding her and thought furiously: how would she, a Filipina American, contribute to the war?

That question would have a complicated answer. Panlilio's response is the subject of her 1950 memoir, *The Crucible: An Autobiography by Colonel Yay*, originally published in the United States. The book narrates her incredible experience as a journalist, triple agent, leader in the Philippine resistance against the Japanese, and lover of the guerrilla general Marcos V. Agustín. Panlilio's sweeping focus moves from the war-torn streets of Japanese-occupied Manila, to battlegrounds in the Philippine countryside, to the rural farmlands of central California. Written in a style that blends wry commentary, rigorous journalistic detail, and popular romance conventions, *The Crucible* weaves together appearances by well-known military figures like Douglas MacArthur and Carlos Romulo, dangerous networks of espionage, and a tumultuous romantic relationship that recalls the plots of Hollywood war films, or at least, as Panlilio's good friend and fellow writer, Lydia Arguilla noted, "a pulp-magazine love story" (chapter 35).

For Yay Panlilio, however, *The Crucible* was meant to be much more than a good story, and certainly more than a mere account of her life experiences during the war. Rather, she saw the book as a necessary act of political redress and retribution. Ever the consummate journalist, Panlilio published *The Crucible* with clear objectives: to publicize the important yet unrecognized contributions of the guerrilla resistance in the war against Japan, to recognize the role of Filipinas in wartime efforts, and to articulate a nationalist formation of *mestiza* Filipina identity. The book is a complicated and often vexed attempt to champion Philippine independence and Filipina American feminism. To appeal to a U.S. audience, Panlilio uses organizing metaphors of motherhood and domesticity (what she calls "guerrilla motherhood"), emphasizes her dual Filipina and American heritage as the biological foundation of her ability to represent both countries, and fosters a potential sisterhood that includes U.S. readers.

But unfortunately, *The Crucible* failed to significantly influence how Americans or Filipina/os remember World War II.[3] Despite the many war-era books that mention Panlilio with admiration and respect, her name is now relatively unknown. Today, few Americans are aware of the guerrilla resistance in the Philippines, and fewer still know the details of Filipinas' involvement. And although Macmillan's 1950 release of *The Crucible*, one of the first Filipina-authored works of literature published by a U.S. press, was a landmark in literary history, the book was never recognized or studied by scholars of Filipina/o or Asian American literature.[4]

More than fifty years after its original publication, we return to *The Crucible* with renewed attention to Panlilio's original goals and their contemporary ramifications. For today's readers, *The Crucible* serves as a reminder of the complicated and interconnected histories of the Philippines, the United States, and Japan. As a rare example of Filipina American authorship in the mid-twentieth century, the book invites new intersections in studies of Filipina/o, Asian American, and American literature. As a memoir that details a *mestiza* woman's role as a guerrilla, the text diversifies our knowledge of resistance in the Pacific War and explores the complexities of mixed-race and transnational identity. And as a document of how the war affected and still continues to affect the lives of Filipinas and Filipinos, *The Crucible* is a call to reconsider how we tell the story of World War II.

Intersections: Yay Panlilio and Filipina/o American History

Yay Panlilio (1913–1978) was born in Denver, Colorado, to a Filipina mother and an Irish father. She grew up in Colorado in a working-class family that included her mother, her stepfather, and her half-brother, Raymond. According to Panlilio, her mother was a stowaway and one of the first Filipinas to enter the United States. In installments of "Where a Country Begins," a post–World War II column that she wrote for the *Weekly Women's Magazine* in Manila, Panlilio remembers her tempestuous relationship with her mother, who, aware that she herself would never again set foot on Philippine soil, persistently encouraged her daughter to return.[5] Initially, Panlilio rebelled against this maternal mandate, until the two found common ground in Panlilio's desire to become a writer. In the essay, "My Filipino Mother," she recounts the pivotal day her mother surprised her with a typewriter. For young Panlilio, the gift represented her mother's long-awaited acknowledgment of her talents and sparked her curiosity about the Philippines.

While Panlilio's writings about her childhood and her life immediately after the war are quite forthcoming, her days in Manila are relatively undocumented. What we do know may be pieced together from her columns and newspaper articles, the work of other writers, and the small details she tells us in *The Crucible*. She left the United States when she was in her teens. During the 1930s, she strove to accomplish her dream of becoming a journalist. In "Where a Country Begins," she recalls her early newspaper days as filled with long hours of anxious excitement. These pieces reflect her memories of the profession and the obstacles she faced—both as a woman in a field dominated by men and as someone who was not born in the Philippines. On the staff of Manila-based newspapers, and later, as a broadcaster for the radio station KZRH, she established a reputation for the personality traits that are recurring features of *The Crucible*; she was headstrong, feisty, and fiercely intelligent. In *Orphans of the Pacific,* the American writer Florence Horn described the familiar sight of Panlilio scouring the streets of Manila in her trademark white sharkskin suit, always in search of a good story.[6] Doris Rubens, who also broadcast at KZRH, remembered her colleague as "well known in Manila as a tough fighter for the underdog."[7] Panlilio quickly rose in the ranks as a photographer and reporter, in part through the sponsorship of her editor Carlos P. Romulo (who would eventually become a war hero, U.S. diplomat, and Philippine political figure). She also joined a prominent circle of Filipina, English-language writers, and this close community of women offered valuable support, a model for the network that she would later highlight in *The Crucible*.

Though the text of *The Crucible* encompasses only a few years of Panlilio's life, the book must be read in the broader context of shifts in U.S. and Philippine relations throughout the first half of the twentieth century. Panlilio's emphasis on Philippine nationalism and independence is a response not just to the Japanese regime in the Philippines

(1942–1945), but also to the Philippines' longer struggle for independence from the United States. In the late nineteenth century, the United States began rapidly expanding its territorial borders. As part of the treaty terms that ended the Spanish American War, in December 1898, the United States acquired the Philippines from Spain in exchange for twenty million dollars. In part because of racist perceptions that cast the people in the Philippines as uncivilized and in need of democratic tutelage, the U.S. government designated the Philippines as an unincorporated territory, ultimately ineligible for statehood. The Philippine-American War (now relatively unknown to most Americans) began soon after, and despite President Theodore Roosevelt's 1902 proclamation that the war had ended, resistance movements continued for over a decade.

By the time Panlilio returned to the Philippines to begin her career as a journalist, Filipina/os had been asking for their independence for more than twenty years. Competing interests in the United States complicated debates about when and how to emancipate the Filipina/os. On one hand, U.S. foreign policymakers saw the Philippines as a strategic military and trading location between the United States and the rest of Asia. On the other hand, the desire to retain the Philippines was questioned by American anti-imperialists, and later, anti-Filipino labor and anti-immigration advocates (especially on the West Coast, where tensions were high because of the large numbers of Filipino migrants). In 1934, the two governments finally reached a compromise. In exchange for substantial limitations on Filipina/o immigration, the Tydings–McDuffie Act granted the Philippines commonwealth status for ten years as a transition to an eventual republic. The interim period was interrupted by the outbreak of the war in the Pacific and the Japanese occupation of the Philippines, and the United States formally recognized the Philippines as a republic in 1946, almost fifty years after the Spanish American War.[8]

Because the Philippines was officially designated an unincorporated territory, for much of the early twentieth century, the status of Filipina/os within the United States was ambiguous. While Japanese, Chinese, Korean, and Indian people were subject to multiple exclusion laws and immigration restrictions, as U.S. nationals, Filipinos and Filipinas could travel and migrate to the United States, even though they were ultimately ineligible for citizenship. Nevertheless, until the 1920s, the number of Filipina/os in the country was quite small, consisting primarily of students studying at universities or government diplomats, officials, and representatives.

In the usual context of Filipina/o experience in the United States, Panlilio's story is rather unique. Her mother's arrival took place years before a sharp spike in Filipina/o immigration. In the 1920s, the number of immigrants dramatically swelled, as agricultural industries began recruiting Filipino men as laborers. The growing presence of Filipinos was controversial and eventually incited alarm in Western states such as California and Washington. In these states, Filipino men often lived in bachelor communities, which soon became sites of race-based tensions. The increasingly volatile situation reached its peak in the late 1920s, when anti-Filipino sentiments led to eruptions of violence. In a desperate response, in 1935, the U.S. Congress passed the Repatriation Act, which offered to finance the expenses of Filipina/os' return to the Philippines. This endeavor was largely unsuccessful, but the legislation, along with the passage of Tydings–McDuffie's limits on Filipina/o immigrants, signal the extent to which Filipina/os had become an unwelcome presence. During World War II, Congress repealed many of the exclusion acts, but a large resurgence of Filipinos and Filipinas entering the United States would not be seen again until a new immigration pattern arose after 1965, the year in which the Immigration and Naturalization Act revised the national quota system and inaugurated what many see as a key shift in immigration.[9]

Because of these dynamics of immigration, Filipino and Filipina Americans in the United States today can trace their family lineage to whether or not their parents were part of a generation migrating to the country in the first or second halves of the twentieth century. The population of the earlier generation is aging, and the documentation of these men's and women's lives has thus become even more pressing. Materials authored by and about Filipina women are especially scarce. Scholarly and publishing efforts in the past decade or so have resulted in the publication of memoirs that account for the lives of men and women who migrated to or were born in the United States in the early twentieth century. Adding to known texts published in the 1940s, such as Carlos Bulosan's *America Is in the Heart* (1943) or Manuel Buaken's *I Have Lived with the American People* (1948), the recent publication of memoirs such as Peter Jamero's *Growing Up Brown* (2006), Evangeline Canonizada Buell's *Twenty-Five Chickens and a Pig for a Bride* (2006), and Pati Navalta Poblete's *The Oracles: My Filipino Grandparents in America* (2006) as well as Angeles Monrayo's diary, *Tomorrow's Memories* (2003) provides much-needed glimpses into the historical roots of the Filipina/o American community, which is today one of the largest ethnic groups in the United States. *The Crucible*, along with Buell's memoir and Patricia Justiniana McReynolds's *Almost Americans* (1997), also answers a growing interest in the experiences of mixed-race Filipina/o Americans.[10]

What, then, makes *The Crucible* different from these other works? Even among such an important resurgence of texts, Panlilio's memoir is notable because of the book's original, mid-century publication, its direct engagement of a Filipina's unique experience during World War II, and its predominantly Philippine-based setting. In *The Crucible*, Panlilio remembers her life as a complicated negotiation of multinational relations among the Philippines, the United States, and Japan. This subject matter complements that of many of the above-mentioned memoirs, which center on migration from the Philippines to the United States. Instead of articulating the challenges of building an American life, *The Crucible* asks U.S. readers to adjust their perspectives, to move from the predominant framework through which we understand Asian American experience—one that would begin with movement from Asia to the United States—to a story that also addresses Filipina American experience abroad.

The Pacific Theater: Shifting Stages of Philippine, U.S., and Japanese Relations

The Pacific War completely altered relations among the Philippines, the United States, and Japan. Panlilio's text is a product of this changing climate, and reading *The Crucible* today thus demands knowledge of key events in the Pacific theater. As part of a surprise offensive against the United States that included the attack on Pearl Harbor in 1941, Japanese bombers flew to the Philippines and destroyed much of the U.S. Air Force stationed at Clark Field. The Philippines and the United States quickly espoused an official position of unity, which was fueled further by dual military efforts against Japanese forces. On December 23, U.S. and Filipino troops left Manila for the military strongholds at Bataan and Corregidor. Japanese bombers attacked Manila for multiple days in late December and entered the city on January 2, 1942. In March, in a move that shocked Filipina/os and Americans alike, General Douglas MacArthur departed for a command post in Australia and vowed to return to the Philippines.

After suffering tremendous losses in Bataan, on April 9, 1942, U.S. and Filipino soldiers surrendered to the Japanese and were marched from the Bataan province to the Japanese military prison at Camp

O'Donnell. Conditions were grueling. The Japanese military was unprepared for the number of prisoners; wounded and exhausted Filipinos and Americans traveled in the intense heat, and many, suffering from ill conditions and abuse by Japanese soldiers, did not survive. Although the exact number of victims remains unknown, estimates of deaths range from the hundreds for Americans to the high thousands for Filipinos. After such debilitating losses, on May 6, General Jonathan Wainwright surrendered at Corregidor.[11] The withdrawal and defeat of U.S. forces was surprising to many in the Philippines. In Manila and throughout the country, Japanese troops rounded up American citizens and interned them at locations like the University of Santo Tomas, where they would remain for the duration of the Japanese occupation.

The Japanese regime moved quickly to break the Philippines' ties to the United States. Almost immediately after they entered Manila, Japanese officials initiated a large-scale distribution of propaganda. Circulated primarily through closely monitored and censored newspapers and radio programs, Japanese materials congratulated Filipina/os on their liberation from Western tyranny and promoted the Philippines' new membership in the Greater East Asia Co-Prosperity Sphere, the community of nations that represented the Empire of Japan's vision of Asian independence from Western domination and oppression. Former Philippine political parties were disbanded. The contents of national libraries were examined, and many materials were burned. Schools were reopened with an education program that diminished Western contributions to the Philippines, and textbooks were purged of references to British or U.S. influences.[12]

Even in this restrictive climate, large- and small-scale resistance movements in the Philippines were persistent and widespread. With MacArthur in Australia, guerrilla forces, which had already been active against the Japanese, continued the battle. Scattered throughout the islands, these troops included Filipinos, Americans, and other foreign nationals. At first, most worked in isolation, but as the war continued, guerrilla units began to consolidate. Some even affiliated (or claimed affiliation) with the United States Forces of the Far East (USAFFE). To encourage guerrilla involvement, the U.S. military promised many guerrillas back pay as soon as the war ended.

The guerrilla resistance was marked by the extraordinary achievements of many who had never had prior military service records. Yay Panlilio's lover, Marcos "Marking" Agustín, was a former bus driver and boxer, yet he led one of the most successful guerrilla outfits in the

Philippines. Panlilio's contributions to the operation soon became even more celebrated than Marking's accomplishments. Her name is mentioned in World War II publications ranging from Carlos Romulo's *I See the Philippines Rise* (1946) to Doris Rubens Johnston's memoir *Bread and Rice* (1947), and her expertise prompted filmmakers to ask for her guidance in the filming of *Merrill's Marauders* (1962).[13] In these works, admirers refer to Panlilio as a key figure in the resistance and as the master strategist behind the outfit's exploits; they frequently emphasize her leadership as truly remarkable, not only because women were not usually commanding officers, but also because of her brilliant military strategies and her ability to inspire her troops.

Across the Pacific, the American and Filipina/o experience of tragedy at the hands of the Japanese began to alter public perceptions of the Philippines and Filipina/os. At first, news from the Pacific filtered into the country in bits and pieces. For many Americans, the Philippines, unlike the battlegrounds in Europe, seemed far away and unfamiliar. To alleviate American fears, the War Department employed Filipina/o nationals in the United States, who toured the country and gave lectures to audiences who were increasingly worried about the fate of troops deployed to the Pacific.[14] In U.S. media representations, Bataan and what became known as the "Bataan death march" were focal points. Quite quickly, the joint experience of war galvanized American public opinion in solidarity with the Philippines, which was soon reflected in newspaper articles, films like John Wayne's *Back to Bataan* (1945), and literary texts.[15] These works represented the new relationship in metaphors of brotherhood and pointed repeatedly to the joint suffering of U.S. and Filipino soldiers in Bataan, a region of the Philippines that, hitherto unknown to many American citizens, soon became a byword.

The glorification of the Bataan brotherhood reflected a desire to recognize the extraordinary bravery of Filipino and U.S. servicemen and to mourn devastating losses in the Pacific. At the same time, though, the rhetoric of the Bataan brotherhood has some troubling ramifications for narratives of U.S. and Philippine history. Indeed, the metaphor of brotherhood refigures another familial trope that was crucial to the justification of the occupation of the Philippines. At the turn of the twentieth century, pro-imperialist rhetoric depended upon terms that were both infantilizing and fraternalizing; future president and Philippine commissioner William Taft described the Filipina/o people as "little brown brothers" who needed American guidance and tutelage.

I underscore some of the potential complications with the Bataan brotherhood not to diminish the extraordinary feats of those who survived or their suffering. Nor do I wish to claim that the coinage of this metaphor was a deliberate recalling of imperialist rhetoric. Nevertheless, these representational strategies have had, and continue to have, contemporary repercussions. To this day, the emotional memory of Philippine and U.S. brotherhood, crafted in the war, shapes the discourse of U.S.-Philippine relations. The image of MacArthur triumphantly returning to the Philippines and making good on his promise of "I shall return" has lingered, and the tendency to view the two nations as jointly united in terms of a special relationship continually resurfaces. In recent years, the language of familial and friendly terms between the countries has resurged with Philippine President Gloria Macapagal Arroyo's pledge of support for the Bush administration's "war on terror." In a 2006 state visit to the Philippines, President George W. Bush stood with President Arroyo and proudly commemorated the anniversary of the U.S. liberation of a country held as a territory for almost half a century. This longstanding and complicated relationship between the United States and the Philippines informs the representational strategies that Panlilio uses to appeal to her American readers and how we might respond to them today.

Recognition and Retribution: *The Crucible*'s **Appeal**

The Crucible was published in a postwar market that was saturated with works recounting the varied experiences of Americans in the Pacific War. Written testimonies included those of Bataan survivors; USAFFE military officers; white American, Canadian, and European guerrillas and intelligence agents; U.S. military nurses; and civilian internees. Panlilio's contribution complemented a relatively small number of U.S.-published texts from the Filipina/o perspective, such as those authored by her former editor Romulo.[16] She clearly addresses *The Crucible* to an American readership, and the text details her wartime experience from a perspective that mediates between this audience and herself, as a representative from the Philippines. In approaching *The Crucible*, readers should keep in mind the instructive suggestion offered by American journalist Kate Holliday in the original introduction: Panlilio, who "has underplayed herself in every page of what you are about to read," should never be underestimated.

The Crucible's call to recognize alternate forms of Filipina and Filipino resistance has contemporary ramifications for two forgotten narratives of World War II history: Filipino war veterans and Filipina comfort women. By the time Panlilio published her memoir, the role of guerrillas, and, to a larger extent, Filipina/os in the war, was already fading from American memories. Indeed, the vision of an idealized, happy brotherhood between the two countries fails to incorporate the embittered experience of Filipino war veterans, who have long struggled for recognition of their efforts.[17] The unresolved issue of Filipino veterans' rights underscores the importance of reading *The Crucible* today. On July 26, 1941, President Franklin Delano Roosevelt called over a hundred thousand Filipinos who were enlisted in the commonwealth army to duty. As the war progressed, the United States authorized the recruitment of Filipinos for military service in the United States Armed Forces of the Far East.[18] In return, the administration promised Filipinos the same benefits accorded to other U.S. veterans. But soon after the war ended, Congress determined that, because the Philippines was now independent of the United States, the Philippine government should be responsible for veterans' benefits. In 1946, rescission acts repealed equal benefits for Filipino veterans, drastically cutting death and disability payments and stipends. For many Filipinos who served proudly in the war effort, these acts of legislation were unexpected and extremely hurtful.

Requests for guerrilla recognition further complicated the debate. In the days of the war, the United States had offered backpay and benefits to guerrilla resistance units. Postwar procedures for guerrilla recognition were long, complex, and difficult, and they were hampered by political motivation on the part of both Philippine and U.S. administrations overseeing the process and individuals who took advantage of opportunities to receive backpay. Although Marking and Panlilio's regiment was one of those recognized, not all guerrilla outfits shared this outcome. The most infamous exclusion was the communist-affiliated *Hukbalahap* guerrillas, an organization that advocated for laborers' rights and against capitalist interests, which remained active even after the formation of the Philippine republic.[19]

The movement to restore Filipino veterans' rights gained national media attention in 1998, when about a dozen Filipino veterans staged a hunger strike in Los Angeles, chained themselves to a statue of General MacArthur, and eventually had to be hospitalized. Congress passed legislation expanding veterans' benefits in 1973, 2000, and 2003, but even in 2009, Filipino veterans' struggles continued, with Congress still debating the terms of compensation (how much money and who is eligible) over sixty years after the rescission acts repealed them. In February 2009, payments to Filipino veterans were incorporated into the economic stimulus plan passed by Congress and President Barack Obama's administration. About 18,000 of the remaining veterans will receive lump sum payments of $15,000 for citizens and $9,000 for noncitizens, a fraction of the amount originally promised. The question of Filipino veterans' reform was interwoven with troubled relations between the U.S. military and the Philippine government. Military base agreements between the two nations, for example, provided for U.S. supervision and leasing of lands for bases in the islands well after the Philippine republic was inaugurated. These complexities of U.S.-Philippine military relations extended to recent controversies in the veterans' benefits debate, which often pitted the rights of Filipinos against those recently returning from service in Iraq and Afghanistan.[20]

The Filipino veterans' campaign for recognition and retribution parallels the unfortunate experiences of the Japanese military regime's so-called comfort women. In both the United States and the Philippines, civilians were well aware of the Japanese military's brutality in China (such as in the much publicized "Rape of Nanking"). Rumors of the likely tragic fate of women in the Pacific abounded, and were fanned by media coverage that alluded to the horrific violations perpetrated by Japanese military forces. Carlos Romulo expresses this fear when he asks in a 1944 *New York Times* article, "And the women? No one dares ask. He is afraid always, to think what is happening to the Filipino women."[21] Such anxieties and fears were not unfounded; many women were raped by Japanese soldiers, who reportedly focused much of their attention on Filipina civilians. These individual cases of violence were part of a systematic exploitation of women by the Japanese military. Throughout Asia, the Japanese regime forced women into sexual slavery in so-called comfort stations. But after the war ended, many victims remained silent, fearful of public exposure to their families and communities. Although rumors of sexual slavery may have abounded during the war, the specifics of what actually happened to women—in both the disturbing extent of this practice and details of the victims' harrowing experiences—truly only began surfacing in the early 1990s, as growing activist movements encouraged Korean, Chinese, Filipina, and other victims to testify and mobilize for recognition and reparations from the Japanese government. In 1992, Filipina comfort woman Maria Rosa Henson began speaking publicly and eventually published her autobiography, *Comfort Woman: A Filipina's Story of Prostitution and Slavery Under the Japanese Military*. Despite international recognition of the cause of comfort women, the Japanese government has yet to answer calls for a formal apology and compensation.[22]

Panlilio's memoir does not explicitly respond to the troubling lack of response to World War II comfort women, but *The Crucible* is interested in significantly complicating the representation of women—and especially Filipinas—in the war. When the book was first published, U.S. public discourse had valorized the exploits of white American military nurses stationed in the Philippines, whose courage was met with much acclaim. These women, many of whom later became known as Bataan's "Angels," were deployed with American forces to Corregidor and Bataan; most were evacuated before the surrender.[23] In the past ten years, as part of a larger effort to rethink emphasis on men's achievements and experiences in research on the Pacific War, several book-length studies have called for attention to these women. Yet although Filipina Red Cross nurses were also stationed in Bataan and Corregidor, even contemporaneous published diaries authored by nurses and more recently published histories only briefly mention the service of Filipina women.[24]

In addition to the more circulated narratives of white American nurses, the publication of memoirs by white American, Canadian, and European women also documented a spectrum of wartime experiences that ranged from the amazing to the quotidian. Like Panlilio's *The Crucible*, some of these books sought to publicize the contributions of women who were spies. Panlilio was part of a larger espionage circle that included Margaret "Miss U" Utinsky and Claire "High Pockets" Phillips, whose memoirs were also published after the war. Other works, such as Johnston's *Bread and Rice* and Louise Spencer's *Guerrilla Wife* (1945), followed the lives of women in internment camps or wives whose husbands were fighting in the resistance.[25] Many of these texts present detailed accounts of domestic life, in which even the everyday task of keeping house becomes extraordinary and difficult in the context of war. Spencer's *Guerrilla Wife*, for example, delineates a version of guerrilla wifehood starkly different from that of Panlilio's; much of Spencer's memoir describes waiting faithfully for her husband and hoping for his return.

Panlilio thus emphasizes her unique experience as a Filipina guerrilla to counter a version of World War II history in which the experiences of women and Filipina/os have been marginalized. Ever the rhetorical strategist, she appeals to her American readers in multiple ways. She stresses her dual Filipina and American heritage as both the biological and cultural foundation of her ability to compel her audience to recognize the contributions of Filipino and Filipina guerrillas. The book highlights the importance of women who were significantly involved in the war effort, in spite of the overwhelmingly male organizational and power structures of the U.S. military, Philippine journalism, and the guerrilla resistance. This emphasis extends beyond Panlilio's representation of herself as the "brains" behind Marking's operation, and her recognition of other Filipina guerrillas, to other women who supported the resistance with funding, supplies, and letter-writing campaigns. Similar to the sentimental appeals of nineteenth-century texts authored by white and African American women, Panlilio's narrative strategies promote a sisterhood, engaging a sympathetic response and emotional affiliation with her cause.

A dominant strand of the main text's fabric is the recurring emphasis on racial and cultural mixture as the foundation for Panlilio's U.S. and Philippine patriotism. Holliday's original introduction to *The Crucible* picks up this thread and heralds Panlilio as an apt and ideal representative precisely because she is biracial and a U.S. citizen. For Holliday, both *The Crucible* and the *mestiza* body of its author had the potential to unite the two nations. *The Crucible*'s description of the benefits of racial mixture must be read in both U.S. and Philippine contexts. For much of the early twentieth century in the United States, intimate relations between Filipinos and white American women were sources of much controversy, especially on the West Coast.[26] Until the California Supreme Court ruled otherwise in 1948, state laws prohibited marriage between Asians and white Americans. Because Filipina/os' racial classification was somewhat uncertain, legislation was eventually introduced to specifically prohibit interracial marriage between Filipina/os and whites. Nationwide, antimiscegenation laws prevailed until the 1967 *Loving v. Virginia* Supreme Court ruling. Panlilio's biracial heritage as Irish and Filipina would have presented added complications; in the 1950s, Irish, which was not synonymous with "white," would have signaled significant ethnic, religious, and class differences from other European Americans. The tensions surrounding racial mixture in the United States are complicated further by definitions of ethnic and racial difference in the Philippines. In part because of a long history of multiple colonizations, many people in the Philippines have *mestiza/o* heritage. Nevertheless, as Panlilio herself explains, in the Philippines, a hierarchical structure (or, as she puts it, "There are *mestizos*, and there are *mestizos*") categorizes mixed-race Filipina/os. Those who can trace heritage to a Spanish ruling class still take pride in their aristocratic bloodlines and are viewed far differently than the children of Americans, especially in locations with proximity to military bases. Horn's *Orphans of the Pacific* thus describes Panlilio as doubly out of place in Manila circles—for her flouting of gendered restrictions and her mixed-race identity.[27]

Despite the anxieties surrounding mixed-race bodies in the United States and the Philippines, Panlilio takes care to highlight racial mixture as ultimately beneficial to her formation of a combined Philippine and American nationalism. In *The Crucible*, these valences of Panlilio's *mestiza* identity provide for high drama, as she clashes with Marking because of her American sensibilities, which she characterizes in terms of blood and biology. For a contemporary reading audience familiar with the debunking of biological notions of race (the idea that certain race-based personality traits are the product of genetics), Panlilio's frequent use of such essentialist claims in her discussion of Filipina and American sensibilities may seem surprising. But for Panlilio, racial mixture is a true benefit, one that allows for the best possible combination of national, inherited traits.

Panlilio always underscores her American heritage as the source of her commitment to principles of democracy and fairness, and the premise for her staunch belief that women are equal to men, even in spaces of war and combat. Without an awareness of the long history of debates surrounding Philippine independence, readers might easily assess this book as uncomplicated in its positive representation of the United States. It is important to read the text carefully, for while its pro-American sensibilities are more readily apparent, the book as a whole also consistently champions an independent Philippine republic. Even when registering her frustrations with the U.S. military, Panlilio's stance is one of unflinching faith in the eventual return of MacArthur and the Americans. In *The Crucible*, Filipina/o support of the United States during the war provides a potential pathway to eventual independence and the formation of a free Philippines. For Panlilio, the guerrilla resistance proves its right to self-government because the guerrillas accomplish what even the might of U.S. military force cannot do alone.

In addition to emphasizing biological, blood-based racial characteristics, Panlilio also stresses a bicultural identity that is central to her evolving departure from gender norms in both countries. These descriptions—which point to both her Filipina and American identity alongside her combination of military and maternal attributes—are crucial to her revision of popular World War II representations of women. She carefully manipulates traditional notions of femininity that would limit women to the roles of wife, mother, or, in the specific case of war in the Philippines, victim. *The Crucible* attaches her ability to become a leader in Marking's regiment to her mixture of Filipina and American upbringing. Throughout the memoir, she consistently reminds her readers that she is able to accomplish what few women and men can do. *The Crucible* defines a unique formation of what Panlilio calls "guerrilla motherhood" and posits the camp as a combination of military and domestic spaces. As colonel, wife, and mother, Panlilio merges the trappings of motherhood, her devotion to her "boys" and Marking, and her fierce desire and need to protect and care for them with her construction of herself as the "brains" of Marking's operation. She frequently reminds us that even though she initially decides to join the guerrillas because the sight of forlorn troops speaks to her maternal instincts, motherhood itself is somewhat unnatural to her. Thus while wielding a gun, traipsing through the jungle, and orchestrating complex military strategies seem second nature, she finds the stereotypical tasks of motherhood intensely frustrating, and she describes the steep learning curve demanded by the domesticities of camp life. Yet she nevertheless disciplines, encourages, and cares for her guerrilla boys, defending them from Marking and insisting on applying a fair and democratic system of rules. This reconstruction of the Filipina mother and wife as a military, nationalist figure becomes the foundation for building relationships among women. In the Philippines, she forms a network of Filipinas who contribute to military resistance, from combat to sending money and food to the camps.

The Crucible matches such relationships in the Philippines with a potentially powerful transnational sisterhood of female readers. While the dominant narrative of wartime brotherhood uses the traumatic memory of war in the Pacific to effect ties between U.S. and Filipino men, *The Crucible* constructs affective, triangulated ties among a Filipina mother, a U.S. GI, and the absent figure of an American mother. This strategy is best illustrated when the outfit shelters a GI who stumbles upon the guerrilla camp after escaping a Japanese military prison. In this scene, Panlilio sympathetically shelters an "American mother's son" who represents "a little of the flesh and bone that had survived" (chapter 13). She envelops him within an assessment of the underestimated guerrillas ignored and unaccounted for by others, constructing herself as having a special ability to recognize the unique potential of those who "maybe... looked like nothing to anybody else; but mother-eyes are sharp, and it is the world that is blind." In recognizing the needs of this American son, she forms an affiliation between herself and her U.S. female audience.

Panlilio also employs a recounting of her romance with Marking to encourage an emotional affiliation with her readers. She represents this relationship in terms that range from lofty and sappy to tumultuous and anxious. Yet this recounting of her romantic involvement with Marking both enables and complicates her claims of power and influence in the camp. Marking's guerrilla outfit gives her opportunities to participate actively in the war. As a guerrilla, she fights for and quickly earns the respect of his men. She casts herself as willful, headstrong, and defiant. But scenes with Marking often contradict this self-portraiture. As his lover, she struggles with the duality of their relationship. While she sometimes asserts her will over his, he can always trump her orders as a commanding officer. Her relationship with Marking as his guerrilla wife also takes on more disturbing terms. Her accounts of his emotional and physical violence and her excuses for him and his abusive actions are difficult to reconcile with a book that wants to be read as a liberating story of a woman's independence. While she sometimes does so ostensibly in the name of promoting their great romance, these problematic elements of the text cannot be ignored.

Readers may also be troubled by Panlilio's representation of the Japanese military and indigenous peoples of the Philippines. Panlilio's discussion of the Dumagats, who are indigenous to the Philippines, relies on both idealized and primitivist characterizations. While she is clearly grateful to the Dumagats for sheltering and guiding Marking's outfit, she represents them as alternately child-like, savage, and innocent. Similarly, her descriptions of Japanese people require careful attention. Panlilio wrote *The Crucible* within a context in which Americans and Filipina/os, still reeling from the tragedies and horrors of World War II, consistently characterized an entire race of Japanese people as enemies. Readers should certainly be critical of the text's generalizations about the Japanese; they should also consider the ways in which Panlilio problematically employs the vilification of Japanese people as part of her appeal to U.S. and Philippine anti-Japanese sentiments. She casts the Japanese in race-based stereotypes; they are bar-

baric, ignorant, and violent. The book also uses dialect as a method of reportage to mock Japanese people speaking English. These characterizations underscore both the complicated, postwar relations among the Philippines, the United States, and Japan, and the strategies that Panlilio uses to reach a pro-American and anti-Japanese readership.

I underscore *The Crucible*'s vexed representation of race and gender not only to point out aspects of the memoir that deserve critique, but also because these elements perhaps contributed to the text's eventual fall into obscurity. In addition to these factors, *The Crucible*'s Philippine-based setting and its appeal to pro-American sensibilities would have made it a questionable candidate for inclusion in 1970s and 1980s formations of an Asian American literary canon, which, at the time, centered on works that explicitly engaged the lives of Asians in the United States or represented the development of politically resistant Asian American positions.[28] Yet Yay Panlilio's *The Crucible* should nevertheless be read today precisely because it emphasizes what is difficult to encounter in print, and for what has been and is still challenging to remember. The memoir thus asks us to recognize the unfamiliar and the unacknowledged—not only the involvement of Filipinos and Filipinas in World War II resistance, or Filipina authorship in the mid-century, but also the tangled skein of relations among the Philippines, the United States, and Japan.

Notes

1. The date reflects the time difference between the Philippines and Hawaii.
2. Filipinas and Filipinos use *mestiza* and *mestizo* to refer to someone with mixed racial heritage.
3. I use the gender-inclusive term *Filipina/os* when referring to both men and women.
4. For contemporary reviews of *The Crucible*, see Donna Flintan, "Guerrilla Warfare Seen Through Woman's Eyes," *The Los Angeles Times*, February 5, 1950, D9; and Chandler Thomas, "Too Untrained to Give Up," *The New York Times*, February 5, 1950, 179.
5. See "My Filipino Mother," in Yay Marking, *Where a Country Begins* (Manila: Manila Times Publishing Company, 1961), vol. 2, 9–41.
6. Florence Horn, *Orphans of the Pacific* (New York: Reynal and Hitchcock, 1941), 59.
7. Doris Rubens Johnston, *Bread and Rice* (New York: Thurston McCauley, 1947), 162.

8. Mae Ngai presents a useful discussion of these events in *Impossible Subjects: Illegal Aliens and the Making of Modern America* (Princeton: Princeton University Press, 2005), 96–126.
9. The above summary of Asian American and Filipina/o immigration to the United States draws from Sucheng Chan, *Asian Americans: An Interpretive History* (New York: Twayne, 1991); Linda España-Maram, *Creating Masculinity in Los Angeles's Little Manila: Working-Class Filipinos and Popular Culture* (New York: Columbia University Press, 2006); Augusto Fauni Espiritu, *Five Faces of Exile: The Nation and Filipino American Intellectuals* (Stanford: Stanford University Press, 2005); Dorothy Fujita-Rony, *American Workers, Colonial Power: Philippine Seattle and the Transpacific West, 1919–1941* (Berkeley: University of California Press, 2003); Lisa Lowe, *Immigrant Acts: On Asian American Cultural Politics* (Durham and London: Duke University Press, 1996); Ngai, *Impossible Subjects*; Rhacel Parreñas, "White Trash Meets the 'Brown Monkeys': The Taxi Dance Hall as a Site of Interracial and Gender Alliances Between White Working Class Women and Filipino Immigrant Men in the 1920s and 30s," *Amerasia Journal* 24, no. 2 (1998): 115–134; and Ronald Takaki, *Strangers from a Different Shore* (Boston: Back Bay Books, 1998).
10. Carlos Bulosan, *America Is in the Heart* (Seattle: University of Washington Press, 1974); Manuel Buaken, *I Have Lived with the American People* (Caldwell: Caxton Printers, 1948); Evangeline Canonizada Buell, *Twenty-Five Chickens and a Pig for a Bride* (San Francisco: T'boli Publishing, 2006); Peter Jamero, *Growing Up Brown: Memoirs of a Filipino American* (Seattle and London: University of Washington Press, 2006); Pati Navalta Poblete, *The Oracles: My Filipino Grandparents in America* (Berkeley: Heyday Books, 2006); Patricia Justiniana McReynolds, *Almost Americans: A Quest for Dignity* (Santa Fe: Red Crane Books, 1997); and Angeles Monrayo, *Tomorrow's Memories* (Honolulu: University of Hawaii Press, 2003).
11. There have been many historical analyses of the Pacific War. Those of special relevance to *The Crucible* include John Dower, *War Without Mercy: Race and Power in the Pacific War* (New York: Pantheon, 1987), and Teodoro Agoncillo, *The Fateful Years: Japan's Adventure in the Philippines, 1941–1945* (Quezon City: University of the Philippines Press, 2001). For an account of the guerrilla resistance, see Jesus A. Villamor, *They Never Surrendered* (Quezon City: Vera Reyas, 1982).
12. For specific studies of life during the occupation, see Agoncillo, *The Fateful Years*, and Thelma B. Kintanar et al., *Kuwentong Bayan: Noong Panahon ng Hapon, Everyday Life in a Time of War* (Quezon City: University of the Philippines Press, 2006).
13. Carlos Romulo, *I See the Philippines Rise* (Garden City: Doubleday and Company, 1946), 165–179.

14. Bienvenido N. Santos's well-known short story, "Scent of Apples" features a narrator who (like Santos himself) was one of these speakers. In *Scent of Apples: A Collection of Stories* (Seattle: University of Washington Press, 1997).
15. See Sharon Delmendo's analysis of this phenomenon in *The Star Entangled Banner: One Hundred Years of America in the Philippines* (New Brunswick: Rutgers University Press, 2004), 86–114.
16. Romulo's war stories were featured in major U.S. newspapers. He also produced several books, including *I Saw the Fall of the Philippines* (Garden City: Doubleday and Doran, 1942), *My Brother Americans* (Garden City: Doubleday and Doran, 1945), and *I See the Philippines Rise* (Garden City: Doubleday and Doran, 1946).
17. Noel Izon's documentary, *An Untold Triumph* (Center for Asian American Media, 2005), is one relatively recent attempt to document this experience.
18. Adrienne Croll, "Legislative History of Title VIII of the Social Security Act," *Social Security Bulletin* 64, no. 1 (2001–2002): 27–31.
19. Luis Taruc's memoir, *Born of the People* (New York: International Publishers, 1953), describes his leadership of the Huks and their cause.
20. See Satoshi Nakano's work on Filipino veterans' rights, especially "Nation, Nationalism, and Citizenship in the Filipino World War II Veterans Equity Movement, 1945–1999," *Hitotsubashi Journal of Social Studies* 32 (December 2000): 33–53; and Bernie Becker, "Filipino Veterans Benefit in Stimulus Bill," *The New York Times*, February 16, 2009, http://www.nytimes.com/2009/02/17/us/politics/17vets.html?_r=1&scp=1&sq=filipino%20veterans&st=cse (accessed April 13, 2009). I thank Candice Williams for her assistance with this material.
21. Carlos Romulo, "The Philippines Await their D-Day; General Romulo sees his people united and eager to renew bonds with America," *The New York Times*, October 22, 1944, SM 5.
22. See Yuki Tanaka's introduction to Maria Rosa Henson, *Comfort Woman: A Filipina's Story of Prostitution and Slavery Under the Japanese Military* (Lanham: Rowman and Littlefield, 1999), as well as Norma Field, "War and Apology: Japan, Asia, the Fiftieth, and After," *Positions* 5, no. 1 (Spring 1997): 1–49; George Hicks, *The Comfort Women: Japan's Brutal Regime of Enforced Prostitution in the Second World War* (New York and London: W. W. Norton and Company, 1995); and Hyun Sook Kim, "History and Memory: The 'Comfort Woman Controversy,'" *Positions* 5, no. 1 (Spring 1997): 73–106.
23. It is important to recognize that in comparison to stories of male valor, the history of U.S. nurses in the Philippines is also quite unknown. See Theresa Kaminski, *Prisoners in Paradise: American Women in the Wartime South Pacific* (Lawrence: University Press of Kansas, 2000); Elizabeth Norman, *We Band of Angels: The Untold Story of American Nurses Trapped on Bataan by the Japanese* (New York: Pocket Books, 1999); and Evelyn Monahan and Rosemary Neidel, *All This Hell:*

U.S. Nurses Imprisoned by the Japanese (Lexington: University Press of Kentucky, 2000).
24. Kaminski's *Prisoners in Paradise* attempts to address some of these gaps, and even includes mention of Panlilio. Kaminski, *Prisoners in Paradise*, 177–179.
25. Claire Phillips, *Manila Espionage* (Portland: Binfords and Mont, 1947); Margaret Utinksy, *"Miss U"* (San Antonio: Naylor Company, 1948); Johnston, *Bread and Rice*; and Louise Reid Spencer, *Guerrilla Wife* (New York: Thomas Y. Crowell Company, 1945).
26. See España-Maram, *Creating Masculinity*; and Parreñas, "White Trash."
27. Horn, *Orphans of the Pacific*, 57–60.
28. For a useful discussion of the formation of an Asian American literary canon, see the introductions to Jinqi Ling, *Narrating Nationalisms: Ideology and Form in Asian American Literature* (Oxford: Oxford University Press, 1998), and Viet Thanh Nguyen, *Race and Resistance: Literature and Politics in Asian America* (New York, Oxford: Oxford University Press, 2002).

A NOTE ON THE TEXT

This edition is based on the 1950 edition of *The Crucible: An Autobiography by Colonel Yay*. The text has been reproduced with minimal editing to correct inconsistencies in punctuation and grammar. Words and phrases in Tagalog or Spanish have been uniformly italicized. Translations appear in brackets for terms that are not translated by Panlilio or in context; repeated occurrences of Tagalog words are defined in the glossary. Panlilio's versions of some Tagalog words and Philippine place names differ slightly from contemporary orthography.

THE *Crucible*

THE MARKING GUERRILLAS' CREED

April 9, 1942
Fall of Bataan

... IF THE LEAST WE DO IS FERTILIZE THE SOIL WHERE WE FALL, THEN WE GROW A RICHER GRAIN FOR TOMORROW'S STRONGER NATION ...

WE, "MARKING'S GUERRILLAS," BELIEVE it is the right of every Filipino to walk in dignity, unslapped, unsearched, untied; to speak freely of honor and injustice alike; to assemble freely; to mold our destiny as a people.

WE BELIEVE that we owe allegiance to America, and that the only flags to fly in this sweet air are the Stars and Stripes and the Philippine flag until such time as the Philippine flag flies alone. We want no independence by treachery. Our independence will come to us in the benevolent manner consistent with the way America treated us for more than twoscore years, or we will get it in due time, on the field of battle if we still want it that badly, without the help of an aggressor who transgressed us and calls us brother and now whips us to arms against those who would help us and punish him.

WE BELIEVE that it is the right of every Filipino to raise his or her weapon against the enemy, be that weapon a rifle, a bolo, poison, or a sweet I-don't-know-a-thing smile. And we believe that it is the right of every Filipino to hide, help, and arm every American who comes within reach of Filipino hands, and to feed and comfort Americans within the concentration camps.

WE BELIEVE that the greatest and the humblest, the richest and the poorest, the wise and the childlike, the oldest and the youngest, the best and the worst, the men and the women, with or without military training—that all these are brother Filipinos and that they have the right to fight the enemy.

WE BELIEVE that the nature and function of the guerrilla is threefold: (1) it harasses the enemy, occupying as many enemy troops as possible in their own "occupied" territory, thus keeping them out of their own front lines; (2) it is a secret self-government, where there is justice and aid for all "of the people, by the people, for the people"; (3) it is an opportunity for a small minority of bums, loafers, ex-convicts, and Welfareville boys to risk their lives on the toughest assignments and thus prove their loyalty, their valor, and their intelligence, and by association with the majority to gain a new standard for living and acting.

WE BELIEVE THAT GOD IS WITH US ALL THE WHILE WE DO RIGHT, AND THAT VICTORY SHALL BE OURS IN THE END.

FOREWORD

This story was lived by one of the most gallant women of our time, a woman of whom two nations should be proud.

Colonel Yay did not see the Philippines until she was eighteen. Born in Denver of an Irish father and a Filipina mother, she grew up in the freedom of the United States, and she took with her into the hills of Luzon not only the American ideals of justice and pride but the Filipino traits of courage and unselfish devotion. In the crucible of war, in herself as well as her adopted country these qualities were blended into greatness.

She is what the Islands call a "*mestiza*," a mixture. Thus, she is small, too thin, with olive skin and black hair and eyes. These are her Filipino heritage. And the Irish in her comes out in delicate bone structure, long-fingered hands, a pointed chin, a casual yet fluid manner of using her body, an intensity of mind.

I first saw her in 1945 in one of the crummiest hotel rooms I have ever entered. Fresh from the blood-drenched provinces she had defended, she had brought her three children by army transport to their grandmother in California. The Red Cross had arranged for available shelter, and I found her on Los Angeles' "Skid Row" in a corner room furnished with two enormous double beds of brass, an ancient dressing table, and a rug brown with the droppings of humanity. There was a telephone hanging from the woodwork by the door, and a cubicle which boasted a three-foot tin tub.

Yay, hearing I was in the writing racket, had asked me to come down. The newspaper business was and still is one of her greatest loves. Before the war she was the finest woman reporter in the Philippines, and she had begged for a "chance to talk the language."

When I saw where she was living I was shocked. Then she made the statement which, more than any other, indicated what the preceding three years had been for her.

"But it has walls, Kate," she said. "It has walls!"

At that moment, I hoped she would write this book, if for no other reason than to let the people of America balance their part in the winning of the war against hers. But she had a larger reason for writing it: she wanted to tell the citizens of the country in which she was born about her "boys." In that, I thoroughly agreed, for they—and the man who led them—made an army out of legend.

Yay has underplayed herself in every page of what you are about to read. Such is Yay. For the story, as she saw it, was the men in the outfit and what they endured. She only allowed herself to enter when it was necessary for her to fight with them for "principle," for "the American way" which is so very dear to her.

Yet someone should tell you what Yay herself endured. Someone should point out that although, less than a year before the occupation, she had broken her leg in an automobile accident and it had not healed properly, she marched over mountains with the rest of them. And that although, shortly before the bombs started falling, she had spent three weeks in a hospital with her heart packed in ice, suffering from a cardiac condition from which the doctors thought she would never recover, she worked eighteen hours a day in the hills, lived on less than nothing, fought her own war against the Japs. And that she too had malaria and dysentery for months, lay in muddy huts when she had the awful chills and fever, marched in the few hours a day when she was free of them, rarely had the solace of drugs of any kind.

This takes courage. Yay has it.

And she has pride, as you will discover, humanity which was fed on tragedy, and the faith in God and man which passes understanding.

Yet she is humble. Her importance in Marking's outfit has to be inferred. She makes herself a shrew, if anything, a gnat singing about them all. But Marking himself has told me that at the end there was not a man among his followers who would not have given his life for her.

Many of them did, in fact. Gladly.

Hers is the only story I have heard in years of reporting which bears endless repetition, endless examination. To me that is the test, both of the woman and of her history. This is that history, three terrible, valorous years.

Kate Holliday

CHAPTER 1

*W*ar came thundering over the Philippines, and seven months after the bombing of Oahu, I, Yay Panlilio, reporter and United States Army agent, had a price on my head and lay alone in a remote foothills farm hut, freezing and burning with my first attack of malaria. To that hut where I lay alone, badly needing help from somewhere, God brought the guerrillas.

I had tried, since the Japs had landed on the Islands, to fight them in my own way, on my own. It had been impossible. Now, like thousands of others before and after me, I took the only course open: I became a guerrilla.

The torch fell in Bataan, igniting the Philippines from Aparri to Sulu. The light flickered out in Corregidor, flamed again unseen in loyal hearts everywhere, in cities and towns, in rice paddy, jungle, and forest. "To you from falling hands..." And thus it became ours, forever to hold high. We did what even America in her greatness could not do. We kept her flag, and our own, hoisted in occupied territory. The enemy ripped it down again and again, and again and again we ran it up on bamboo poles to float proudly on the winds, to glorify the mobile upland camps of freemen who hit and ran and were attacked and retreated, over and over again.

The first sixty days of those seven months, I had risked occupied Manila. I had to risk it. Captain Ralph Keeler, assistant chief of Intelligence at Fort Santiago, told me to. Major Each-Hair-in-Its-Place Diller, aide to General Douglas MacArthur, refused to order me to Bataan with the army, refused even to allow me to catch a ride with the troops.

I thought I had a right to be on Bataan, for, long before we saw the war coming inevitably, Keeler had sworn me in as a United States agent, Badge No. 67, following orders from Colonel J. K. Evans. I was to continue to cover Manila as a reporter, picking up everything interesting to S-2 as I went along.

When the Japs struck, instantly I became primarily an agent. Reporting was secondary. Through the Baguio bombing, the Cavite bombing, and the dog-fighting over Manila, I kept my eyes open. I shuttled from the Fort Santiago Army Intelligence headquarters at one end of the Walled City to Victoria No. 1 at the other end. There MacArthur was busy ordering his already battle-worn forces up from the far south, through the defenseless city, and down into Bataan.

Over at Victoria No. 1 I had to go along to Bataan, too, I said. I could drive a truck. I could pound a typewriter. In a pinch, I knew which end of a rifle was the shooting end.

I would plead with Diller.

"I have to go!" I said.

"You can't go," he answered.

Back I went to the Fort. Trucks roared in and out of the tunneled walls. Like a two-way crossbow, I pulled my front in as a truck shoved me one way, yanked in my rear as I was shoved the other. Trucks were as good as bullets those days; you could get killed just as fast.

Inside, S-2 was confused. No telephone in its cradle did anything but ring. No swinging door did anything but hurl this way and that, holding hard to its hinges, split seconds between swings. The only spot out of the traffic was a corner, and from there I made timid signals to my friend Keeler, as he strode to and fro in an awful sweat with a sheaf of papers in both hands.

My signal, a teacher-may-I-leave-the-room affair, caught Keeler's eye. "Stick around," he said. One hour. Two hours. My signal caught him again. "Stick around," he said.

Finally I came out of the corner to stop him in the middle of the floor by blocking each direction he plunged. So he said, "Wait for orders."

I went back to MacArthur's headquarters to Diller. Diller said, "No! No, no-no-no! What do you think this is, a picnic?" I showed him my badge. By the middle of December, I had found it again in the bottom drawer of my desk under newspaper mats, old negatives, and what not. He waved me off. "Go home," he said. But he was still too polite, too unruffled, to say what he meant. He meant, "Get the hell out of here before I toss you through a window!"

So I went back to the Fort. Back and forth. And once in a while to the *Herald*, to sleep on my desk, to cover a world flying apart, to drink coffee out of a tin can.

And then toward Christmas, as I went salmon-leaping up the stream of army trucks, Glass came by, and he wasn't in plain clothes any more. I looked at his cap—overseas. I looked at his coat—khaki. "So long, kid," said this agent, who had been kind to me and taught me a little of sleuthing. I said nothing. I think I kept looking at him. Glass said, "Take care of yourself."

Words came to my tongue: "Where to?"

Glass poked his head out of the car window. "Off to the wars, kid."

We were talking swiftly, in urgent sentences. I said, "Let me in." He shook his head. "Nope, kid, I can't."

"Glass, I can drive. I can type. I can shoot. Really I can. Just show me how to get the bullets in." And, hopefully: "You never handled a rifle in your life."

He said, cheerfully, the way we used to talk making the night-club rounds, "They tell me the wooden end goes against your shoulder." "Let me in, Glass." And I tried to get the door open.

He pushed me away, slapping my hands big-brother fashion, and turned his head to the driver, saying, "OK, buddy, roll!" To me he called back, "Save the country if you can, kid."

At radio station KZRH, where I had been doing programs for fun, I couldn't save the country, but I tried at least to steady both myself and it by broadcasting preparation for war programs. And at the *Herald* office, squeezed in with the *Bulletin* after incendiary bombs burned us out of the Walled City, I wrote into my column advice for the women: "Let your children look back and remember how their mother faced the war."

From Keeler in Intelligence: *Stick around*. From Diller close to MacArthur: *Go home*. From Glass: *Save the country if you can*. And again from Keeler: *Wait for orders. We'll send you orders.*

That's all I had to go on.

The Japs occupied Manila on January 2, 1942. All the world knows that story. I saw my friends behind the Santo Tomás fence, helpless individuals herded in with the thousands. I clung to the fence, looking, and I was unable to reach out or speak words of comfort because they were ordered back. I hung there for a while, my eyes pulling at the figures, then walked a few steps to sit on the curb and retch into the dust between my feet.

I needed to think. It was two blocks home. I stood up to go home. I walked roundabout, halfway across the city, seeing the Japs taking over like a newsreel, thinking all the way and still thinking when I found myself in front of my own house. It was the first real thinking I had ever done: If orders were coming through, best to keep reminding them that I was alive. No use merely waiting, better be ready to fill the bill when it came. As an agent, get in close. As a fool, get the children out of the way first.

I had separated from my children's father, Eduardo Panlilio, long before the war started. He was in the mountains of Palawan Island at his job of mining engineer. So the safety of the kids was up to me. I took them to Herbert and Janet Walker, elderly Americans exempted for the time being from internment. They would hide my nine-year-old daughter Rae, my six- and three-year-old sons Junior and Kerty.

In the first week of the occupation, I met one Victor Takizawa, who for fifteen years had been "of Davao." In 1939, when I had been turning out a newspaper supplement on the Davao plantations we had been congenial. He had shown me around, even had had a huge tree felled for my special benefit. I had taken pictures, written articles, collected advertising money in advance. One of the pictures had shown the Jap flag alone on its pole flying over a Jap schoolhouse in the heart of Davao, still technically part of the Philippines, and when Jesús M. Integnan, city editor of the *Herald*, saw it, he patted me on the head and passed the picture along to the proper authorities and up started a rumpus between the American High Commissioner's Office and the Japanese Consulate. Two years ago—1939, and here was Takizawa, of Davao, a conqueror.

Faint heart never won any war. I climbed out of the *calesa* to answer Taki's greeting, and I walked swiftly, with dignity, to keep my knees from buckling. We met once again as friends.

There was in the group a newspaperman of the *Philippines Free Press* staff, denying that he had anything to do with its last issues, the finest they had ever printed. He held a Jap, a former clerk in the Japanese Consulate, tightly by the hand, and wheedled for a pass. The former clerk, no longer obsequious, taunted, "Why do you need one? You are a civilian. You are safe." The newspaperman kept on wheedling, pleading. The clerk maliciously swung him around by the hand and wrote with his forefinger across the newspaperman's back, "We'll give you a pass. We'll write 'Stool pigeon.'"

That was the cue on how far to go and when to stop.

So, with Taki, I discussed the need for gardens. The people must eat, I said. The people were my greatest concern. Taki showed concern over my concern. He took my telephone number, and two days later he called. Luck! Shining luck, for he had been assigned to reopen KZRH, and I was familiar with the station. Would I help him? I couldn't help him fast enough.

On the air with news reports, Jap news reports. Would Evans, would Keeler, would Diller with MacArthur's forces, hear my voice, know it was I, listen, listen sharp, realize where to find me to deliver my orders, my orders or anybody's orders? Would the Voice of Freedom "from somewhere in the Philippines" answer and think twice and be careful—sort of remember where I was?

While I waited, I tightroped and triple-talked in and out of the Japanese-censored scripts, trying to accomplish three things: advise the truculent, unarmed Manilans to look before they leaped; tip off the Voice of Freedom what to say instead of what it was saying; inform the Filipino-American forces by the most delicate innuendo what was going on behind enemy lines, innuendo so obscure sometimes that only mental telepathy could decode it. Between broadcasts I chittered and chattered with the Japs, covering my tracks in advance by looking and sounding even more of a fool than I was.

Taki was around a lot. He wasn't running the station any more, but he was still around.

He drifted in one day, eased a thigh over a desk corner, talked idly. He squirmed, but I couldn't tell whether happily or otherwise until he pulled out of his pocket a badge covered with Japanese characters and a flower design. Then I was sure he was happy.

"This is the miritary interrigence badge of the Japanese Imperiar Forces," he said.

I liked Taki. "Congratulations," I smiled, for many reasons glad to know. Some day the knowledge might save my skin. "Looks like a reward."

"You rike one?" asked Taki.

In the old days I could have said, "Sure, pal. I'll tie one on each end of a string and play them both." But now I said, "Those are for their very own whom they can really trust, like you." Taki nodded proudly. "Need any more rumors?" I added.

Through me, loyal elements, certain guerrilla units which were only beginning to form, had been giving the Japanese military police the run-around. Antonio M. Bautista, lawyer and founder of the Civil Liberties Union, had had me tell Taki that I had heard of something suspicious going on in South Manila, with the result that he and his confreres had haunted it while Tony and his own confreres had run guns through North Manila.

Quickly, Taki answered my question. "Yes, what have you heard?"

"That it isn't South Manila, Taki. It's North Manila. I don't know what's going on, but there's a stir, sort of."

Taki may have been joking when he said, "You better be carefu'—you know who I am now," because he hied himself away, happy and proud, to check up on North Manila. And Tony Batista sent something south, something on two legs with a price on its head.

That night, straining to hear the jammed-out Voice of Freedom talking to Manila, I thought I heard my cue: "*There are those who speak ... Listen to them within the bounds of honor.*"

Corregidor had recognized my voice.

"Damn that woman!" the great MacArthur had burst out, turning on his aide, Major Carlos Romulo, who as Manila newspaper owner before the invasion had been my boss. "Isn't that *your* Yay?"

The boss hung his head, and I, talking my way to a saber execution, would have kicked him by television if I'd known it.

General Willoughby was bright. "That woman," he said, "is trying to give us information." And he lined up the stenographers to take it down. They couldn't get a tenth of what I tried to say: only the bay between us and yet ... I wasn't that good. Sometimes with the Japs at my elbow I was plain yellow—that was when I reached High C singing their praises. But—God bless Willoughby—HQ [headquarters] did get some of it.

The Japs were catching on, bringing in English-speaking Intelligence men of their own who could understand my triple talk. Run, or stick it? They could pick me up at any time, but it was my contacts they wanted, a whole network of them. Friends of other days now could be divided into three classes: those who had fallen away and could no longer be depended on; those who held aloof and would keep for the day when all could be explained; and those who fell in step, knowing the score, ready to pay the price—but not stupidly. A word of warning to these spread swiftly, silently, and by common consent I walked alone. America was no farther away than the Philippines, and where before my days had been numbered now it was the hours.

The Japs held off. I held on. And then, somehow, I knew when and how to go, and why. Not to die, but to fight and survive to fight again.

It all came to a head one afternoon early in March. The Japs were combing the city for Romulo. Thinking I knew where he was, they tried to trick me with a letter for him. They thought I would lead them to him, or take the letter and be followed. I was eager to help them, but blank: Romulo, when he had last been seen, was with General MacArthur. Did they know General MacArthur? Both might be found in Bataan. Did they have a map, and would they care to send me there? No. No, they wouldn't send me there. "It is very dangerous," they said.

They left. Because of a conference at the Jap High Command, the radio station was almost empty—only a few sentries and a handful of small-fry collaborators there to earn a living. A telephone call could order the sentries to arrest me, but probably the radio officials were occupied with bootlicking their superiors, or might doubt a little longer before taking action. If I talked carefully, easily, like any blurb ...

And so, for all of Romulo's former staff members, I said goodbye. I broadcast to Dr. Carlos P. Romulo, pronouncing his name clearly and in full: "Wherever you are, put up your feet and listen." In essence, I told him to keep going; and, in straight words: "We to whom you were a father—we will keep faith."

We did, too. Not one of Romulo's writing staff sold out to the enemy. Integnan, his city editor, died by torture to keep that faith.

I snapped off the mike, faded in the music, waited the remaining minutes of my program to turn the booth over to the regular announcer, then tried not to walk too fast out of the station, into the street, around the corner. The Japs had recently kept check by tuning in on what went over their air. Within fifteen minutes of my leaving the station, the order was out for my arrest.

It took four days of side-stepping to clear the city. Ding Moskaira, whom no one knew I knew, with whom ten years before I had scraped up an acquaintance in the aisles of the markets, she with her basket, I with mine, gave me refuge. Late at night, an inch before curfew, I knocked at her door. She opened the width of her hand, then wide to pull me inside, and she asked, "Have you eaten yet?" That was all she ever asked.

When her husband Roger came in, he led me up the back stairs, pointed to the window ledge outside below the sill, the wall top lower down, and a door open several patios away. "If anything happens, climb out that way. Straight through that house. I'll meet you on the other side of the block—somehow." That was all he ever said.

And the disguise that passed friend after friend, sentry after sentry, was simply girl's clothes—worn for the first time in years. A masculine escort, lipstick, powder, a dress. No customary slacks, no boyish bob visible under a frivolous kerchief. I simpered, clinging to my escort's arm, and he said, "That's it, damn it. Overdo it, you idiot! ... Don't turn your face when we pass a sentry. And don't talk. Think about the weather." And, through teeth gritted to keep them from clicking, I said, "Funny, how cold the tropics are now."

And so in one slow day we passed into the province of Rizal, and through the town of Tanay, and into the foothills, and to the tops of the mountains. From there we watched Bataan, a rough dark line against the horizon, a No-Man's-Land where, in the minutes we stood there, Americans and Filipinos alike were fighting and dying. The entire sky was a gun-metal mauve, and through it as through a curtain with a hole cut in it was the round, rayless, blood-red sun. In all the gamut of Philippine sunsets, from brazen to pastel, there had not been one like that.

A small, cold wind swept up the slope. It was like a bad omen.

Then, as we watched, the curtain broke apart and the clouds reformed, a cluster of mauve islands in a sea of red. "Bathed in blood," I said. "Let's get out of here. I'm seeing maps in the sky."

When the Japs found I had gone, a price was set on my head and I was to be shot on sight. My children were to be taken hostage.

Through weeks of waiting for America to come back, through weeks of learning to live as a hunted creature, my heart was in Bataan. Where were the reinforcements? Slowly the Japs were seeping out of Manila into the towns: excess soldiery, not needed any more to hold Bataan, not needed even to crush it. And then I found myself in the hut of Igi, the farmer, and began to think.

While I was thinking, shaking with new malaria, alone in a place I hoped the Japs weren't patrolling, while I was wondering whether to join the guerrillas in the north or the guerrillas in the south, the guerrillas joined me. They joined me by rolling up on my doorstep and sweeping me along with the tide.

CHAPTER 2

They rolled up in the middle of the night, ragged, soaked with the night's drizzle, on weary retreat from a three-point attack by the Japs on their Tatala-Binangonan Camp. They stacked their rifles wherever they could lean them, wrung out the remnants of their shirts and warmed their bare backs at the fire, which Igi the farmer had covered with ashes and they had built up again into a fine, crackling blaze. It was July of 1942.

I had heard about the guerrillas and had thought about joining them, but realized honestly that I was kidding myself. It was hardly my line. A broken leg that had set awry gave me a bad knee, and a tired heart muscle made me huff and puff on the climbs. Also, I was shortsighted: would I see the Japs first, or they me? And I was a woman—not a juicy morsel, but there are times when any old horse looks like fresh meat.

But as I looked at the gaunt faces in the firelight, the maternal instinct in me was awakened. My heart tightened, and I loved them so much I got gooseflesh. So I climbed down from the bamboo-slat shelf where I slept, one more sardine with Igi's wife and kids.

"Boys," I said, "better get some sleep. Take the rice loft up above, and two of you squeeze into my place. The rest of you will have to make out as best you can. At least, the ground is dry." I indicated the floor.

Nobody moved.

Then a face familiar to me said in the dialect to anybody who was listening, "It's a helluva life. We fight. We don't eat. We don't sleep. We got no blankets. And now we take orders from a woman."

In a flash, love turned to hatred, and I leaped off the last rung of the little ladder. "You do as you're told. This is my house, by God! I got here first. Up into the loft! Line up beside those kids—and don't wake them up, or they'll squall until morning. And shut your traps!"

Also, I identified the familiar face. Two months after the fall of Corregidor, he had almost ridden me down on a trail, galloping madly by on what once had been a race horse. Spluttering, he had said, "You can't see the Major!" "Who's the Major?" I demanded, wiping mud off my chin. He said, proudly: "Marking. Major Marcos V. Agustin." "Well, I don't want to see him." "You can't see him anyway."

In the firelight, looking gaunt Ming Javellana in the eye, with the taste of mud again in my mouth, I said, "As for you, look out!"

They bedded down, mostly because they were worn out. I propped my back against a post and slept hunched, knees against chest, head pillowed on knees. The loft was full of guerrillas, the ground covered with them. Periodically until morning I woke up, ears cocked, on guard for them and for me, for the Japs follow up an attack. Through the mud, the Filipino fighters had left their tracks. Poor, hunted devils. Brave. Sassy as hell, but sweet. I, who wanted to help, on that night found something to help. My fever had cooled. Was the quinine licking the malaria? No matter—tomorrow we might both be dead, the malaria and me.

At dawn I discovered more of them in the larger farmhouse Igi the farmer used as an outpost up front to guard me in the hut farther back. The Jap garrison knew that outpost, and having patrolled there before, would know the trail in, especially following tracks, and the lay of the land when they got there.

The men were in no condition for more retreating. One was lying in his wet clothes on the farmhouse table, a boy not more than sixteen, groaning with appendix pains. He wouldn't unbutton himself, nor let me. I had no patience and, poising an arm to give him a back-slap, managed to unbutton him with the other and slip in a cold canteen over the pain. Tears welled up in his eyes, and he said, "Ma'am, I don't want to die that way."

"You won't," I said. "Just do as you're told."

Upstairs another, Robert Velge, stripped to the skin was lying on the bare floor—his only garment a pair of torn pants hung on the sill to dry. He was delirious in dry fever. Five days on the run, no time to stop. He needed cathartic pills.

There were so many. They packed both the farmhouse and the hut, and overflowed outside under the trees. They lay everywhere. They walked everywhere. They cooked in a huge caldron they lugged along with them, and stood in line for rations of boiled rice in coconut shells or cupped leaves.

"You've got to get out," I said. "This is the last place you should stay." I didn't know then that the people everywhere, fearful of being caught in the crossfire, forever urged them on. By what I said, I was merely another cowardly, selfish example. So they didn't move.

I harangued. They referred me to their officers. Cunanan referred me to Rodriguez; Rodriguez referred me back to Cunanan; Cunanan referred me to Cabalhin; Cabalhin wasn't there yet. I stayed around, insisting they move.

Cabalhin arrived with more worn soldiers who had been "covering the rear," to give the weakest and least experienced a start and a chance to rest. He eyed me with suspicion, and I eyed him back, curiously, for by this time, as far as I was concerned, it was up to them if they wanted to get wiped out. He had perfect up-slanting cats' eyes with the upper lids almost straight across the eye, hiding part of the pupils. High rosy cheekbones flanked the button of a nose, and an elfin grin curved up from a boy's round, half-formed chin. The eyebrows were sharply defined, and above a good brow was a shock of stiff black hair that, short or long, jutted in all directions like coconut husk. For the rest, he had fine, broad shoulders, a Colonial Dame waist, short, bandy legs. He might have been five-foot three, twenty years old, a hundred fifteen pounds. Some of the guerrillas were twice his size or twice his age, but when his eye fell upon them they were all respectful attention.

He, too, was respectful—hostilely respectful. "What do you wish, please?"

Nothing to lose. I repeated from memory, "Get your men out *behind* my hut instead of all over the landscape in front of it."

"Why?"

"The Japs know this place."

"How far is the other place?"

"Just around that spur, maybe half a mile."

"I cannot act without orders from the Major."

I sighed. "All right, where is the Major?"

Quick, narrow-eyed suspicion gleamed behind his half-dropped lashes.

I gave up. "Look, I don't care where your Major is, nor who he is. If you want your men killed, it's your fault, not mine. I just felt sorry for them."

"Who knows the place?" That was Leon Z. Cabalhin, the man who was to be my enemy and my friend. When he made a decision, it was made.

Igi stepped forward. Cabalhin gave the order, and the men began to move.

By late afternoon, only the guards were left up front. Content now that the rest were safely bedded down a full two miles from Tanay town,

I crawled up on the shelf amid the cooties and the chickens and the kids, for the sun was setting and morning might bring the Japs. Then I would be out in front, if the tired guards fell asleep; I had better be awake and have my shoes on.

No sooner was I well asleep than the hut was full of guerrillas again. Wearily, I pulled myself awake. Igi lit the *kingki* lamp. One of the kids whimpered. A chicken squawked. So I eased to the edge and swung my feet down. There was undoubtedly the Major, with Cabalhin a foot behind and to one side of him and other shapes sensed rather than seen outside the faint circle of light.

Tall, well muscled, but lean, Major Marcos V. Agustin, alias Marking, stood with his fists on his hips, his feet planted wide, and his head high and a little back. In the flickering light his small eyes were challenging, beady. I eyed him sleepily, in no mood to be challenged in the middle of the night awakened out of a sound sleep. Sleep was precious. For seven months, I had slept with one eye open if I slept at all. It helped through the food shortage. I was living on gruel; sometimes I didn't have to eat at all; blue of lip and ice to the marrow, I huddled in my blanket until the chills turned to blessed fever. That saved the noon meal and the night meal—it was a waste to force food down and promptly upchuck. Five months of that. Now sleepily, grumpily, I eyed the Major.

Came the challenge, "What are you doing out here?"

I had as much right to the backwoods as he, and I preferred it to Fort Santiago under the Japs. Still, Marking and his men were armed and I was not. They might shoot; then too late my friends would say, "My God! You—it was a mistake! She was *all right!*"

Dead, I wouldn't be all right. So I said, "Helping the guerrillas," and pulled up my legs to stretch and sleep again. I had helped many long months, here and there, and I was tired.

Marking tossed his head and scraped his boot. "Nobody's been helping *me!*" he flung.

All sleep fled, and with it discretion. "Pick up your heavy feet," I flung back. "You're stepping on somebody's toes!" Money and guns that the townspeople had been urged to collect had gone to various loyal elements, among them Marking.

Hotly we looked each other in the eye. I saw a fighting man. He saw a defiant woman.

We burst into laughter, having found each other. We asked and we answered, told stories, explored each other's minds, matched information, and in the background his men shifted from foot to foot, squatted wearily, exchanged meaning glances, hid their disgust behind blank faces: *Cherchez la femme* [Look for the woman] . . . They could see dainty horns coming out of my temples, a forked tail curled about one ankle.

I could see other things. The man had his troubles. In that summer after Pearl Harbor, he and 150 followers were fighting blind, not knowing how long they would last, not caring. They were armed with anything from army rifles to .22s, riot guns, shotguns, 44-caliber buffalo guns, one-shot *paltiks*, and pistols. Anything would do—it was how it was used. He had added farmers to his soldiers, drilling them until he was hoarse, knocking a blockhead flat, stringing up a hardhead by the wrists: "When I say, 'Right face,' I mean right face, and I don't mean left face!" They had policed the countryside and warned the budding collaborators, "Whaddya mean, what will you tell the Japs? Tell them to go to hell!"

Gallantly, within two months after the Death March, they had attacked the Lumban prison camp in Laguna. Marking sent friends to "case the job": one was Sammy, troublemaker, who had been conductor on the fine, shining, vacation-resort bus Marking had driven before the war; the other was Mendy, good-time acquaintance, barker at small-town fairs. "You go see," he told them, "and come back and tell me what you see. I'll get the men in shape for the job."

Mendy and Sammy cased the job, but not too well. So Marking stuck his .45 into his belt under shirttails hanging out, and went to see for himself. He saw grave after grave—six, ten, fifteen a day. He saw Americans knocked flat with rifle butts, kicked where they lay, beaten to their feet again. He saw drooping, dying soldiers with desperate, dull, glazing eyes.

Straight back he went, his heart aflame, to get his fighters. Launches and sailboats brought them across the lake from Tanay. Under cover of night, he took them up the Lumban River. Cabalhin with twenty men crept to position on a rise overlooking the schoolhouse garrison, to fire on possible reinforcements the moment they came out of the garrison. Other men proceeded to a halfway point between the garrison and the prison camp, to string barbed wire across the road. The Lumban mayor, in on the raid heart and soul, had all lights out and every dog tied and waited himself for the guerrillas to tie him up as alibi to the Japs.

On through the town to the camp Marking and some forty-five men moved, slow and silent, picking their way over each dry branch and loose stone, feeling with their hands through the blackness, crawling.

Inside were the helpless men they would save. It *must* be a success; it *had* to go right! They were tensed to life, and death.

Marking shot a sentry, signal for a tensely aimed volley, and the guerrillas sprang into the clearing to shoot and bludgeon the remaining guards and grab their guns.

"Out here! Come with us!" yelled Marking.

Commotion within. Then, "Who are you?"

"Filipinos! Hurry up!"

One soldier, George Lightman, leaped through the door, calling, "Where are you? I'm an American! Where are you?" An American captain barred the way after him.

Marking bellowed, "Over here! Bring everybody!"

And the captain at the door shoved back the surge toward liberty: "Don't go! I order you to stay!"

"C'mon," said George, floundering, panting. "They won't come! Let's go!"

And so, having pulled the perfect raid, with launches to carry the Americans across the lake to the hills and safety, Marking and his men returned with but one rescued soldier. It had not occurred to them to rescue by force. A captain's orders were still a captain's orders; it was up to the Americans to obey or escape, and only one had come.

Out of the raid, one lone American and rifles that brought Marking's strength from seventeen .30-calibers to sixty. Not a Jap had come out of the garrison to reinforce the camp guards. Marking had raided primarily to save Americans, not to get rifles. And the next day, the Japs killed ten, ten of the youngest and strongest among the dying prisoners.

Sick at the thought, never again was Marking to attempt the rescue of prisoners. He talked about it. He planned it. He envied other outfits' raids that brought some through, safe and sound. But he who had guts for suicidal fighting had no guts for the rescue raids that saved one and murdered ten.

For the one American they had rescued, fresh Jap troops hounded the guerrillas everywhere. That was how they rolled up on my doorstep, worn out with pursuit, in shreds, sore-footed, eating when and where they could.

Blind fighting. Suicide. No good.

Marking and I argued. "All right, give me a squad of men, and I'll show you a camp," I proposed. "You can rest and make plans and a last stand too, if you're fools enough."

He gave me the squad. Four miles farther back from the main highway I took them, to an old revolutionary fighting ground where plows still turned up shells marked 1898. Here among Kalinawan's limestone crags, bat caves, and underground rivers, they might have a chance. The squad mapped Kalinawan and the vicinity, and I sent them back to Marking.

The Japs went after him and his men again.

They dragged back to the haven I had shown to the squad, and there was safety but little food, for the harvests were still in the green and it was far from the town. Bathing Suit, the scout, lamented, "We should stick it. We should fight. They have sardines! And bread!"

Meager supplies in. Heavy patrols out. The camp full of sick men. High spirits for some, too high. Bewilderment for others. Fever, wounds, boils—"But it hurts, ma'am." No rules yet. No creed. No long-range plans. Nor short ones. Hit and run, hit and miss; from pillar to post and run again.

I found early that it was hard for him to bear the shackles of leadership, as it would have been for anyone. And I made him hate me because I insisted on it.

It was a Philippine custom, a never failing courtesy, to indicate departure. A Filipino might, in the excitement of renewing acquaintance or the weariness of duty done, forget to give greeting: "I have returned." But to give farewell, "I leave you here; *I shall return*," was a politeness never overlooked because its omission might be interpreted as a deliberate insult.

And so Marking fell in his fighters when they had eaten and rested. Turning to me, he said, "I leave you here." "Why?"—bluntly. "Because I am going now." "Going where?" "To raid." "Why?" "Well!" exploded Marking. "Am I to stay in this camp and be a woman?" "What's wrong with being a woman?"

The fighters waited in line, waited for Marking to walk down the file of them, waited for him to fall in at the head of the line and lead them out as he had for the same five months that I had, alone, tried to fight the war and win. There were scowls on their faces.

Patiently, wishing to leave me in a good frame of mind, Marking started all over again. "I leave you here. You will be here. I am going."

Again I said, "Where? And why?"

He flared. "I am going anywhere I can fight—that is where and why!"

Coldly I said, "You are going where you can get yourself killed."

"I die for my country."

"Phooey!" I said. "What good are you dead?"

There were mutters as well as scowls from the waiting line, but only Marking could hear what I said.

"It's my life," he said.

"All right. Go ahead and lose it. Be a damn fool."

Swiftly Marking countered, "Is my life more precious than the lives of the fighters? Will I ask them to do what I will not do myself?"

"Go ahead and get killed," I said. "Don't let me stop you. Somebody else will lead them when you are dead. He probably won't be as good a leader. He probably won't care what happens to them. He'll probably have enough brains to lead them *into* ambush, but not out of it. But you're in a hurry, of course. Don't let me delay you."

Sullenly and stubbornly, he repeated his farewell, "I leave you here."

With a deliberately sarcastic smile, I said, "I won't be here."

"You will be here. If you leave, you will be a prisoner."

"OK. Take me prisoner. Execute me. One way or the other, I won't be here."

He was cold, stiff, slow in his movements because of suppressed anger. He turned to the fighters, addressed the ranking officer, "Go ahead. I'll follow you up."

I had won the first round.

He sank down on a log, his back to me, watching the fighters file out. I bent to the typewriter again, rushing "contact" letters to be taken by the most trusted couriers to prominent citizens in Manila, to rich people, to loyal people, to keenly intelligent people whose opportunities and powers of observation would supply us with valuable advice as well as material aid. My years of newspaper work had given me a priceless mental file of knowledge. I knew whom to ask and where to find them. Carefully I avoided addressing any letter, but wrote into it just enough to identify myself to the receiver beyond a doubt: "Remember the day your baby was born? No matter what I thought, I said he was beautiful, didn't I?" That would bring a smile at memory of the long-gone occasion when a young mother had said, "He's such a raw looking mite, isn't he? Tell me the truth, Yay." She would know the letter could be from none but me, and she would intercede with her influential, wealthy father for information or money for the resisting forces.

The resisting forces, in the person of Marking, still sat twenty feet away on the log, but the shoulders that had been square and obstinately unmoving now drooped.

Letter after letter came off the typewriter.

Under the trees, where the westering sun could not filter its last rays, it grew cool and gloomy. The day began to darken around Marking, to enfold him, and he looked small and forlorn against the boulders, fallen logs, and thicket. I could no longer read what I wrote. I stopped, stretched aching back and neck muscles. Marking was hardly visible. I swung my legs around and over the log, stood to stretch other muscles. Was the guy still sitting there?

He was.

"Come," I said, "let's talk about it."

He made no answer. I took my hands out of my pockets and sat down beside him on the log.

"Now," I said, "let's begin again. I've said it over and over. I'll say it again, *for the last time.* After this, I won't talk. I'll just stymie you if I can, one way or another, as I stymied you this afternoon. For in this one thing I am right and everybody else is wrong. I am one against all of you, and some day you will thank me for it ... Are you listening?"

"No."

"OK. No good army, no really crackerjack army, gets its best brains blown out first. You are the brain of your fighters. Who teaches them to pick a high spot over a pocket in the road with at least two possible retreats? Who teaches them to spot the enemy and outthink them? Who keeps their morale up? Who is strong enough to control them by force when they won't pay attention to reason? Who knows more about guns than you? And who do they look to more than to you? Are you listening?"

"No."

"OK. This outfit of yours is going to grow bigger and bigger and harder and harder to control. Only you who brought it into being can keep it in line. How many times a day do you have to untangle them? They're a bunch of hotheads. They're freemen born. They're rugged individualists and, as Filipinos, are sensitive and proud. One fighter jostles another, the second says something he shouldn't say. Both are sick or tired or distressed by personal troubles. Both have buddies. Pretty soon half the camp is ready to settle matters with bullets meant for the enemy. Who is the only one who can step in and knock their ears off? You are, Marking. You know it.

"This war isn't going to be over tomorrow. It's not going to be over this year. Take my word for it. I will draft the propaganda any way you want it—and your guess is as good as anybody's. But there are authorities on world affairs who know what they're talking about, and they tell us it may take five years—"

"It *won't* take five years!"

"OK. However long or short, there is a job to be done. One man can't win the war. It takes many men. Any man can learn to fire a gun, but not every man knows when to use it and when not to. Not every man knows the difference between commandeering and banditry. You can recruit and train the thousands to fire guns, but who among them can you trust to remain strictly honorable? A rifle *should* be a trust; *actually, it is power over life and death.* That feeling of power can make a man drunk, unless he can carry that kind of liquor. Are you listening?"

No answer.

"OK. If anything happens to you, who will be the authority over these men you love? You do love them. They are your sons. You are thirty-six years old. They average from sixteen to twenty-five. Ordinarily, youth should be free to make its mistakes. That is part of the privilege of living. But these are not ordinary times. These are times of war. Life can be taken or lost in the split second. Girls can be ravished in the desperation of the moment. There can be lawlessness because there is no authority."

I spoke slowly. "This is your duty; your responsibility, your cross. Nobody can carry it but you, for you were marked for it and it was marked for you. Jesus was a little guy, but He carried His. He was a fighter, too, and He fought for exactly the same principles—equality, justice, human dignity, kindness, mercy . . . Oh, God, where am I now—off on religion?"

I began again. "Look, Marking, if you really give a damn about these men you'll save your own life a little longer. You're not going to live through this. Neither am I. Neither are most of the men with us now. But we can live long enough to do more good than just getting ourselves killed tomorrow. Look how the newcomers brag and act big just because they've got guns. I heard you bawling one out this morning, and you were right. Look how some of the old-timers have sickened and dropped out. Who will take care of them if the organization breaks up? They will drift through the countryside. The Japs will hunt them down. The traitors will find them and betray them. Some will go hungry and finally turn the gun against the helpless. By staying in camp, you will miss a lot of the fun, maybe. The glory will go to somebody else, maybe. You're going to be lonely in the crowd, but by holding the reins, you will be able to face God some day—and look Him in the eye.

If you live through this war, you will be a great man, believe me. You will be great because you were willing to be humble, because you did the dirty work, because you made the sacrifice of staying in camp—"

"I don't want to be great," Marking mumbled. "I want to fight."

"No. You just want to be proud of yourself. You haven't the courage *not* to fight. You want to leap over the ramparts and die a glorious death and stand in stone on a pedestal. You want the hooey, the baloney, the tripe."

"I want to fight."

"You want to show off."

"I want to fight."

It was an impasse; but he had heard me and would perhaps, for the safety of all of us, take it to heart. There was a moment of silence. "There's soup in the kitchen," I breathed, at last. "C'mon. Want some soup?"

"No."

"I finished thirty-three letters."

"Letters don't kill Japs. Bullets kill Japs."

"We need some iodine."

Silence.

I squeezed my hand under his folded arms into the crook of his elbow, stood without pulling him but also without removing my hand. He rose, and together we picked our way through the darkness toward the cook hut where dying embers lifted a low glow in the night.

The hot soup was comforting. It was a hunk of beef in much water, well salted to make it go farther. There was rice, and we soaked it with the salty soup, giving body to the liquid. Only the interior guards moved about the camp, stumbling sometimes over roots, slipping in the mud. A sick man tossed in fever. Together, cautiously under the blanket against the wind, we sponged him down with a rag dipped into a coconut shell of water. It was sketchy work in the darkness, but the sick man quieted.

"We'd better get some rest ourselves," I said. "The headquarters *kubo* is finished. It will be pleasant, not sleeping on the ground."

We picked our way into the *kubo*. Robin, the bodyguard, was already curled in his corner. That left places for two. Out of courtesy, I delayed picking my place, leaving the choice to Marking. To do so without making a point of it, I felt along the log seat with my leg, sat down, swung my feet over, groped for the typewriter and pulled it toward me. I could not write letters for lack of a light, but I could type out a list of reminders for the next day's work.

"What is that?" The sound of Marking's voice indicated that he had lain down on the shelf.

"Reminders," I replied. "I'll be finished in a minute, so the noise won't bother you."

"Your place is next to the wall on my other side."

"Thank you," I said. He would sleep in the middle between the bodyguard and me, my bodyguard against his bodyguard. I was the only woman in camp. I felt grateful to him, as I shortened the spell at the typewriter and groped away from the log to the sleeping shelf and over to the corner left for me.

I pulled myself up and squeezed against the farther wall in as straight and prim a line as I could make of myself. No need to add to the man's troubles, or my own. But Marking reached for me.

"I love you." "Man, man, get away from me. We have work to do. We need sleep." "Please!" "I'll think about it." "When will you tell me?" "Tomorrow." "Tomorrow might not come. Make up your mind tonight."

Tomorrow might not come...

When a man gives his life for his country, how little a woman's heart! I turned my head, to meet his lips. War was our marriage, the guerrillas our sons.

In a week the Japs were on us again. The outpost sighted three on the trail a quarter-mile away. Scouts were sent to check—all youngsters with the orders: "Don't touch. If they go away without knowing we're here, so much the better till we're ready for them—and their reinforcements." But one lad, a doctor's son, sighting his shotgun ("I was just pretending—I didn't mean to pull the trigger!") brought one Jap down, and the remaining two Japs hot-footed it to the garrison to tell the tale of their woe and our glee.

The boys bore their trophy in on a pole and dropped him like a sack of rice into a mud puddle six feet from my long, chipped-enamel plate of rice porridge. He was dead, but still warm with the blood flowing through the Double-Zero buckshot holes in neck and chest. He bounced once, heavily, as he hit the ground, and his arms and legs flopped loosely.

I had to keep on eating. I had to tell Robin not to pull the Jap's gold teeth: "It won't fit that gap in your face, Robin. You're pretty enough anyway. Let him alone." And another: "Stop kicking him. He's dead. Go after the live ones."

I had to keep on working. Finally, after three hours banging away at the typewriter—what a typewriter!—I lifted my eyes. There we were, the Jap sprawled on his back, and I.

"Marking," I said, "you've got a Moro prisoner. I'll vouch for him. How about untying him and, for God's sake, letting him bury that Jap?"

So Daud, the Moro, was untied and became a guerrilla with the untying. He expertly hitched a rope to the Jap's ankles and dragged him out, only to circle back out of my sight and bury him under the kitchen lean-to where the earth was soft and the k.p.'s [kitchen patrols] too harassed by hungry mouths to care what went underfoot. It was lucky Daud didn't lay him on the trestle with the cow. It was stew that day.

Early the next morning, Japs. Ten Japs, where the day before there had been but three. The outposts and later the scouts counted them. Just ten. Our raiding parties had rolled out at dawn and were long gone—an hour on their way, too far to call back; only the sick and seventeen for guard duty were left. The seventeen clamored to jump the ten. Daud the Moro with a .30-caliber; Velgo the *mestizo* with another; a farmer with a *paltik*, the barrel of which had to be unscrewed and screwed on again for each loading; shotguns and riot guns and .22s.

"Are you sure how many?" Marking asked again. "Exactly ten?" The boys were sure, and impatient.

"All right," said Marking. "Hit, then scatter in different directions. There are thirty-five sick men here without arms or guards. Retreat in any direction but this."

The boys raced one another out of camp, eager, hot for the kill. Ten minutes. Twenty. Then the *boom-bang-ping* of the medley of firearms. That should have finished it. What it did was begin it.

From somewhere behind the ten Japs, a full company let go at our seventeen. Velgo, still wobbly from his illness, headed straight up a mountain. The toothless farmer took off up the Koyambay trail, his *paltik* butt in one hand, the unscrewed barrel in the other; when he glanced over his shoulder and saw the Japs in chase, the old boy flew. Daud, instinctively the bush fighter, backed up into the brush and faded away after the others who had plunged through. The rest skirted the fray, leaving the bushes to take the beating, and turned up downtown, bathed, in clean clothes, sauntering idly down Tanay's streets, their eyes peeled for activity at the garrison. For a full hour the Japs machine-gunned and mortared the countryside; then they sent for Volunteer Guards, *the Japs' forced enlistment* of the people, who were also Home Guards, our *volunteer enlistment* of the people, to come up and help bury the dead. When this was done, the Japs ordered them to say nothing in the town. Promptly on release some circled back to our headquarters, where the day before they had carried rice for the fighters, to report, "Sir! We got twenty-three killed and many wounded." The rest sped townward to spread the good news to wife, brother, cousin, and friend, to the last happy, gory detail.

And the seventeen, reporting in by ones and twos and threes, strutted in glory: "Out of ten, sir, twenty-three! And they didn't get any of us!"

Marking said, "After this, count all of them, not just what they stick out in front. Know where the bait is and how big the hook. *Before you cross the river, look for the crocodile.*"

CHAPTER 3

*T*he Japs patrolled oftener and oftener, in groups ranging from 30 to 150. We moved back. We moved forward. We side-stepped. We sat tight. For more than eight months—from August 1942, to April 1943—the main base, our guerrilla headquarters, played blind man's bluff in a strip four miles long and two miles wide, and little crossroad *sitios* were to be consecrated in suffering and death: Kalinawan, Rawang, Makantog, Sulok, Mayton, Kanumay.

Marking and his men learned self-sufficiency the hard way. The first camps never knew where the next meal was coming from. Pooling resources from empty pockets was irony. The farmers brought their own rice and shared. Sometimes there were unaccounted donations from unknown donors, and somebody from somewhere carried it up to the camps. Never in the hurly-burly of volunteer assembling was there enough.

Many were sickening to death and, with eyes yearning to fight on, dropped out because they could not drag through.

Marking was the "father" of a hungry family. He had given refuge to lost soldiers, among them Cabalhin, and with no other place to go they stayed on day after day, weeks, months, until the outfit grew from 17 armed men to the "original" 150 in August 1942. Against his army pay, coming "some day soon," Marking borrowed from his friend the town barber, from his close-mouthed uncle Mang Esio, from his *compadre* the chief of police, one Peping Oliveras. The boys shared rice, and finally they added more and more water to the rice and shared gruel, and Marking kept them close under his wing around the hearth fire of the mountain hut. The Philippine custom of hospitality bound him to give and them to receive. While there was food, all would eat; when there was no more, all would starve.

Meanwhile, the countryside was being terrorized by Sakdals, the Philippine Fifth Column which had been trained by the Japs, and these looted and betrayed at will.

"Marking!" A farmer friend had come running. "They took my *carabao!* They took my good suit for the mass!"

And from Antipolo town, an old woman had panted into the hills, "Good sir, it is my son! My Philippine Scout U.S. Army son! They have pointed him to the Japs!"

And from town after town, "Protect us! Protect us!"

And always, a basket of eggs, a banana-leaf bundle of sweet rice, a clean, untorn shirt for one of Marking's men.

More and more fighters came to him; more and more of the helpless besought his aid. His refugee soldiers, lectured by him on right and wrong, grew into a chivalrous, patriotic brotherhood. Knighthood flowered again.

But cold and hunger were weakening his old fighters, and the new were untrained.

Leaving me in charge of the main base, tending to the guerrilla household of official mail, sick fighters, distribution of the little we had—a sliver of soap, a shred of tobacco—the father went forth to fend for food. One jump ahead of the Japs, one jump behind, for the towns were heavily patrolled by Jap troops, Marking implored the people to send a little more, give a little more. Defiant of the enemy, impassioned and humorous by turns, pleading for his fighters, weeping for the country, his feet braced upon the crest of a precarious spontaneous leadership, he touched the hearts of the people, and their pockets.

There was one who heard, and acted.

Miss Trinidad Díaz became a Home Guard.

She held the responsible job of cashier in the cement factory at Binangonan, the wharf town on the Laguna lake shore. Before the war, into the occupation, she was popular with the employees—strict on the job, yet kindly enough to fish up from her jeans numerous small loans until payday or to buy the baby's medicine herself. She had a following ready-made. Each weekend, she carried the pay roll from the factory to the quarry two miles away. Often she made the trip alone, armed with a revolver she had never had to use. The people loved her, and there was a picture of her, in jeans, with the gun at her waist. Against the background of tradition and the gentle, bashful womanhood around her, she stood out as a tomboy, but so gracious of heart she gave offense nowhere.

Before Marking left the vicinity, Lieutenant Díaz sent him gunny-sacks stuffed with clothes and food and funds contributed through her to "the people's army." For several weeks, she continued.

Then, abruptly, she went into combat on the spot, policing the district with her own men, liquidating a spy, laying an intelligence network to catch more of them.

The factory was on the lakeside for easy loading of the launches. Lieutenant Díaz saw temptations come and go, in the form of Jap-manned launches. She was not content with being a Home Guard. To become a guerrilla with a combat record intrigued her. Eventually the temptation to do in a few of them was too strong. Without much preparation, she and a half-dozen of her men struck, pulling a clean, quick foray on the wharf, killing all five Japs and hiding the launch for guerrilla use. With one order, she stripped the bodies and disposed of them; with another, set men to making armored plating for the launch.

"Sir: Please find enclosed the Japs' clothes and caps," she wrote. "The launch will be ready for your use two weeks from date."

Four of the Japs she killed were just Japs. The fifth was a naval architect, and soon the Jap High Command sent military police looking for him. The trail led to the wharf. Lieutenant Díaz held her people steady, and the investigators found nothing.

Time passed, and all seemed well.

The dead Japs had long been cement, and other Japs were all unknowingly pouring them into special earthworks in Bataan.

More clothes, more money, more food came from the indefatigable girl.

Then, unexpectedly, she was arrested. The Japs showed her a photograph of herself in jeans, with a revolver.

"Yes," said Lieutenant Díaz, "that's me. It was taken before the war."

That was not the point. The point was that she was "different."

"So, you are a brave woman!" they said.

She was hung by the heels, lashed, burned with cigarette butts. A Jap doctor revived her when she lost consciousness; then they strung her up again. They varied the treatment by tying her to a tree outside her room at the factory, leaving her there weak and fainting for twenty-four hours at a stretch. She was allowed no water but given a thin rice soup once a day.

All her friends who could get near enough were casing that job with hearts almost bursting. They counted the Japs in the garrison. They marked where the patrols passed, and where the sentries were placed. They estimated the minutes between raid and possible re-enforcement from near-by Cardona, from Angono, from Morong and Tanay. They marked alternative getaways. But no matter how they plotted the rescue, they knew they could save but one life and lose a hundred.

After three weeks hemorrhage set in, and her strength was the more rapidly reduced.

Still we watched, hoping the Japs would lessen in numbers, or at least in vigilance.

Long before her arrest, as if she had foreseen her fate, Lieutenant Díaz had told the guerrillas, "If anything happens to me, don't strike! If you do, it will be the helpless that will suffer. The Japs will take it out on the town. Wait for me. I'll get out of it myself."

Pending her escape or release, Marking promoted her to captain, and armed men awaited her leadership.

For thirty-two days and nights, she endured, admitting nothing. She knew no guerrillas. She knew nothing about a missing Jap naval architect. She loved the Japanese people and was serving them well at the factory.

Finally she was too weak to give the answers. She stopped answering at all. She hung crumpled in the ropes.

None was at her execution but the Japs. Did they shoot her, or behead her?

It was the Japs who called her brave.

From the old battleground at Kalinawan, we shifted to Rawang with its great mango tree on the hilltop and its little river that shot out of an opening in the mountain's side to cascade in eleven distinct bridal veils. After a rain, there were seventeen, a frothy bubbles-and-lace picture as seen from the bank below, where the river made a sharp left turn.

Jap patrols found Kalinawan, a half-hour away, and pressed hot on the scent, posting little flags along trails they had already patrolled, and each day starting up a new one. They were painstakingly mapping the trails.

Low on bullets, we were set to use our heads and our feet until the ammunition situation improved.

Then, when there was only one unmarked trail left in Rawang and it led to our camp—the garrison was transferred, and new troops came in. The guerrillas could not understand the change. It was inefficient. No sooner had the original troops learned the general terrain well enough not to need the guidance (?) of the Volunteer Guard, than off they went to some other part of the Philippines.

I knew that one, I thought. Back at KZRH a Jap official had asked me what the people thought of the soldiers. Cautiously I replied, "Well, you can't expect them to love your army. Look what your army has done to our country—" He interrupted by pointing through the window to the street below, where a Jap sentry had left his post and his stern attitude to share some pictures with a couple of passers-by. Even from our height, the sentry looked hungry for affection, eager to please. "Look," said the official, "look what your country is doing to our army." I was surprised. "You mean you have to keep them away from the people?" He nodded. "Otherwise they go soft."

That experience set our official guerrilla policy regarding the townspeople and their association with the Jap garrison troops: "Kill them with kindness. Make them want to stay forever. Wine them and dine them, and poison them with love of mankind and enough arsenic to make sure they won't die on the town's doorstep."

Now, new Japs in the garrison. Home Guards and our combat patrols had plucked away half the tiny paper flags the earlier Jap patrols had posted as markers. The new Jap patrols started in all over again, very confused by the rough sketches left in the office by the earlier garrison, because maps and markers failed to tally. So they patrolled and patrolled, and our patrols kept tab on the Jap patrols, and our outposts were on twenty-four-hour alert lest the new Jap troops blunder up the right trail by mistake.

Again the main base was undermanned.

Cabalhin was out. Rodriguez, the fat one, was out. Cunanan, the thin one, was out. He was never to come back. He had gone home to rest for three years. Postrade, the "real army sergeant," was out.

Runners brought back their reports to Marking. The fighters ambushed four trucks on the Emy-Emy, the zigzag in the mountain road between Antipolo and Teresa. They had routed a Jap patrol in Bulao, a *barrio*, accounting for a dozen Japs and grabbing up rifles and ammunition.

A new group reported in, having raided first to come up complete with the arms they had had before the raid and the arms they had taken in the raid. They lined up before Marking, "Sir, we are here." Marking sized them up, accepted them, dispatched them on another raid. They were the nucleus of what was to become one of Marking's toughest units—the Mata men of San Guillermo near Cardona, Rizal.

And the people, the small and the big, the weak and the strong, were ever present.

Home Guards came in long lines, loaded down with as much as they could carry of rice, salt, and sugar. Marking had them pile it where he could see it, and watched the rationing with a sharp eye, for each time Cabalhin and the others rolled in with their men, they needed not only rest but food.

In the milling about the camp, a friend slipped up from behind to sit beside me on the rough board bench from which I was giving free advice to nobody who wanted it. I turned, and there was Roger Moskaira's virile baby-face with its large, sultry-lashed eyes, and modest smile.

My mind flashed to the organization—there was a loophole somewhere. Somewhere, somebody had slipped up.

"How did you get through the Home Guards?" I asked.

"I made them bring me. I said they could kill me when we arrived at the main base if you refused to identify me."

"Some day, Roger, you'll slip up somewhere."

"What can I do?"

"What do you mean—what can you do?"

"I'm joining Marking."

"Well, of all things! What about Ding?"

"Ding's brave."

"Hell, I know that, but—"

"May I introduce Joe Mapa?"

"How do you do? . . . Roger, you go home before Ding comes up and knocks all of us for a loop. It was bad enough when the two of you hid me out—"

"Will you introduce me to Marking?"

"You've done enough. You go home."

"Shall I introduce myself?"

"Aren't there enough of us—Ye gods, ye gods! All right. Come along and throw your life away."

Marking and Roger fell to talking.

I talked to Joe Mapa, looking him over. Well educated, so refined that he seemed a sissy beside the drilling, arguing, lounging, tough-mouthed guerrillas. Handsome: curly hair, broad brow, good eyes, infectious white smile. Healthy: clear, bronzed skin, well-built body heavy in the shoulders, light of foot.

"It's a tough life," I said.

"Let's see."

"Let's see what?"

"Let's see if it's a tough life."

"It's up to you."

"I'll try." The man spoke quietly, stuffing his pipe with slow, strong fingers. Calm son-of-a-gun.

"Have you a blanket?" I asked. That always stumped them. We used to ask lowland volunteers, "Whaddya think we're running up here, a hotel?"

"I have a blanket, ma'am."

"What! Well—do you have a change of clothes?"

"And medicines."

"How many clothes? Your whole wardrobe?"

"Enough, ma'am, to carry easily."

"Well, the first volunteer who comes prepared! What were you, a boy scout? Don't be offended. The best—the most able men in the outfit had some sort of boys' training."

"I just came prepared, ma'am."

Marking and Roger worked out their plans alone, under the mango tree. Roger was to return to the city and find men who had joined Marking months before but lost contact after the Kalinawan fight, in which one premature shot brought on a big fracas.

Mapa was to stay.

The men were eying him—neat and clean and very polite, a perfect gentleman. They would find out in their own good time whether he was a man or just a gentleman.

For the moment I was being domestic. Not knowing that up to then the bodyguards had washed out Marking's clothes, however clumsily, I rolled his air mechanic's overalls around my own lighter garments and betook myself between typing spells down to the narrow, deep torrent below the waterfall. I had a fine, fat bar of Chinese laundry soap, and with it I undertook conscientiously to wash each garment and each spot by hand, native-style. Not even a handkerchief had I washed for years before the war. I rubbed, I soaped, I rubbed.

In two hours the chills took me—malaria again, encouraged by the cold water. I turned blue, shook with ague until my teeth chattered. It was torment to rinse the clothes and spread them on the bushes before returning uphill to the headquarters in the farmhouse under the mango tree.

Marking took one look at me and dug for the quinine pills. I tried to smile, to apologize, for there was work to be done, all kinds of work.

"Get up on the mat," he said. "Change your clothes."

With relief, I did as I was told. He handed me the pills and a shell of water, then climbed up to roll me in the blanket and pile an army coat on the bundle that was me.

"I'm sorry," I said. "I had it before."

He said nothing but climbed down, and I heard him calling one of the men usually dispatched on errands to the towns. I huddled deeper in the blanket. If I could relax, the chills would ease; my body would stop its aching and its shivering, and fever would come and I would sleep. Occasionally, I felt his hand under the blanket, feeling my hand or my foot. Fever came. I slept.

In the night, he awakened me, and I saw the little Montoya, a medical student, preparing a syringe for injection.

"Hello!" I said. "Last time I saw you was where?"

"In the mountains. I'm always getting called from the town, and I always go into the mountains." The syringe was ready. "This is the best injection for malaria."

"Arm or hip?" I asked.

"Hip," said Montoya.

Marking frowned, then climbed up to pull the blanket aside and himself bare the exact spot and no more for the needle. The moment the injection was completed, he pulled my clothes together, over the very small patch of skin that had been exposed, and quickly drew the blanket over the whole.

"Sleep," he said.

All that night he held me close, though sweat drenched me. As quickly as it came, the malaria passed. It would be back again on the hour each day like a clock. In the meantime the mornings were clear. I who had hiked between malaria chills could type between them. I could work.

Business proceeded as usual until the day Postrado brought back to camp a guide whom he suspected of treachery, with nothing more than circumstantial evidence.

"We'll kill you," said Marking.

I looked around the post and recognized Pascual, who had given refuge to three Americans for several weeks, and whose wife and daughter had given me a night's rest and the best food in the *barrio*.

"You don't mean Pascual, do you?"

"He betrayed us," said Postrado. "That is why our raid on Sta. Maria failed. The Japs came before we could destroy the bridge. Pascual used a light—"

"But I know this guy. He's all right if ever a man was all right. Of all the—"

"If he betrayed," said Marking, "he will be killed."

"He didn't betray," I said. "I know this guy."
"He did betray."
"Poppycock. Circumstantial evidence isn't proof."
"We'll kill him for betrayal."
"You'll *prove betrayal* first."
"We'll *kill* him first."
"Not unless he's guilty."
"Postrado!" said Marking. "Prepare a firing squad."
"You *can't* kill him, Marking."
"Ma'am," said Pascual, "I am innocent."
"I *will* kill him," said Marking. He pulled his .45 from his holster.
Quickly I stepped beside Pascual. "Then shoot us both."
Marking paled with anger, and his knuckles whitened as he gripped the butt of the .45. Slowly the fighters in the headquarters eased farther out of the line of fire. There was no sound, not a word, only alert eyes.
I said nothing, but looked as steadily at Marking as he at me, my eyes wide, his narrowed to slits.
For him, it was a showdown on who was boss.
For me, it was a showdown on what was just.
For the men, it was a test of courage.
The moment held, then Marking whirled, flinging at me: "You know I can't shoot. *I love you.*"
"Huh?" I was surprised, not because he had not shot me, but because love had nothing to do with justice. Even then I could not believe that Marking cared deeply for me. Later, as I came to know him better and better, I realized that Pascual had not been in great danger, for Marking had a keener sense of justice than I, and through him I learned the capacity of the Filipino to love a woman.
Out of this was born one of the outfit's legends—that I had courage; for I had stood up to Marking with the most courage of all and was fit to be "with him." The fighters were to come to me, in their troubles, for intercession. They were to leave to me the brunt of crossing or prodding him. And a companion legend to the courage legend was the love legend. "Filipinos die for love" is as true a saying as "Americans are free." It was not his love they doubted. It was mine. And thus they loved him for all things including his love for me, but pitied him because they doubted my own capacity to return it. They need not have.
Closer and closer to Rawang the Jap patrols were combing. To Kalinawan they had taken a dimpled, obedient lad picked up in town. He had been sent from Rawang on errand, to deliver orders to the town

units. In our old camp at Kalinawan, they beat him up, demanded to be led from there to a place named Rawang. One of our patrols kept tabs on the Jap patrol from the ridge dividing the two camps, but did not recognize one of our own among them. A courier running from the town to tell us of Benjamin's plight missed the way in a maze of trails. There in Kalinawan, a half-hour away, Benjamin died. Bullets or no bullets, we could have saved him had we known, or he could have saved himself by betraying us.

CHAPTER 4

Benjamin was my first personal loss. I lay in the night, cocooned in a blanket, held close in the curve of Marking's arm with my head pillowed on his shoulder. The cicadas thrummed and shrilled in the thickets around the camp. Without stirring, I lay remembering young Benjamin of the eager, gentle eyes.

"Sleep," mumbled Marking. "You sleep."

I neither answered nor stirred. He would think me asleep if I kept silent and made no move.

But the arm around me tightened, shook me once, imperative and possessive. "You sleep," he commanded.

"Can't," I said.

"Sleep!" And his other hand groped to tuck the blanket more securely about me. "Tomorrow, next day, another camp. You will have to walk. No horses. You sleep."

Worn by his own full day, he himself slept again.

Somewhere Benjamin slept. The maggots had him. They work fast in the tropics, the maggots. They would be in his eyes, in and out, working around the sockets, leaving them fleshless, sightless. In Benjamin's eyes I had first found adoration, the adoration of the boy who, right or wrong, sees in someone else the personification of an ideal. Benjamin's ideal had been patriotism. The look in his eyes had inspired me to be better than I was, to try.

Late in the afternoon of a drizzly day, Benjamin had come to me in Rawang. Marking was out, exhorting the people, begging for food. I was in command of the camp in his absence, and all able men were elsewhere on raids or administrative missions. Thus, it was a business of my hoping the Japs were too busy to attack a camp in which the sick lay huddled in their rags and an occasional gunny sack, the fit but weaponless stood guard to give warning and help evacuate the sick, and one foolhardy woman issued orders: "Don't kick off that sack. Do you want pneumonia on top of malaria? . . . Don't use the laundry soap for your shirt. There's only enough for your face . . . Until there's a latrine, go farther into the bushes. Don't just squat where you are. I know you're sick. You need a doctor, a nurse and a bedpan, but you've only got yourself. Here, hold on to me and we'll go together."

Benjamin came, breathless from a five-mile half-running hike: "Ma'am, where is Sir?"

"Out, Benny. Binangonan, I think." "Ma'am, the Japs are coming here." I stood quiet: "Benny, keep your voice down." "Yes, ma'am." "Have they left the town garrison yet?" "They were getting ready when I left." "Are you sure they were coming here?" "Yes, ma'am. Not exactly, ma'am. They have a guide for Kalinawan." "Who is the guide?" "A Sakdal, ma'am."

"Are you hungry? Have you eaten? Get some soup at the kitchen anyway, while I figure out what to do."

"Ma'am, perhaps they cannot arrive here tonight. I came most quickly. Also the Japs are not good in coming up. They rest every time. They breathe like the horse is tired."

"Have your soup." While Benjamin sipped hot broth from a shell I thought with outward calm and inward panic, and, as I thought, the panic abated. The Japs were headed for Kalinawan, a half-hour away. They would not go into it at night. They would wait for morning. In the meantime Marking would be cutting back, or Cabalhin might check in with his fighters. Or, if Mata's men struck somewhere, the garrison might recall patrols for their own protection. Anyway, there was time. There was time to think on it.

"Ma'am?"

"Yes, Benny. You did well to warn us in time. Go home now. Send word to me if more Japs leave the garrison and come in this direction. Take care of yourself. Tell the other Home Guards to find out more about the Sakdals. They know more than the Japs. They are more dangerous than the Japs."

"Yes, ma'am. I leave you here, ma'am."

I called Quimbo. "Quimbo, take several others with you. Go to the ridge overlooking our old camp—"

"Kalinawan, ma'am?"

"Yes, Quimbo. Use one man at a time to inform me on what the Japs are doing. There will be a patrol arriving there late tonight. They won't go into the camp, probably. They will stay in those empty houses at the crossroads half a mile away. If they enter Kalinawan, send a runner to me."

"I will comply explicitly with your immediate orders."

"Quimbo, some day you will get one too big for you, and it will choke you to death."

"I adore the English language, ma'am."

"So I notice. Now, what did I tell you?"

"I will proceed with the men under my command to surveillance from the highest point the enemy maneuvers within the terrain abounding Kalinawan, and by frequent communications acquainting my superior officer with the exigencies of the situation develops—"

"Quimbo, *get going!*"

"Yes, sir."

"Don't 'sir' me."

"No, ma'am."

"Quimbo!" Then, less impatiently: "Keep out of sight."

"I depart, ma'am." And Quimbo departed, tripping over a rock hidden in the ankle-deep mud.

Sleep that night was fitful. Twice I rolled out of the blanket to shove warm feet into wet, muddy tennis shoes and slog through the mire to the barracks twenty feet from my *kubo*. Each time I decided to spread my blanket over the sick, then decided against it. Marking would rage if he found out about it, and there would be the long-drawn arguments about the difference between what he provided for me and what was for general distribution. In the dark hour before dawn, sloshing in the mud brought me alert.

"Ma'am!"

"*What is it?*"

"None, ma'am. Quimbo reports that no Japs are anywhere. A farmer passed at night. The farmer said the Japs returned to the garrison. They took a wrong fork."

Relief flooded me. "Tell Quimbo and the men to return to camp and sleep." Promptly I lay back and slept.

Full daylight and the sound of feet in the sucking mud brought me awake to duties. I sat up, pulled my eyes open, and all around me were waiting men. They sat on the rocks. They leaned against trees. They stood around the split-sapling table in low conversation. Across from them I sat still in my blanket, hair tousled, eyes still gummed with sleep, like a witch in a little bamboo and grass cave set on stilts. Between them and me there was a sea of mud now churned up to a depth of six inches. In the center of the muck a boulder humped up like a hippopotamus. Around the boulder and through the mud came the patriots, to hand me reports, inquiries, personal letters, and receipts to be signed indicating delivery of supplies. They indicated other men "to be sworn in, ma'am."

All the dreary morning routine had me in its grip. I scarcely saw the faces behind the hands giving and receiving papers that somehow acquired small smears of mud, however careful all hands. I refused to sign the supply receipt until the rice and salt arrived in the camp before my own eyes. We had but one meal of porridge left for the sick, and I had not eaten the night before nor this morning, lest there be none for the porridge.

"Please, ma'am, I have eighteen years." The boy saluted.

"You're fourteen if you're a day," I said, after one look. "Ma'am, I am seventeen." And again he saluted. "You said you were eighteen." "Please—please, I will be a good soldier." "Tell me the truth: How old are you?" "Almost sixteen, ma'am"—with a third salute. "All right, wait for the 'Old Man'—your tears will break his heart." "I am not with tears, ma'am." "Hold up your head. Salute only twice: once when you come, once when you go. And you don't have to salute at all if you don't want to." "Please, ma'am, I want to."

"*Hold up your face!*"

"My eyes hurt only—"

"So! You're a crybaby!"

"I will ask the Old Man."

"You will have to, because I *won't swear you in.*"

But by the oath of the United States Army, as presented in the Rules and Articles of War, I swore in the others: "All right, repeat after me, 'I'—and say your name—'do solemnly swear to bear true faith and allegiance...'"

From the Fall of Bataan, April 9, 1942, Marking had sworn in his followers by the United States Army's own oath, and Marking himself had taken the oath first, down on the rice paddies in the moonlight, repeating the sacred words after Lieutenant Russell D. Barros of the Ninety-first Infantry Division, to whom, with other stranded American officers, he had given refuge. Barros was to go elsewhere, serve the cause, and become a lieutenant colonel. Marking was to remain throughout the war in or near Rizal province and become the most famous guerrilla leader in Philippine history.

As fast as routine accomplished itself, more men filed in with more reports, receipts, and letters. There was a note from Marking: "Darling, keep the camp quiet. Not a million Japs can find you in that place. I will be back soon."

It was the seventh day of his absence. Everywhere men had seen him pass. All over the countryside, from *barrio* to *barrio*, he was campaigning for solidarity against the enemy. "Give us your hidden guns! Give us your bullets! Never surrender them to the Japs, never, never—for the Japs will use them against you! Give us food and clothes for the fighters! Send us the wanted men, the hunted men, the lost soldiers! Give them a chance to fight, to save themselves, to save their country!" However he stumbled in English, there was nothing he could not say in his own language, Tagalog, and he lit the darkness of fear and despair like an unquenchable torch. "For me, there is no surrender!"

Again men filed out and men filed in.

Into the mud at my feet fell a short, fat man. He struggled to rise, to wipe the mud from his face with both hands, and I saw then that he had been flung there, for hands grabbed at his collar, yanked him back to throw him on his face again.

"Hold it!" I ordered sharply, with awakening indignation. "Traitor! He is a spy!" said a voice vibrant with its own indignation. It was Fulgado, ex-soldier, now guerrilla.

"Hold it!" I said again.

The man gained his feet, wiped away the mud, and when his eyes met mine he sank into the muck again, this time on his knees. "Mercy!" he quavered.

Fulgado kicked him in the ribs and shouted, "Because it is a woman, you ask mercy!"

To Fulgado, sharply again, I said, "To man *or* woman, any human being may plead for mercy. At *least*, your own leader demands fair trial. Doesn't he? Answer me!"

Fulgado looked hotly into my face. "Yes! But this one does not deserve it!"

"What did he do?"

"He told the Japs that the Volunteer Guards were our Home Guards—"

"He *what?*" The significance struck a chill all through me. Thousands could die on that report alone. The Japs could line up all the men they had forced to be Volunteer Guards in the service of the Japanese Imperial Forces, men who were also the auxiliary enlistment, the true underground, supporting the combat units or guerrillas in the hills— they could line them up and riddle them with bullets. Their lists of Volunteer Guards were the key. We should lose the faithful enlistment that kept tab on the enemy, gathered and gave and carried food to the fighters. We should lose even Benjamin, the small-town boy who had come five miles through a driving rain to tell us "just in case" the Japs were really headed our way. We should lose our future full-fledged guerrillas a-borning, for they would never live to carry arms.

Fulgado waited.

I looked at the fatness of the man cringing in the mud. He was slobbering into his hands, "Mercy, mercy!"

"Quimbo!" I ordered, without looking up.

From the circle of men pressing toward the figure hunched over its hands came Quimbo's reply, "Sir!"

"Put this man under heavy guard. Under no circumstances let him escape. Hold him for the Major's return."

"Yes, sir." Quimbo collared the fat man with a vim and hauled him roughly to his feet.

"Quimbo."

"Sir?"

"A man is innocent until he is proven guilty."

Quimbo's answer was to swing the prisoner around and shove him along.

Fulgado spoke. "There are many witnesses. We were all in the garrison, preparing to guide the Japs to another place where there was nothing for them to see. Then this fat one came running, and we heard excitement at the commandant's desk. The Japs were very excited. This fat one thought we were also informers like himself, and he told us that the guerrillas had caught him yesterday. This morning he escaped. He came as quickly as possible to tell the Japs what he had discovered *since joining one of our Home Guard units*. He was among those who carried rice to *the Kalinawan camp*. He was the guide last night when the Japs started to Kalinawan, but he lost the trail in the dark because he had only been there once. Already in the town two have been arrested by the Japs because he identified them as among those who carried rice. This morning this fat one was caught by the other Home Guards because they had already suspected him but were not sure before the arrests were made. Ma'am, I have the greatest respect for you. You are an officer. I ask only that you do not allow your woman's heart to hear his lies."

"Fulgado," I said, "your word against his is enough. However, there should be a trial. Final decision should be made by the Major—"

"The Major left you in charge of the headquarters. He gave you authority to act for him—"

"He will be back soon. Fulgado, understand this. If he is a spy and the orders are for *me* to kill him, I will. It is true that women are soft. It is also true that women can be the most bloodthirsty and cruel of creatures. I want to be neither. It is enough to do my duty."

"He should be killed."

"If he is guilty, he will be."

"He is guilty."

"The Major will make final decision."

"If he escapes, thousands will die."

"I understand that. But thousands may die anyway. He already has given that information to the enemy . . ." In my heart I felt again the chill. All our loyal Benjamins—no chance to fight.

Fulgado read my mind. "Ma'am, can you not share the blood on our hands?"

"There is nothing you suffer or dare that I will not share." "Then kill him."

"No."

"Then order him killed."

"To kill or to order the killing are the same, Fulgado. Sometimes the pen kills more than the sword."

"Will you let *me* kill him?"

"No."

"Is he going to be killed at all?"

"I don't know."

Quimbo had shoved the prisoner through the crowd that gathered, and pushed him along to the far side of the circle. As the crowd thinned, I saw both prisoner and Quimbo, himself the guard, hunched on separate rocks.

"I am going now," said Fulgado. He was as dissatisfied as the men who had listened to his testimony. "If he escapes—"

"He will not," I said. "You can trust me."

I had tested my authority and won.

More men came from the town. Among the reports was one from Benjamin that the fat man was a Sakdal from Palatiw, Pasig, a *barrio* known to be a nest of traitors. For a long time, gazing blankly into the mud, I thought that over. Benjamin loved people, and he was very careful what he said about them, even what he thought about them. So this was a Sakdal.

At one time the Sakdals, or Ganaps as they were sometimes called, had been nothing more than discontented farmers. There had been reason for their discontent. Under the cacique system—an absentee landlord system—they had labored in an economic slavery that kept them in debt years ahead of their hours. Their food had been measured by the handful; their wives had but one good dress, none too good; their children were rickety, and pale and potbellied from hookworms and roundworms. They bathed wounds with the liquid from boiled guava leaves because they could not afford pennies for mercurochrome. What little the landlords left them, the usurers took. Usually landlord and usurer were one and the same person.

Then an opportunist named Benigno Ramos organized a group of the disgruntled, helpless farmers, and their membership dues paid his way to Japan before the war. He returned in high style, riding the Japanese conquest, honored by the conquerors for the fifth-column work well done by traitors who had cut communication lines in Luzon ahead of the invaders. The despised, poverty-stricken, ignorant farmers followed Ramos straight into the arms of the Japs. When he handed the Sakdal membership lists over to the enemy few could escape collaboration even if they would, and the majority believed their day had come. No Sakdal could be executed simply on the strength of membership in an organization founded to aid and elevate him, for there were Sakdals and Sakdals. There was Pito, who had been arrested and brought to Marking and was at this moment with him as bodyguard and barber.

Marking made Pito dig his own grave. He dug it, making it deep, not hedging or pleading, or scooping a shallow pit against the inevitable. Marking ordered him into position for the shooting. Pito stood to take it, his homely, simple face without emotion. Marking fired over his head. Pito did not flinch. He also thought he was dead, and looked surprised that being dead was so much like being alive. Then Marking asked him his trade. "Barber, sir." And Marking said, "Cut my hair right or you'll be dead again." And Pito the Sakdal began running the gauntlet with Marking, guarding him through the night hours and exhorting his own family to send rice to the fighters. To me Marking had said, "See? Because he was brave. Never kill a brave man. A brave man can be reformed, but not a coward. If the fault is not too serious, save the brave man. If he has fault and is a coward, kill him."

Now I became conscious of looking at the mud. God, what muddy mud!

"Sir, is there coconut oil?"

"No," I said. "Yes, a little." And I remembered my .22, uncleaned, unoiled, fast rusting in the rainy season. I had cleaned it myself, for no real reason except that it was mine, given to me by Marking—my accolade as a soldier, like the men's addressing me as "sir." And so I said, "Wait. Let me dip my patch in it and you can have it."

I turned toward the rifle lying within reach and lifted it with my right hand to swing it around and drop the barrel into my left hand. There was a loud plop into the mud and a scream. "Mercy! Kind lady, mercy!" On his knees in the mire, his hands pressed together as in prayer, was the fat man I had forgotten.

Quimbo and I looked at him. Then suddenly Quimbo's foot flew out and kicked him, and he rolled over on his back, plastered with mud.

"Hold it," I said to Quimbo. "You do that again, and *you'll* be under guard." To the prisoner I said, "Get up. Stop that sniveling." Suddenly halloos rang through the camp, and laughter faintly from the distance. Soon a line of men filed in, a different breed of men from the Home Guards. They rolled as they walked, and the rifles slung from their shoulders or balanced on their shoulders seemed part of their bodies, so casually did they handle them. There were feathers in their battered hats, and their trousers were tied around their ankles. Their walk was not half so cocky as their grinning faces. "Hello, ma'am. We have returned." By the men who filed in—Cambusa of the large, heavy face, Pedro the clown, who had to be dragged out of a fight, Azores, who could make a guitar talk, Postrado, as military a soldier as customs of the service could produce—I recognized Cabalhin's group.

"Where is Cabalhin?" I asked.

"Coming, ma'am," said Cambusa. "No good, Antipolo." "Were you that far north?"

"Yes, ma'am. No Japs outside the town. No raid. Japs next week maybe. Long walk for nothing."

Quimbo collared his man out of the mud, propped him up on a rock. "Next time I kick you," he said, "there will be development in the region of the thrombosis."

The fighters looked at the prisoner, looked at me, said nothing. Cabalhin arrived. His impassive face was unfriendly. There was no greeting. "Where is the Major?" he asked.

"In the lake towns," I answered as impassively, then thought there was no sense in this. Whether he was friendly or not, I ought to be. He *was* a person I admired, and pride was pointless. "Have your men eaten? There is a little rice—"

"They have eaten." Cabalhin gave no thanks for my concern. "When will he be back?"

"I do not know."

"Who is in charge here?"

Hesitantly, I replied, "I am."

Cabalhin turned on his heel and walked back through the mud to the barracks. I sat quiet. Every fiber of me wanted to stand up and fight, but squabbling was childish and unmilitary, and ours was an army that was growing. Perhaps these disaffections were our growing pains. No longer was Cabalhin closest to Marking, for whom he would die without question. Marking had said, when he found him brooding, "But you're no woman, Cabalhin. I can't sleep with you."

But for dangerous months before I came Cabalhin had been Marking's bodyguard. He had rolled the trails with him, fought beside him, shared food with him, groped through the darkness for the blanket to tuck it more snugly around the leader he loved. Now, there was a woman around whose back the leader tucked the blanket though his own might be exposed.

My rifle was still uncleaned. I lifted it, and into the mud went the fat man again on his knees.

"I'm not going to shoot you, you fool!" I exploded.

The fighters still perched around on the rocks to rest roared with laughter. Cabalhin returned, and the mask dropped from his face as his eyes opened in amused surprise.

"He does that every time," I said.

Cabalhin turned his head slowly, and the mask was again in place. "Why?"

"You know better than I. You've handled this before."

Quimbo, who like most of the fighters loved Cabalhin, began to tell the story, throwing in many a five-syllable word.

Cabalhin's face grew darker as the facts presented a tighter and tighter pattern. Again he turned to me. "What are you going to do with him?"

"Hold him for Marking."

Cabalhin and a dozen of his men stared directly, unblinkingly at the fat man, who hunched even lower and turned his pig face from side to side to avoid their gaze. Then unexpectedly the prisoner stood up, hurried around the boulder on the far side from Cabalhin and his men, and, trying not to kneel in the mud, cringed toward me. He blubbered, "It is my father who is the Sakdal, not I. I will lead you to my father's house. Take him, not me."

"What does he say?" As yet I understood little of the dialect. Quimbo told me, in short instead of long words, and I gasped,

"He would betray even his own father?" Quickly, without realizing what I said, "Give it to him, make him talk!"

Instantly all the men except Cabalhin circled the rock, and the Sakdal was lost to sight. I scrambled to my feet, and Cabalhin stepped back, leaned against the rustic table under the tree. The Sakdal came into view, his face contorted with fear, making strange sounds. A fist smashed into his face. When he tried to cover it with his forearms other fists smashed into his ribs, and he was hidden by a mass of bodies pushing to get at him. He came into view again as Pedro and Cambusa stepped back to spare another fighter who had fallen also underfoot. Then an open hand smacked him full on the back of the head, tumbled him across the boulder toward Cambusa, who pounded him on the back, then kicked him as he rolled into the mud and was temporarily lost again. Other fighters hauled the traitor to his feet, yanked his bent elbows away from his face as he sought to protect his head, struck him in the ribs to straighten his bent body. Full in the face, they struck him again, and the yellow mud was tinged pink by blood. The blow carried him across the boulder on his back. The fighters spread out, in a circle around the boulder. As he rolled off, they caught him up again, stood him straight, landed more crashing blows to arc him across the boulder, back and forth, blow after blow, arc after arc, a game of human volley ball.

"No," I said. "No." I became conscious of my hands, cold and clenched, and looked up to see Cabalhin's sardonic gaze upon me. The fighters closed in again. Pedro, his eyes bloodshot, was beating at the Sakdal with both fists and whichever foot was free. He was shouting imprecations now: "You betray! You betray!" Others were grunting, "Son of a bitch, ass-kisser, cuckold!" The Sakdal groaned, and a blow in the belly brought a sickening gasp. He no longer protected himself, and he was limp each time he landed on his back on the boulder. Two of the fighters had to hold him up while a third struck him. There was a frenzy in their faces, a fierce, cold gleaming in their eyes. They had become strangers to me, and the horror held me helpless. Then, as the Sakdal spread-eagled, his legs on the boulder, his head in the mud, I saw Pedro kick for his groin and miss, shove another fighter aside to aim the final killing blow. I came to life, urgently, wildly. Down in the mud I went, against Pedro, to spoil his aim. Quimbo recognized me, pulled away, but was shoved against me.

"Stop!" I said, through a dry throat. "Stop it! Enough!"

The scrambling, maddened fighters still grabbed at the body, now nothing but a bulge in the mud, and Pedro shoved me aside unseeing. I pushed at his chest, and shouted in his face, "Don't kill him, *don't*." In the madness my small strength was nothing, and a blow not intended for me deflected and struck my hip. Even my voice was thin, unheard.

Then a sharp bellow cut the air: "Enough!" A figure not much bigger than mine plummeted at Pedro, then at Cambusa, and it was over. The fighters stepped back. Cabalhin, who had given the order and, smaller than either Cambusa or Pedro, almost spun them away from the prone figure in the mud, waved all the fighters to the barracks. They muttered but filed away one by one, still looking at the Sakdal, who stirred but did not rise.

"Quimbo, pick him up." It was all I could think of.

"Yes, sir."

I turned to thank Cabalhin. He stood looking at the Sakdal, and his face held a hate and scorn even fiercer than I had seen on the faces of his fighters. Then he followed his men to the barracks.

Weakly, I sat upon my *kubo* floor, my feet dangling in the mud. I faced the fact: I could command the fighters to do what they wanted to do, but I had no magic to stop them once they had begun to do it. They might respect me, but they had no physical fear of me. Of Marking, yes, and of Cabalhin. I sought in my mind for another, but the only officers the fighters feared were Marking and Cabalhin, and these two men they also loved most. My weakest word would be sufficient as permission, but I could scream at the top of my lungs for all the good it would do in stemming the tide of vengeance. I knew then that my strength would lie in preventing violence, not in trying to stop it once it started, and I knew the meaning of violence. I knew, too, that I was against it in all unnecessary forms. If we killed, we should kill outright, as mercifully and humanely as possible, so that our fighters would not be scarred by their own brutalities and would return to normal life without the blood lust I had seen so stark in Pedro and the others.

I came out of thought to see Cabalhin and his men filing out of camp on their way back to their sector near Antipolo—Cabalhin without a word to me, with a soldier's acceptance of authority, which at that moment I did not feel. First, last, and always he was a great soldier.

The dreary, drizzly day drew to an end without a sunset.

A runner came: "There is word from Benjamin's father. Benjamin has been taken by the Japs to guide them. Benjamin will guide them only to Kalinawan. You are not to worry. The father thinks the Japs suspect Benjamin, but wishes to assure you that his son will never lead the Japs to this Rawang camp because Benjamin knows you are here."

Soft-eyed, idealistic Benjamin, the first of the fighters to look at me with glowing eyes, as if I were a great and wonderful person. "Quimbo!"

"Sir!"

"Have you killed yet?" I spoke to the student as a friend to a friend.

"Not yet, ma'am."

"Do you want to?"

There was hesitation, then, "I love my country, ma'am, and I want to be a good soldier."

"You love big words, too, and want to use them all, don't you?" Quimbo smiled shyly at the friendly raillery, and I said, "I will teach you a lot of new ones—one at a time."

"Now?" he asked eagerly.

"Yes." I thought, then said, "like 'juxtaposition.'"

Carefully, he tried it: "Juxtaposition. That's easy."

"Don't you want to know what it means?"

"I like them anyway."

"Oh," I said, "I know that. Quimbo, this is something serious. There always has to be a first time. Are you ready to kill?"

"You mean this dirty coward fool, this, this—"

"Yes, Quimbo."

"Yes! Right now!"

"Wait. You might have fever afterwards. This man must be killed because—"

"He's guilty, ma'am!"

"Yes. But more. If he escapes, more of our men will be arrested. He knows more of them now, since his arrest, than before. And he has reason now to avenge. The Major may not come back for several days yet, and tomorrow there will be Japs very near here. We will have to be quiet. We will have to keep a sharp lookout. And we must not have this prisoner on our hands."

"I will do it right now—"

"There is more I want to say. It must be done quickly, mercifully. We cannot waste bullets. That is an over-all order. You must use the bayonet right through the heart. When I send you and your men to kill and bury him, you must not beat or kick him any more. He is dying anyway.

Perhaps he has internal injuries. He must be put out of his misery as quickly and kindly as possible. Do you understand me, Quimbo?"

"No, ma'am."

"What do you mean?"

"He is no good. He would betray his father, his brother. He is only for himself. He would sell the Virgin Mary. He would crucify Jesus. He is a Judas."

"But it is not for us to punish. Even killing is wrong, but now it is self-defense. We kill to preserve ourselves and our country. It is kill or be killed. Do you remember Benjamin? Well, Benjamin has been taken. Only this man in contact with the Japs knew those who brought rice supplies to Kalinawan—and now the Japs are arresting them, very quietly, one by one. Perhaps Benjamin can fool the Japs. Perhaps the other two can talk their way out of it. But Fulgado had difficulty convincing the Japs that this man was only reporting people who were his personal enemies. Fulgado could convince these Japs because when the man escaped from the guerrillas he ran to the nearest garrison and he was not known at that garrison; it was at another garrison that he was known, the garrison that is now arresting Home Guards. Soon that garrison will give the information to the other garrisons—"

"Ma'am, I understand everything. I will now proceed to my patriotic duty—"

"Quimbo, merciful. Take him far and finish him quick, understand?"

Quimbo snapped to attention. "Yes, sir!" Quimbo picked his men, and off they went, shoving, half carrying the Sakdal. I dug out the quinine bottle and essayed the mire to the barracks to portion out double doses. Those in fever needed sponging. Purgatives cleared the fever sometimes, but without bedpans or receptacles of any kind the sick men had to struggle through the rain to the bushes. Even when the quinine brought the malaria under control, there was no food to rebuild them. Beef broth was becoming infrequent, and there was only rice porridge, watery and tasteless—starch, starch, starch.

It was night and yet not night. The grayness of a day without sunset at the sunset hour left the last hour without identity. I could see my way around, yet it was dark. Somewhere outside the camp a human being was dead by my hand—or dying. I hoped the men would carry out my orders, yet knew more violence might have been committed in the name of patriotism. How many I was to kill by order, I had no way of knowing then, nor can I remember now. The number killed directly by my own hand is but one man, and I lost no sleep over that.

Over the lonely camp, the night finally fell. There could be no lights, neither *kingki* lamp nor campfire, for those were Marking's orders to keep us safe. Our number had dwindled to forty-three, for some of the able-bodied I had sent back to their civilian homes. For there was not rice enough for all, and soon the able-bodied would starve and sicken. I felt very much a woman and very much alone.

Quimbo reported to the *kubo*, slipping and stumbling through the mire as he felt his way.

"It is done, sir."

"Good. Sleep."

"Yes, sir."

In my thoughts as I fell asleep was Benjamin, who on the morrow would lead the Japs.

And on the morrow, Benjamin led the Japs. When they reached Kalinawan and he denied any knowledge of any other camp, they tied him up.

"You know where Marking is. You know where the half-breed woman is. Talk."

"I do not know," said Benjamin.

They beat him to insensibility. He revived. "Talk."

"I do not know." "Kneel." Benjamin kneeled. "Bow your head." He bowed his head, and one of the Japs unsheathed a saber. "Now *talk*." "I do not know."

The Jap struck the blow, and Benjamin's head rolled from his body to lie with eyes half open in a pool of clear rain water.

It was Benjamin who first thought me a heroine. But I didn't feel like one. At the moment that he died, I was counting quinine pills and swearing in more fighters. I was sure that Benjamin would die before he would betray us, but I did not know that he would *have* to die. And Benjamin was only one of many.

CHAPTER 5

*B*arr, an American, and his wife, Nene, were swept up by the guerrilla movement, and joined the headquarters, Nene as a registered nurse, Barr as a willing worker. An instinctive trail man, Barr found Makantog, the one blind spot the Japs, in all their patrolling and attacking, never found. They shaved by time and again, but always, somewhere along the line, they took the wrong fork, and Makantog remained the hidden valley cupped by high mountains in the heart of a labyrinth of mountain paths leading up and by and away but never in. One wrong turn could take a runner five miles off the beam.

Barr found the valley with *kaingin* rice coming to a head, and up into its safety and food Marking moved the fighters. Nene set up the outfit's first *kubo* hospital, prodding the convalescents into transplanting wild flowers and cutting trim pathways around it to keep them in the morning sun. They worked hard, Barr and Nene, and received little satisfaction, for they wanted a home and each other, and a guerrilla camp is no place to be at peace with the world.

To Makantog from all over the country came contact men, freelance organizers, couriers, city officers, and from the immediate vicinity of Rizal and Laguna provinces Marking's combat units, now grown to two hundred rifles, reported in and out on raids and patrols.

Roger from Manila brought in convoy after convoy of volunteers, clothes, medicine, and bullets. As he had brought Mapa, he brought Armando de la Rosa, to become the outfit's "Big Boy Bernie"—a handsome, six-foot Visayan, a bit inscrutable, always diplomatic, incorruptible, and given to scrutinizing the details, background, possible consequences, and significance of each and every incident and situation.

Alora came, Pablo Alora of Cavite. He mumbled humbly. "Howzat again?" asked Marking, and grinned at me, for he remembered the scrap of *The New Yorker* and its Howzat Again Department. I had read it to him and he had reread it for himself. "We need rifles and bullets," said Alora, very serenely. "So do we," said Marking. "I give you authority to organize to get them for me, not me for you." "But we want to fight, sir." "You get some more rifles and I'll let you fight."

It was a bad day.

A Manila volunteer came up. "Sir, I will go home." "Why?" asked Marking. "I will see my mother." "Why?" "She is worried about me." "Why?" "This is a hard life, sir." "Two days in camp and you want to go home!" roared Marking. "So it's an easy life you want! Borres! Put this pansy on k.p.!"

One of the regular fighters came. "Sir, it is broken." "What is broken?" "The firing pin, sir." "Let me see it. A Springfield! Why, you dirty son-of-a-bitch, don't you know how to take care of your gun? You don't deserve a Springfield! Give him an old Enfield! Give him a God damn shotgun! No! Give him a *paltik!* No! Disarm him! Borres! Put this man on k.p.!"

"Sir, there is no rice." "What do you mean, there is no rice?" "We ate it, sir." "All of it?" "Yes, sir."

"Cabalhin!" yelled Marking. "Do the other men still have rice?" "Yes, sir." "Then why doesn't the outpost have rice?" "Perhaps they eat more than their regular rations, sir." "So that's it! Glutting themselves. Halve their rations! Give them half of what everybody else has until they learn to skimp!"

Seneres, Alejandro Seneres, the oldest of three patriot brothers, came in. "Sir, I wish to go to Australia." "How?" asked Marking. "I will find a way, sir." "Swim?" "Batal, sir, by sailboat, sir. Please give me letters to take." "Why?" "To get arms and ammunition." "From whom?" "From General MacArthur, sir." "Bataan is closer than Australia. Go rake them up from Bataan!"

"Cabalhin! Read this report. Is this the kind of soldiers we have? Juanito Santos . . . Arrest him! Send men to pick him up. Five bullets!"

"What goes?" I asked, leaving the typewriter for a moment, stretching an aching back, twisting a sore neck.

"Remember Juanito?"

"I think so. What has he done now?"

In explosive bursts, Marking told me. Hungry and tired, Juanito had climbed up to an old *kubo*. Inside the *kubo* was an old woman, and tethered to the doorpost was an old chicken. He asked for the chicken, nice and proper, the way we had taught him. Said the old woman: "We've been together for years, that old chicken and I. No, you can't have it." Then Juanito forgot the rest of the lesson. He turned his rifle down and fired five shots. The chicken fluttered and squawked, and the woman fluttered and squawked all over the place. Home Guards passing by heard the commotion, investigated, and sent up the report.

This time I made no defense. Juanito was going from bad to worse.

"Sir, here is Juanito."

Juanito said, "Sir, it isn't true. I didn't get the chicken!"

"Did you fire five shots at the chicken?" "Not at the chicken, sir." "Where did you fire them?" "Around, sir." "Around what?" "Around the chicken." "You mean to say you fired five shots at that God damn chicken and didn't hit it once? Five whole bullets! I scratch my fingers raw, and you can't even hit a chicken! . . . How far was it?"

"Just there, sir." Juanito indicated a spot ten feet away.

"Mapa! Keep this man under heavy guard. Charge: wasting five precious bullets."

"Marking," I reminded, "he was breaking the Rules and Articles of War."

"Also the Rules and Articles of War," Marking amended. It was a bad day.

"Sir, we are ready to drill." "Sir, Major Salvador is here." "Sir, shall we distribute the *tapa?*" "Sir, more of the Manila men are sick." "Sir, Tomás left the camp without permission." Again: "Sir, we are ready to drill."

Marking to me: "Yay, I will be at the outpost."

And I: "Thank God!"

Ruffled, Marking demanded, "Why?"

"Because I can hardly think when you're around."

More ruffled: "I don't bother you. I never interrupt you any more. You don't want me around."

"It's not that, Marking, but where you go the *whole camp goes!*"

"I can't help it."

"I know you can't. Go along to your outpost."

"I'll stay there the whole damn day!"

It was still a bad day, but he was off—at last.

I opened up some freshly arrived reports—to find out what had happened to our last batch of counter propaganda.

Into the hands of the Japs, *in toto*—all our "paper bullets."

From the beginning of the war to the end of it, whenever the Japs got too thick for our numbers, or we were low on bullets, we pulled our fighters far back into the hills and using courier and Home Guard distribution, turned to counter propaganda. We fired the paper bullets with zeal, mostly because it ired the Japs and lifted the hearts of the people.

Ernesto Felix, battalion commander in charge of Home Guard enlistment in Cardona, Morong, Binangonan, and Tanay, who was most eager to render any patriotic service, organized a group of the loyal. The group grew, and among them he went to get all that he could "for our army in the mountains." He fed his children with one finger, and devoted the other nine to the fighters. He was ready, willing and able around the clock. Years of education, experience, and travel in America fitted him for a multitude of assignments. Furthermore, as a small-town businessman, he was practical.

To Major Felix went an order for two reams of a certain handbill, "copy attached." His men did a flawless job: not one typographical error; no smudging of ink; margins straight. Then he took upon himself the risk of transporting it. From Cardona, where the mimeographing had been done in the municipal building, he sailed across the lake to Tanay. It was late at night, but the wind was high, and along the lake trips depend on the wind, not the clock. He arrived around one in the morning. Mischance, not betrayal, placed the Japs on the shore when his boat came into the shallows and it was too late to pull out and land at another point. The Japs too had learned to cross when the wind was high. There was no retreating into the lake. The telltale propaganda was found in the boat, and he was captured before he could get away.

In a hut on the shore, they pulled his arms back and up and strung him in the "butterfly swing," his feet a yard from the ground. Then they proceeded to beat him with a club, steadily, killingly. On his way that night to deliver the propaganda direct to headquarters, Felix could have ended his suffering with a few words: "Marking is at Makantog." He could have told, and won employment as a spy which would have enabled him to feed his seven children more than they had ever eaten before in their lives. Some have done it.

But not a man of Felix's caliber.

At dawn, his arms gave way in their sockets; his toes scraped the ground as his body swung limply, to and fro. They cut him down and dumped him on the floor of a car in which they took him to the dread Antipolo garrison for some more.

He was dead before they arrived and, because the Japs concerned had no business beating a man to death when Fort Santiago could apply the "finer" tortures and keep him alive—and maybe talking—for months, they stuck him in a hole behind the garrison and hurriedly covered him up.

Felix's grave is marked by a depression in the earth, and there are other depressions in that desecrated, and consecrated, schoolyard. The question is, which here is which?

CHAPTER 6

By October of 1942, the outfit was growing by leaps and bounds: full-time fighters in the hills; part-time saboteurs, working for the enemy and undoing all they had done; propagandists writing, printing, passing their down-in-black-and-white defiance; men and women training themselves as intelligence agents, learning to observe and retain and evaluate what they saw and to convey the information accurately and quickly; a countryside, bending its back to a double load: the Jap army that took by force, and their own patriotic army that begged, begged, begged.

"Marking's Guerrillas" was not the only organization, although it was the largest and most active and was based in the province closest to Manila. There were several other big outfits, and hundreds of small, compact groups everywhere, namelessly, cautiously striking, delaying, negating the enemy. There were the "USAFFE Guerrillas," the "Hunters," the "Fil-Americans," the "Quezon Guerrillas," and the activities and organizations overlapped one another. There were Peralta of Panay, Kangleon of Leyte, Fertig of Mindanao, as in Luzon there were Marking, Anderson, Terry, David, Clark, Vaulkman, and a score of others, of all of whom great things are said. History will do its own winnowing.

As his organization grew, Marking turned more and more to training his fighters. His was the personality—magnetic, intricate, young, golden with laughter, fragrant with tears, complex, contradictory, filled with surprises—that drew and held the following. An ornery streak kept him of earth and made him understandable to his men. And his was the ability to whip raw civilians into a discipline and tradition of their own. None could outshoot him, nor outfight him, nor outthink him. "While you're still on the way to church," he would say, "I'm already coming home." And it was true. Sometimes it was too true, and, overzealous in keeping the organizational record clean, many a fine officer was cruelly hurt by flat, unfounded accusations that he was loafing, cheating, or breaking the rules. Through three years I was to spread my skirts protectively between Marking and one or another of his best men.

Marking was growing restless. No born field man can be chained long to a desk, though that desk be nothing more than the focal point to which every decision is sure to come. I could advise and plan, but Marking had to decide. Marking was sick unto death of deciding, yet it was his outfit, and he was running it. He tired of the administrative burden and sought to drop the onerous details in my lap. Fair enough, but he still had to decide.

Felimon Aquino came in, dapper despite the season, muddy only halfway up his pants legs when the half-dozen men with him had splatters belt-high—he had stepped around the puddles in the trail instead of plunging through. This darkly handsome man with the slow twisting smile was reticent. He was a man of the world without ever having been out of the Philippines. So sure was he of his charm that he made no effort to keep a softening waistline lean; the poker table and the cockpit claimed his waking hours, and a likely lass could share the rest. How had this cool assurance warmed to the heat of battle? He was manly, but his own words were, "Why live by your muscles when you can live by your wits?" Marking disapproved of him for a number of vague reasons, but he could not deny Aquino's courage and loyalty.

Said Marking, "I catch him gambling with guerrilla funds, and pft! there is no more Aquino." And he watched for three years.

Perhaps Aquino kept his own funds and the collections all in the same pocket, but they always added up right, and he could lay the money on the line even when without warning Marking called him to account in the middle of the night, and always there was Aquino's slow smile, which drove him insane.

"I catch him this time," said Marking. But he never caught him. Aquino, saluting, explained that once again there was difficulty in soliciting aid. "The people say they do not have it. They say no in many ways. Your orders have been not to use threats or force. Do those orders still stand?"

Marking sat bent over his small typewriter, absently wiping it with a rag.

Across from him, in front of my own machine, I continued writing. But as usual half my attention was on events around me. The words ran along the line, the bell rang, and I swung the platen back for a new line:

"and it is imperative that all subordinates realize how necessary it is [new line] to preserve this leadership which is both inspiration and control [new line] for leaders are born, not made, and we who strive in lesser capacities [new line] will not soon again find among ourselves or elsewhere another like him. [New paragraph.] To the people he is already a legend. They come just to see him. [New line.] Personal contact with him fires them to take part in what [new line] he himself is doing toward eventual victory. Let us keep the legend of Marking alive [new line] like a jewel in cotton, to be shown on rare occasions and always [new line] to be guarded for the precious thing that it is."

Marking said to Aquino, "I will go down with you to the people, and I will tell the great need we have."

"There are too many Japs, sir," said Aquino. "I will keep you informed. You are too badly wanted to move freely. There is a price on your head."

"I will go with you."

Without too much pause in writing, without looking up, I asked, "Why?" It was the same old *why*.

Without answer, suddenly violent, suddenly fed to the teeth with my endless pounding, Marking laid both hands on the typewriter that he had that morning taken apart and put together again. He lifted it, swung it, then with all his force threw it ten feet into the mud. As it passed between Aquino sitting on the log bench and me on the *kubo* shelf, we noted its flight but did not exchange glances. I typed one more line: "Whether he himself likes it or not, he must be kept safe."

"I will go!" shouted Marking.

I rose. "You will not go."

For answer, he yelled, "Robin! Fix my pack! Check the bullets in my clip! Pabling! Get ready! I take but five men!"

"All right," I said. "Go. But don't expect to find me here when you come back."

My statement brought a quick thought, part of the past which was a challenge to him. He grasped at it eagerly.

"So, you will go away! Let the men stop you, let them show tears in their eyes to hold you! Let them beg you to stay! Let them be fools to want a damn woman! As for me, you can get out! Right now!"

I stood looking at him.

"Well, go!" he shouted. "Get out! Right now!"

I still looked at him, coldly, without love. "You forget." "What?"

"What I told you I would do."

"What you told me—" His eyes narrowed, and he remembered the even greater threat I had once made out of exhaustion and irritation with his fractiousness. If his rage could be more intense, it was then. Gritting his teeth, he said, "We will see."

Quietly, I went on: "You *will* see. It will teach you a lesson you will never forget."

"I will be very sorry." There was sarcasm and disbelief in his voice.

"It will be too late to be sorry, but that isn't the point. If I can't hold you as I have been doing, I can hold you that way. You will remember my words, all I have said and said and said until I am sick of saying it. You will remember—"

"Phooey!" said Marking, and spat. "I do not believe you will do this for me."

"Not for you, Marking. For the fighters. For the people. For the organization."

I turned and stepped along the rustic path of sawed logs he had made for me through the mud, past the rustic table and vine-tied chairs of split saplings with which he had made me a solitary place all my own under the big tree beside the brook, past the pool deepened by scooping and damming where I sponged him down, when I could catch him between hurried activities. Out into the clearing I stepped, into the warm and golden sunlight, and on up the slope to a hummock where for a little while on good days I had sat alone, chewing on a grass blade and watching the clouds as they came over the ridge.

On the way up the slope it came to me how tired I was. Until late at night, week after week, I had been writing. Without a light. Orders and circulars, and hundreds of letters for Marking's signature. Over his protests, I made him read everything he signed, knowing it was easier to read than to write, to think the words on the page. And many times, in things which seemed unimportant to him but were truly important, he refused even to think. So I had thought, put in what became his policies, and when he saw them he knew how vital they were, what precedents would grow out of them. He was grateful for this. He appreciated me. He admired and respected me. But the effort of doing it all had exhausted me completely. I was a one-woman staff who ran all the dangers of the outfit without enough strength to do that alone, much less the rest of it. And the rest included not only hours of paper work but the hours after three a.m. when Marking talked, insisting that I listen, and I reminded him of things, encouraged him, tried to clarify things for him. Constantly, never-endingly, I was at his beck and call—forever "on duty," and now I was almost insane with it.

Going up the hill, I felt neither sorrow nor anger. I knew what I was doing, and, alive or dead, I would be in the fight to the end. Mine would be a victory accomplishing itself until Victory itself was achieved. A little pity for Marking stirred in me. I had taken a wild and free creature and broken it to bit and spur. I had groomed it not for my own horsemanship but for the good of a cause. Discipline galled the untrained, untamed thoroughbred, but until he stopped rearing and kicking and bucking he was force undirected. Over and over again there had been tears within me, tears for him as he fought free of responsibility, but a country needed him not as he was but as he could be, and out of my own small cunning I had helped to break the stallion to harness.

The day was clear above me, and the clouds were high. They were travelling fast, and that meant strong winds. This will be my death, I said; away out there in eternity, I will have the wind. I will be free in the wind.

I pulled my pistol from its holster, sprung the catch to check on the six bullets in their neat, revolving cylinder, snapped it back into place. It was a pretty little gun, given to me by Marking, who had taken it one day when he and three others had been ambushed by Sakdals and had killed nine of them. It had been cocked and pointed at Marking's head by the Sakdal Patena, and Marking's shot had caught the Sakdal in the head before he could pull the trigger. Ever since, the pearl and nickel-plated .32 caliber snub-nosed Colt had been known by the name of its previous owner.

And so I looked at Patena, and my thumb pulled back the hammer, and I raised it. Marking's hand closed over my wrist. I had not seen him approach, had not sensed the presence of anyone. I looked for others, but only Marking was there.

"Are you really going to?" he asked, challenging but quiet.

I did not pull my wrist away. I said, "You don't have to see it. I thought you had gone. You should go now."

"I won't let you."

"You can't stop me."

"I will take you with me."

"It's not that."

"What is it?"

"Marking, if you don't know what it is, you will. Come, bend your head. This is a kiss for good luck."

"Come with me," he said.

"No."

"Then what is it?"

"It's the principle of the thing."

"What's that?"

"It's American. Filipinos will die for love, and Americans will die for principle. I am half-and-half. I die the same way."

"Come with me."

"No"—and again I felt exhausted.

In defeat, he put his arms around me. "I will not go any more. I will stay."

"No," I said. "You go. I am tired of arguing. I am tired of everything. If I do this, all the arguing will be over. You will remember all I've said, but I won't have to say it and say it and *say it*."

"I will stay," he repeated. "But it will kill me to stay in camp."

I knew. And I should have to watch his slow death. Trying to be patient, I said, "When the garrisons are light and there are no big patrols, you can roll. You can't go now. There's a flood of Japs throughout the province. The reports show a heavy garrison in every town and tight patrolling between towns. You cannot pass without risk of encounter, and an encounter will bring enemy reinforcement and encirclements everywhere. It's all a trap, wide open to snap you up, a trap with doors everywhere. That's why I want you to stay out of the towns and foothills—that and to protect the people."

I stopped, suddenly overcome with weariness. "Marking," I asked, my eyes directly on his, "have you any idea how *tired* I am?"

He turned his head over my shoulder, to hide his face, and said nothing. But I knew he had heard. I sighed—the victory was a bitter one. And the endless work pressed down.

"Come," I said at last, "you've got a dozen letters to pass on. And you haven't decided whether to establish that training camp for the Home Guards."

Marking helped me to my feet, taking Patena from my hand and unobtrusively slipping it into his back pocket. Past the rustic table and seats along the log walk we walked slowly. The fighters were absorbed suddenly in small tasks, folding a shirt, cleaning a gun already cleaned, cutting brush. They had watched us in the clearing through the screen of trees, but nobody made comment.

Borres the cook-bodyguard brought a large coconut shell steaming with imitation burnt-corn coffee and Marking took a draught and handed it to me, turning the shell in our private way so that I would drink from the same spot on the rim.

We sipped the coffee back and forth, then remembered together: "Aquino! Where is he?"

"Oh!" said Borres. "I am to say to you that he left. He made the farewell to me."

"When did he leave?"

"Very quickly, ma'am. As soon as the Old Man was not looking." Borres grinned at me behind Marking's back and slapped down a banana leaf for our scoops of rice, steaming and white. "Porridge," I said, "—not hard rice. We're short, Borres." Imperturbably, he said, "Porridge for everybody. Rice for you."

"Porridge," I said.

"Rice."

"Orders were for porridge."

"Yes. I give you rice." And then Borres produced a surprise: *tuyo*, the small salted fish so much a part of a native meal.

Marking picked the biggest and most crisply toasted and placed it on my scoop of rice. I picked it up and laid it neatly upon his scoop of rice. He returned it. I put it back.

Borres spread the rest of the fish with his stubby forefinger, found another large one, placed it on my rice, saying patiently, "Same size, same cook."

That night, with a great man's arms ever more tightly about me and the day's happenings hours behind me, I shivered.

"Cold?" Marking pulled the covers around me.

I made no answer, and he slept again. Boy, I thought, that was close! I might have killed my fool self. Was I bluffing? Would he have called it? What happened, anyway? I shivered again, he pulled me closer, and we slept.

A day passed.

A week passed.

There was the eternal camp routine. I said nothing more about staying in camp. If being nailed down irked him, nagging would be of no help.

Finally he slid right out of it and was off into the Sierras, Robin Hood, Richard the Lionhearted, Errol Flynn, and Tarzan all in one, flipping his cares away. "You do it, darling," he said.

"Don't you 'darling' me, Marking."

But he was already on his way with a hundred armed men or more, and neither straight talk, nor crooked talk, nor crocodile tears availed. He was gone.

When I looked at what was left behind, I braced my aching head between palms, one by one checking off every vile word I knew. There, with the Japs practically at the mouth of the valley (for they had found Rawang), with some fifty sick fighters, weaponless recruits, and square pegs for which there weren't even round holes, with no rifles in the camp worth mentioning and *only twelve shotgun shells* in all three outposts—there I was, in charge. Mine, this time, the decision.

Stick it, and with twelve shotgun shells give enough delaying action to pull the men out of an attack? How many of the shells were good? How many of the sick men could walk how far? The Japs *could* be on top of us in two hours from the moment I sat there cogitating.

So I fished around among the men who knew the countryside, and lo! one of them knew a good place with wood and water galore a little farther away from the Japs. Late in the afternoon and through part of the night, we stumbled and dragged and crawled through vines for lack of a *bolo*, to reach one of the prettiest camps we were ever to have—limestone basins in easy drops with deep, smooth, shaded pools all up and down the river, Roman baths for everybody—and everybody needed it, including me, what with the rivulets in Makantog drying up before our eyes. That was the only thing wrong with Makantog: it was seasonal.

CHAPTER 7

*R*unners and sick men reporting back from Marking gave me juicy bits of gossip. He and his "expeditionary forces" were having their troubles. After the headache he had left me, I was maliciously gleeful, and plied each man with questions. Blisters, cut feet, lack of food. Those were the answers. A hundred men all armed was big stuff back in October '42. The knack of feeding them en route had to be acquired by teaching them to go hungry first.

Marking had led them forth, then stepped out of line occasionally to check each platoon as it filed by, sweating and panting on the rough mountain trail. There were swollen feet and raw knees; shoulder thongs of bark or rattan bit deep. A morning rain greased the trails; then the sun came out full blast, and the world steamed, and the trails turned to glue.

Marking observed each man, corrected pack carrying, eventually wound up at the end of the line, prodding them up the mountains, coaxing them down.

When he caught up with the "main body" at the bivouac area, the fighters had rested in a sugar-cane field and not a cane was left standing. The field was covered with guerrillas and bagasse.

Pale with anger, his eyes narrowed almost shut, he fell-in the whole lot—officers, enlisted men, guides. Then he spoke. His words were short, to the point, and he challenged each man and all of them together.

"You men, who gave you the order to eat all the sugar cane—even one piece of it? You officers, did I tell you to order the men to take as they pleased?

"You will listen to me before somebody gets killed. I did not organize to prejudice the civilian. I did not organize to be the leader of bandits, even the bandits of sugar cane. I organized to fight the Japs, who do exactly what you did here on this very day in front of my own eyes. Do you know how many the mouths we are? Do you think the farmer can say no to you when you have the guns and he has no gun? From sugar cane you will take a horse. From a horse you will take a *carabao*. From a *carabao* you will take a woman. All this you will take because you have guns and nobody says to you, 'No, you cannot take my horse, my *carabao*, my daughter.' You think you can take it because it will be your habit. And I shall be the leader only of bandits, to my shame forever."

He flung at them. "I *did not ask* you to *join me. You asked me to accept you as my followers* . . . Who is it teaches you how to fool the Japs? I do. Who teaches you the smart precaution? I do. Who makes excuses every time for your mistakes? I do. You made me the leader, and what is your fault is my fault. It is *my good name* you ruin with your foolishness!"

He remembered something. "Do you think you can live and fight without the people? They will betray you. If you continue like this, they will *have* to betray you, to protect themselves and to keep their *carabaos* and their wives. Or they will hide their food. They will give nothing, nothing. How will you eat? On the grass side by side with the horse? Because you do not yet starve to death, you think it is easy. It is not easy. Always I beg for you. I *beg.*" He looked at them as if they were two inches high. "For myself alone I do not have to beg. It is for you I beg. All my life I work with my hands. I owe not one debt. Instead, it is other people who owe me. Now, for your sakes I beg!"

His voice lowered. "Let me tell you something. I do not want to be a leader. It is harder for me the taking care of you than taking care of myself even if I am the most wanted man in Luzon. All day I must think about feeding you. I must drill you. I must teach you to take care of your firearms, which are my firearms, which are the firearms of the United States Army. I must teach you to eat salt to keep your strength, and not to drink too much water at once after a long hike. I must take care of your sickness and get the medicines to cure you. I must look for your clothes and your blankets, and almost I go crazy getting more bullets all the time, more bullets. And—God damn it—will you keep your eye open and *squeeze slowly?*" He paused and went on. "I am so tired of being a leader I don't care sometimes if I get killed. You came to me, and that is how I became a leader. If you all go away I will not be a leader any more, and I will not be sorry. Here I am today teaching you to force-hike, and what am I teaching you instead? I am teaching you what God teaches you in the church. I am teaching you the difference between right and wrong, and maybe I better just blow off somebody's top. With all the great big army of MacArthur, he has not my headaches because he has real soldiers and America feeds them and makes bullets for them and also makes blankets. Here I have to make even the soldiers. The only one officer who helps get more guns and money and medicine is Major Yay, and I tell you I would make that woman also a combat officer *to shame you*, but she is shortsighted and sick. And I ask you, Have we no men left in this country that women must fight?"

He stopped suddenly. "Stand up straight while I am talking to you! Attention! Or somebody sure will get killed!"

He went on slowly, point by point, "I will now speak in a language you will understand: The sonumbits who disobeys my order will shoot it out with me. I am tired of being ashamed of you. Locusts, look at that bagasse! Look at it! Hell! *Hell!* HELL! Who wants to challenge? Step forward!" A pause. "Speak up! I will tell you with a God-damn bullet between your God-damn eyes. That is what you understand. Come on! Are you cowards? Am I also the leader of *cowards?* Come! You are one hundred and thirty! I am only one! Are you afraid?" Scorn again: "You'd better be!" Resignation. "Now I will pay for the God-damn sugar cane. Where do you think money comes from—the sky? At ease!"

After Marking had finished, his voice deep and full, his hand on his .45, no fighter in his sight ever touched a farmer's crop—not one cane, not one sweet potato—without asking first. Marking would offer to buy a whole crop. If the farmer said no, it was no. Marking might persuade like a Fuller Brush man, evaluating freedom in terms of corn, but no was no. For the sugar cane eaten by his guerrilla locusts, he paid double its value.

There were Japs in the backwoods at Daraitan, but not many, and they were far from any town. No helpless population to be caught in the crossfire. There were Dumagats, the aborigines of the district, but no bullet could catch those fast-footed babies.

So Marking and the Expeditionary Force began to stalk the Japs. They stalked and they stalked, and into their midst fell a Jap mortar shell.

Mario Lacson, forever sitting down to tell funny stories and to rest a minute, landed on his feet running. His feet pounded up and down. His arms flailed the air. "They got me, they got me!" he squawked, all humor gone, his eyes bulging, sweat rolling down his temples the size of corn kernels.

Marking caught up with him, unhooked the vine from across his throat. "There," he said, "now you can make headway."

Another shell punctuated that, and Mario leaped away and fell into a hole. "My God," he panted, "what's got me now!"

Marking was helpless with laughter, but worried too about the rest of the men. For everybody else had flown and fallen and flown again, and it took a full two hours to reassemble his command. Only veterans like Cabalhin, Mata and Lucio stayed steady. Then his scouts reported that the Japs who had scattered his more-than-a-hundred guerrillas numbered exactly sixteen whole Japs. It was the first time the Japs had the drop, and under real fire the recruits learned to sink into cover, to wait for orders.

Covered with more scratches than glory, they dragged back to Makantog, and thence to the new camp. Marking hobbled in, his boots unlaced and flopping. He sank to a rock, pulled tenderly at the loose boots, winced as his socks came off bringing blistered skin with them. He had been gone three, or was it five, days?

No welcome from me: "Why did you come back?" "Aw, honey, my feet hurt!" "Why are you back?" "Because I forgot to leave you any protection." "And when did you think of that?" "On the way back." "Then what did you do?" "I got back quicker. Excuse?" "Gimme your foot." "It hurts. They all hurt." "You've only got two. Stop wiggling." "Ouch! . . . Ouch!" "Shall we take it off with a *bolo*?" "I'm so good to you! I come back all the way. I even don't rest. You are a not-kind lady. Ouch!"

The camp of the pretty sunken gardens on a mountainside became the camp of False Starts.

The Japs were coming so close that the outpost swore it could see the whites of their eyes, and one day, jittery, it fired not upon Japs but upon the supply lines coming in. A double-zero shell sprayed around Home Guard Inabayen of Antipolo, taking off his hat, shattering his walking staff, nicking his clothes somewhat around the edge. It was worse than hitting the Japs, whom the supply lines were forever side-stepping, for it took two weeks to find them, reassure them, and get them to try it again. In the meantime, other town units were pinned to the lowlands because of Jap vigilance in the foothills, like a network between mountains and towns. The camp went on half-rations, then no rations, until relief came.

Came the day the Japs were surely coming in. They couldn't miss. They were on the trail, and only twenty minutes away. There were no forks that close to headquarters. All they had to do was keep coming, and the outpost assured us, "They're *coming!*"

To let the Japs in, we drew up out of the hollow at the head of the waterfalls. Once in the hollow, they were ours for keeps, they and everything on them including their twelve to sixteen bullets apiece. That would bring our bullet count up again, or at least cover the fight—thirty Japs should take not more than fifty bullets.

So Marking pulled the men into position, dispatching Bathing Suit to keep check on the Japs in case they should take the brush instead of following the trail and pop up behind us. Bathing Suit should have been back in ten minutes. We waited one hour. We waited two. In the third hour he reported back, his ugly mug spread in a wide, triumphant grin.

"No more Japs, sir." "Where are they?" "I took them away"— proudly. Marking paled with sudden anger: "You *what!*" Less proudly: "Why, I took them away, sir."

Bathing Suit on the way out had circled the incoming Japs and come up behind them. That day he wore a fine new oversized American suit-coat, the sleeves five inches too long, the tails down to his knees. He unrolled the sleeves, to flap scarecrow. So, down from the jungled mountain and out in the rice fields with their occasional hillocks he slipped up a hillock on the Japs' off side, whistled and yelled and hooted, and the Japs turned to give chase. As they pursued, he ran down again and came up, gopher-style, behind another. When they pursued again, he ran down and popped up elsewhere, farther and farther away. All with the best of intentions.

Marking, fists clenched, held himself steady. To move meant to kill Bathing Suit, and scouts like Bathing Suit are hard to find. *But why the hell do they get inspirations?*

The Japs might come in again, and they might not, or they might come up behind us through the jungle and push us down the mountain into the open where they would have us proper. So, merely for security reasons, on we moved, skirting the range and picking another waterfall facing the same rice-paddy stretch of Pinugay. Marking found a shelf halfway up another mountain with clear water running through it and no feasible approach from the rear, but a good back-way retreat. It was to become one of our famous camps, thrice attacked and thrice pulled out of.

We didn't expect to stay long. Instead of the usual *kubos*, we built grass wigwams, matted the ground with dry *cogon*. We were in fine spirits.

CHAPTER 8

At sunrise on January 3, 1943, the Japs came straight up the trail to the wigwam camp, led by a Filipino unknown to us. They were almost lost to sight in the brush at the foot of the mountain when the outlook in camp, using binoculars, spotted the end of their line. It was a five-minute warning, for the head of the line was well up the mountain, almost at the outpost—one turn more in the zigzag trail, and the boys there would be firing.

As usual, the regular fighters were out on raid or patrol. Only the sick men, new men waiting for arms, a couple of administrative officers, and a handful of bodyguards—bodyguards, fortunately, had automatic weapons or Springfields—were left in camp. With Betsy, the water-cooled Browning machine gun, the bodyguards, and several shotguns and .22s, some fifteen armed men in all. Marking ran forward, throwing an order for me over his shoulder: "Assemble the men and send some on. Have the *bayongs* ready to carry. Wait for me here."

While I scrambled everything back in the *bayongs* and simultaneously gave the orders necessary, a shot went off, right flank.

On the run, Marking stopped short, then bellowed profanity at the barracks used by San Juan's men. One of them, rattled, had fired off his gun, tipping off the Japs that we were wide-awake and waiting, almost as bad as having them already in the camp, as the shot at first indicated. Only the pause to curse, then off again.

He had the men deployed, Betsy set up where she could do the most good, and, because there was so little time, was on the way back from the outpost to help me with the desperate, necessary work of evacuating the camp and the sick men when the firing started. Half of the seventy or so men were already toiling up the back way; I had told them to keep going awhile. Others were still loading up, and these Marking hustled into line as the firing out front ceased, then started up again. He eased the line out the side trail, the two of us stepping in halfway along the line where he could control both ends.

"Hey!" I said. "I sent Borres and the others out the back way." "Why'd you do that? Why don't you do as you're told?" "I did! You said, 'Send some of them on.'"

"I didn't say *that* way!"

"You didn't say *this* way!"

Bullets were pinging the leaves over our heads. Jap bullets. The Japs' .25-calibers had a sharp, singing, light report compared to the American .30s, which we used—when there were any in camp. Betsy was doing all right, and she was a .30.

"You did too say that way," I picked up again. "You scouted it when we got here the first day and said it was a good retreat." "Shut up!"

Another ping and a leaf fell between us, picked clean off the twig.

"Keep your head down," I said.

"Keep your own God-damn head down."

We moved upright along the narrow side trail at a regular pace, still arguing. "Marking, you needn't be so damn nasty." "You shut up."

"I won't!"

A greenhorn broke past, running, but Marking collared him. "Where you going? Fool!" The boy twisted and started to run back, his eyes wide. Marking held him, shook him hard. The boy quieted, fell into the moving line again.

We climbed the slope, out into the open.

"My God, Marking, why don't you keep the boys under cover?" "Oh, God damn you, God damn! Shut your God-damn mouth." "OK, OK. Do it your own way." "You write. I fight. See?"

"OK, OK."

Far up on the Taranka trail we stopped to scan the rice fields below. The firing had stopped, and even Betsy, still hot from the fight, was with us again. On the top of the mountain we had just left, tiny figures emerged, and a distant hallooing and waving indicated they were up and out of the attacked camp but wanted to be told how to get down to join the CO [Commanding Officer].

The CO looked at me. "Look what you done."

"Marking, you said that was Sulok's best retreat."

"Look what you *done!*" He was in good mood again, teasing.

I didn't care what I had done. The purgative I had swallowed half an hour before the attack was beginning to tell. I stepped off into deeper grass, twenty feet away.

"I told you not to take those pills," he said.

"Oh, hush!"

Silence, then excited chattering among the fighters.

"Yay! Come and see."

"I'm busy."

"We got eleven of them because they're only nineteen left. Look! You can count them!"

"Are they coming this way?"

"No."

"Then don't bother me."

More swift talking among Marking and the men.

"They're burning them!" he called again.

"They're what?"

"They put the dead ones in a house, and they're burning them. That's why the townspeople can't tell us any more how many we got! They don't let the townspeople see. They burn 'em up, and then they just go back and tell the people they killed *us!*"

Down on the flatlands thick smoke and the shimmer of flames with very small objects moving around the burning hut made a picture like a movie. Beyond stretched the skyline, with Mount Payong like a peaked cowboy hat and Antipolo nestled high in mountains to the northwest. To the southwest the sky and Laguna de Bay melted into each other, clear and cloudless.

The Japs had pulled out their dead and the fallen rifles, and now were cremating the bodies. Sometimes the dead were not quite dead. On the premise that they would be, Jap noncoms sometimes chucked the dying in with the rest and lit the pyre. Native farm huts are highly inflammable, but they burn too quickly to do a good job. On one such occasion, a farmer passed by after the Japs had left and among the half-charred bodies, one still moved, still groaned. If he had had a chance, the fire had taken it away. He died within the hour. The farmer, appalled, helpless, watched him die.

Lounging in the grass, we ate fistfuls of cold rice from Borres's tin cans and clay pots. The boys grabbed for the hard, browned rice along the bottom; but three of my molars were aching, and I couldn't eat anyway, not even the soft rice. Off and on, I was out in the grass. A fighter not looking where he was going almost stepped on me there and got bawled out by a dozen voices, including Marking's. One of them reprimanded the little tenderfoot: "Haven't you any education? With you, it doesn't matter, but when Major Yay goes in the grass, don't go there. She's a girl."

"Woman," I said. "I'm getting old."

We climbed the Taranka trail; toward afternoon, Marking urged us on. We had turned an attack into an ambush; sorer than ever, the Japs would have reinforcements swarming all over at least three mountains by morning—the one we had left, the one we sat on, the one we were last seen climbing. The next day could prove an interesting one. The sick dragged. Without being exactly sick, I made poor time. We waited for the line to catch up, then pushed on again. I lagged, refused to go on. Marking stepped behind me, stopped each time I stopped, refused to proceed without me. I struggled on. But night and a rain caught us far from even a *kaingin* hut.

Trying to short-cut, we lost the way in the blackness and started down a cliff before we realized it was cliff all the way down, down, down.

"Walk on your behind," said Marking. "Are you weak?"

"No." But I was.

"Here. Give me your foot. Where are you? Stay where you are till I find you. There. Give me your foot. Hold on to anything solid. Come down slow."

Others were struggling down, and we heard a rattling and a crash. "Who's hurt?" Marking sang out.

Silence. Then a faint voice, far below: "None, sir."

"Take it easy, boys. Go slow. Feel your way. Help me with Mammy."

"Mammy, here." Somebody's hand groped. I took it—a firm, big warm hand, holding me up as my foot swung, feeling for Marking's hand.

Braced somehow, he moved my foot to his shoulder, then to a rooted foothold. "Hold her there."

"Yessir," said the big, warm hand.

Another crash below us: a cussword from one, laughter from others, and so it went, until we reached a river tearing down the mountain. In the darkness we could hear its roar, feel its chill waters, sense its power.

"Dangerous for the sick men to try to cross," decided Marking. So there we "slept."

Soaked through, hunching and lying in the continuing drizzle, we had nothing in the *bayongs* but the boys' extra shirts, as threadbare as the ones on their backs and, too, as wet, a blanket for Marking which he threw over me. At our feet a boy chilled and burned by turns in a heavy coat discarded by some patriot soul in Manila and brought along by Seneres No. 2, second of the three patriot brothers named Seneres. At my head, lying crosswise, his head not a foot from my own, another fighter vomited through the night. The acrid smell ran with the rain; nor could we have a fire to heat a can of water to ease him as we rested on the great, flat boulders or sought the scant shelter on the ground between them, for Japs had been and might still be in the general direction we were taking.

In the gray dawn, chilled to the bone and hungry, we followed the torrent down until the forest began to thin. Then we filed into a *kaingin* where the farmer and his wife spared rice from their homegrown, foot-threshed, hand-winnowed supply for more than half a hundred men. The men wolfed their fistfuls. I couldn't eat, but shrilly I lashed them for not sharing with Marking, who had brought them to safety. Shamefacedly, they ate more slowly, and one rose to offer food to their leader. Marking himself frowned at me from where he sat, worn and haggard but indomitable. With all my heart I pitied him and his men, but mostly him. These men were new men, for the old-timers were on patrol. The old-timers, because Marking forever put them first, put him first. Cabalhin especially was one who ever thought of Marking, and no rice ever went into his mouth until there was a coconut shell or banana leaf of rice for Marking. I was to discover him time and again not eating at all, and hiding the fact, to feed Marking. But with these newcomers my patience broke, and I lashed at them.

From the *kaingin*, restored in spirits, we followed the advance patrol into the pretty village of San Andalis, heavy with grapefruit, cocoa pods, and tamarinds. The *barrio* was empty, for Jap hobnail tracks were in the road, and the people had fled and not yet returned.

At each end of the *barrio* Marking placed guards lest Jap patrols surprise us; then, because the fruit was dropping on the ground with none to tend it, he told his hungry men to help themselves. He sent another fighter to borrow a chair from a porch and bring it to the middle of the road, where, with mock gallantry, he seated me in state: "Mother of the Guerrillas." Then he himself went to pick the fruit for me, trotting back gleefully with his arms loaded with the great gold-green citrus balls. The men brought fresh coconuts, hacking off the tops and making a hole through the soft shell from which to drink the rich, almost carbonated juice.

There was no rain in San Andalis. The sun was shining; the grapefruit, crisp and sweet.

CHAPTER 9

*T*hough it was defendable, we could not make a camp of San Andalis; once discovered there, it would be marked a war zone for the duration, and none might return there with safety. Out of consideration for the helpless people, we serpentined our way up over the brow of a *cogon*-covered mountain, dropping out of sight into rolling country dotted with *kaingins* and threaded with shrimp rivers. Here the men, sick and tired, crowded into farm huts and threw up additional shelters of saplings, bamboo slats, and *cogon*. Headquarters—Marking and his bodyguards and key officers—built a smaller camp within the larger camp on the rocky parapet-peak of Mount Mayton. Water, far down the slope, had to be carried up laboriously in bamboo poles. Food was limited to sweet potatoes and leaves out of the patches around the huts and shrimps out of the river, never, never enough for all. We turned to shooting wild cows, counting our precious bullets over and over, and too much meat and too little starch brought boils in clusters on the men's backs, buttocks and legs. An occasional ear of corn found its way to me, prized, procured at the cost of begging it in my name by a boy fighter or by Marking who denied himself that I might eat.

Sickness came oftener and finally Marking himself, a former boxer, broke down. From a week's stubborn but fruitless patrolling, trying to bait into the hills Japs who stayed safely in their garrisons because they were few at the time and we, the guerrillas, had an even chance, he returned with a high fever. In delirium, he shouted orders: "Steady, boys, steady. . . . Ready? Ready, everybody? . . . FIRE! . . . *Pendejo sila! Avante!* [You sons of bitches! Ahead!]" And as the sweat broke: "Pull out, boys. Back to the base."

Cabalhin, Marking's "Sonny Boy No. 1," came at a forced march over the high sierra and across the treacherous rivers, from Infanta, Tayabas, where he had been dispatched to get arms that were not there, though there was reasonable evidence that American submarines had been seen in the vicinity.

If Marking suffered in fever, Cabalhin suffered double for his stricken leader. He brooded. He was pointedly surly around the camp—I was giving the orders. He left without permission and without orders, to arrest any doctor within reach if he refused to come. In the meantime, following orders, Pabling Jornación, who as a small-town boy who had followed Marking around in his boxing days when he had been a local hero, made the Tanay-Koyambay trail, a seven-hour fast hike each way, four times nonstop. Robin, the reform-school kid whose real name was Ruben Ricabar, did the same. Pabling brought the doctors and their satchels. Robin brought the nurses and anything good to eat in can or jar or leaf wrappings that he could beg, borrow, or steal.

Marking pulled through, and Cabalhin steadied.

Through the convalescence, Cabalhin carried Marking's full burden of feeding the fighters, assigning the officers of the day, keeping the outposts alert with only sick and hungry men to man them. Everything was done to prove his devotion to Marking, and his hostility toward me.

All around me, the enmity of Cabalhin and his men. Cabalhin had come to Marking first.

He had come in the first month, February 1942, when the Original Seventeen shared Marking's rice. Of them all only Cabalhin was to fight on through with Marking to the end of the occupation and into Liberation. Cabalhin was one of the great guerrillas to come in off the mountain trails and climb into the foxholes with the American GIs.

Somewhere along the line, the seed had been sown: "She doesn't care for him as we do. She's just using him."

While Marking recovered, I fell ill. With five abscessed molars, unable to eat even gruel, sleeping on *cogon*-matted ground under the night sky beside the campfire to keep the canteen hot through Marking's illness, emptying the borrowed bedpan, carrying the usual administrative work, and making decisions for the Manila, Bulacan, and Cavite units as wisely and cautiously as I could, I was alone in an atmosphere so hostile that the few friendly ones made their kind gestures in surreptitious fashion. A tired heart muscle was aching, and through the ache there were sudden stabs of pain. The old malaria threatened. If the guerrillas were a lost world, mine was a microscopic lost world within it.

Fever came ...

Marking brought doctors and a dentist for me, sending runners as I had sent them. Luz of Teresa and her cousin Milagring, who had nursed him, nursed me and called me Mammy; and I would turn to the grass wall of the *kubo* to hide the childish tears that rolled out though I gritted my swollen jaws and pinched my eyelids shut. Anesthetic, old stock, was not too effective against the agony of the dentist digging for fragments of three teeth and two others as abscessed, including a crookedly rooted wisdom tooth. How sorry I felt for me! I was soaked with tears of self-pity.

Then I too was up and out.

Greater appreciation for each other permeated a joint convalescence. The wind was bone-marrow cold; the food, poor; the precious evaporated milk, long consumed; the fighters, suffering all around us. But for a few days, on top of a mountain, in a flat thirty-by-fifty-foot headquarters area dotted with small shade trees and enclosed by a twenty-foot crown of limestone crags, we did nothing but get well.

Juanito Estocapio of Cardona was brought up, under arrest for a practical joke.

"Why did you go to that wedding party?" asked Marking.

"I was invited, sir—"

"But why did you take all your men?"

"We were only twelve, sir."

"Why did you take them at all?"

"Well, sir—the circular said that each in-charge would have to feed his own men."

"So, instead of asking your friends to spare a little rice, you went to a party."

"Well—the boys were so hungry—"

"But why did you say the Japs were coming when the Japs weren't? Everybody ran away. This report says that the groom almost forgot his new bride. That isn't funny. Stop laughing."

"Sir—sir—"

"Stop that laughing! Is that the way you boys act in town! Do you know how many complaints there are against you! Half the letters I get complain about you young fellows who sing and dance and play jokes! I know you do your duty; I know you're doing your share against the Japs, that you're obedient! But you God-damn have to behave yourselves. The people are scared enough without you scaring them some more. What will the people think is going on up here? A circus?"

"I'm sorry, sir."

"What did you do after the people ran away?"

"I told my boys to eat well."

"Then you can afford *not* to eat so well. You will be assigned up here and go to town only when you are sent on errand."

"Yes, sir."

The lad took the discipline cheerfully, enjoying life with a cocky air. Then, on an errand over the lonely Taranka trail high on a mountain spur running down through the *cogon* from the forest camps to the distant lakeside towns, ahead of two guerrilla pals—the sky blue, the birds and crickets singing—he strode head on into a patrol of sixteen Japs.

Face to face—and the Japs in the hills always came shooting.

They were already firing as Juanito shipped out his pistol with one hand, and with the other waved the other two into retreat. Covering his retreating buddies, he fought it out alone, backing down the slope, wounded through the thigh, empty shells and flattened *cogon* marking his path. The Japs captured him in less than twenty yards. His body, found later by his superior officer, Felimon Aquino, regimental commander in the Home Guards, showed signs that the gay, reckless boy, already desperately wounded, had been tortured with cigarette butts, and bludgeoned.

The sky was his cathedral, the birds and crickets the only requiem for the dead.

The days went by, filled with administrative details and scratching for food. And humor.

One day, not strong but already well, Marking tied empty milk cans to tree branches and began swinging one with pellets from the .22. He invited me to join him, and I joked, "Watch me cut the string."

Aiming at a can, I pulled the trigger. Promptly the can dropped to the ground and the severed string snapped up.

Marking's eyes widened. My mouth fell open. I am no sharpshooter, and Marking was and still is the best shot in his outfit. How explain the miracle?

There was appreciative laughter, quickly hushed, from some of the men. Marking raised the .22 and, with beads of sweat forming on his forehead, said, "I will cut the string or resign as commanding officer."

He aimed long and steadily, lowered his arms once to rest, and aimed again, squinting his left eye—ordinarily he shot with both eyes open. Slowly, gently, steadily he squeezed the trigger. The can dropped. The severed string snapped up.

Marking leaned against a tree, visibly shaken. "I am still commanding officer," he said. He laughed as if relieved of a terrible doubt. Then he turned to me, smiling. "I'm proud of you."

The comradeship between us drove Cabalhin farther away. I tried to win him over by inviting him to conferences on policy. I reminded Marking that his twenty-one-year-old second-in-command should take part in important decisions, if only to keep him informed and that his opinions should be consulted, if only to train him in administration as well as field work. When they were together I would leave them and either return to my little rustic table or walk over to faithful Borres in the kitchen. But my overtures in behalf of Cabalhin were from Cabalhin's point of view morsels of charity, probably poisoned. Whoever had sown the seed of distrust in him was an artist whose work endured.

Then the Japs got wind of Marking's illness, and swarmed into the hills again, certain of their quarry. They would run him to earth or run him to death. From our rocky parapet, we could see them a thousand yards down on the trail, snooping around, waiting, looking for the smoke of our campfires, listening for an accidental shot that would mark our direction.

Cabalhin, more fiercely loyal and devoted to Marking than any other in the outfit, said, "Let me fight, sir. Let me hit them farther down, to draw them away . . ." And, answering his commander's hesitation: "Do you have no trust in my ability, sir? Do you doubt my courage? Am I nothing to you that I cannot serve? Are others more than I?"

So Cabalhin struck the Japs an eye-opening blow in February '43. Up to then, raids had netted a score or so of Japs each. Other guerrilla outfits were doing the same. It was a jabbing everywhere, at any hour, hit and run, wearing the enemy down. Cabalhin, the quick, tiny-waisted, broad-shouldered, bandy-legged, cat-eyed second-in-command, picked the best of the weary, worn-out fighters.

He deployed his men at a sharp angle along the Koyambay-Tanay trail. Besides the old rifles, he had a few Browning automatic rifles and an air-cooled .30-caliber machine gun recovered from a plane. Closest to the trail he placed the Brownings. In the middle of the line, farther from the trail but on a knoll with a fine sweep, he planted his machine gun. Farthest from the trail he set the few Springfields, superb for sniping.

Craftily, carefully, Cabalhin observed the Japs approaching—some 150, more than twice his own number. Unlike the guerrillas, who rolled along in single file five to ten paces apart, ambush-wise, the Japs were treading on one another's heels. His keen eyes noted with surprise that this was not the usual expedition into the mountains after guerrillas. It was a convoy. Before and behind, the Japs were heavily armed; the main body was made up of better-dressed figures, and their loads were carried by others. He guessed that these must be the engineers and radio men for the Angelo mine, to build the something-or-other that rumor had it the Japs were planning in the interior.

The Japs climbed into it. Cabalhin held his men in, his eyes intent slits, his face red as it gets in a fight or from embarrassment. The Japs came on until their advance almost rolled by. His boys couldn't miss. A bird shrilled. A vagrant breeze rustled the leaves. On their short legs the Japs came plodding along, the advance patrol out of sight, the advance guard pulling up the last climb.

Then he signaled for the volley.

A crash of sound! Volley after volley!

The machine gun jazzed. The Springfields boomed, and all up and down the line the Enfields, carried from the battlefields of Pozorrubio, Infanta, and Mauban before Bataan, and others dug up and pieced together after Bataan, banged vengefully in fulfillment.

Fifteen feet from the trail, the Brownings had their hands full. And their laps. "Gimme that God-damn clip," cursed Badidles. "Load it, you fool, load it!" And, as the Japs scattered, and one ran to cover in the wrong direction: "Kick the son-of-a-bitch! Kick him in the balls! Gimme that Goddamclip!"

Then Cabalhin cursing, "Pull out of it, pull out of it! God damn you, Pedro! *Tarantado!* [Fool!] *Punatero!* [Shithead!] You'll taste my .45. *Putang ina ninyong lahat!* [You're all sons of bitches!]"

Already those less experienced were on their way, tearing through the jungle. One in leaping pierced his scrotum through and through but received no comfort other than, "Maybe ya lost 'em. Maybe ya dropped 'em in a birds' nest. Maybe they're hanging on the bushes back there." All in the vernacular, more pungent than any translation.

Red and gold the campfire, black the night, glowing the fighters' faces as they relived the fight in boisterous talk and scored the boobs for their blunders and the butterfingers for lost clips, and fell significantly silent when one dared join in who had proven yellow.

From a wild cow the meat squad had cornered there was hot beef soup, and as special concession, hard rice instead of gruel. Down to the stomach, the rich soup; up from the heart, the talk of victory; sweet, exulting music from the singers, Tumol and Bugarin, Hawaiiano and Ming and Maring:

"Oh, more victories ahead of all,
For we the faithful and the free are marching!
Above, burning sun or stars that fall;
Below, the hills, the rice fields parching!
Let our feet be light and never drag,

For in our hearts we fly the same old flag!
Victory! Liberty!
More victories ahead of us we see!"

Cabalhin and his boys netted 93 out of the 150—most of them technicians, precious little jewels to dig and build the robot Jap army to supremacy in the Far East. He knocked ninety-three stones out of their crown in three minutes flat. It was only one of many such raids, pummeling the enemy everywhere, and it indicated the growing strength of the guerrillas. Close after the young Cabalhin, other Marking officers were emerging as leaders of men: Mapa, marine engineer, with smiling eyes and quiet ways; Lucio, the bearded hurly-burly, who fed 500 armed men ("But it takes both my hands, and I gotta use my feet too"—for the Japs wanted him, badly); De la Rosa, virile, broad six-footer, meek and mild until the fight came (then, "they asked for it"); Roger Moskaira, beaten and imprisoned for fourteen months, who kept the secrets that would have hauled half Manila's prominent into Fort Santiago; Salvador, loose-jointed, boyish, who sobbed in the bushes when the Japs took his family hostage, "Now I really won't surrender, damn them!"; David, handsome-Hindu type with boring black eyes and a flashing, up-curving, can't-catch-me smile; Seneres, highly emotional chief of intelligence, forever mixing his facts and feelings, forever whipping his starving agents on; Bert Mata, whose crack fighters were brothers, uncles, cousins, nephews, and his unit a clan: Major Mata, Captain Mata, Lieutenant Mata, Sergeant Mata, Corporal Mata, Private-First-Class Mata, Buck Private Mata, No-Standing-at-All-Mata-just-do-as-you're-told. They called each other by nicknames, and sometimes a private, riled, would stiffen and say, "Major, don't forget I'm your uncle!"

CHAPTER 10

Except for the limestone parapet, Mount Mayton had no cover except isolated clumps of trees and bamboos, and the Japs had learned how to deal with that—they burned it off. For an encirclement, it was perfect for them and death for us.

Across the valley loomed heavily forested Mount Kanumay. Down from the parapet we picked our way, across the valley, and up the steep sides of our next camp. The two-hour hike took some of the men the whole day.

Kanumay was the kind of natural stronghold that looks good before a fight, not after it. The approach from the main trail was straight up a narrow ravine which had tricky spots where climbing meant clinging to roots and rock ledges. Approach from the other side was simple: the trail rolled in of its own accord; but a rise commanded a trail junction and a *cogon* stretch, and unless the Japs were allowed to slip up flankwise it looked good from behind the machine gun for which the Schaffer-Farretta team had engineered a nest, getting down and digging part of the hole themselves with one eye cocked for gold. The rest of the mountain, flanked by the *barrios* of Santa Inés and Tinukan, was not unscalable; it was merely unlikely that the Japs would come through leeches and thorns.

A depression in Kanumay's top formed a shallow, rolling basin that kept the campfires from shining across country and was roomy enough for *kubo* after *kubo*, barracks after barracks, until the camp looked like a small *barrio*. A spring gave sufficient water, and after making a pool to draw from, its rivulet disappeared underground, leaving no telltale waterway for the Japs to patrol in their usual searching of the countryside. It was probably ten miles from the nearest town, a long distance for Jap troops to climb, and the Japs, in all the time they spent in the Philippines, liked the jungle least of all.

No camp ever saw more serious work. Little by little the dialect was becoming familiar to my ears, and I could understand ordinary conversation. It began to make real sense, to mean something the instant I heard it without the necessity of translating the words and then shifting them around. More and more I could concentrate on the business in hand and still know what was going on around me to the point of throwing in a word of advice, praise, or rebuke, though the group be ten feet from me and up to then oblivious of all but themselves.

There was nothing so irritating as the term "Sir." It opened the day. It closed the day. It woke us up in the middle of the night. All through the hours it was the trickle of water on the stone of our endurance. It was either "Po" in Tagalog or "Sair" in English, and, whichever it was, it meant work, work, work. We went crazy with it.

"Sir, here are thirty for training."

"Sir, here are eleven to stay. Six of them are wanted by the Japs."

"Sir, the people are afraid the Japs will harvest the *palay*."

"Sir, I need an authorization to collect supplies. The Manila men always pass by my place, and I just haven't got anything more to feed them."

"Sir, Ming Pasio's son had a gun before the war. May we find out if he still has it? Will you give us a receipt to give him for it?"

"Sir, Luis is abusing. He doesn't ask in a proper manner. He just tells the people to give. It is not good."

"Sir, my child is very ill . . . I will report back when she is better."

"Sir, we are out of salt."

"Sir, I said it three times three different ways to Major Yay but she is better in English."

"Sir, the patrol has done as you ordered. They did nothing you told them not to. When may they?"

"Sir, Major Yay is angry. She says if I ask again she will shoot."

"Sir, better I go home. My wife is writing that if I stay up here any longer she will get another man. I will be a Home Guard, sir."

"Sir, my brother surrendered, but he did not surrender. He was captured and thus he surrendered."

"Sir, Major Yay says there is no more thread, and I cannot drill and hold it too, for it is largely torn."

"Sir, may I tell my side before you read the complaint?"

"Sir, there is not enough rice for tonight."

"Sir, a PC [Philippine Constabulary Member] says this camp is known to the Japs."

"Sir, Sunia's squad will not pound *palay*. They pounded it yesterday, and they say it is my squad who must pound today, but we pounded yesterday also."

"Sir, I want to report something good . . . May I speak with you alone?"

"Sir, I am sick."

"Sick, he is *not* sick. There is a fiesta in his town."

"Sir, Pepe borrowed my shoes when you sent him on errand, and now he is returned and he will not give them back. He says they are old now—why do I want them?"

"Sir, Major Yay says you must approve this roster before she makes the commissions."

"Sir, Mang Pepe says he has given to the guerrillas everything he has, and he has no more, and one of these days he will give his life because the Japs are already investigating him."

"Sir, there is a woman who wants to meet you. She says you are the most famous man in the Philippines."

"Sir, we cannot go down to the town because the Japs are looking for us. This is my wife and baby. They said you would baptize him for us."

"Sir, the meat squad has not come back yet."

"Sir, I am a runner from Cavite. Here are the reports, also a new roster for your approval."

"Sir, my brother joined the guerrillas. May I see if he is here? Our mother sent him a blanket and some soap and a religious medal."

"Sir, Rubén is courting a girl who is also courted by the PC working for the Jap military police. There will be trouble."

"Sir, Roger's convoy was scattered in Marikina. There were sixty-five in the convoy bringing arms and ammunition and clothes and medicine from the Manila units for the hill units. They had an accidental fire, the gun went off, sir. The Japs heard it and came out of the garrison and everybody scattered because they only had five guns and there were a hundred Japs. Sir, Roger ordered me to report that he is finding the convoy. He will be here tomorrow or the next day. He is very sorry, sir. Also, sir, he is bringing you army boots and a woolen shirt for Major Yay and something nice for Cabalhin and Mapa. Also, sir, he has a bottle of good whiskey for Sergeant Schaffer and Farretta for their medicine for the soul. That is all, sir. Have you any orders for Roger and the Manila units?"

"Sir, there are too many people in the camp, and there is no rice. There are four hundred fighters and more than one hundred supply men ready to return to the town; but first they must eat, because it is far and also they carried much and Truadio has too many Dumagats in the camp and they eat more than everybody else and there are at least fifty visitors. Sir, there is rice only for Major Yay, and she declares she will not eat. Yes, sir, I told her it was your order, but the rice is still not eaten."

"Sir, the meat squad was surprised by a Jap patrol that was also stalking a wild cow and also, sir, the rich people in the town say these cows are not wild cows but their own cows that they have not counted for a long time."

"Sir, have we iodine?"

Suddenly, Marking exploded, "Don't say 'sir'!"

Scared out of his wits, the boy asked with trembling voice, "What shall I say, sir?"

"Don't say anything. Just God damn shut up!"

And then, as before, for hours Marking made decisions, settled squabbles, enforced discipline, planned ahead, while I wrote the answers and the appeals, gave suggestions, defined policies, and worked out the details of more plans. Between times, he drilled the men along with drilling instructors he had developed, and I continued to pound the typewriter or talked with officers and runners. Together, or taking turns, we checked up on the sick. Periodically, the *kalaws* broke in with hoarse caws announcing the hours, then went heavily winging their way from treetop to treetop. They were pelican-headed, with great wings and small, bony bodies that we roasted once in a while for none-too-appetizing, wood-hard, fish-flavored gnawing. When night fell, there might be an hour with the boys around the campfire, and in that brief period entertainment was spontaneous. Marking, who enjoyed his own stories as much as his audience, told them in the dialect with much arm and leg action and with humor edging on the ribald. Each clique among the fighters pushed forward its own singers in good-humored competition. Good guitar music invited dancing, however rough the ground, and the burliest fighters were pressed into service as "the ladies" and hilariously advised on how to lean, cling, sweep and swoon. Here one hobbling on a cut foot—never mind the cut. There another sang, though his face was pinched with hunger. A dark, ragged throng they were about the glowing fire, with the tall, dense jungle pressing close about them. Exhausted with their awkward capering, they would sit to hear the stories of other lands. Once I told them of King Arthur and the Round Table, of Elaine floating down to Camelot, of Excalibur. When I finished, the knights in shining armor and their caparisoned steeds were still there, but the fire had sunk to warm, white ashes.

At night I learned the history of the one I followed. Sometimes in those moments of peace we would walk with linked arms or hands, going to and fro in the camp, up and down the paths, past each barracks in a final check-up on our brood. There would be the murmur of prayer and the faint click of the rosary beads through the whispering of lip and of breeze in the treetops.

"Marking," I said once, "fancy two like us with a following of Catholics."

"My father was not a Catholic," he answered. "I am not a Catholic."

And I said, "If I ever joined a Church, it would probably be the Catholic."

"Anyway, you've been baptized"—as if baptism took care of everything.

"No, I haven't. I went to be baptized once, and they wouldn't have me. I disagreed with them. It wasn't an important point. It was about the Immaculate Conception. The priest asked me if I believed it, and I tried to be absolutely honest—I said I couldn't see that it mattered. So he didn't baptize me."

"It is not good," said Marking, "not being baptized."

"Look at that moon—b'r-r-r!"

"Yah, there will be Japs again."

"We'd better get some sleep."

But he could not sleep. We never slept well in the Kanumay main base, and it had less to do with danger than with the logs upon which we lay. There was little bamboo to be had on the mountain. By natural inclination the fighters built with what was nearest, and it seemed there were no straight saplings on the mountain, for, however they were put together, they did not fit. In one spot under me there was a six-inch difference between logs, one humping up and the other bending down. On Marking's side, five different bumps made him sleep like a pretzel. *Cogon* grass was piled high upon the logs and stuffed into the depressions. The grass matted or shriveled and dropped between the cracks. We folded our few extra garments into the worst spots. But still, all night long in the darkness, we bumbled around like rabbits trying to find the sleep that escaped us.

Marking stood up again. "I'd better inspect the outpost."

At sunset, he had inspected the outpost. That was sufficient. The trail to the outpost was dangerous. One slip meant, if not a broken neck, a broken leg.

"Come," I said. "You're just restless."

"I am *not* restless," he said, prepared to quarrel—just name the subject.

Somewhere I had read, in a Macfadden story title or subhead, perhaps in the *Ladies' Home Journal* or in a medicine wrapper, that the best way to hold a man is to make him talk and avoid interrupting him. Also, not to sleep in his face. I couldn't sleep if he went groping along the precipice, so I resigned myself to sleeplessness with the organization's precious jewel safe at my side.

"Come, sweet," I said. "I can't sleep either."

"Want to go with me?"

I thought of the precipice and shuddered. "Let's sit on the lovely rustic bench you made me."

"Okay."

We sat on the lovely rustic bench he made me. We sat five minutes. Then he stood up.

"Well, I'll check up on the outpost. You go to sleep."

"Oh, come!" I said. "You talk."

"Why?"

That had me for a moment. Guilty conscience. "Well, I like to hear you talk."

"I don't want to talk."

"Then let's sit here. Well, don't sit at the other end of the bench. Sit here—near me. Let me put my head on your shoulder."

He moved over, stiffly put his arm around me. "I don't like woman." More vehemently: "I *hate* woman. I am a real woman hater all my life, forever and ever, amen."

"Even when you were a little boy?"

"No. That was when I fell very in love."

"No kidding."

"My teacher." He relaxed, curled around me with his legs crossed and one hand thrown across my lap. "She was beautiful. Every morning I said, 'Good morning, dear titser,' and then Marta, a little girl, said. 'Oh, wot *pretty* plowers you hab!' and I said, '*Yes*, I put dem on my table.'"

I burst into laughter at the singsong that for more than forty years, thanks to the Americans, [Filipina/os] had obtained in the first grade. The laughter brought coziness to us, sitting in the moonlight, for it was honest laughter, and moonlight was ever made for lovers.

"You know," he mused, "my life was hard."

A question from me would have broken the spell. He was talking to himself, with someone to share his listening.

"She beat me bad, that time. She beat me and beat me. The pot, it was boiling, but the rice was not done. There was still much water. I did not put more sticks in the fire. The fire was all right, not time to scatter the coals because not time to steam the rice. One stick was long—"

"Where was the pot?" I asked, out of necessity. "On the fire." "Was the fire on the ground?" "Yah. There were three big stones—to hold the pot above the fire." "Was it a regular rice pot, round bottom, small opening, red clay where it was not blackened by the fire?" "Yah. It was most red. It was a new pot." "What were you wearing?" "Nothing." "Naked?" "No. You know kids wear the *camisets,* the undershirt." "Did you have on pants, the short ones with a drawstring?" "Yah, maybe. I was big already. I was nine years old." "What happened?" "It was not a great fault. She beat me." I said nothing.

He continued: "One stick was long, like a sword. I made the sword salute—like this." He stood and, snappy, like any ROTC [Reserve Officers' Training Corps] lad, he made the saber salute. He settled again beside me, crossing his legs, lifting his arm over my head to encircle my shoulders with his elbow on the bench. "I dreamed some day I am a soldier. Some day I am a leader of men. Some day I am a great man with many soldiers."

I said nothing, and the moment in the moonlight was quiet. The wind picked up, bent a bough, and the lace pattern on the ground at our feet shifted, then was fixed again.

"I heard the guns. I saw the smoke from the cannon. I smelled the smoke."

Another moment passed.

"It was the rice. It burned. It burned as burned as possible."

"I can see your mother beating you."

"My father," said Marking, "was a wonderful man. He loved my mother very much, like I love you. They quarrel, yes; they separate, no. One time my father taught my mother something. She was a gambler. All day with the cards, she played *paguingue,* and when she wanted to spit the servant brought the can for her to spit in and then the servant carried it away. A convent girl, my mother, and my father loved her much, much."

The bough swayed; the pattern lost itself, then became fixed again. Down the slope, the guards changed, and against the rules there was the glow of a cigarette.

"It was so happen," Marking related, "that my father at that time was the president of the town, which is the highest position. He was a lawyer—a good one—and the people honored him. There was not much work. It was only important. He was the important man there, so he was also the president. Well, it was so happen that it was against the rules to gamble in the town. But my mother continued to gamble. She could not gamble with herself only," he explained seriously—"Therefore other people came to gamble with her. All this gambling was therefore in the house of the president of the town because my mother was the wife of the president.

"When my father said to her, '*Hija*, you break the law in my face,' my mother called the servant and spit in the can and the servant carried the can away. So my father went down to the municipal building and he said to the chief of police, 'Is it not against the law to be gambling in this town?' and the chief of police said, 'It is true all that you say, sir,' and my father said, '*Compadre*, do your duty—arrest all violators,' and the chief of police said, 'But you know like myself who is the violator, the very leader of the violators,' and my father said, 'Are you the chief of police, or are you afraid of my wife?' and the chief of police said, 'Mr. President, I do not wish to have misunderstanding with you, but it is also true that your wife broke a platter on your head, no?' Whereupon my father said, 'Who will be the chief of police if the chief of police is himself in the jail?' and therefore the chief of police called all the policemen including also others and together they went to clean up the vice in the town. My mother was very, very angry. They held to each of her arms and also pushed her behind and pulled her in front, and they succeeded, but not in stopping her mouth as to what she said about my father who was the president of that town. They put her in the jail, and each time the door was to be closed they pushed her back in the jail to close the door, and in time they succeeded. When the door was closed, the chief of police reported to my father, the president, saying: 'Well, your wife is in jail. Also it was I who put her there. Also I *will not be the one to let her out*, even if I am discharged. Anyway I resign.'

"Well, my father took the key and put it away in his pocket, and then he went to visit my mother in the jail. '*Hija*,'" he said, 'why are you here?' And my mother said, 'You foul animal, you, let me out immediately! It was by your order, because who would dare this outrage?' But my father looked at my mother between the bars. 'Am I the president of this town?' said my father, and my mother said, 'You are the president of hell. Let me out of here—I will break your head.' And my father just smiled, and he said, '*Hija*, you are dear to my heart, but I cannot take you out of jail.' My mother was very angry, and she cried, and then she cried only little pieces like the hiccups, and then my father said, '*Hija*, if I leave you here, you will sleep alone.' My mother was not smart, because it was my father who did not want to sleep alone, but my mother cried because she was very, very alone inside the jail. So my father was a fool, he took her home, and she cried in little pieces, and my father put her to bed like his child."

"What a story!" I said. "Sounds like a wonderful family life."

"No," said Marking. "She threw away all his money. She treated my sisters better than us brothers. I never had shoes. My sisters had shoes and shoes. My sister made a face at me, and I knocked her down, and my mother said she wished I, her son, had died when I was born. So I ran away from home. I left Ichu—"

"Ichu?"

"My baby *carabao*. When we crossed the river in the flood, if I fell off Ichu would swim to catch me with his side until I could hold his tail. Sometimes I fell asleep on his back, and he would stop when he came to the river and not cross until I opened my eyes and saw we were to the river already. Then I kicked him, but if I kicked not hard he waited until I kicked hard, to show I was exactly awake and not one eye open only. One time I beat him for something. He would not talk to me for many days. He hid away in the forest."

"Ichu must have been good if he could talk."

"He could talk," said Marking, with conviction. Then, reluctantly: "He did not talk really, but I told him everything in my whole heart. He loved me very much. He would look for me, going everywhere until we met."

"When did you grow up?" This question I asked with a smile carefully concealed.

In all seriousness, Marking answered, "Maybe when I ran away. I had to eat. I liked servants always, and played with them even more because my mother scolded. And when I ran away it was not the rich people who helped me but the poor people. The old woman at the showhouse which I swept to see Tom Mix as my pay for sweeping took me to her house and let me sleep there. She also gave me food. I worked as a servant. I learned to drive. I learned about the motor of the automobile. I was a professional boxer. I worked in a hospital in the surgical ward. About the autopsies, for one week I could not eat meat. I got thin. I was a secret service man in Antipolo, the fiesta town. I fooled around with many women, but not one was to me how I love you so dearly."

He looked serious.

"My father told me that in my age of thirty-five to forty years I would find a woman, and when this woman came to me my star would shine. When I saw you I remembered my father's words. He said it would be a *mestizo*, a half-and-half. He said my heart would know. He said right away inside my heart there would be a voice and I would know, 'This is the woman.'"

Slowly, closely, he kissed me.

"I am my father again. I used to say to my friends, 'Why do you die for a woman? Go get another one. There are many. Have them all.' But now I am my father's son, and my father's word was prophecy. I am more lucky than my father. I have a better woman than my mother."

"Don't say that," I said. "She was your mother."

He slipped his lean, strong arm under my knees and lifted me to his lap to cuddle me there. I smiled within. My friends would have stood mouths agape to see me cuddling. I liked it, too. I cuddled for all I was worth, and felt weak and sweet in the arms of a real man, woo-woo.

The guards changed again.

"How'd you get into the war?" I asked.

"Oh, I was air-raid warden, like everybody, and then the Army called for motorcycle riders, and I convoyed troops to Bataan. That was bad, very bad. The Jap planes caught us every time on the open highway. Once the officer in charge did not take my advice and therefore instead of scattering the men in the rice paddies away from the highway and leaving only the empty trucks, he kept on going, and when I reached Bataan, out of my fifty trucks there were only eight trucks left, and I reported to the officer in charge there that there were only that many from so many. He said very roughly, 'There is no sentimentality in the Army,' and it was then that I felt the tears on my face and discovered myself crying. I hated the officer for that, and I said to myself, 'It is not so with me. Life is precious—not mine, but other lives that are mine to keep safe. For me there will be sentimentality always, because I will not let anybody be killed if it can be avoided.' If I find that officer again some day I will show him the army I am myself all alone making and leading, and I will say, 'See the sentimentality in my army, see?' And then I will knock him down and maybe jump on him with my feet. That officer is one man I do not like."

It was too late for us to talk more, yet the hours were magic. I could not rouse him to take himself, and me, to rest. These were his hours of communion with himself, and I did little more than induce them. To me he could bare his heart. Whatever his pose with others, when he held me on his lap he knelt at my knee in confession. And jumbled though his speech, with thoughts rambling or leaping helter-skelter, I could sense the sweep and force of the man, and the wistful seeking.

This had been his real beginning, the start of the legend that was over the Philippines:

His last convoy, in the week before New Year of 1941, was cut off by the momentous blowing of the bridges between Manila and the enemy's approach from both north and south. The convoy was cut off because he was not in command: he merely led it, clearing the way for it with siren and dare-devil riding that swept the two-wheeled *calesas* and bullock carts off the road, and zipping past the horns of a *carabao* to make it high-tail back into the paddies.

"Hurry it up," he had urged. "We can make it—we *can make it!*"

"Yes," said the officer in charge. But the dawdling continued.

"Are we going? Let's go!" demanded Marking.

"I am in command," said the officer.

"Bullshit! Let's go!" But the convoy stayed where it was, though filled with men eager to stand up and fight in Bataan.

Distant detonations shook the countryside.

Marking gritted his teeth. "When I am in command," he told himself, "I *will command! When there is a command to be given, I will give it!*" But the bridges had been blown on the hour, and the deliberate delay had stranded the convoy in Manila. Swiftly, another order went into effect: "To the Port Area and destroy everything."

Case after case of bullets went into the Pasig, nosing into the silt, digging deeper as the tide pushed in and the river rolled out. Marking counted the Garands, as he threw them upon the fire—one hundred twenty of the finest guns of the time. "I cannot," his heart said. But everywhere the orders were being carried out, and "It must be done," said his head.

From "scorching the earth" he turned to an armored car, and all his love for automobiles—this one had bullet-proof glass and holes for the rifles—rose and like to burst him within. "No," he said, "to hell with the orders. This beautiful car, no. Not in the fire with the fine guns." He was done. As dusk closed in, he climbed behind the wheel, placed gentle hands upon it. Reverently, he put the car into gear and pressed the accelerator. A gun, a car, and a woman—these always called to his heart, brought response.

Southward he sped out of Manila toward the little mountain resort where the Virgin of Antipolo had her shrine. Already the Japs were straggling into the outskirts of the city. His headlights picked out three of them, to the side of a bridge ramp. He jammed on the brakes, but not too roughly. He reached for the Enfield stacked against the seat.

Through the hole for it, he took careful aim, three times, in quick succession, and the first notches for it were cut in his mind.

Through the town of the Virgin he roared, and as far beyond as the car could be driven, off the road into the fields and up from the fields into a bush-covered ravine. Then, on foot he returned to the town to speak with friends in the night. Around his waist were two bandoleers of a hundred fifty bullets each. In his right hand was the Enfield. He thought of the Garands. But the Enfield had been issued to him, the Garands not. Through three years of patching riot guns together, of repairing Enfields and Springfields, of looking with bitter eyes at the clumsy, undependable, usually one-shot native *paltiks*, he was to grind his teeth and see in his mind's eye the flames upon which, by orders, he had tossed one hundred twenty fine Garands. It made him sullen. The next fighter who said "sair" to him was likely to get the *paltik* wrapped around his neck. The fighters knew that. Whenever he was repairing guns, they said "sair" at a good ten feet.

In a farmhouse a few miles behind the town, Marking sat, a Thinker in truer brown than Rodin's bronze. Why had he been disbanded? Why had he and the others been ordered to the destruction and in the same breath told to "go home"? Home was no place for a man whose country was at stake. The officer had told him to "wait." Wait for what? Wait how long?

He couldn't wait.

He left his gun in trusted hands, dressed in civilian clothes instead of the air mechanic's overalls he loved because they were "army" even if he himself was not strictly an army man, not having taken oath because none had time in the flurry to swear him in.

Down to the town he went, and from the town, squeezed in with the frightened, sweating crowd in a rickety bus, he proceeded to Manila. He found the house of the officer, the officer he called "coward" over and over in his mind.

"I am waiting," he said.

"Wait," said the officer. "I will call you."

Gritting his teeth, Marking returned to the farmhouse in the hills. Again, all unconsciously, he did a native take-off on Rodin's Thinker.

Again, he could not wait and again he went to the officer's house. "I am *still* waiting," he said, and he was in ugly mood.

The officer said, "You and Lieutenant Vidan will try to get through to Bataan. Are you willing?"

Marking looked at him in surprise. What did being willing have to do with it? To himself Marking said, "The sonumabits." To the officer, he said, "Yes, sir."

"You will do your best to get through. If one of you is captured or killed, the other will not proceed but will return to me. Is all understood?"

"Understood," said Marking aloud. To himself, "Why don't three of us go?"

In civilian clothes, Marking and Lieutenant Vidan, Filipino army man, made it through to Pampanga where the Japs were massing in heavy lines across the northern boundaries of Bataan. They were allowed to rest in an isolated farmhouse hidden in a bamboo thicket, and in the night had to creep out a back way because the old people and the young parents begged them not to be found there when a Jap patrol pounded at the front door. Lying flat in the thicket, they bounded up at the sound of screams, struggling, a groan, and the young girl's pleading sobs.

Vidan caught himself in time, then struggled with Marking. "We have a mission. They are too many for us. We have no arms. Our mission—it is of paramount importance."

Marking heard and realized, and a harsh, helpless sob tore its way out of his breast. "It is the little girl," he said, "the *dalagita,* the child not yet a lady."

Vidan held him flat.

"Animals!" choked Marking. "Beasts! Devils!"

After a while it was quiet, and together Marking and Vidan crept to the house to find the grandfather dead, the grandmother dazed from the blows and the horror. On the earthen floor lay the eleven-year-old girl, unconscious, with blood smears on the small thighs that an older brother and a young man with a baby in his arms tried to cover with her little skirts even as helplessly they sought to recall her to consciousness. Marking and Vidan lifted her to the bamboo pallet.

"But a baby herself, but a baby herself," choked Marking, and he was weeping because he had never been helpless before.

They left. Dawn found them between the lines, crawling on their faces, snaking beside the rims of the rice paddies, lying dead beside the dead when the voices of Japs came to them. What were they, patrols? Or walking radios? They rolled over a paddy lip, used every tuft of dry grass for cover, signaled to each other when they could but stayed far apart to give each the best chance of making it alive. There were voices in the strange Jap monotone that nevertheless was nasal and high-pitched, then a shot. The voices went away, and Marking crawled on while the shells whining overhead marked his progress. He came upon Vidan. There was a neat bullet hole in Vidan's head.

Marking lay still, the ground hot beneath him, the stench of rotting bodies all around him, the warm, limp body of Vidan under his hand. Go on? Go back? Vidan had been a soldier. Vidan had said, "We have a mission." Marking had liked Vidan. And so, Marking pulled Vidan's coat straight, turned about on his belly and crawled back the way he had come.

He saw bodies in grotesque positions all along the railroad tracks. In places, they had fallen in heaps, as if piled on purpose. Here and there a body lay alone, and he noted that some were less decomposed than others. So others had been trying to get through?

All through the afternoon, exhausted, in terrible thirst, faint with hunger for he had not eaten since breakfast of the day before, he wormed along, and there was no cover for him but the tufts of grass, the paddy rims, and the dead.

At night he found a freight car on a siding far from the pinging of snipers' bullets. Heavily, with great effort, he pulled himself into it and lay not knowing that he slept. Jap voices awakened him. He was hauled to his feet and thrown out of the car to the ground. It was not yet morning, but the sky had begun to lighten. They were the men of a dawn patrol. He expected death. He tensed to fight, to die fighting, but he was herded along at the point of a bayonet. Despite the ignominy, hope rose and cunning quickened. He could give them the slip, the yellow bastards.

But they were conscientious soldiers. They herded him to a frontline headquarters where systematically he was questioned. The officer in charge, with an automatic, routine gesture, felt his shoulder for the callus caused by long drilling with a rifle. There was none. They asked his age, his place, his reason for being in the vicinity.

"I am a student," said Marking. "I am looking for my parents."

The patrol was eager to do its work well, and did it too well. One of the men pointed to Marking's hands and jabbered excitedly.

On his right hand in the fleshly portion between thumb and forefinger was a tattooed star. On his left hand, a twin design showed clearly—a heart with a girl's name long since blurred past reading, much as his memory of her had blurred.

Marking's heart did not sink. It rose to the fight. The greater the odds, the bigger the fight he put up.

"Sojer mark!" ejaculated the officer, jabbing at the star, at the heart, with his forefinger.

"Student," said Marking.

The patrol pulled his shirt apart, snapping off the buttons. And there, spread in all its glory, unpinioned and unshot, was the American Eagle with the Stars and Stripes forever unfurling behind its proud head, and in its talons a banner proclaiming, "Love unto death."

The Japs were beside themselves with rage. They spat upon him. Happily they had found what they were looking for, and so they were terribly, terribly angry.

Shoving and yanking, they dragged Marking to a barbed-wire inclosure in which Filipinos lay half conscious or knelt on their knees with their hands tied behind them and fastened to stakes. They drove in a stake for Marking, struck him to his knees and bound his hands behind him to the stake.

The sun climbed higher and higher. There was no water. There was no food.

The sun sank and the night came. The wind blew cold with the sudden extreme change typical of the tropics.

His muscles ached. His head swam. There were pains in his stomach. He twisted at the stake, but the bonds held. He squatted as best he could, then knelt again. He was too tightly bound to the stake to lie at length.

The morning broke, and more prisoners were brought in.

At noon, a Jap soldier passed with a bucket of cold rice that looked like leftovers. Stopping beside each stake, he put down the bucket, scooped up some of the rice, pressed it into a dirty ball, and thrust it into the prisoner's mouth. The prisoner gagged on the ball because of its sourness and its size.

When the Jap came to Marking, Marking spat the rice back at him. The Jap drew back his rice-sticky hand and slapped Marking full across the face. Marking gathered spittle in his mouth and spat that at the Jap. With the back of his hand, the Jap struck the other side of Marking's face. Blackness came over Marking for the moment, but he slobbered weakly, trying to spit again.

In the full heat of the afternoon, the Jap came again, with his hand spraying water into the faces of the prisoners, "like to a flower."

On the third day, the prisoners were unbound from the stakes. They stumbled. They fell.

They were kicked to their feet again. One was dead on the ground. Marking leaned dizzily against another prisoner. "Where?" he asked. Thickly, through swollen lips, the other answered, "They are going to drown us. They will put us in the death truck and take us to a place to throw us in. They will not untie us. So we will drown." And a Jap shoved them apart.

The truck came. They were tied and could not climb. They leaned over the back end of the truck and the Japs shoved them up like sacks of potatoes. In that way some got great splinters in the face.

Marking leaned against the side of the cattle truck. He worked at his bonds, twisting, pulling, twisting, feeling the blood warm on his palms, desperately twisting against the pain.

There was one Jap at the wheel. One was on top of the cab with a tommy gun. A third was at the end of the truck with an automatic rifle of strange make.

Marking vomited weakly, swayed along the side of the truck, the weight of his body purposely shoving other prisoners who were too weak to hold him and had to give way. Again he vomited, and again, though only a drop of spittle came from his gaping mouth. When he swayed next to the guard at the end of the truck, he leaned weakly and showed only the nausea that he truly felt. He was no longer twisting his hands behind him, but they were behind him.

The truck sped on. As it approached the ramp of the Calumpit bridge at the boundary of Bulacan on the way to Manila, Marking turned his head and saw that the bridge's bombed superstructure dangled toward the water far below. The bridge itself had been repaired, makeshift but strong.

Then they were roaring up the ramp.

Marking brought up his hands, the left clenched, the right open, struck the flat of his palm with all the strength left to him, ramming his elbow with stunning force into the pit of the guard's stomach. He turned, leaped to the sideboard, poised and bent his knees to spring from the truck straight over the bent and hanging superstructure down into the water far below. He missed the wreckage by inches, dived deep, grazing his face on the hard-sand bottom and clawed with the current to stay deep. He heard the *rat-tat-tat* of the tommy gun and kept going on the river bottom. When he no longer heard it he still clawed along on the river bottom with lungs bursting. When he could no longer endure the suffocation, he kicked to the surface and swam weakly to the side where bushes grew into the water over a flooded bar. He lay in the shallows for hours, his head propped against a half-sunken log. When dusk came, he dragged himself up the bank to a stretch of sand. He scooped out a hollow. He removed his shirt and pants to wring them out and spread them on low bushes. He lay naked in the hollow and raked the sand over him.

He slept in his burial bed until the light shining through his eyelids brought consciousness and he opened his eyes to a sun high in the heavens. His clothes were damp, but not wet.

Awkwardly swaying, he propped himself against the bank to dress.

Away from the river he walked. His head was light. His feet were lead.

He neared a farmhouse. A dog barked. Chickens scattered. He waited, watched. Slowly, keeping to cover, he approached it from behind. Inside, on the earthen floor, a young woman lay, shreds of her clothes still on one arm and about her waist and under her. The mark of a bayonet gaped over her heart. Marking stood swaying, back and forth, seeing her in a haze. His eyes went from her violation to her glazed eyes. Then he saw two feet not far from her head, two feet standing up, and he lifted his eyes to the knees in short farmer's pants, to the waist, to the chest bent forward and held by the post to which the arms and the waist were tied. There was no head. There was raw meat and blood clotted black and the buzzing of flies. I must find the head, thought Marking. I must find the head. Why he must find the head, he did not know. It was compulsion without reason. He took a step. He looked. Slowly, with great effort, he turned. There was the head. There was the head of the young husband. Yes, there was the head.

He sat down upon the hollowed log, upright for pounding rice. He must eat. Yes, he must eat. He stood up, carefully stepping around the two bodies. It was their house. He must be polite. In the Philippines, it was the custom. People were always hospitable, and people were always polite. Sometimes foreigners thought people should be frank, but no, people must always be polite. They must be polite until they can no longer endure, and then they must die for their love or their pride. They must be polite until they can be polite no longer. Frankness was rudeness. Rudeness hurt. There must not be hurt until there was no recourse but death. No hurt but the final hurt. No hurt but death.

There was no food in the house.

In the garden he found the tiny, marble-sized native tomatoes. Beyond the garden he found sugar cane.

He walked and walked.

He tried not to walk upon the highway where the Jap trucks went up and down. He tried to use it only for a bearing. Out in the fields, stumbling along, he paralleled the highway.

Night came, and he was tired. He must be tired. He pulled at his leg. Nothing happened. It did not move. He pulled hard. Then he sat down—forward because, when he bent his knees to sit, everything gave way. When he came to himself he was on the ground, lying, not sitting.

He rested. He must have rested. The sun was up again. He was sure it went down, but it came right up; so perhaps it had been up all the time and he had merely fainted.

Again he paralleled the highway. Leaning against a tree, he saw an automobile. It was not moving. It was not on the highway. It was beside the highway. The hood was up, and a man was looking into the engine. Marking rested a long time. The man and the car were still there.

Marking walked, this time toward the highway. He turned and tried to parallel it, but again he was walking toward the highway. He was walking toward that part of the highway where the car was.

The man came out from under the hood. Marking stood directly behind him. The man turned, pliers in hand.

"You fix?" he asked hopefully. "You fix?"

Marking looked stolidly at the Jap. He felt a little flicker of fear, but it passed.

"I fix," said Marking, reaching twice for the pliers held toward him. The first time his hand had stupidly fallen short.

Strength came to him with the feel of the pliers and the familiarity of an engine. He fixed it. Now he would use the pliers on the Jap, even if he was a civilian who had lived many years in the Philippines.

He turned, pliers in hand. The world turned and tilted. He regained his balance to find the Jap supporting him.

"You not eat?" said the Jap. His eyes were filled with concern, for, though he did not know it, he had acquired too much of the Philippines ever to be Japanese again.

Marking looked at him.

The Jap pursed his mouth. "In," he said. "You in car. No sit seat, sit f'oor." And he tugged to help Marking into the car and down on the floor. "You close eyes. I take you city."

Marking closed his eyes. This was not a Jap. This was only a man, a kind old man, not too old, not young.

The motor started, the car rolled back on the highway.

"You go now," Marking heard. "You go now." He came up out of a pile of gunny sacks. When had the Jap piled the sacks on him? No wonder he had slept. The Jap was insistent. He opened the front door and climbed down, opened the back door and gestured. "You go. You go home. No go city. No good Manira. No good you. No good me."

Marking climbed out.

The Jap asked, "You go money, yes money, no money?" Marking said nothing.

The Jap took out a worn wallet and extracted two one-peso bills. "You eat first. You go home." His eyes fell upon Marking's raw wrists. "You no go city. Many sojer. Many sentry."

Marking nodded. The Jap thrust the money into his hand, climbed into the car, leaned out. "You go home, no go city."

And so, forewarned of the "sentry situation" obtaining in Manila, Marking worked his way around the city southward to the small towns where a bus line still rattled its way through the town of Antipolo. He was to sleep a night, eat a meal, and treat his wrists before going to the officer in the city to report Lieutenant Vidan's death.

"Well," said the officer, "well, I guess there's nothing more to be done."

Marking returned to the hills, to brood by the campfire, to live in the jungle rather than surrender. It was then that others like himself began to wander his way, and he took them in and fed them.

Among them, Cabalhin swallowed the hot gruel slowly, his eyes grateful, and the seed of loyalty grew deep, strong roots.

This had been the beginning of Marking. I learned it, piece by piece, in the black nights, and I remembered it always.

CHAPTER 11

Kanumay was the main base of them all.

From Manila and seven provinces—as far north as Baguio, as far south as Mindoro—reports flooded in, and from the towns and the subcamps near the towns all roads led to our guerrilla Rome.

To fortify the more obvious entrance on the San Andalis side, Marking built what we dubbed his "Wizard of Oz" creation. It was a bin, a broad shelf made of logs and suspended by vines, thick and strong, overhanging the steepest approach. Working with his fighters, heaving and pushing, Marking loaded it down with boulders of all sizes, from fist-size to twice the circumference of straining arms. Kanumay was boasted as a fort; the rock bin, snickered at.

Morning, noon, and night saw a seething activity. More truly than before or since, Kanumay was "Headquarters"—couriers in, patrols out, convoys in, rice carriers out; new volunteers tucked under the wings of the veterans; accidental fires; the key officers from everywhere discussing problems, arguing, setting dates and places for contact and action; Marking doing whatever he happened to be doing, in the heart of the confusion always and unmindful of it; somebody always misplacing something and somebody always looking for it—under everybody's elbows and feet in the middle of what somebody was doing; platoon leaders reporting malaria, dysentery, tropical ulcers; officers explaining, officers asking, officers listening, and a pressing need not only for good officer material but for the time and patience to develop it; reports the Japs had spotted the camp, counter reports they hadn't—it was the supplies coming in; final reports that it was both; tall stories everywhere; and the bragging and belittling of the fighters, sounding one another out as to who would go with whom and where they would go next.

Alora was doing splendid work in the Cavite Navy Yard: "Sir, we were unable to damage the planes because surveillance is still too strict. We could not burn the pier. We also have not completed the work of organization. Therefore we used the Molotov cocktail as instructed to. Five shops now out of order because we successfully accomplished our mission. Also, we finished repairing the ship and thereupon pulled the seacocks, and now we are helping to raise the ship, and it will take some time as the ship is beneath the water, not very far of course because the water is not deeper. Sir, my boys are being employed to bring in much lumber. Shall we float it to the tide at night? It is a pity to waste it, but if it is found in our homes surely our families will suffer if the Japs catch us with the best Philippine hardwoods which they desire for themselves."

Written and verbal reports indicated that Manila units were doing well. All manner of aid was coming up by convoy—especially bullets; nor was the work of gathering it dull. Some of the boys had an outpost in Tondo in the thickest of the city population, recruiting, instructing, laying their own plans. . . . We kept warning them. Guerrilla business shouldn't be carried on like a prosperous news-stand concession. But they carried on, fired with patriotic zeal and the kind of adventure known as *pasikat* under the enemy's very nose.

Up drove a *jitney* one day, full of Japs and Jap-employed police. It was a raid.

The outpost boys, lounging at an intersection to see what was coming and give warning, opened up with .38s and .45s, and tossed a grenade. The *jitney*ful let go with automatic fire, scattered before the grenade; then one with "presence of mind" threw it back and that scattered the guerrillas around the corners, down the alleys and over the back fences. But neither side pulled the pin.

The Manila men brought troubles with them to the main base. No sooner was the camp in good shape than too many Manila recruits for the combat units brought influenza with them. For a month, one batch was flat in the huts, another coming down with fever and sniffles, another on its way to its feet only to relapse. We *tried* to isolate the cases. But everybody had it anyway, either coming or going. Marking was the fighters' only doctor, and when I gave up they nursed one another. Helplessly, I tried still to help, and Marking patiently taught me to crush the quinine, boil it in a spoon, pull the liquid into the syringe, jab the hypo needle in the right spot, injecting it neither too hot lest an abscess form nor too cold, when it was already coagulated. I made the rounds of the malaria cases, and he, haggard, short of temper, made the rounds of everything. Hot soup, hot water, hot soup—but nothing quick enough nor good enough to check the worst scourge, beriberi, once it started.

By way of making cheerful conversation, I asked Marking, "C'mon, tell me the truth. Where did you learn what you know about nursing?

You're no real nurse, but you've learned a lot and had some little experience somewhere. Wherever you learned it, you can be darn glad you know it now."

Lifting out a sterilized needle with tweezers, he answered, "ICS." Quickly he added, "Don't tell even *anybody*."

I didn't get it at first, but then I blinked. "International Correspondence Schools! That's wonderful!"

Fighter after fighter, recruit after recruit, had to be sent out of the camp, even those wanted in the city, because it was death for them to stay. They dragged themselves up over the basin's rim and down the long slopes. One, left behind to catch up later or fall in with others, took the wrong fork, wandered along a little used trail, stumbled and fell, rose and stumbled a little farther, fell and lay for a while before he crawled, starved, and crawled until he died, unknown. Days passed before he was found.

The pressure of work, the strain of hunger and sickness, the sheer desperation brought matters to a head between Cabalhin and me. He said something, I said something, he placed his hand on his sidearm, I challenged him to pull it and reached for my own. Marking leaped between us, pulled his gun on Cabalhin. I protested, and Marking's angry voice drowned me out. Cabalhin, with his arm crooked over his face, plunged into the brush at the camp's edge, sobbing like a child. I followed, soothed him, came back to cool Marking's head, brought them together—Cabalhin was catching his breath in dry, convulsive sobs, and tears were in Marking's tired, sunken eyes—and left them, to crawl into my *kubo* and rest my aching head and raw nerves.

Then Bathing Suit came stumbling up the incline, shot through both lungs. He and Maring, the girl fighter, pals, had been lounging in a sunny spot between duty assignments. A favorite game among the guerrillas was Russian Roulette—loading a six-shooter in only one chamber, twirling the chamber, and snapping it in place sight unseen, twirling the gun on the finger cowboy-style and in the middle of the twirl bringing the barrel against the temple and pulling the trigger. It was a guts-tester. Maring was practicing the twirl for the real test some day, and kept swinging the pistol around, backward and forward, training her index finger. She failed to unload it, though it had a hair trigger and all six chambers were full.

There was a sharp report, a silence, then Bathing Suit came, supported by Bugarin and Tumol and a shocked, tearful Maring.

"Sir! I'm killed!"

Marking took him in hand, laid him flat on a clean mat, took from my hands as he needed them the alcohol, iodine, cotton, bandage, and plaster, cutting the gauze into strips to use as drains for the wounds. Each time Bathing Suit whimpered, Marking cursed him. "Shut up. It's just a scratch. Ya wanna die? I'll kill you myself." So Bathing Suit lay quiet, turning his head to catch the looks between Marking and me; but Marking and I exchanged no glances. The shot had pierced his left lung under the armpit, passed through behind the heart, cut the right lung and come out just below the right shoulder blade. Schaffer, Farretta, and George Wicks, USAFFE buck private, took turns sitting through the first nights with him. For the duration, if anyone spoke of them in their absence, Bathing Suit would leap to defend them and annoy all who liked them too and were just talking to pass the time.

Three weeks later, Bathing Suit was carrying his rifle. He had to. We needed anyone who knew the business end of a gun, for finally, once again, the camp gained its collective feet.

Marking fell-in squad after squad, platoon after platoon, dispatching them separately to an area halfway between the main base and some town, where they could ambush the enemy and find better foraging grounds. Too, the Japs were seeping into the hills again as the town garrisons increased in strength. If the fighters strengthened themselves on good food and exercises, and the Japs came out of their holes into the hills, there might be action to our advantage.

Sidney Gorham from No'th Ca'lina, USAFFE corporal, was becoming our pride and joy among the youngsters. Short on words but long on guts, he, like Cabalhin, had been one of Marking's bodyguards. Sometimes, if they scouted by moonlight, Marking would kid him, "Now, look, Paleface. Every time you get in front of me, you expose us both. Me, I'm khaki like my shirt. Behind me, boy, behind me!" Sincere, courageous, drawling Sid was Marking's favorite, and John Paul Schaffer and Alvin J. Farretta, American mining engineers, were close seconds. Schaffer was of German extraction; Farretta, of Italian. After a Hitler-Mussolini argument, they often refused to speak to each other. All three might have been neck and neck in Marking's favor, but where Sid patrolled, Schaffer and Farretta would start out patrolling and wind up prospecting. They would roll out. There was a war on, and they were to find some Japs. So Schaffer and Farretta would walk around over here and walk around over there and eventually they would come nose to nose with an outcrop or fall over a float. When they came back in, Marking would ask about enemy movements. "What enemy movements?" Schaffer would ask. Farretta would prompt him, "The Japs—you know. *Where are the Japs?*" "Oh, yes, the Japs. How the hell should I know where they are? *They're everywhere, anyway!* Look, whaddya say we give the war a week off? There's the prettiest little vein up the creek around the mountain . . ." So Sid was closer to Marking's heart.

All through March, Sid and his two squads of guerrillas rolled back and forth in the foothills east of Antipolo, Teresa, Morong, Baras, and Tanay. Marking gave him wingspread to see as much as he could see, in and out of the smaller areas steadily patrolled by others. They policed the countryside and reported by courier to headquarters what the Japs were doing, how many were doing it, where they were doing it.

At first, Marking worried about Sid, who knew little more than yes and no in the dialect, was hotheaded and reckless at times and might not be able to control his men, all fully armed and as spirited as he. We discovered there was no cause to fret. Sid's men loved him and told him what they ought to do; he thereupon commanded them to do what they advised, and they obediently carried out his orders. Because they never wanted him to get in wrong with Marking, their advice was on the up and up. He didn't know the rules; they did. He was learning to distinguish between trails, but in an emergency cross-country trek they brought him through. It was a headquarters joke, but Sid never knew. From his point of view, it was only fair—as well as democratic—to discuss trail problems, etc., with his men, especially when they knew the country and customs better than he. All he could see was that he commanded, and they obeyed.

Of course, there were complaints.

One report stated that the Gorham patrol was harassing the chickens instead of the enemy. Sid, enraged, retorted, "My men must eat. And I ask properly and don't insist, and give receipts when the people finally say yes."

There was also the report that night patrolling including serenading the farm girls for miles around. Marking ignored it, and so did Sid.

Then once he and his squads flattened themselves on a rise in the hot sun in the thick grass, waiting for the Japs they had spotted to come through a choice spot on the trail. And the Japs, who had spotted the guerrillas, picked another rise over another choice spot where *they* waited for Sid and his men to come through. Both sides were still there when the Home Guards carrying supplies arrived at the main base to report that they had tiptoed through unscathed because both parties concerned had drowsed off, it being a fine day.

That brought a reprimand from headquarters and much laughter from other patrols.

Thus the laughter and the tears of our first base at Kanumay.

More and more Japs . . . The garrisons were packed . . . That meant business again. Soon the Gorham patrol and all the other patrols were sidestepping the Japs in ever-increasing numbers. Reports became repetitious: *The Japs know where the main base is. They have had informers in previous convoys. They have maps of the mountain and the surrounding countryside.*

Up to Mount Kanumay came a letter. The Japs had caught a farmer and given him directions, just in case he was not a guerrilla, which he was. He delivered it direct, and told Marking that April 18, 1943, was the deadline for surrender. If Marking refused, he could expect the Japs on that date. The letter was addressed also to me, incidentally changing my sex:

April 8, 1943

Mr. Marcos Agustin
Yay Panlilio
Rizal and Laguna Provinces

Dear Mr. Agustin and Mr. Panlilio:

I am now sending you the last advise [sic] of the Chief Central Luzon Military Police of the Japanese Imperial Force, as if you have at present antipathy to your friends and to your countrymen; the Independence of a New Government as it is promised in the near future that the Philippines should be a Country free as of those in GREAT ASIA.

I hope you will understand this present situation, and be a historic man for the establishment of the New Philippines so that you will be consider second to Rizal.

I am sure that the day may come that you will repaint if you continue the nothing dispute against the New Government or the Japanese Imperial Force.

I am going to serve you as a man of real Philippines if you come to me and surrender, I will do the most possible way for your security and protection, as I, Chief of Central Luzon Military Police.

Yours truly,
CAPTAIN IKEDA
Chief Central Luzon Military Police

Marking read it and turned again to the riot gun disassembled on carefully spread sacking. "Whatever he says, no." He scrubbed and oiled each part; his forefinger stirred anxiously among the tiny screws. Riot guns are intricate, and he alone in the outfit could repair them.

As usual, all patrols were out. He had left in the headquarters about thirty good men and sixty weaponless, unfit, or sick.

He was busy with the gun.

"Marking," I said, "they're not kidding. The runner says they'll be up the Eighteenth. We can't defend the base."

"Where's the plies?"

"Pliers."

"Plies."

"Pliers. Marking, you've got to decide what to do."

"I don't give a damn. I want the plies-pliers-plies!"

"You want the sick butchered, that's what you want."

"You damn woman, you keep your damn mouth shut!"

The blood rushed to my head. I saw the canteen sail through the air, saw his elbow go up and deflect it from his temple, saw it bounce into the sacking and parts of the riot gun fly in every direction. On his haunches, running the flat of his palms over the ground, Marking's whole heartsick attention focused on finding the tiny screws, picking up the springs and levers. "You ruined my gun! You ruined my whole one gun!"

I stood aghast. What lives had been risked to get those guns! What lives given to keep them from falling! "Marking, I'm *sorry!*"

"My nice, beautiful, one whole gun!"

"I didn't mean to throw it. I'm so sorry."

He rose to his feet, rubbing his elbow. "Order the sick to go home and lie low. And next time you throw a canteen, darling, empty it first."

April 18, at dawn, the Japs came. They came from every direction. They poured out of the towns into the hills. And more Japs from the north and south poured into the towns to pour into the hills.

Cabalhin sent a runner: "Sir, shall we come in to strengthen the base?"

Others sent runners: "Sir, the Japs have guides who have been there before."

Sid was most frantic of all: "Sir, *we can't stop them. Get off that mountain!*" He didn't have the faith of the others in the Old Man's sagacity. "Sir, retreat *now!*" Sending runner after runner to no avail, Sid talked it over with his men, as worried as he, and together they headed for the main base, hiking a hill behind the Japs, a mountain ahead of them. Sid was on his way to reinforce Marking, disobeying orders to stay away, foolhardy, scared for another, not for himself.

"Sir! Japs!" "Where, and how many?" "Many many." ... "Sir! Japs on the river side!" "How many?" "At least three hundred, sir!" ... "Sir! Japs out in front on the Taranka trail—hundreds, sir!
Can't see them all!" ... "Sir, they're coming up the ravine." ... "Sir, they're in Tinukan! They're in Santa Inés!" ... "Sir, shall we fight?"

With his *bolo*, fifteen-year-old Victor, mountain lad, filled four trucks with Jap dead. He saw them swarm up the ravine, following the dry streambed, so narrow and sheer on both sides that they slung their rifles and used both arms to hoist themselves up, clinging to the jagged rock ledges, pulling up by the tough roots. Victor waited. They climbed in a frenzy. Still he waited. The head of the swarm was nearing the bin. When the ravine looked like a broad, moving line of ants, and those in the lead were too near for comfort, he raised his *bolo* and chopped at the first vine, ran nimbly over the rocks as the bin creaked to cut the second, then leaped to safety. Down dropped Marking's log shelf, flinging tons of rocks into the upturned faces, bouncing and ricocheting and rolling to bounce again; and while the Japs screamed, and our handful of shotguns, a few rifles and one Browning sprayed the tumbling mass, Victor slipped through the jungle and over the rim to the secret base to report.

By eleven o'clock the Japs had taken the central camp, and the fighters there followed Victor to us fifteen minutes away.

At one o'clock, firing again—the machine gunners at the back entrance. There was a spitting for five minutes, then a lull, then a furious spit-spitting for a full half-hour. Sid had come in just as the machine gunners started to pull back up the mountain. It was he who fought the half-hour.

The boy was beside himself.

Fully seven hundred yards away, the Japs hoisted their flag.

Upright, in full view, Sid deployed his two squads and his scouts Ming and Maring, and, with the tears streaming down his angry face, ordered his men and the sixteen-year-old-girl to fire anyway, fire defiance! Untouched, the Jap flag, white with the red spot, waved against the green and brown.

"Gimme an American flag!" wept Sid. "Just gimme an American flag!" He shouted at the Japs to come on and see what they would get.

"C'mon, you dirty skunks! You cowards, you!" And the Jap flag furled mockingly while Sid's fighters threw their precious bullets to the winds, and each time the firing of the girl's .30-caliber knocked her flat, she picked herself up and snatched her rifle up and fired again. They potted a few with the fusillade.

Then the Japs rushed them. Fighting until they were almost pinched by the Japs' flanking movements, Sid and his men pulled out and pulled the machine gun out with them, so that Marking's runner found only the Japs coming in and sank quietly into the undergrowth to circle around and scout for the boy farther up the mountain.

Late afternoon passed. It was night when Ming and the girl Maring, exhausted and in tears, found the secret camp to report.

Against all Marking's lectures, Sid had sent no one ahead to scout—a regulation even when no attack was on—but had charged ahead of his men. Innumerable times he had been ordered, "Sid, walk between your two squads. Always send somebody ahead. Never take chances." But Sid had charged ahead, and because he had six-footer legs and his squads were made up of the shorter Filipinos, he outdistanced them no matter how hard they pushed themselves; nor would he hear their advice. Devoted to him, they pushed on after him against their better judgment.

Thus, instead of coming to the secret camp, Sid bore straight up the mountain, over the basin's rim, down into the captured camp. It was an early moon and a white moon, and the whitest moon throws the blackest shadows. There were figures near the little *cogon*-thatched "hospital," first *kubo* from the trail by which he entered.

Headed for the old headquarters office across the rivulet, Sid was striding through the group, who he thought were guerrillas, when they jumped him, pinning him to the ground. He was a big fellow, Sid was. We used to put him in loose pants, and in two months he had grown out of the seams.

They had him flat, a Jap on each arm and one on each big leg and a fifth gagging his mouth.

Sid heard pebbles rolling on the trail. He quieted. His faithful two squads were coming in.

Then he gathered all his strength, yanked one big leg loose, kicked the Jap off his mouth by a blow full in the face, yelled, "*Japs! Retreat! Retreat the men! Japs!*"

The first of his men had seen him pinned to the ground. Whispering the urgent word back up the line, they eased themselves along carefully and quickly into fighting position. But as Sid shouted one of the Japs grabbed a rifle and fired, apparently at Sid, at close range. The fighters thought him dead, knew resistance was useless, retreated back up the basin's edge. From seven in the evening, when Sid was captured, until close on midnight, they scouted a mountain with more Japs on it than guerrillas, looking for Marking.

At midnight, Ming and Maring, and the others, reported Sid's death.

The next morning, the Gorham patrol returned to the central camp. The Japs had left. Sid's men scouted the ground, looking for his grave. The *kubos* had all been burned. So had the *palay*. Clay pots were bashed in. Only the great *kawali* caldron, iron, was undamaged.

Automatically, with guerrilla thrift, the boys picked it up and carried it to the new secret camp.

The Japs came back in, looking for the *kawali* themselves. It was gone. Questions began to buzz in their heads. They checked with other Japs. Huge iron pots do not vanish into thin air.

And finally they guessed that the guerrillas were still there. The hunt began in earnest.

For four days Marking and the forty-nine of us left to him—he sent the Gorham patrol out to deliver strict orders to all others to stay out lest other officers repeat Sid's gallant but tragic mistake—retreated around the mountain, evading the Jap patrols. And still he was not taking his chances alone. Alone, he could have Kit-Carsoned himself out of it. But he had the rest of us, only half with arms to speak of, counting the five it took to handle a machine gun, yet it never occurred to him to do anything but bring us through.

That was Marking's greatness: he never ran out on his following.

I brought the chance of escape to his attention: "Take the best men and go on through. Six of you could make it safely. Leave me in charge of these others. We'll take our chances."

He looked at me. His face was inscrutable.

"It's the sensible thing," I said.

And he said, "I am the Commanding Officer."

"Don't be a fool!" I was impatient. "What difference does it make? I mean, because you *are* the No. 1 and the outfit needs you, get out of here and find Cabalhin and the others."

"Shut up," he said. "I will leave you when I am dead." It wasn't me alone he wouldn't leave. He wouldn't leave anybody.

The Japs had a system: the mountain was surrounded, then the patrols cut through, over and over again, like cutting a pie. To go where they had just been was safest—for a while.

Seldom before had the Japs lingered longer than the day of an attack, but the missing *kawali* had given them ideas.

Marking thought he had rice and concentrated food for fifty for a few days, and so we settled down into a game of hide and seek.

I never did like the damn game. "So! Positional warfare, is it?" I poked at him, the anathema of them all, for guerrilla warfare loses all point when it bites off more than it can chew. It loses points, and the enemy makes them.

Marking was in a stubborn mood. He wouldn't give up his mountain unless he had to. As far as I was concerned, there were always new ones.

Toward the fifth day, the food for fifty turned out not to be food for fifty. We found ourselves on the outer flank of the mountain, far to the north, creeping down into territory through which we had never been. The Japs were still too close, too close for comfort, too close even for cooking.

And we discovered two "items of interest" that last day: Mount Kanumay was in no way connected with other mountains by concealing jungle, and the Japs on Mount Kanumay were not the only Japs around.

In greater detail, Mount Kanumay was an island in a desert of *cogon*, and the Japs had burned the *cogon*.

There were Japs in all the *barrios* around the mountain, Japs in camps between *barrios*, Jap patrols, Jap sentinels, Jap outposts, Jap lookout stations equipped with transmitters. The Japs had even taken down telephone systems in the towns and lugged the equipment into the mountains and were stringing it around the mountain. Every river and creek mouth was watched, every trail guarded. Through the night, there were Japs lying flat in the trails. A canvas tent high on the highest neighboring mountain, Susungdalaga, indicated not only an observation post with transmitter but high-powered glasses.

Japs waiting inside. Japs waiting outside.

Starvation for sure if we hesitated.

There was no choice. Marking decided to go through. The moon was still full—one reason why the Japs were in the mountains too. A brisk wind filled the sky with scudding clouds. We had a long way to go, and a chance of making it. At the last minute, as the sun went down, we noted that we were also fortunately downwind from the dog at the nearest Jap outpost. More fearful than any Jap were the bloodhounds used by the China-campaign veteran, Captain Okada, for the hounds could bring a swarm of Japs. It would be risky business sidestepping bloodhounds with the rivers and creeks under surveillance. There would be no throwing them off the scent, once they caught it. Sizing up terrain, time, and the odds against us, we crouched in the jungle at the base of the mountain. The sun sank in a last rosy flare.

"Remember that I love you," said Marking, "and keep going. Whatever happens, even to me, keep going, darling."

In the dusk, we stepped forth. No use crawling. We were in full sight anyway, if their eyes were good or they had a searchlight. Best to move quickly, straight through.

There was no moving quickly. The men were heavily loaded, worn out from strain, weak from half-rations.

Leaping a gully in the darkness, I fell short to strike with my chest a boulder imbedded in the opposite bank. I saw stars and colored pinwheels and fought for breath. Hands reached for me, others boosted me up.

Silence, invisibility, and speed were our only weapons. We kept going until midnight.

We had passed the burned area and entered *talahib*, which stabbed many an eye, cut many a hand. We groped across narrow, deep streams, knowing there might be crocodiles. "Carry Mammy," said Marking in a low voice. In water up to the armpits, I was carried across on somebody's shoulders.

A fighter sneaked a cigarette, not realizing how great the danger. I knocked it from his hand, crushed it underfoot. Another whispered, whispers became undertones; I hushed them harshly, in sharp hisses.

Marking's .45 had slipped out of his holster when he rested, waiting for the others to follow the trail he had broken. He wanted to go back for it, but dared not leave his men lest anything rattle them into scattering, and so starving or being hunted down one by one.

Wicks and Bob Burns, his friend, had colds; Wicks especially was drowning in phlegm, but his cough, which boomed like a California bullfrog, could not be allowed him. And Marking would have swapped both for Sid.

One and all, we had our troubles.

I was retching since the fall.

In a fringe of trees growing on the banks of a small river, Marking let us halt. Most of us fell leadenly to the ground, slept heavily. But Borres, the cook, cooked. He cooked to put something warm into Marking, who was up again and again to check the guard, to protect the brood, unable to rest.

In half-sleep at dawn we ate. As we prepared to move, Marking looked out from the fringe of trees in a last check-up, and there was the same large encampment of Japs we had detoured. In the darkness we had made a horseshoe turn, and now we were nearer it on the other side!

They were in plain sight, exercising before the rising sun, and perhaps had seen our fire in the middle of the night. "They'll be coming" said Marking—but he allowed breakfast, a gulp apiece. Once again, he took the lead. We were out in rolling country with no concealing jungle at all and very little brush. Cannily, he threaded the long line of weary fighters along the streams in the grass and small trees, or kept a tree, larger than the rest with spreading branches, between our creeping, crawling line and the Jap encampment, threading around a rise or hogback, zigzagging back and forth across country. He paused just long enough for stragglers to come in sight, cursed them roundly, pressed on, yet would wait again for them to catch up.

"Keep them coming and keep them down, *very* down," he ordered me. We had reached unburned grass and could snake through with less detouring, but it would have to be very flat snaking. To get a rump down, I punched it.

The two Japs in front of the tent on Susungdalaga were taking turns with the binoculars.

Hour after hour—broiling sun, *talahib*, no water.

Crawling, Marking came across a lavender wild flower. He thrust his hand through the grass, pulled the flower to him, roots and all, then turned on his side to hand it back to me, also crawling. I was to carry it, like a talisman, for many days; carry it until it withered and turned brown, until even the leaves were gone and the stem was split and doubled in my palm.

On the last grueling push, Marking brought forty-nine people and himself into *kaingin* country and food: two of the forty-nine, Americans; three of them, women. And still he was unable to rest, for only Marking the showman could sweet-talk the backward mountain people out of their rice and into the river to catch fish and shrimps. He spoke with awe of the great United States Army that would back the receipts with gold, and thus he brought food to us who were famished.

While we rested on a high mountain *kaingin*, four planes zoomed and swooped over Mount Kanumay five miles away. We counted the blasts—nineteen, twenty, twenty-one!—and pricked our ears for the strafing, burst after burst: "The Americans! The Americans!" It was still April 1943. It was *not* the Americans. Disappointment was tempered by the later contentment, "There goes some more of their war material."

There was joking. We let them have the mountain. Were they grateful? No. They knocked the hell out of it.

But there was, too, a sobering thought: it was the first time they had used planes against our puny forces. And we remembered Sid, the Paleface.

Marking knew the pursuit was not yet over. Feeding and resting us, he prepared to pull us relentlessly on again. The men began to pick up. "No more tails dragging," was Marking's only comment. To Santos the magician he had said, "This is the time to turn yourself into that watermelon seed." But Santos had been nothing more than another hunted human being; his card tricks and his sleight of hand rendered him no less vulnerable to bullets and bloodhounds than the rest of us, even if he could still squeeze out of ropes knotted about his neck, wrists, and ankles, with his ankles drawn up to his wrists and his face flushed and the neck veins angry from constriction. He could wiggle out of them, leaving the knots intact. We would look at the loops and the untied knots and marvel, believing yet not quite believing. And so the boys rested and swam in the river, lazing in the sun, talking idly, recovering. Three days, five days?

Then down the river came a patrol of thirty Japs, and they were dressed in civilian clothes to resemble us—a trick apparent throughout the network. Only a scrutiny of their short legs and their teetering waddle-walk revealed their true identity. Marking sent a few of the boys back to check up. At a bend in the river where very deep water and steep banks made climbing the cliff bank on a vine ladder necessary, the boys discovered—Japs. One boy fired pointblank. With his precious Browning rifle, he fell into the river. The Japs had been resting, and so the boys had not distinguished them in time by their walk.

That stage of the long, three-week retreat was a fast flight straight down the river. Marking had hired Dumagat guides, primitives who knew the mountains as bookworms know the classics. They saw trails everywhere, walked up and down precipices, nonchalantly paddled in and out of river rapids. When the firing was heard upriver the Dumagats knew the trails; but they didn't wait for us—zip!

It was our good fortune.

We missed the trail to the left where another Jap patrol was coming in, climbed the face of a low, silly mountain—Mount Purro—with loose rocks everywhere, and exhausted ourselves more on its loose, steep face than ever on a towering mountain, coming down on a vine swinging over a concave cliff, barely making it.

There, around the bend, below the waterfall, we rested, puffing native tobacco—chopped by us, sun-dried by us. Up above the waterfall, where we had missed the trail and gone into an impossible climb and drop, the pursuing Japs were resting before taking the trail that would bring them face to face with more Japs. Their Filipino guide, who later fled to us, gave us a day-by-day account of the Kanumay encirclement from the Jap angle. Every close call, checking our notes with his, we breathed, "God took care of his children."

As we drew out of danger, closer to safety, Marking began releasing those among the forty-nine who could fend for themselves for a while, hiding with relatives and regaining their health. Bathing Suit was all but dead on his feet. Ming could barely support the girl, Maring. Borres' eyes were sunken, and Darol wanted nothing more than to be left somewhere to die and each time Marking pulled him on, kicked him on, brought him through. Darol did not know that he was almost safe, nor that he was still taking turns carrying the machine gun. The two Americans, Burns and Wicks, went off, striking slightly north in a search for new friends and food. The two young Filipinos, Maring and Peggy, drifted off with their teammates. The sick were assigned to people along the way who would care for them. The prisoners, because they had learned "what it's like," were forgiven and sent wherever they wanted to go. No prisoner pardoned under these circumstances was ever known to betray again.

Pain in my right chest, left side, and lower abdomen was increasing hourly. Sometimes, for an instant, the river and its jungle walls blurred before my eyes, and oftener and oftener I lost footing for no reason at all. There was so much pain in me that I no longer felt hunger pains. Like Darol, I was ready to die.

The simple mountain folk behind Montalban, Rizal, gave us refuge. After a talk among themselves, one among them guided us up a near-by mountain, and there in a hidden clearing were huts with huge *palay* baskets filled to overflowing—more than a hundred *cavans*.

We rested for a week or so in what seemed a quiet place. If I lay quiet, the various pains receded. I lay quiet, ate doggedly. Those who have almost starved cannot eat immediately nor well. There is no taste and little desire for food; forced feeding brings cramps. We had difficulty eating in the midst of plenty.

Then a restless Marking pushed on. Intuition, perhaps. We left on an afternoon (May 6?), and before dawn of the next day, two hundred Japs raided the cluster of *kubos* where we had rested. One among the farm folks had betrayed us all, and the *kubos* with their secret stores were burned to the ground.

The food and rest had not strengthened the half of us left. On my feet, moving again, the pains heightened until I felt disembodied and apart from the triangle they formed. We dragged through, through the day, through the night, and in the night, I fell, struggled up, fell again. With none of my own sex to turn to, I turned to Marking and his ICS background. It was a hope for help. Hesitantly, I confided my trouble.

"How long?" he asked.

"Since the fall in the ravine," I said slowly, thinking back.

"Why didn't you tell me?"

"I didn't know. And there were so many other things of greater importance. I didn't pay much attention—"

"Damn!" said Marking, and "Darling, darling!"

I had been in slow hemorrhage for eighteen days.

"You've got to be carried," said Marking.

"No. No!" Without seeing them in the dark, I knew what worn, sick men drooped in the group around us.

On we went.

After hours of increasing internal pain, I collapsed. Fumbling in the darkness, the men tied two ends of a canvas strip to a bamboo pole. Marking put his shoulder to one end, saying, "Borres, we will carry first." Soon others relieved them. For hours, heavy-footed guerrillas took turns at the improvised hammock. In the dawn I must have seemed shrunken, for Marking spoke to me comfortingly but avoided looking at me. Looking up at him, I saw a skeleton on a stick. The last lap had been the hardest for us all. Losing direction in the night, he and the fighters had almost walked up to a Jap outpost. Only our rule of silence on the trail saved us. We heard them and then saw the red gleam of coals before the Japs heard us. A quick, noiseless backing up, cutting across country again, brought us to farmlands where only the mountain tops retained crests of forest. Up into little caves hidden by thicket we went—mountaintops are traps useful to the encircling Japanese. Our defense would be half secrecy and half the Japs' ignorance of which mountain to patrol.

In a roomy cave, headquarters set up work again. To the towns Marking sent relatives and friends who were farmers of the district and had passes from the Jap garrison at Antipolo. They procured a Claudin injection that might stop hemorrhage, and they gave Marking the chickens, eggs, milk, and vegetables to build me up. Down on the flatlands, Mang Esio of the clean-cut cheekbones, the quiet voice, and the steady eyes watched the countryside while he ostensibly performed his farm chores. Each morning he brought fresh milk, warm from the *carabao*. I had not seen and was not to see again a man more quietly courageous than Mang Esio.

Reports flooded in. I could read them but not answer them. Marking and his bodyguards went scouting, setting up an observation post on a hill between two main trails. No forest or brush on that hill; only a crown of sharp-edged rocks half lost in the *cogon*. Before dawn they crossed the open to reach it, and all day they watched. They could see the Japs going up and down the two trails. There were long caravans of horses and men loaded with supplies for the Japs still trying to ferret us out in the interior, and enemy patrols at regular intervals watching for any movement that might indicate our presence near the towns—and all tallied with the reports of a tight network. Japs were catching everybody except the men they wanted, and were disgusted. So were the people caught and released over and over again, usually after rough handling. At night, Marking returned to grope into the cave where I lay on a trestle bed, and there, with the waning moon shining through the vaulted entrance of the larger cave that was my penthouse, he told me the day's news. I told him how a great rat had bit my finger as I slept with arm outflung; how I woke with a jerk to see it turn and disappear into the rock walls as gray as itself.

First of all the officers to find us was Cabalhin.

One day Marking did not return to the cave. Cabalhin came. With him were picked fighters, two of them carrying a native hammock.

"Ma'am," said Cabalhin, "we must move."

"Where is the Old Man?"

"He will be coming, ma'am."

I pondered two things—Marking's not coming and the "ma'am." Wild horses could not have dragged that from Cabalhin. If my illness awakened pity, to hell with it! By this time, I was inured to enmity; it was a norm to have my intentions, efforts, and small achievements unappreciated; in fact, the inuring was a sick super-sensitivity that looked for slights and ugliness, found them even where none was intended, passed them off as far as action was concerned, yet piled them up in a vague, deep resentment. Without effort, I held control over myself, with definite reservations in a manner that still persisted in being friendly.

In broad daylight, at three in the afternoon, Cabalhin was moving us across the open rice paddies. There seemed to be an urgency. It must be emergency, to cross so much in the open. On and on we went. Sometimes, to strengthen my legs and rest the carriers, I walked, but soon I had to lie in the hammock again. After dark we stopped in a cozy farmhouse, and Cabalhin outdid himself in offering good food. Looking into his unique face, I saw sincerity and concern. There was no mistaking the change, but after long suffering I was slow to forgive. At thirty-two I was no less a child than Cabalhin at twenty-two.

A mat was spread, and a blanket offered, and even a pillow borrowed from the farm folk. Then late at night came Marking, and piecing his and the boys' talk together, I realized that Cabalhin had come ahead to snatch me out of the flood of Japs going that way, and Marking and the rest of the men had covered the maneuver. One woman was hardly worth that much risk and effort; the glacier within melted a bit.

Cabalhin left the next morning with Marking's fighters and his own, carrying on his broad, little shoulders the entire weight of feeding, basing and hiding them from the Japs who swarmed everywhere. A dozen of the best fighters were left as bodyguards to Marking, for small groups can hide where large groups must fight.

The story of Sid was patching together. He was only a few miles from us in Antipolo.

Captured, he had walked in on his own two big feet.

"I am Sidney Gorham, from No'th Ca'lina, age twenty-one. Yes, I'm a guerrilla. I'm a captain; no, I'm a major." Sid was a captain, for he not only held his small combat unit but could give orders to the general supply enlistment in the towns near which he patrolled. We later understood why he boosted his rank: sometimes the Japs treated majors and up a little better, and he was using his head. Sid was to clarify that while he was only a captain in the guerrilla, he was a full army major—and make them swallow it.

But it was probably his own personal charm that got him off easy. That, and courage. The Japs at that time had a grudging admiration for brave men.

During the interrogation—he was not maltreated as far as we could check—the Japs told Sid that Marking and the guerrillas were bandits.

Sid riled. "You just don't know him. He's a swell guy. He's like my father. He's honest and he's kind. And he sure was good to me. They were all good to me." When Marking heard about this, he was inconsolable. He laid plans for raiding Antipolo.

Then Sid was whisked away.

Down in Laguna at a bigger garrison, he was cutting hair. It is no trick cutting off all the hair, as the Japs do it. Probably Sid was saying to himself, "I ought to cut off yo' haid." The Japs kept him supplied with cigarettes. He was even allowed to go alone to a store. Marking gave orders to his men to help him make a getaway.

Again the boy dropped out of sight.

Marking offered five thousand pesos in war notes for any unit rescuing him or aiding in his escape. He was found working on the piers. Then came the Talim encirclement and through three months of peril and broken contact, the thread was lost again.

Escaped Americans told us he had been executed with a group of others, including Thorpe and the heroic Barker, who when forced to make a speech after his capture said, "The fate of the Philippines will be decided in this war between America and Japan, I thank you," and promptly sat down, stony-faced. People turned away from the young face under its Pershing cap, turned away to hide their tears of pity and respect.

Then, in August 1944, sixteen months after the date of his capture, it was verified that Sid had been sentenced to two years' imprisonment. And finally, after the Liberation, it was believed that he had died in a hotheaded fight in Old Bilibid in which prisoners took over one of the Japs' machine guns and gave the last twenty minutes of their life in the name of Old Glory.

No American ever loved his flag more than Sid.

And he gave his life for it and for the Filipino leader he loved.

CHAPTER 12

Something more than Japs was troubling Marking in the early days of May 1943. Time and again I caught his eyes upon me, brooding. My health had improved. I had gained weight. I was almost happy. Yet Marking followed me with morose eyes.

"Do you really like roast pig?" he asked.

Food was all he could give me, when he would have liked to give the moon, or a guaranteed safety, and I made a point of appreciating all he could offer. I did appreciate it, and I took special pains to express my gratitude.

I grinned. "Where is this roast pig?"

"Soon will be your birthday. You will have it for your birthday." On May 22 a fine pig squealed its last. Borres scraped the bristles away with a *bolo*, and his k.p.'s filled coconut shells with hot water, pouring it over the spot he scraped. It was a fine pig, truly. And Borres prepared the bed of coals for slow roasting. The k.p.'s cut and pointed the sapling to thrust through the pig and keep it turning over the coals.

Father Aramil, our "fighting priest," smiled at me, then at Marking. Marking grinned.

Lamp, the agricultural student, arrived.

"Did you get it?" asked Marking.

"Yes, sir, the parish priest was glad to send even more." Lamp and Father Aramil entered the farmhouse; Marking examined the pig.

Word came down from the lookout: "Japs very near, sir."

Borres and the k.p.'s lifted the golden-brown pig by the sapling. "Which way, sir?"

"That way," said Marking.

Into the brush with the precious pig they went.

"You, too," Marking told me.

"You be with her, sir," said Father Aramil, "and we will stand guard here."

"No," said Marking. "You come with us."

Man by man, we all followed the pig.

We waited, wondering how much scent a near-done roasted pig threw off, yet reluctant to depart from it, ready to carry it through enemy lines rather than leave it behind. Father Aramil climbed a tree, perched himself securely in the fork with his pistol drawn. Marking skulked through the bushes with rifle ready. The bodyguards deployed toward the Japs' possible approach. Minutes, then an hour went by.

New word came from the outpost: "They followed the river instead of the trail, sir. The fisherman said it was an ordinary patrol and they probably will not be back."

Borres grumbled: "Damn Japs. Pig got cold—skin won't be crisp, not cooked yet inside. Damn Japs." We pushed out of the brush, and Borres straightway rushed to the fire and repaired the coals.

I looked around at Marking and found the new, brooding look in his eyes again.

Father Aramil asked, "Shall we start now, sir?"

Lamp said, "Sir, even the proper vestments are in the package." There was more in the air than the birthday pig.

"Let's go up in the house," said Marking. All three began to mount the rough board stairs. "You, too," he called to me. "Come." Reluctantly, not knowing why, I followed.

In the main room of the farmhouse, Father Aramil was drawing a priestly garment over his ordinary shirt and trousers. Lamp handed him something: "Here is the water, sir."

I felt Marking's hand across the small of my back. "Come on," he said.

"What goes on?" I asked. "You're going to be baptized." "What! *I will not!*" "Why not?" "Because I don't have to be." "Darling, *you have to be!*" "Why?" "Because—well, you know what the dangers are. We may all be dead tomorrow, even tonight." "What of it?" "Well, all of us will go to heaven, and where will you be?"

"It's OK by me." I stood with my feet braced, obstinate.

"Darling, please. Everybody has to be baptized."

"I've been baptized and baptized and baptized!"

"But it wasn't a real baptism. You did it because it was a hot day and all the church people went down to the river and you kept getting in the line for fun—you told me so."

"Marking, I *won't be baptized!*" "It's against God if you don't." "So— it's just to be on the safe side, you want me baptized!" "No, darling. I want us both to go to Heaven." "Oh, God, oh, God—" "Who do you want as your godfather?" "I don't want one." "Please, Yay. For my sake."

Now I understood the troubled, brooding look. I softened. "Marking, what if I don't?"

"Nothing." He meant he would make no issue of it, yet I knew then that on impulse he might flop me on the floor, pin me there, and have me baptized by force. The indignity I pictured angered me.

"So! It's really at the point of a .45 that I enter the Pearly Gates!"

"You got to be baptized," he said stubbornly. "Please. For my sake."

The bodyguards were grouped at the door, surprised and listening.

Borres laughed. "Mammy's birthday, Mammy baptized."

"I'll have Lamp, I guess." Thus I picked my godfather.

Quickly Lamp stepped into position, Father Aramil bent his head in prayer, Marking stepped back, leaving me to the Father's administrations. There was the salt, there was the holy oil, there was the water blessed by the Catholic priest unable to come from the town but in on the secret.

"In the name of the Father, the Son, and the Holy Ghost," intoned Father Aramil.

"Amen," said Lamp.

I looked sideways at my old friend Lamp. "Amen, amen," I said sourly.

Lamp grinned. It was all over. As I turned to leave the room, Marking cupped my elbow in his palm and walked me toward Father Aramil again.

Father Aramil turned and said, "What God hath joined together, let no man put asunder." And he smiled.

Touched by his good wishes for our happiness, I smiled back. "It's nice of you to hope so, Father. The pig awaits."

Borres called through the partition, "Sir! Shall I cut the pig now?"

"OK," said Marking. "Let's eat."

"This is some birthday," I said half ruefully to Father Aramil as he folded the vestments. "Now I go to Heaven, of all places."

"It's a good birthday—one of the best I've ever had." He explained, "Because May 22 is *my* birthday, too."

The Japs were to come within a hundred feet of us before we finally cleared the rice paddies around Teresa. Kiko Pakiko, regimental commander, whose real name is Francisco C. Francisco, was guide and contact man for us throughout. He carried on ceaselessly, day and night. When the Japs came too close, we huddled in farmhouses or lay in scant brush patches, and Kiko would amble down the trail to meet them and talk with them and guide them elsewhere or, staying so that he could return to us, would steer them a few miles out of the way. In his hand lay our lives, and for Marking's head and my head alone, he could have collected a couple of hundred thousand.

Through Cardona, where the people smiled at us and sped us safely through, we stepped into sailboats. Brisk winds swept us away.

"Yay." "Yes, Marking." "It was eight thousand Japs at Kanumay." "I saw ten." "Not joking. It was eight whole thousand." "The boys ought to have uniforms, or something drab." "Yes. That was the worst part of it—the white shirt and that colored sweater." "Khakis are best." "Can't afford it. Can't get the material any more." "Poor lads! Gad, but a white shirt stands out! Gives away the whole line."

The sails, released, flapped loosely. The boat rocked. Other sails dotted the lake, skimming by as we lazed along. A month before ... Kanumay loomed purple to the east. With my eyes on it, I was remembering the three-week retreat, and I wondered what other unseen struggles like ours were going on everywhere, in Europe, in Asia, and in our own little Philippines. My hand trailed in the algae-yellowed lake waters, cool and calming. Haven at last. How long *would* it last?

"They're still up there," said Marking, following my eyes.

"No! What for?"

"Looking for us. They swear we're dead."

"What're they looking for then?"

"Our bodies."

"They can have them"—and I returned his smile.

"Eight thousand ... They had everything ... We can't fight them fair, not with less than five hundred armed men."

"But they can't lick us foul."

"No. And the Americans are coming back."

"Who told you so?" I challenged, for fun, to point up a rumor. Marking's face sobered.

"You did."

"I did not. You did." Again we could smile.

"Isn't that a launch? We'd better move on, don't you think?"

"Damn Japs," he muttered. "They've got everything now, even the launches."

CHAPTER 13

*W*e needed rest desperately after Kanumay, and at last in the summer of 1943 we found it. But only for a moment.

Cabalhin and Salvadore took our sick fighters and gave us fighters from their units for our protection. Thus, with thirty bodyguards and heavy reserve enlistment guarding us, we retired to Talim Island, a lovely paradise of forest, farm, and duck yards. Marking held headquarters there, picking up the threads of organization, changing plans, renewing assignments—and renewing himself. We set up in style in a little dispensary in Lambac *barrio*. There were beds. There was a floor underfoot. There were chairs and a table. We eased around, trying out the furniture.

"It took centuries to evolve a chair," I said.

"Let's put up the flags!" Marking, too, was excited by all the civilization around us.

Happily we draped them on the wall, the Stars and Stripes and the Philippine flag, both a little soiled, a little torn. "Let's change the chairs around."

We changed the chairs around.

"Sir!"

"Oh, hell!" The never-ending greeting had interrupted us again.

"Sir, we have arrested an American." "You what?" "An American—we arrested him, sir." "What for?" "He escaped from Nichols Field, sir."

That caught my attention. "Don't arrest him," I demurred. "Help him."

"He might be a spy, ma'am. Sometimes they don't escape. Sometimes the Japs send prisoners of war to find out about the guerrillas."

Marking dusted off the already dusted desktop. "Well, bring him in."

"Yes, ma'am."

"Don't call me 'ma'am.'"

I laughed.

"They better know who's running this outfit," said Marking.

Contentedly he drifted through the swinging door into the bedroom for a nap. The springs creaked. Then soft, regular breathing with now and then a snort. I sat in the office, waiting for the prisoner, making notes of work to be done.

When Pivet was brought in he looked as if he had come out of a coal mine at the end of a double shift. The grime on his face ran up into the smudge of a shaved pate growing out and down into short, dark stubble. His eyes were red and wide and flighty, though their gaze was steady except for occasional quick glances to the side. He kept his back to the wall, but he did nothing else. He just stood there, his arms hanging. Beneath the grime and stubble was a sensitive, intelligent, and possibly high-strung young man.

"Sir! Here are his papers." "Don't call me 'sir.' The Old Man's asleep. I'm ma'am."

"Yes, sir." "Ma'am." "Yes, ma'am, sir."

Pivet's eyes flickered. Perhaps the flags on the wall . . .

"Albert Carron," said one paper. A picture of a five-year-old boy in front of an American home said, "Good family." Calendar leaves, drawn by pencil with each day laboriously crossed out told of long, desperate weeks. There was a note from an American in another prison camp asking Pivet how it was at Camp Nichols. I could answer that one: Camp Nichols was the hell of them all.

"Come inside, lad."

He followed me like an automaton into the room where Marking slept.

"Over there. Sit down and relax." I smiled, in the practiced heavy-mother role, to put him at ease. I had to smile because I don't have a great, bulging bosom upon which to pillow a troubled head, and if I don't ooze with kindness I look thin, dark, and mean.

Obediently he sat down behind the small table in the corner of the room, regarding the lanky Filipino spread-eagled on the bed. Sitting there, he looked cornered. He sat in the corner as if he had to because I told him to. Marking slept on.

So this was a little of the flesh and bone that had survived the tragic Death March out of Bataan in April 1942, had even survived the worst prison camp of them all—Nichols Field. Where thousands had dropped of exhaustion, had been clubbed to their feet or bayoneted or shot on the ground because they could not rise, not again, this young American with the bloodshot eyes had marched in spirit if not in body in the long cavalcade of surrender. Where thousands had died like flies, hundreds in a day, at the infamous Cabanatuan prison camp and at other lesser camps, this American mother's son survived. He had survived with the courage still to make the perilous break toward freedom. He was hardly fit for soldiering, either physically or mentally. What, I wondered, could we do with him? But he was an American, and for any of us that was enough.

Marking woke, swung his feet to the floor.

"There's nothing suspicious in the papers, hon." I spread them out: picture, calendar, letter, name card.

If Marking has the man, he pays no attention to papers. Rubbing his eyes with thumb and forefinger, elbow propped on knee, he asked, "Where'd you come from?"

"I escaped from Nichols Field," the boy answered in a mechanical tone, as if he expected to answer the same question again and again and to stick to the same answer.

"Who brought you out?" We had a network for aiding individual prisoners to escape and guiding them into the foothills. "Nobody."

Marking looked up. "How'd you get through?"

"I kept going." "Nobody help you?" "Only after I reached the Rizal side." "Must've been our men." "They were Filipinos." "Then what?" "People brought me to this island in a *banca*. They arrested me here on the island."

Of course. The loyal population was like a wall around us. Where ordinarily anything could pass through with nothing more than eyes marking passage and tongues relaying warning, the people were alert and quick to catch when Marking and his headquarters were in their midst. It was protection of the guerrillas and protection of themselves for harboring us.

Voices in the outer office. Marking pushed through, called me.

Pivet was left alone in the room. The window was open, and his feet pulled at him to keep going. But he had seen a flag, his own flag, and he had heard a woman "talk American"—me ... Outside, hilarity.

Cabalhin, Mapa, and Mata, crossing the lake in a shell to report, had capsized, and they had clung to its bottom all night. The Home Guards had respectfully rescued them, saluting them as they bobbed up and down in the water and cursed, gurgled, cursed. They were blue with cold, dripping.

Marking was laughing at and with them. Cabalhin, Mapa, Mata, three of our best—we might have lost them all. Digging for my denim jumpers which would fit Mata, I was sharp-tongued: "Now you know what I mean, all your eggs in one basket. What if a Jap patrol launch caught you floundering in the water? What kind of a fight could you have put up? . . . Marking, stop laughing. You only encourage their shenanigans."

Nagging, scolding, pounding at them, I wondered what had happened to me. Where was the girl who had wandered far and fast and been reprimanded by Romulo at the top of his lungs in the days when he was no general and the *Herald* was the liveliest paper in town? No reckless scrapes for me any more, and no reckless scrapes allowed even those around me. With or without bosoms, a fretful, no-good-end-predicting Mamma. Gone my once jaunty shoulders. Gone even a sense of humor.

"Here, Mata," I said, "go drown yourself again."

"Yes, ma'am." He smiled.

The impatience dropped away. After all, they hadn't drowned; the Japs hadn't got them, and there were no signs of pneumonia. I sighed, and smiled back.

Hot coffee came in—something to pour into three handsome, swaggering buccaneers, figures out of a storybook. Maybe they looked like nothing to anybody else, but mother-eyes are sharp, and it is the world that is blind.

And there was the American boy inside, beyond the swinging door: another one. I was a mother with too damn many sons.

I put the coffee before the escaped one, and it steamed up as he bent his face forward, his hunted eyes holding mine, not believing.

Marking called, "How about sending him along with Mapa?"

"Come join the boys," I said.

Pivet rose.

"Bring your cup," I said. I felt rich, saying it: we had a house; we owned a cup.

Outside, the boys were free and easy, and Pivet was limp and awkward in the shaking of hands. He had nothing to say, but the hunted look in his eyes began to change to one of bewilderment. Anyhow the boys had too much to say—raids, gains, losses—and soon the silent Pivet was forgotten in their joshing and clowning. Offered a chair, he sat down, watching. His eyes picked at the pistols strapped to their thighs, the ornamented clip belts, the fancy lanyards with the guerrilla tassel on the gun butt. He gazed at their eager, alive faces. Steps on the stairs; the hunted look again. More fighters in, more greetings, more jokes; a relaxing.

A rice delicacy, *suman*, came in.

"Here," I said, "have one. Have one quick. Learn to grab. These guys have big appetites."

While I unwound the wrapping and dipped the rice cake in the brown sugar, Pivet beside me helplessly held his wrapped *suman* in his hand. He smiled his first smile.

"Like this." I unwound it. "Then dip it." I demonstrated. He ate, bite by bite; it was the sugar he was after.

"What did you eat at Nichols?" "Garbage. They clawed at the garbage and the guards kicked them away like dogs. I wouldn't." "Wouldn't what?" "Wouldn't fight for garbage. I'd starve first. They forgot they were American. I didn't." "Have some more coffee?" "No, thank you." "What did they call you at home?" "Pivet." "Like it?" A real smile this time, "Yes, Mammy."

The noisy bunch were making their goodbyes, off on new assignments. I interrupted, "Marking, his name is Pivet."

"Want to go along?" Marking addressed Pivet over their heads. Suspicion in Pivet's eyes. I thought, My God, what do the Japs do to them?

"Where are they going?" he asked me. "To the highland camps. Guerrillas." "Are you guerrillas?" "Yes." "You, too?" I laughed, "Yes. You'd better fall in. More fun and more people killed!" "Is that why—" "Why we fight? No."

He looked up at the flags, and I nodded, "And everything they stand for. This one's our flag. That one's yours."

"I've got my knife."

"Where'd you get that?" It was a little, battered, nicked, rusted penknife. The most it could attack would be a pencil.

His eyes were wide again, remembering. "I had it all the way. I had it open, in my hand. Anybody touch me, I'd kill 'em. Jap or Filipino or anything else."

"What you need is that camp in the hills. They'll give you a rifle up there. Keep it clean. Don't lose it. Drop everything, but drag that through. They're leaving. Are you going?"

"Will I see you again?"

"Sure," said Marking.

"Sure," said I. "When something flies by with the Japs on its tail, that's us."

"Goodbye, sir. Goodbye, Mammy."

The fighters loved him. He buried his green bananas for ripening, and shared them with his comrades. He learned a Tagalog love song and lined up with the boys in any *barrio* serenade. He wiped himself on a broad nettle leaf and hobbled for days, plaintively trying to walk around the itching, burning, swelling, and the fighters laughed at him and loved him.

Five months later, at another headquarters, he swaggered in with the rest of them, a free man again. "Hello, Mammy! Ya got an extra shirt?" And I said, "Get along with you. I got no extra shirt." He laughed, "I'll have the one off your back!"

The Jap swarm in Rizal passed over the lake to Laguna and great Mount Banahaw, where another guerrilla outfit was operating. Then, mysteriously, the Japs were less and less in evidence. It was July 1943. The towns had light garrisons—fifteen to thirty soldiers we could have knocked out in as many seconds. Manila seemed empty. There were few Japs in the north, few in the south, but more than we could ever turn about and handle still pursued us. The only Japs in the country seemed to be those immediately after Marking and his fighters. We sidestepped them about the lake, touch and go, thumbing our noses. Once they almost got us. Twice they almost got us. But their cordon was thin. The people, too, became bolder and bolder as the Japs lessened in number. An uprising? We toyed with the idea. "Let's have us an uprising," said Marking, and "Let's!" said I, and "When, sir, when?" demanded the people.

As usual, the Japs had thought of that.

They played their trump, "zoning." All of August 1943 was devoted to zoning.

Fifty Japs could surround a town, one town after another or several towns at the same time—surprise it, pouncing by truckloads, dumping men there at dawn, or creeping into sentry position before day broke.

Anybody could come in. Nobody could go out.

Women and children were herded into the garrison or church. Men were lined up while a hooded creature, his eyes peeking through two holes in the sack over his head, passed down the line. Where his finger pointed fell torture and death. Out of the line the victims were yanked to hang in the butterfly-swing or simply be lashed to trees and fence posts; beaten with clubs or rifle butts; burned inch by inch with cigarette ends, matches, or tufts of cotton soaked in gasoline and ignited; slow-roasted head down over an ever replenished fire. Whole bananas sometimes were thrust down their throats at the end of a sharpened pike or trained dogs were sicked on to tear out the calves of their legs and leave them bleeding to death; for others, days of slow starvation and hanging in the ropes intervened before death released the drooping victim. Women too, expectant or not, could expect the same for having a patriot husband, brother, or son.

And so the Japs punished the people of Talim because there, after sixteen months of backbreaking effort and heartbreaking setbacks, Marking had been able to draw his breath, reassemble his fighters, reorganize the reserves, shift assignments, pick up old plans, make new ones—he had been able to recuperate free from the pursuit that was wearing him down. Talim had guarded him and his mobile headquarters by a wall of secrecy for more than fifty days. Here on Talim he had slept like a tired child, protected by a patriotic people who loved him. Here he had eaten ripe avocados with a little fresh milk. Here he had had fresh fish and homemade sweets. Here he had met old friends and new, among them Lydia Arguilla, woman writer, who was to become his aide, and Lydia's husband, Manuel, the Philippines' outstanding story writer, who was to disappear in the Japs' torture cells. Here he had gone swimming in the lake, frolicking like a porpoise; seen the sunrise; traced the sunsets. And here, too, we had danced at a little party the *barrio* people gave us—"Pappy" and "Mammy" climbed down from dignity and authority to open the country dance officially and, with boots still caked with mud and our guns strapped to our thighs, we had waltzed and rumbaed and congaed and finally, to the whooping of our boys around us and their clapping hands, we sedately and modestly closed our number with a little boogiewoogie.

Most wanted of men, hardest pressed, Marking had turned to Talim Island, and the people there opened wide their arms and took him in. It was not yet peacetimes in that July of 1943, but it was an hour's surcease from war. He "rested" at desk work, and the people outdid themselves giving him the all of the little available.

Then somebody on the fringe of this haven breathed a word to the wrong party and ushered in the awful month of August.

The Japs came, bringing hell to paradise.

Though the thousands were gone, they came by hundreds from everywhere and made a couple of thousand, still too much for us.

An outer encirclement guarded the lake from every side. Within the larger circle there were many small, tight circles as each *barrio* on the lake's shores and on the island in the lake was surrounded for "zoning." We lingered, sidestepping, not knowing what zoning was, and it was for our own safety, not their own, that the people begged us to go.

Once the zones were set, those inside faced hunger, for no one could bring in food. Those caught outside were promptly tortured and dispatched or sent to the mainland garrisons for "prolonged interrogation."

And, then, within the zones, one lone, cringing specimen of humanity fawned upon the enemy and eagerly pointed—even at his own son-in-law. He ingratiated himself into a personal safety that brought upon a helpless, kindly population the full hate and retribution of an armed enemy. Women and children were segregated; for three days and nights, they were foodless and without water. For many more days, they grew weak on gruel and fright. Throughout the *barrios* rang the shrieks of those beaten unmercifully, clubbed to death. Through the night, the groans. Kicked, a woman lost her child before term. Some of the tied died in the ropes, tumbling stiffly to the ground in the grotesque shapes produced by hanging in the ropes until rigor mortis set in.

In the *barrio* of Lambac alone, seventeen men "failed to return." Some had been sent to the mainland; others, dumped into a well. When the Japs left two weeks later, the bodies were too decomposed for identification. To this day, families still hope, for the members of each bereaved family think, persist in thinking, that maybe it was somebody else, not their own father, not their own mother.

During the punishment, the terror induced by such wholesale cruelty and the tearing, helpless grief at losses they had never in their worst fears imagined reduced the population to a cowering, punch-drunk herd ripe to follow the first leader. One had pointed. Beside themselves, two more broke. It was enough to bring more punishment, and brokenly the people surrendered, not all, but hundreds, leaving great gaps in what had been solid Home Guard territory.

The hours of tragedy were climaxed when a handful of weak characters, formerly held in check by guerrilla control, helped to hunt down guerrilla organizers, their staff members and bodyguards. Some of our finest became the blood sacrifices on the altars of their fear, for the weaklings did not offer them up alive to the Japs but delivered them dead because the dead tell no tales.

Guerrilla Colonel Jesús Deniega fought it out. Months before, in the Kanumay encirclement, his pal Ricardo Postrado had died and was laid to rest in Daraitan, far in the interior. Deniega fell on Talim, and the team was no more. Ben Romero, Bataan boy, fought it out. Peggy, a fair, vivacious, cameo-faced girl of fifteen, pleaded for her life, was *bolo*ed to death, then violated in death. Captain Felipe Feliciano bent his head to light a cigarette offered him by one of his trusted men and was *bolo*ed from behind, his head rolling from his body.

Mario, his handsome, loyal bodyguard, died beside him.

Across the lake on a peninsula, a net of Japs closed in on Lieutenant Colonel Hugh Straughn, retired army officer who until Christmas 1942, had been adviser to Marking.

"I told him that peninsula was a pocket!" sobbed Marking. "I told him to come with us. I told him to get farther back. I told all of them. Why didn't they listen?" Unashamedly, with the men around him, he wept for old Straughn.

"Perhaps they'll spare him because he's a high officer," I said, but without any manifestation of grief. Disliking him, I could not weep any tears except crocodile tears; I sincerely would have wished him safe, and I pitied him—but without tears.

With fighters we could have called in from our scattered camps, we could have held the Japs for an hour or so. But that would have had no lasting effect, and we had no time to get our forces anyway. It was, furthermore, the unarmed the Japs were after, and we did not have the strength to save them. The enemy would kill and kill and kill. We pulled away, heavy of heart, vowing vengeance some future day, but helpless in the hour.

The thirty of us slipped through, not in sailboats, but in *bancas*, under cover of night, gun barrels on the thwarts, alert to each minute of a possible last fight. Up to the now empty peninsula, along the shore we went, resting in a lone house with the machine gun on the porch. Before dawn, out and creeping through the brush, and to the house we had just left, the Japs came and set up two machine guns, one pointing over the water, the other up the hill. On again, resting in houses the people tried to guard by running to warn us of the Japs' arrival, and leaving by moonlight to grope through the boulders and bushes and twenty minutes after we left to hear the rattle of machine guns strafing the houses where an hour before we had lain in restless slumber. On again, to flatten beside a highway where trucks carrying Jap troops to hunt us down thundered by in the darkness, shrinking lest headlights expose us. On again, to find hobnail tracks fresh in the trail we were following. On again, to file across highways, quickly, rifles loaded in the chamber and ready, between the Japs' speeding convoys, all in our honor. Through open fields to short-cut danger and thereby take an equal risk instead.

On, on, and on.

Everywhere, suffering and death among the people. And we without the strength to help them.

The wails of the widows, the sobbing of children.

Harsh, wild words from the people running from us in terror lest someone see and tell, words of blame through the cries of grief and horror. Now it was for their safety, not ours, that the people bade us go.

With our own hearts breaking for them, on and on and on, away from them to protect them, to lead the Japs away in pursuit of us. Through *kaingin* country, where the Japs came later to kill six farmers only because we had passed within a mile of the home of one or had drunk from the brook of another or had stopped at the door of a third to buy salt to take with water as we pulled farther and farther away from the people.

One little clubfoot farmer gave us rest.

Someone broke and told.

The Japs pierced his side with a bayonet and dropped him in a hole and kicked dirt over him.

He regained consciousness, pushed his way out of the grave, went home to his wife to give her the few coins in his pocket, then lest greater retribution come and perhaps strike down his wife and his pert daughter in their little dooryard of roses and *sampaguitas*, he reported back to the Japs.

"Sir"—to the Japs, holding his wounded side, lopsided because of his clubfoot—"I am here again."

And then they really killed him.

Up and up into the jungle we fled, our spiritual suffering so great that hunger and cut feet and cold winds and rains went little noticed. Our wounds were deeper than bullets or sabers could make in flesh.

Farther into the interior than we had ever been, poised at the edge of unexplored territory, gathering strength for the last pull over the divide, we looked back upon a lost land. Would we, *could* we, ever return? With the last *barrio*, Karakatmon, at our feet, long we looked at Sampaloc, a handful of thatched huts, brown against the plateau's green. Long we looked at the apple-green and gold of rice fields in their patterned paddies and the slopes of *cogon*, crested with the darker green and the gray of brush and limestone, dropping and rising, rolling and lowering to the lake's lily-padded shores, mountain after mountain, hill after hill, paddy after paddy. On the slate mirror of the far-away lake, white specks meant sailboats scudding along, careening before full and fickle winds. Sprawled on the shores and nestled against the slopes were the towns in which the many helpless suffered and over the distant horizon's rim, veiled in the low-lying clouds, the Manila we loved and a Bataan forever with us.

Not for our own sakes, the renunciation of battle. We could have fought on, taking our chances. But the enemy turned viciously upon the helpless through whose lives we passed unbetrayed, even succored, and to leave them was to save them. For their sake, forsake them.

Up into the dark, wet jungle, we the hunted struggled upon our way, falling, sliding, climbing, pressing on our way.

"Give me your hand, walk in the exact middle." Falteringly, I picked each foothold, close behind Marking, my right hand in his left extended behind as he faced forward, keeping his balance for both of us as we crossed high above a ravine on a fallen tree whose decayed bark was spongy with rain and fungus.

"Rest." We rested. Scarecrows squatting on their heels, rifles upright between their knees, sodden, bleak, silent, dwarfed to futility by the immense wilderness, by our impotence to stem the horror in the valley we had left behind.

"Up." We dragged on, pinched with hunger, trembling with fatigue.

"Mammy, we will carry you."

"You can hardly carry your loads. I can make it. All I carry is me."

"Up."

"Rest."

"Yay! The river!"

"Beautiful!"

"There are the *kaingins*. Food for the men. Corn."

"Corn! Will they sell?"

"Remember when I organized Truadio? Well, these are Truadio's people. I sent him ahead to have corn and cassava collected. See my foresight? More than a year ago, Yay."

"I take off my hat—"

"You can't, darling. You lost it again."

CHAPTER 14

We lingered by a stream called Kaliwa, left-fork headwater of the Agos River flowing east through Tayabas province to Infanta on the coast. Bottle-green and white foam, the water splashed and rolled and roared along between high rock walls and steep, thickly forested banks. Already, three days into the interior, there was comparative safety. The fighters lolled around, as Marking and I did, talking idly. Sweet corn and blessed sunshine and finally Truadio's *banca* men with a new kind of craft. I marveled at the graceful shells, technically dugouts, yet thin almost to frailness and shaped to canoe points—a craft made to shoot rapids.

Not all could ride. In four *bancas*, we loaded what *bayongs* they would hold without capsizing; then Marking ensconced me against the baggage in that of Pulo, rifleman from these parts and expert riverman, and Pulo with his sapling pike swung the *banca* into the river. We were off.

"Relax!" yelled Marking from the shore, as I sat stiff and straight gripping the thwarts of the *banca*—so narrow there were but three inches to spare on either side.

For hours, as we slipped between boulders or bumped and stuck and bumped again and the river boiled around us, I stayed tense. Then, worn out, I became inert as the baggage stacked at my back; my troubles were over. The water cascaded into a broad stretch and became as silent and silken as it had been wild.

"Pulo! Where's everybody else?"

"We wait here, ma'am."

"How will they get here?"

"Walk, ma'am. Do you want to sit on the bank? I will take the water out of the boat." He was unloading the baggage, stacking it ashore.

"A lot of river got in, didn't it?"

I pulled my sopping pants legs through the shallows, sat on a rock, then leaned back on an elbow, and finally rolled down on the clean, brown sand. Heaven ... A wild mountain river, the high green walls through which it tumbled, a clear sky with fleecy white clouds, sand warm in the sun and a clump of tiny wild flowers ... War? *What* war?

"Ma'am, they are coming." I raised my head. Far upstream tiny figures, no larger than the wild flowers in their rock-and-sand cranny, threaded a way in and out of the boulders, across the spits, always on the left bank, growing larger and larger until, across the still, slightly swirling surface, I could distinguish the girl fighter Maring's little-Indian-maid face and Pagayunan, the electrician, with the assured step and lean, broad-shouldered body. Others were catching up with them. All came to a stop, hallooed to Pulo.

"Pulo, what do they say?" For no reason, alarm brought me to my feet.

"Nothing, ma'am." He was grinning. "They can't get across."

"Why do they have to cross?"

"They have to, ma'am." He pointed to the sheer granite wall, scalable only with both hands and maybe picks and ropes. At its base the river was deep and dark and a tree branch, sweeping along, was promptly sucked out of sight.

"Pulo! Maring can't swim!"

"It's all right, ma'am. This is the first crossing. Everybody, even the mountain people, must cross here by *banca*. We stop every time to bring them across."

"How many crossings are there?"

"Many. Maybe eleven, maybe fifteen."

The group on the other side had grown to thirty or more.

"I go now, ma'am." He stepped into the *banca*, kneeling instead of standing, checking up on his paddles, using the pike to push the craft in lunging starts upriver close to the right bank.

Now where was he going? I watched as Pulo shoved against the current, taking his craft far upstream. The group on the opposite bank hallooed again and again. They were lowlanders and had as little river lore as I.

Then Pulo hallooed back. With a last shove of the pike, the *banca* shot out into the middle current. He lifted the pike clear of the water, laid it carefully the length of the *banca*, and, as the light shell bobbed and swung broadside down the current, used a paddle lightly to turn the prow upstream, then held it deep and hard against the river, breaking the swing of the *banca*, slid out of rough mid-stream into the swirling backwash as part of the river curled upon itself before rolling on again. He stepped up on the opposite bank, a figure of competence and authority in his own land, and those who had ridden and belittled him in Rizal kept their lips buttoned in Tayabas. To the girl fighter and

Pagayunan and Ming and Badidles and one nameless k.p. who had been kindest to him, Pulo gave the courtesy of the first fording. The others would have to wait until His Highness condescended to take them across. He would have to ford them all, for Marking was the CO and left none except in good hands; but Pulo could take first those in his favor and make the rest wait, just as Borres fed the disciplined fighters first and served last any loafers and braggarts, regardless of their position in the line and the number of times they shoved their coconut shells or cupped leaves under his rationing hand.

Another halloo when Pulo had brought the first five to join me. Marking's erect, authoritative head and full, deep voice zigzagged down the stream toward us. He was sitting in a *banca*. Behind him more and more *bancas* could be distinguished.

"Hey, Pulo," I asked, "where'd the other *bancas* come from?"

"The Old Man made Truadio get them."

"Whose are they?" "The Astovesas.'" "You're Pulo Astovesa, aren't you?" "We're all Astovesa on the Kaliwa. Over on the right fork, the Kanan, they are all Marquez." "You mean all interrelated?" "No, ma'am, just cousin-cousin."

Marking swept up, stepped ashore. "Darling, we'll eat when the sun is like that." He raised his hand in the Fascist salute. Pulo, pushing upstream for another load, laughed. That was time in the interior: morning was at dawn, noon when the sun crossed the strip of blue sky between the towering green walls through which the river tumbled, evening when twilight fell. We would eat about eleven o'clock.

"Where?"

"About two cigarettes from here."

The fighters sprawling around us on the sand laughed. They had learned that one too, and were gleeful at my blank face. Mammy was at the bottom of the class.

"Say it again, dear."

"About two cigarettes." Marking was gleeful too. Nothing like putting the old girl in her place. She didn't know everything—yah!

"You better explain it." If I didn't get it, I didn't get it. I was piqued, and the boys knew it and loved it.

"How long does it take to smoke one cigarette?"

I had figured that out long ago, making them last. "Oh, about twelve minutes."

"Then, how long does it take to smoke two cigarettes?"

There was a catch somewhere. I took my time, knowing they would make a fool of me. "With self-restraint, half an hour." Then I got it, and it was all over my face as I felt my eyes open. "Is *that* the way they measure distance out here? What if you smoke cigars?"

Amid laughter, Marking motioned the fighters up. Down the right bank they proceeded, toward the next crossing. The *bancas* were ready to take the baggage.

"Marking, Maring's the only other—She's a girl. Let's put her in a *banca*." "I told her to take any of them. It makes her sick, she said." "I got a little dizzy, too." Baggage had been readjusted, piled a little higher in other *bancas*, less of it in mine. "May I ride in your taxi?" asked Marking of me.

Back to back with the baggage between—frayed *bayongs*, ragged blankets rolled and tied with vines—we rode down the river. Pulo, at the helm, was happy too, back in the old familiar groove of river-running, hallooing to relatives laboriously pushing and pulling their *bancas* up the rapids. Pulo was back from the wars and important in company with the great guerrilla chieftain, Marking. Curiously the people eyed me, and comment was unanimous: "She is not beautiful." With a chance to pick, they wondered, why did Marking pick me?

And when the sun was like heil Hitler we did eat. The boys had rice, gathered by Truadio, and they squatted about, cooking it in tin cans and battered old pots, in bamboos cut eighteen inches long, or wrapped thick in banana stalk. Sitting cross-legged in the river sand was a three-year-old Dumagat, a child of the primitive hill people, all tropical chocolate in one package with a comb of fuzzy hair. All he had on was a string tight around his potbelly. At the river's edge his mamma was working her way along, up to knees and elbows in the water, feeling under the edges of flat rocks and in pools where mud-caked dead leaves lay on the bottom, giving the shrimps refuge from our watering mouths.

"You mean she catches them with her bare hands?" I asked.

"I'll show you." Marking walked to the river, squatted, fumbling in the water under the stones. He pulled up a hand and something flipped into the sand. I jumped a little, looking down. There was a real live shrimp, in color a kind of transparent speckled brown.

"See?" said Marking. "And the country's full of wild pigs and deer. You'll never starve."

The baby's papa came up. He dropped a fat, eight-inch fish on the sand, and the baby reached for it, patting it as it flopped. Unable to get a lifting grip on it, he bent his head to taste. Mamma Dumagat kept on catching shrimps; Papa Dumagat gave a betel-nut smile, dark brown and bloody, and dived into the river again, his steel needle and elastic band ready in his hand to spear another fish.

"They sort of don't bother with their clothes," I said.

Mamma Dumagat had bark cloth wrapped around her hips like an overlapping dish towel, very rough, very dirty. As she moved along, bent over, her breasts hung fat and pendulous like great, brown pears.

Papa Dumagat wore even less. A strip of bark cloth was tight around his waist; another strip disappeared between his buttocks to come up snugly in front and then under the waistband, from which it hung, stretched wide and fringed a bit, like an apron. It was a very tiny apron, six inches wide, eight inches long.

"You know, Marking," I said, "it's all inhibition, this complete covering up. Comes a cold spell, and of course you cover yourself all over and pin the flaps shut. Then you get used to the idea, and you think you've *got* to be covered."

No answer, not even a grunt.

I looked around. There was his shirt on the sand. There were his wet trousers. Twenty feet away, he was fumbling in the shallows for shrimps without even a G-string.

"Marking! That's indecent! You come back here and put on your pants. Or you borrow a G-string."

No answer. Then he rose upright and flung a long-clawed shrimp at me, and slapped his wet hands on his thighs, haw-hawing as I shrank aside. It was his first real laugh in many weeks. He had laughed, yes, but this was from all the way up, a real ho-ho!

Then I laughed.

"What you laughing at?" he demanded.

"You. But never mind. Bring home the bacon, Pappy."

"Sir, ma'am. Let us eat." The boys were already eating, and some, finished, were off downriver getting a headstart.

The fish were broiled over the hot coals of a Dumagat campfire. In the can the shrimps had turned a brilliant salmon-pink. An *anahau* leaf—that fan-shaped, fan-folding jungle leaf of a million uses—lay spread out with rocks pegging it open, and on its glossy green the rice piled snowy and steaming.

"My God, Marking," I said, "who says rewards are in Heaven?"

Mamma Dumagat dumped the shrimp can upside down on the leaf beside the rice pile. With the shrimps and a few small ungutted fish, out rolled something round, the size of a walnut, brown outside, orange across—a great fat snail!

"Marking, look what she's feeding us!"

Promptly he picked it up, pulled it out, popped it into his mouth; picked up another, did the same. "I'll leave you some," he said.

"Oh, no, you won't!"

"Here—you eat it!"

"Marking, get away with that monstrosity! It would creep around inside me for days."

"It tastes wonderful. Each snail, one whole bite."

"It's big enough to take me in one whole bite." But I was curious. Everybody was eating them with gusto. "Gimme one. If it kills me, bury me."

Delicious? It was the most succulent mouthful this side of France.

Down the river eastward we went, through the rapids, over the still, deep pools, around the bends, lifting the boys at the crossings.

Some had forged far ahead, swimming across or fording up to their chins, making for the forks decided upon as bivouac area. Even Maring, the diminutive riflewoman, had pushed on, refreshed and singing. The plucky kid could not swim, but she had accepted a dare. At the crossings Pagayunan would hold her by one wrist and Badidles by the other, while the fighters made a line across the river to hold everybody fast. In the line of heads, above the sliding waters, Maring's head could not be seen. Then, up from where she was walking on the river bed holding her breath, they would pull her for a gasp, and down she would go again, floundering bravely along. She preferred it to nausea in the *banca*; hers the right to choose between hardships.

At the point where the two rivers flowed together to form the Agos was Pinagsahangan, a *sitio* like a park on a high bank. Ferns made natural beds in natural lawn, and in the background tall trees festooned with vines and moss were a wall to emphasize the park.

"Not here," said Marking. "Planes could find us from the air."

Northward up the Kanan River we went, and there we found a farmhouse full of a widow and her children and everybody they had married and begot.

"Not here," said Marking. "They are *mukhang perra.*"

I could read his mind. There were two kinds of people Marking hated: the *mukhang perra* ("money face") with greed written on it in large letters, and the *matapobre* ("kill the poor") with the same message. The *matapobre* was the rich ogre, and the *mukhang perra* all the little hungry ogres grabbing and stealing and cheating one another. Marking was sandwiched between, a very thin but defiant filling between the high and the low. Some day the Philippines will have a great middle class, too, full of people like Marking; for there will be a yanking down of the high, and a kicking up of the low, and all will be seething activity and progress and democracy and then the rest of us parasites will have to work for a living.

Marking looked at the opposite bank across the river. "That's it—we'll be Dumagats."

"We'll *what?*" Then I realized I had indulged him too far. "Marking, we'll get that itchy skin disease, that boney! And we'll get lice, *tuma!* You and the boys go native if you want to, but not me, *not me!*"

He himself had a horror of the skin itch. The skin all over the body turned rough, dry, and flaky, and looked as if slugs had left a network of tiny trails. It started with a spot and spread and spread and spread, until there was no inch untouched, in the meantime spreading to everybody else. Except for itching and appearance, there was nothing to it. Nobody ever died from it.

He didn't want the skin itch, but his heart was set on being a Dumagat. I could understand that. If a New York businessman had to live with the Indians and bears in Yosemite, he might as well make the most of the experience. So across the river we went and piled ourselves and our *bayongs* high upon a clean sweep of sand.

"All right," I said. "You do it and I'll endure it."

Marking called his six Dumagats around him—fortunately they understood Tagalog. Singsonging it their way and pantomiming the general idea, he made known his plans. The Dumagats giggled. Then they ambled off.

"All right, Heap Big Chief Sitting Bull, what now?" I asked, sitting squaw-fashion on the sand. "We will have the house of the Dumagat!" "I didn't know they had houses." "Oh, yes, they have houses."

The Dumagats ambled back. They were singsonging in their queer language, and having a leisurely, happy time. They dropped *anahau* leaves and saplings hardly more than sticks upon the sand. Then they sat down on their heels and opened up their *anahau*-leaf pouches and scooped lime out of old shotgun shells and smeared it on betelnut and green leaf and took a fine mouthful of the hot, dizzying stuff and squatted chewing and spitting and passing the time of day.

"And when will we have this house?" I asked Marking. "Tonight." "The sun is setting." "You have to be kind to them, or they won't work for you. You have to be polite. Money doesn't mean much to them." "Lucky little souls! What if they decide not to build the house?" "They will go away." "And if they go away?" "I can't catch them, and besides it isn't right to make people do what they don't want to do." "How about making the boys keep their rifles clean? They don't want to." "That's different. They got to do what I tell them because they took oath of allegiance and I am the Commanding Officer and I tell them what to do." "OK. You tell these Dumagats to build that house." "I can't. They're free people, not even under oath, and I can't fire them because even if I don't pay them they can't starve to death. In fact, I am nice to them so we won't starve to death. Tomorrow they will spear us some more fish." "Oh, my goodness! Then don't offend them." "They will build the house when they feel like it"—restlessly. "Wait till America hears about this!" I laughed.

Then the Dumagats rose from their heels, stood three sticks in a triangle, and tied the tops together.

"No good tepee," I said. "It's lopsided." "That's the way they are," said Marking, who had visited the Dumagat village upriver.

Then the Dumagats tied slats across two sticks, leaving the third as a brace for the two. On top of the slats they tied and piled leaves.

"It's a lean-to," I exclaimed, "and I'll bet you crawl in."

They began to build a fire in the center toward the front stick.

Marking began explaining, "We sleep around the fire." "No!" I said. "Not in it?" That annoyed him (a woman can always annoy a man), and he continued, "And the fire burns all the time, to keep you warm at night, and it cooks all the time—you just put the sweet potatoes in the ashes."

I looked at it doubtfully. "If you survive this, Marking, I hope *I* do."

But he had innovations. Out of a *bayong* he brought a small mat, and spread it behind the fire under the leaf roof. "There," he said, "that's for you."

For no reason at all, I felt like writing. Out of the baggage pile we dragged the battered portable, detached the lid and turned it over tablewise on the sand to support the typewriter. I began typing, and soon the Dumagat ladies with their naked babies in their bare bosoms came squatting around, singsonging their chatter, spitting betel-blood all over the place, regarding me with as much amazement as I had them.

"Marking," I said, "they're spitting all over my parlor."

"You be nice. Their husbands will bring us a huge eel tomorrow. They're spotting him now."

"An eel! Marking, have you seen what they drag out of this river? This morning they had one five feet long and as thick as your leg!"

"Reason to be nice."

"Reason to be nasty!"

Night fell close around the campfires, and the river rolled by, muting the voices of the fighters singing. Away from the firelight, we could see the fallen branches and leaves phosphorescent in the forest. "Marking, it's luminous. Look!" He picked up the rotten piece of log. In the firelight it was dull gray, just old driftwood. Out of the light in the darkness, it glowed like a neon sign.

"What do you call it in English?" he asked.

"Fallen moonlight," I said, in romantic mood.

"Sir, we brought fruit—"

"Hello, Popoy," I said. "You're a sweet lad." Embarrassed, he smiled and returned to their own campfire twenty feet up on the bank.

"Darling, it's sweet!" Marking broke up one, eagerly offered it. "What is it?"

"Rattan fruit! You know—what they make furniture out of, rattan vines."

"Thank you." While I chewed on the sour-sweetish meat, I examined the peel—brown and yellow scales fitting snugly over one another like glazed shingles. The fruit came in clusters like heavy grapes, each fruit the size of a giant olive but the form of a pineapple.

All over the camp, new fruits and new customs were the gist of the chatter. There was talk too of a "beautiful girl" on a *kaingin* where the boys had gone foraging. Up in the mountains anything is beautiful. In fact, in the whole Philippines, it is so. First of all, there seems to be but one word, "*maganda*"—that is, beautiful, lovely, exquisite, divine, out of this world, also good-looking, pretty, attractive, not bad. There is no degree. A woman either is or is not *maganda*, and if she is married her looks have nothing to do with it any more. If she's single: hey, pal, where's that guitar?

Time stood still. Sometimes it was morning. Sometimes it was night. I frittered about in the river, collecting pebbles of every shade—shattered rainbows. There were greens, blues, pinks, yellows, reds in every shade of shell, chartreuse, jade, garnet, sandstone—on and on. Wet, the colors were bright; dry, they dulled. I amused myself, letting them dry, then flicking water on them again. Marking and the fighters were in and out of the river with the Dumagats, and up and down both the Kanan and the Kaliwa and on down the Agos, the boys combined business with pleasure, serenading the mountain girls and bringing back to camp whole sacks of sweet potatoes.

One morning I sat on a flat rock beside the river washing clothes by lightly slapping a wet shirt with a stick while Marking talked idly of his childhood and our future together. Suddenly he stopped, and I looked up to find him tense and pale. He shivered. His eyes, though fixed on the distance, were blank.

I jumped up. "What is it? Are you ill?"

"No." He looked at me without really seeing me.

"There's something wrong with you."

"No, I guess not." He was still pale, though no longer tense. "I just thought of Lamp."

Lamp was our most trusted courier. He was somewhere on his way from the city to us with $25,000, the biggest sum ever collected at one time for our fighters. With the money we planned to give the fighters something they had never had before—five pesos a month each, officers and men alike, for whatever they wanted. They could buy a little sugar or a local magazine. They could buy thread. They could buy a sliver of soap. Lamp was coming through with this from Don Ramón Oriol, who was later to suffer excruciating agony in Fort Santiago. But Don Ramón gave Lamp the sum, and Lamp, the cross-eyed, round-shouldered, thin farm student was on his way through. He would find us. Lamp always found us.

"What made you think of Lamp?" I asked.

"I wasn't really thinking of him." Marking was puzzled. "I was thinking of us. Suddenly I felt very cold. My heart began to beat fast like never in my life—like I was afraid; and I have not been really afraid since the beginning of the war. It was like being afraid when I was a child."

"And then?" I prompted him.

"I thought of Lamp, like I see his face before me, like I hear him call me. I feel like he is in trouble and needs me."

In a flash I knew what it was. "Marking," I asked, "have you heard about mental telepathy?"

"What is that?"

"I think it's what just happened to you. What makes you feel that Lamp is in trouble?"

"I know it. I just know it."

At a week's distance that very hour, Lamp was captured by traitors. He pleaded, not for his life, but—"Let me go once. I will come back and surrender myself. I promise you."

They took his *bayong* pack from his back. They found the money, the newly printed guerrilla money and the Jap war notes for using in the town markets. They found reports and letters. They held him fast, against his struggles. Lamp was to tell me after his torture was past, when he came back to us in the mountains and limped the trails he had once trotted, "Ma'am, in my heart I screamed for the Old Man. I did not call to you because you could not help, you are a woman and not strong. But in my heart I called Marking, if not to come, then to know what happened to me."

In Marking throughout the war there was prescience. He *knew* when something was happening to his men elsewhere, when there was an emergency in the organization. He was uneasy, restless, fractious. He could not sit. He rebelled against the confines of the camp. Allowed to roll where there were no Japs he still lay uneasy in his blanket or walked back and forth, back and forth around the campfire.

He knew when Rodriguez, one of the combat officers, had committed an outrage, and he became easy only in the hour that Cabalhin took proper action. Because I was forever observing him, I took pains to verify dates and hours, noting his periods of restlessness or seemingly unreasonable irritability for comparison with the reports that might come weeks or months later.

His distemper in the Rodriguez case lasted the whole day, and in that day Cabalhin and his officers took Rodriguez prisoner and decided his fate. Not far from where Lamp had been captured, a week of travel from us, Cabalhin had camped his hundred fighters, dispatching other fighters to other camps. His second in command was Rodriguez, a fat, squint-eyed, fighting man of cool, steady nerves. Months before, he had been brought to Marking under arrest for rape.

Marking itched to put a bullet into him, but Cabalhin demurred and signed as guarantor. His winning arguments were: "Rodriguez was not our member when the rape is alleged to have happened, therefore the Rules and Articles of War do not apply to him, sir," and "If you will give him to me, sir, I will see that he is put in the front lines."

To Cabalhin's camp came a woman of intense patriotism. "Yes," she said, in a country already going hungry, "I have rice and I will give you all I can." She did give, and the whole camp ate well from her generosity.

Because his men would not go hungry for several days, Cabalhin went away to check up on administrative work elsewhere, leaving the camp in charge of Rodriguez because in an emergency Rodriguez would fight like a fool. He was a brave man, and was known to have on his person an *anting-anting*. Throughout the fighting ranks there were such charms, and stories were told around the campfires of their powers. Some of them made a man fleet of foot. Others gave him an eagle eye or a keen sense for danger. They were passed down from father to son or given by an old man to the young man whom he chose as best deserving of the inheritance. Always there was acknowledgment that a man would kill to get a charm. The owner of such a charm might talk of *anting-antings* and their properties, but only a brave man or a fool would exhibit it. Rodriguez had shown his charm: a coin that could be rolled up like a crepe suzette, then return to normal, that could be stretched like an elastic band, and return again to being just a coin. Without having seen it, I heard the story from men who claimed they had. Its property was to ward off weapons like a shield. Fighters said that Rodriguez could stand in a hail of bullets and be untouched while they ripped holes through logs and leaves from one side to the other in a straight line across his body. No *bolo* could touch him. But he was vulnerable: he could be clubbed, stabbed, or shot from behind.

As soon as Cabalhin had left camp, Rodriguez carried his sex mania straight to the hut of the good woman who had given the rice. He found her alone and raped her.

When Cabalhin returned, Rodriguez was turned over by the very fighters of whom he had been in temporary command. "Sir," said Alzate, of the high, thin nose and the black, unshorn curls, "it is against the honor of us all, what this man has done." And the woman was brought to testify.

Cabalhin burned red with shame and anger, but his soldier's training held fast: "We must hold proper court-martial, and it is the Old Man who will decide."

"No," said the fighters. "We will kill him now because he is not fit to live."

"The Old Man will decide," said Cabalhin. Then he remembered one of the terms of his guarantee to Marking: if Rodriguez should ever again commit an outrage, Cabalhin himself must execute him. Quietly, he sat down on a log. Rodriguez was a canny, fearless fighter, a man of much experience and full of stories. Cabalhin, who was still a boy, would listen, fascinated, far into the night while he talked.

"Sir," said Alzate, "all of us your subordinate officers will make a petition for the execution of this—of this—of this indescribable one—"

"What petition will you make?" asked Cabalhin, chin in palm. "That the Old Man will kill him as soon as we deliver the prisoner there."

"The Old Man will not kill him," said Cabalhin. "He will send him back to me."

"He might escape during the journey," said Alzate.

"Make the petition. Attach the affidavits as made by the woman and her husband. Write down the testimony of the fighter who found Rodriguez in crime."

"Yes, sir." Alzate snapped to attention.

"And then strip Rodriguez to his underclothes. Take off his shoes. See that there is nothing sewed in the material of what he wears. Do not tell him we are going to execute him. Tell him that we are going to make a show to satisfy the woman. Tell him he is to show that he knows he will be killed, and when he hears the rifles shooting he must fall as if dead. Tell him this is the only way to save him from the wrath of the people."

"Yes, sir!" Alzate saluted snappily, his face blank.

Cabalhin held up his hand. "Wait, I am not yet finished. You will instruct the firing squad not to shoot over his head but to *kill him*. Let him think it is *pasikat*—just vaudeville—but shoot straight. Is all understood? Stand him with his *back* to the firing squad."

With admiration and respect in his eyes, Alzate saluted again. "Yes, sir."

The orders were carried out to the letter, for Cabalhin was a stern if boyish officer and his men were soldiers to a man.

Cabalhin gave Rodriguez proper burial, but no one knows to this day who has the coin.

Many months later, when Fajardo the silent soldier was wounded and retched violently into the coconut shell I held to his mouth for no other reason than hygiene, the fighters said among themselves that I had destroyed Fajardo's *anting-anting*, which was the kind that was passed by spittle. I knew about that. My little old servitor Donny, whom I had saved from execution, wanted to spit in my mouth to give me his charm for a long life. I had refused and hurt Donny to the core. Now, when Fajardo retched and spit the bubbling foam into the shell, I stepped outside the farmhouse, kicked a hole in the dirt with my heel, spilled the spittle there, kicked the loose earth back and stamped it flat.

"It is lost forever," murmured the fighters. "He trusted her to destroy it, and it was destroyed."

Thereafter, sick fighters whispered and pressed into my hand an odd assortment of things that were nothing more to me than doodads. At one time I carried in various pockets eleven different *anting-antings* that I was careful not to lose and returned them to the fighters when they were well enough. Some of them thought that the charm was "too strong" and was responsible for their fevers or inertia. "Please hold it awhile, Mammy. It will not hurt *you*." Once I had jokingly said that Irish blood was its own charm, that no other charm could work against it. Now I found myself a special "charm bank" and stayed a little closer to Marking lest somebody stage a bank hold-up.

Once, in a leisure moment while bathing, I scrutinized one of the charms with Lyd and found strange, Arabic characters written on old cloth of fine linen weave. "Looks like the zodiac," I said. "Looks like it needs washing," said Lyd.

Other charms, at which I had glanced carelessly, looked like sticks and stones and seeds—but radium was mysterious before science defined its true properties, and many a quack hill doctor used the right medicinal roots and leaves in his magic potions. Whatever the chant, the potion had quinine in it.

Up on the Kanan River we explored the land and its little people, the Dumagats. They told us of cannibal plants that caught people and animals both with long twining vines like the arms of an octopus. They told us of the mysterious tree that was never seen twice in the same place but whose great drooping blossoms made it look like a ballet in perfect movement in the wind. I saw that tree. Exquisite. But I could never find it to show others. I found the spot where I knew I had seen it, but it wasn't there. So I was wrong. Months later, when the Dumagats told us some of their strange tales, I shivered a little. Spooks. Dear God, it was bad enough resisting the Japs without having the Dark Ages creep up and jump us.

Then the Kanan went berserk. One minute we were lazing around, and the next we had to scamper up the bank and into the trees, pulling even our feet up as rains far upstream turned the pretty river into a mad, muddy, roiling torrent. Away went our Dumagat houses. Away went the whole river, with uprooted trees tossing and bouncing along in the flood.

The Dumagats edged up as the river rose, threw up more shelters. "It's like this," they told Marking. "It will go down. It will come up. It will go down again."

With the madness, suddenly the pin-pricking began again. The war was with us once more: "Sir, there are no more cassava." "Sir, we have to cut through the jungle." "Sir, there are couriers from Manila waiting in Infanta." "Sir, we cannot use the river: many people are drowned when the river is big." "Sir, we have no salt." "Sir, there are no more sweet potatoes." "Sir, there is no rice." "Sir, we cannot cross the river." "Sir, there is nothing on this side of the river. It is all on the other side." "Sir, the river is up twenty feet—since last night, sir." "Sir, the river is like this three days. It will be like this three more days." "Sir, it will be like this three months. This is the rainy season starting. I asked the mountain people."

Our *bancas* were almost useless, even when held close to the edge. The river tore at them, whisked them away in one careless second. Nothing could come upriver; and, to get downriver, we should have to cut through jungle, thick Tayabas jungle.

To reach *barrio* Baytañgan halfway from Pinagsahangan to Infanta, it took one whole day and part of the next on one of the hardest treks we ever took. Then, dragging along, Marking broke one of our outstanding policies and parked us lock, stock and barrel, bodyguards, fighters, baggage, and all in the *barrio* schoolhouse.

Bernie checked in from Bulacan.

Ruperto Batara reported up from Manila where, like a spider in his corner, he had been reorganizing after Roger's capture, carrying on somehow.

Alora came in from Cavite.

Seneres No. 2. reported in with a load of supplies accompanied by Butch, the Visayan woman, tough-mouthed, smoker of native cigars who was to be the only girl convoy leader in the outfit. How many times Butch trudged the trails, pulling her short legs up the divide, falling halfway down, she alone knows, but Butch was up to any of the men in cross-country running because she kept plugging on her way somewhere, brusque in manner and full of hell.

Checking reports, we found that in our three months' necessary absence the organization—except for the fighters with Marking, and those pulled into Laguna by Cabalhin and Mapa, and those that Bert Mata sent home to till the fields and hide their arms ready to hand—had fallen apart, and its fragments were drifting everywhere.

Day after day, and long into the night, Marking and I conferred with key officers. To us they came, asking, "What shall we do now, sir? Ma'am, what can we do?"

By ourselves, Marking and I talked. "It's hard," he said, "to be a leader." And I, "None of us ever led. They just kept pushing us." On the morrow, I would have to write forty-three letters already listed. On the morrow, he would have to make new plans, authorize new men, check reports, reports, reports, issue warrants of arrest, hold trials, make a hundred on-the-spot decisions. We both wished we could quit. "But," said Marking, "who will care for them as we do? Who will care what happens to them? Who will advise them right? Who will discipline them, keep them under control?"

We thought of Cabalhin. Shift it to him. He was already a leader in his own right. Let him be the top leader. But Cabalhin was young and reckless—and tired, too. More tired than Marking, more burdened by lesser responsibility in his comparative lack of years and experience. We could run out on all the headaches—and never look each other in the face again. Alone, the fighters might sweep to destruction, and take half the countryside with them. Talim—remember the people of Talim. And there were other guerrilla outfits perilously near to banditry. Would ours become the same? Could Cabalhin, who loved the men, hold them down as well as Marking—who loved them too but, when angry, had no compassion to divert him from smashing a jaw or booting a behind?

"If we love the country—" said Marking.

"And the boys," I said, thinking of Cabalhin and Lucio and Mapa and Bernie and Seneres and Mata and Salvadore and all the half-nameless who followed Marking and his key officers.

"I wish I were not a leader," said Marking.

"It's up to you."

"I started out alone."

"So did I."

"And then people began coming to me."

"Are you telling me?"

"And now I can't send them away."

"That's leadership, Marking. You're it, and you can't duck out."

"Yay, do you love me because I'm a patriot, or do you love me because—well—just because."

I had to be honest. "You're half angel and half devil, Marking. I love you for the good there is in you. Perhaps the people love you for the same reason, plus a terrific need for leadership in times of crisis."

"What if I quit?"

"You will be a failure, but the resistance movement will go on. Always there will be someone somewhere fighting for freedom. We're not indispensable. We're just a big help."

"I won't quit, anyway. I started this, and I guess I can finish it."

How very tired he looked, resuming the responsibility! Healthier, heavier from the months on the river—and now again the old, burdened look. To myself I said, "Brave little bus-driver, keep on fighting. If you can, I can."

He was looking at me. "I know you love me, Yay. To me, your eyes are beautiful. You are still fighting. If you can, I can."

It startled me. "Well," I said, "well..."

And then old friends came to visit us at the schoolhouse. Not Farretta, the cherub-faced, hot-headed American mining man who could yell, "Jesus CHRIST, God DAMN IT TO HELL!" He was down the coast on a jaunt to Fertig in Mindanao where the Moros and the Christians and the Japs were raising Cain. But Schaffer, the other of the pair, an officer now assigned elsewhere, came slugging through the mud with an old friend of mine, Bim Manzano, quiet-voiced right hand to Anderson of the "USAFFE Guerrillas." Early in the occupation, in one month's action in Bulacan, Bim and his pal Jesse had armed more than eighty men. We leaped upon them, pummeling and slapping and telling a dozen tall tales all at the same time.

And with them came someone else.

CHAPTER 15

We were in the schoolroom.
"Marking," said Schaffer, "this is Captain Bernard L. Anderson."
Gunpowder and matchstick.
"Captain, this is Yay."
I shook hands, too, and said to myself, Lady, this is going to be historic—you'd better say something too. I said aloud, "How do you do?"
Marking gave me a quick, suspicious look, and so I didn't speak again until spoken to. For he could be a devil as well as a leader.
A week before, in a jealous fit, he had thrown me on the ground, leaped over me to grab me up by my shirt front, slung me up over his shoulder after a couple of stinging slaps, and carried me to the creek to hold me under water, thrashing and kicking and helpless in his big paws. I didn't drown because he was in the water too and it brought the blood pressure down and he came to his senses.
Before that he had fired his .45 twice past my left ear at two feet, trying to put the fear of the Lord in me, and it did, it did.
Another time, having me again by the shirt front, he had slapped me almost unconscious when Cabalhin, the only one in the outfit who dared brave him in his fits, threw himself between us, squeezing his small self in over Marking's arm, hooking his armpit on it, taking the slaps on his own face: "Sir, please! Sir, you'll kill her! Sir, please!" Then Marking cooled and finally cried and begged forgiveness, and none could doubt his shame and sincerity, but it was just as well to avoid it.
So I said just "How do you do?" and let history fly on by without taking a bigger bow. That eliminated personal jealousy at the moment. There was still professional jealousy.
Andy was a rival guerrilla chieftain.
And still it was less professional jealousy, although that was rife throughout the Philippines, for great fighters are great sportsmen and competition is their meat, than the need to survive to fight again. Each leader ran his territory a certain way. Some believed in the mailed fist. Others, like Andy and Marking, knew the iron hand in the velvet glove was not only more reasonable but more effective. Yet neither, upon

meeting, knew the other's ways. Each was an unknown quantity; Marking didn't want to know, but Andy had come to find out.

Marking and Andy, with Schaffer mother-henning them, observed the social amenities in the big, bare schoolroom: "Have a seat." "What do you smoke? This is all we have." "Well, this is fine, meeting each other." Meanwhile I sat at attention, watching it all, remembering back. Marking had brought me to sit within the circle, his big rough hand across the small of my back, propelling me into place. He always wanted me there, to dish up my own opinion later, but something else as well hung in the air: "Don't forget you belong to *me*. I catch you making eyes, I'll black them both." And my unspoken retort, "If I weighed 135 and you weighed 90, it'd be the other way around, buddy boy."

Andy must have felt all this, for he was careful too. To me he was officially formal; to Marking, personally affable. Hostile for the moment toward Marking, I took it out on Andy, without intending to allay Marking, which it did, and Marking's growing congeniality was encouraging. At least, he wasn't going to shoot first.

Bim had wandered out of the circle around the bare desk of the schoolteacher and was talking easily with our fighters, who were pointedly drifting in to eavesdrop and gossip for the next two weeks. The following will give one more point on which to judge a leader: while Andy was sounding Marking out, Bim sized up Marking's fighters. Disciplined? Any ex-soldiers among them? Riffraff, or patriots?

Far back in October 1942, when Marking's guerrillas were becoming an army, a letter had come from an American officer in Bulacan to the north who wrote, among other things, that he would help Marking to be authorized; his advice was to lie low and organize. Just about that time, a resentful question was taking form in Marking's mind—a labyrinthine mind, where questions could buzz and buzz like whole hornets' nests. "What's all this authorization business?" Marking demanded of me, tossing the letter to me. I read it to remember it, and filed it in the No. 1 *bayong*. Marking dug into his prized U.S. Army Rules and Articles of War and answered it to his own satisfaction, and now at their first meeting, when the army was a reality, *an organization of 200,000 men and women under Marking's command*, all the little hornets were full-grown and ripe for the American officer—Anderson.

"By the way," Andy was saying, "what rank do you carry?" Marking stood up. "None," he said haughtily.

"But they call you 'General,'" said Andy, as if he were saying, "But it is a nice day, isn't it?"

It was true, for the title somehow fitted him. Furthermore, since he was, after all, building an army and was the head of it, there was sense in calling him that, and he had made Cabalhin and Roger and me lieutenant colonels, though we had protested, though we did not think we merited the appellations.

"Well," said Marking, "I guess if my people want to call me 'General' that's their own business. If they think I'm their general, then it's up to them."

Schaffer was fidgeting. Bim was listening from down the schoolroom, and the fighters around him were listening. I just sat.

"How do you sign yourself, Marking?" asked Anderson.

"I sign myself like this: 'MARCOS V. AGUSTIN, Commanding.'" (From his tone, he might have been saying it was nobody's damn business anyway.)

"I told you!" said Schaffer. "I told you!"

I turned my head to look at Schaffer. So! There had been previous discussion. Proof that this was Andy's own scrutiny; proof that Schaffer had upheld Marking somewhere at some time; proof that there was something more afoot, and that Andy was fitting Marking into somebody's future plans.

Marking had shuffled among the papers and brought out an order.

"See?" said Schaffer. "See?" And Schaffer was relieved rather than glad. Perhaps he had argued, not too sure of his ground, as mining men in the Philippines often do.

Andy was speaking again. "I might be able to help you get recognized," he offered. First spark.

"Bullshit, recognition!" said Marking. "I don't need to be authorized to fight for my own country, I guess! Are my fighters paid heroes that they can't fight just for nothing? I guess even MacArthur won't tell me I'm doing the wrong thing! I guess even a bus driver can fight for his country—get the idea? And I was the best driver on the line too. I guess I can run my outfit right! Nobody has to give me permission to fight. I'd like to see anybody stop me! I'd like to see MacArthur stop me! I guess—"

"Don't stop," said Andy.

"I won't!"

"I mean, tell me all about it."

Marking was spitting scornfully, legs defiantly apart, elbows akimbo. Between stiff, defiant stances, he strode about with the characteristic head and arm movement, flailing the air, elbows akimbo again, head thrown back. I shifted over a little. He might knock me off the bench, and he'd pick me up and brush me off and maybe sniff my cheek as comfort and then promptly drop me on the cement if Andy asked another question before I got settled on the bench again.

"Sure, I'll tell you about it!" said Marking. "Who gave me, my rifles? I scratched for them myself! Who finds my bullets? My own members! Who feeds my men? I do! And if I catch anybody robbing or raping I kill him, and I don't let my fighters hang around where the people get caught in the crossfire if the Japs come. And I guess I'm a Filipino, and this is my country, and I don't like the God-damn Japs worth a damn, and I guess it's my right, my very first right of all, to fight for my country, and I guess it's a more important right than this bullshit freedom of speech which is all talk-talk-talk and no bullets!"

Quietly Andy baited him. "Recognition means bullets." Like a flash, Marking bit, "How many will they give me?"

Andy sat easily, elbows propped on the teacher's desk in the schoolhouse in which we had bivouacked, chin on interlinked fingers. Marking strode back and forth, head, arms, and legs punctuating and emphasizing his speech. Andy was striking sparks as he pleased, purely for purposes of informing himself on one more guerrilla leader.

To myself I thought: a couple of naturals in two directions, each perfect for his line—one the detail man, the builder, the other the combat man, the destroyer. Andy had come to get a look at Marking's processes. He interrupted only enough to get more, or to swing the torrent into a channel leading to something else of interest to him. One violent; one serene.

Marking wore himself out. Not a hornet left in his head. As the wheels ran down, Andy asked, "Will you take orders from MacArthur?"

"Yes, but not from anybody else!" That told Andy straight that if he thought he was buying Marking out he could keep his bullets. Andy smiled. "I will merely relay the orders." He was barefooted. He was pale, and he had the build to carry forty more pounds.

Marking said, "We are killing a pig for you." To me he said, "Come inside a minute." I followed him into the corner where he had partitioned off a private corner for me. "You talk to him," he said, "and remember, a fish is caught by its mouth."

I riled anew. I hate politics. I hate bargaining. I hate suspicion and distrust. Yet, if I had always had my way, without Marking's wily cunning, we should both have been dead a half-dozen times. "OK, OK," I said.

I walked back to the desk where Andy still sat. "Marking's all fagged out. He's taking a nap."

"All right." Promptly Andy began to give me instructions on the system of army account keeping, the typographical style of army orders, general policies, and army procedures. Then he asked questions that I answered, and I asked questions that he answered, and twice I snagged him just for fun, and his face bloomed like the red, red rose, and he admitted, "Well, it depends..." And we left both arguments depending. From dedication to the methodical, the systematic, the army way, Andy could be neither detained nor detoured. Patiently he insisted, firmly he prodded the guerrillas into doing things the army way. Now, as I write this, the Philippines have been liberated, and where is Andy? Immediately after the liberation, the army got after him hotfoot because patiently and firmly he told officer after superior officer how to do it the guerrilla way!

Andy and Schaffer and Bim finally left—Schaffer backing away from us along the trail while he held the newly split seam of his pants together with one hand and waved with the other. "Needle and thread!" I called. He called back, "I've tried that before—it doesn't work anymore."

We talked, Marking and I. Marking was cagey. I was appreciative. We talked on and on. Andy, Schaffer, and Bim were threadbare and barefooted. We had nothing to give them, and none knew better than we—who were forever digging festered thorns out of the fighters and cleaning up infected sharp-rock cuts on feet swollen to twice their normal size—how great their hardship. We knew what it was to starve, to hide, to drag through the mud, to climb until hearts almost burst and legs gave out, to count the days and months and years and dream of food, food, food. Ours, because of the number Marking carried with us, was the more hectic, the more perilous life; but all we had suffered they had suffered, and perhaps a little more.

Andy had good men, for the good are magnets for those of the same metal. There were Schaffer and Farretta, once ours, who had been whirled away into the interior by the Jap swarm that swept over Kanumay; both had come down with malaria and, unable to contact us, had drifted on, to be taken in and helped by Andy. They had sent word: "We were sworn in to your outfit, Marking. Andy is doing something that will benefit everybody. If you say so, we'll come back, but we would like to stay here and help him." And a mollified Marking had sent word that Schaffer and Farretta were "assigned" to Captain Anderson.

We knew these two: Schaffer would say, "Look at that beautiful outcrop." And Farretta would say, "Where are my glasses, WHERE ARE MY GLASSES?" And Schaffer would say, "Just pick up your feet, my friend, you're standing on them."

They might be cutting across country, with Schaffer falling on his face to rise and trouble deaf heaven with his bootless cries. Farretta would struggle on with his beatific face, stumbling along, pushing through the jungle, until finally, tired of unhooking himself from thorn-barbed vines, would lose his temper and thrash his way, wildly fighting nature as it is in the Philippines. Then Schaffer would wail, "Hey, that's my shirt you're tearing to pieces!" and Farretta would grunt, "Well, go back and get it then," and Schaffer would cry out, "But it's all over the God damn country now!"

There were others: among them Lieutenant Russell D. Barros, whose legs were raw from ankle to knee with tropical ulcers, and who had the best of intentions and forever said and did the wrong thing and somehow muddled through without getting killed; and Gottlieb Neigum, who, in spite of the two little towheaded girls clinging to his trousers, chattering and munching away at peanuts, and the baby boy in his arms, managed to serve the guerrillas. Like Pivet, they were Americans and never forgot it.

Some forgot it. There have been Americans adrift in the backwoods who would be unacceptable in their own country; they lost their Americanism in the war, or perhaps they never had it. Some have been rude, mean, even cruel to the very Filipinos who aided and hid them, and it was bad for guerrilla morale. But the Filipino has a Christian heart, and he could sense if not analyze the circumstances—the destitution and the peril. Lost jobs, lost necessities, lost friends, lost hopes. Pushed into the foothills, then into the fetid jungle. Living on less even than the average Filipino needs. Sick, in rags, slowly starving. Bitterest of all, loss of both personal and national prestige—not in the eyes of the Filipinos forever sympathetic, forever loyal, but in their own minds insisting that the Filipinos must see it so.

Little news of great victories elsewhere seeped through the walls set up by Japan's Imperial Forces . . . Hunted and running and hiding before the eyes everywhere—and seeing both pity and fear in those eyes, pity for the hunted, fear of the hunters. As there is no freer people on this earth than the Americans, so is there actually no prouder people—used to free speech, used to walking with free stride, used to holding the head high, used to deserving fair treatment because they give it . . . Said Marking to his fighters, "What if we were lost and alone in America, like they are here? What if we were being hunted down there and they were the ones hiding us?" And so no guerrilla outfit had greater patience or was more sincerely kind to American refugees in the hills than "Marking's Guerrillas," though the suffering of the refugees made for blind blows that struck and hurt many a forgiving Filipino. "When you're hurt," explained Marking, "you kick, maybe. And the one nearest to you gets it, is it not so?" His fighters nodded, for it was so, and some of the fighters, cut off from the Visayans Islands where they belonged, were homesick enough themselves to understand.

And so, circumstances of occupied territory were a challenge and a crucible for the great individual as well as the great American and the great Filipino. Andy and his men were among the Americans in Luzon who rose to the challenge and made the grade, gloriously, grandly, with many a snicker at the enemy.

That night, after Andy, Schaffer, and Bim had left to return to their own camp far up the Tayabas coast line, Marking and I agreed that it would take an American to pull the local Americans out of the rut—one who knew his own people, and one from whom they could take orders without loss of pride. Andy was it, we said. He was a considerate person. He didn't wander in and out of the towns so that informers could tattletale that the Filipinos failed to catch him. He didn't park in the *barrios* for the same reason. He didn't backbite or curry favor by carrying gossip, and thus throw guerrilla outfits against one another. He didn't criticize or complain. In fact, what we knew about him was principally what he did not do that others did, to the great danger and suffering of the people. Andy was no Statue of Liberty in occupied territory; he had the good sense, instead, and the compassion of heart to keep himself humbly hidden.

For the next six months, while Marking and his following went through more suffering and emerged even more heroic, Andy was a busy man in his own unobtrusive, quiet way. Of a sudden the lone, drifting Americans were gone from the countryside. From their *kaingin* hide-outs where they had hunched, longing for home, quarreling and hateful to one another in their barren, impoverished existence (they had not been forsaken—all of us had tried to help them, but in a country growing poorer and poorer what is there left to share?), they were missing for a while; then all popped up as couriers for Anderson. "Orders from MacArthur!" They were Americans again, doing important work; where in humiliation they had been mean, surly, ugly, all of a sudden in restored importance there was humility and friendliness—and gratitude. The only difference between them and Andy and his men was that they were restored, and Andy and his men never had to be.

CHAPTER 16

We talked and we talked, Marking and I. We sloshed around in the mud by the schoolhouse, and the fighters sloshed around in the mud, and there were boils because we were hungrily glutting ourselves on pork in the paradisical river-bank *barrio* where we held headquarters, a village with more pigs in it than people.

Cabalhin checked in with more fighters than the lad should be carrying. Cabalhin checked out with even more to feed and discipline and direct and hide. Bernie was in close to Marking, studying his ways, learning hill movements and customs where he had specialized in city "terrain" and personnel; from underground organization to mountain combat, Big Boy Bernie was easing himself into position: any ground, any tactics, whatever the cost, he would fight.

Andy's Lieutenant Barros had told us, by way of friendly advice, to "keep the orders going to them." "To whom?" we asked. "To your city units." "Why?" "Because they'll break up or slow down."

"Well, that isn't the way we do it, Barros. If they're tired of fighting, we leave them flat. If they want to fight on, they find us first, tell us what they want to do; then we advise them on how it should be done, and finally we give them orders to go ahead and do it."

"That's not the way the army does it."

"Well, we're not the army, we're the guerrilla." And we explained, "Barros, this outfit is all one big family. Marking's the Pappy and Yay's the Mammy. We can't repeat that too often, and that oath of allegiance is the shield from behind which we shoot their ears off if they don't behave themselves. Whatever they do right is up *to them*; whatever they do wrong is up *to us*."

"Still," said Barros, "you better keep the orders going to them."

"We'll give them the orders when they come and get them. They follow us. We don't follow them. If they're patriots, they'll come. If they aren't, we don't want them anyway."

Word of our whereabouts had seeped into the city, and roundabout by way of Infanta. They began coming for their orders again. Once Marking had said, "If nobody bothered us for authorizations and commissions and orders and advice, it would be simple, wouldn't it?" I grumbled, "Yeah, all you have to do is sign 'em. Look at me, doing the dirty work." And Marking got huffy and hunt-and-pecked at his own typewriter for a week, and the orders he turned out will be in the national archives some day, for Marking makes history every time he writes, direct to the point, profane, let-the-chips-fall-where-they-may history.

Came Ruperto Batara to headquarters, so frail and small, yet so brainy that we called him Nik-Nik for gnat. His was the skillful hand behind the Manila underground. In his small, erect head with dreamer's eyes half the city organization was born, and he had double incentive, for he was carrying on for Roger, who had found and developed him.

And from Nik-Nik and ourselves, matching notes and dates, came the story of what had been happening in Manila, a tale of courage so immense as to be almost incredible. First, there was the sacrifice of Roger Moskaira, the man who had given me haven after my final broadcast at KZRH.

As all trails had led to the Kanumay main base, so, after the Talim zoning, all roads led to Fort Santiago. Wave after wave of arrests had followed in the city.

Verification had reached us on Kanan River that Roger was in Fort Santiago.

"We've got to get him out," said Cabalhin.

"They'll kill him," said Mapa.

"Assemble the fighters," said Marking.

Roger had once given me refuge. Roger was my friend.

"No," I said. "No. I warned Roger time and again. What are your chances, storming the heart of Manila when the city is swarming with Japs? Japs in every big building. Japs in every schoolhouse. Japs thick in the suburb encampments? And have you seen Fort Santiago inside? Do you know what they've got on top of those walls? Maybe he'll die. The Fort is the end of the trail. He who enters it is on his own. At the cost of thousands of lives, one life must go. Roger would not want rescue any more than I."

With Roger's soiled, tattered plea, "Save me not for my own sake, but for the sake of all the others I knew about—I can't stand it much longer," there came in the same cross-country mail a copy of a letter from Roger's brother Turing: "I told my brother to take it." Turing had been beaten unconscious thirteen times, but by sticking to "I don't know, I don't know" had survived to be released. So Turing smuggled in his own message to Roger: "I took it. You take it."

Playboy Roger was taking it. To begin with, he was beaten for six days straight. Regaining consciousness, he denied flatly that he was even Roger Moskaira—a lie so palpable that the Japs were beside themselves. Roger, too, was beside himself. The Japs swung a rifle butt across his jaw; six molars were knocked out. They jammed him into an iron drum and rolled and beat it until the clanging and dizziness addled him. They gave him the water cure, using a hose to pump him full until the pain of distention brought vomiting unconsciousness again and again. They strung him up in the butterfly swing until he could no longer feel pain, but swung back and forth in a haze. Once, with the thought, "I'm going to die anyway," he fought back wildly, desperately, at his tormentors. That, he thought, would bring on mortal blows and end his suffering.

Instead, it awakened the grudging admiration of the Japs. They gave him a week's rest, extended it to a month.

But Roger was the key man in the city, and guerrilla activity continued unabated. Especially, Jap Military Police agents were winding up in the morgue, and little nurses wrote me: "There are shootings all over the city. Here on the slabs all the occupations read 'MP.' Sort of fatal disease, isn't it?" The Japs wondered if Roger was directing it somehow from within Fort Santiago's walls. The Japs had to know.

For another seven days, Roger was tortured. He was never, before or after, so terribly alone, helpless, wondering where we were, wondering why we had forsaken him, remembering me: "Roger, one of these days you will be beyond our help. You take too many chances, and you'll get caught. There will be no rescue. You will be on your own. If you die, we will not forget you. If you live, you know where to find us."

All around him others were screaming and dying, and for some the doors opened. They tottered, were carried, were even shoved into blessed sunlight.

Sunlight. Sweet air. Surcease from agony.

Roger weakened.

Hub of all city organization and activity, he knew everything and everybody, the only one besides Mapa who really did. The Japs had the right man. On his courage hung the lives of Manuel and Lydia Arguilla, writers; Cirilo and Asunción Pérez, librarian and social worker; Ernesto Bengzon, mining engineer; Herbert and Janet Walker and my three helpless children, a girl of eleven, two boys of eight and five;

Helen Wilk, missionary nurse; Reymunda Guidote, champion girl swimmer and "socialite"; national leaders who had given us both aid and advice—Roxas, Yulo, Alunan, even Vargas and Paredes; wealthy men like Salvador Araneta and his wife Victoria, my friend and godmother; intellectuals like Antonio M. Bautista, founder of the local Civil Liberties Union, his wife Adalia, graduate of the University of California; María Orosa, government researcher; Rafael Roces, Jr., journalist we called Liling; and thousands of the enlistment, a cross-section of the city. Once he gave the regimental commanders up, 30,000 at stake ... And the trail would lead everywhere from there.

"We've got to save the others then," said Mapa, "by saving Roger."

"No," I said, "I picked Roger, and Marking OK'd it *because we knew he could take it—some day*. In this whole organization of 200,000 people only six others know what Marking and I know. And the six will only know it between them when something happens to us and, carrying on, they have to match notes. Then you'll find out what Marking has done ahead, and what I have done ahead, against our own *day of death or capture*."

Roger, in the Fort, weakened.

His hip bone was fractured. His left jaw, with tooth fragments loose in the gum pulp, was swollen and feverish, his good-looking face hideous beyond recognition. The rest of him was bleeding, battered to a pulp. He was senseless most of the time.

"We can't let him die!" said Cabalhin.

Unspoken was the criticism all around me, and I answered it with words: "Don't think I don't care. You knew him only in this war. For ten years, he and his wife have been my friends. Ding is suffering even more than Roger, and it is Ding especially who is my friend. If he breaks, my own children will suffer and die. What are we fighting for? For just our own, or for all the world's own? We have warned the city. Some have gone away for a while, to come back when the danger is past. It is the organization that must be guarded, not the individual, for it is the strength of organization that will restore and protect individual rights."

Advice. My advice. They hated the advice, and I think for a while hated me, and so I said, "When this happens to me, remember my own advice and apply it. Let there be no suicidal emotionalism. Keep yourselves intact. Fight on. Never throw something away for nothing. Check the gains, check the losses, play to win."

Still they were restless and set against me, and I had to fight myself and them too. Roger was my friend.

"T'hell with it," said Marking.

"Yes, sir," said Cabalhin.

"Shall we go, sir? Now, sir?" prompted Mapa.

Desperately again I said, "No. If Roger must die, he must die. If I must die, I must die. If all of us must die, so may we die for a world of peace ... If Roger lives through, tell him it was I who held you back."

Nor was Roger more alone than I ... Causes may come, and causes may go. I'm finished with them.

Roger came through his crisis. None were betrayed. Punishment became milder. Soon the Japs changed tactics to bribing, offering of reward. This saved his life.

Roger was cagey, and so they gave him time to think, transferred him to the mental torture chambers of Old Bilibid where human beings sat crosslegged in row after row, bullied against even whispers to one another, with only one freedom left, running around inside the head until the brain wears out. For three months Roger sat on the floor, unable to speak to those at his elbows, unable to nod drowsily, unable to see anything but prison walls, to smell anything but urine— fourteen and one-half hours every day.

Back in Fort Santiago which he had left, others were running the gamut of Jap torture. Hundreds, thousands, passed into those time-mellowed walls, and a few came out, injured for life. That great Catholic school, the Ateneo, almost transferred classes there, the list of prisoners so resembled its roster of alumni.

There was no end to sadistic variety, and Fort Santiago was merely the mirror reflecting the Jap garrisons and isolated incidents everywhere on the city streets, in the towns, in remote *barrios*, and on lonely trails. Variations of the water cure included leaping on the distended stomach of the victim, rupturing the stomach walls, or tying a victim on his back on a bench with a wet towel over the nostrils and water forever keeping it soaked. Hour after hour the victim struggled for breath and slowly suffocated to death. Expert interrogators could dip the victim's head into a bucket, putting him through the agony of drowning over and over again through many days. Beating was routine, hardly to be mentioned. It began in the application of a ruler edgewise to the face and hands, aimed at the bone protrusions such as eyebrows, bridge of the nose, knuckles. It ended in simply pounding the victim to a jelly with a baseball bat or rifle butts. Using prisoners for ju jitsu practice was common and was favored by Japs wanting to keep in trim. It never quite killed the victim but left him bruised and shaken, with broken or dislocated bones. With an internal injury from such treatment the victim might even be released, being found innocent, and never recover.

There was the "cutting" torture. The Jap would rush the victim with bayonet or saber, as if to dispatch him permanently, then would deflect or pull the thrust to inflict a lesser wound or slice off only a nick of flesh. A slip meant death, but what of it? Sometimes there was rollicking fun, too. The Japs, to amuse themselves, would tie the victim's penis, scrotum, or both and lead him around like a dog on the leash, yanking it, laughing hilariously at the pain provoked. It was a favorite for swinging a victim undergoing the butterfly-swing, and even the swing had variations, such as stringing the victim up by the thumbs or little fingers instead of the wrists, and always with the arms pulled behind and up. Striking the genitals with the ruler or, when the parts were tied, to stretch them to the limit, brought raucous laughter among the Japs applying the torture or merely looking on.

The sun cure, especially in the tropics, brought blindness to many, and certainly half-blindness to all who suffered it. It was a simple torture. The victim was tied to a stake in the full heat of the sun with a sentinel to prod him with a bayonet to keep his face up and his eyes opened full in the sun's direct rays. One day of the sun cure meant total blindness for twenty-four to thirty-six hours afterward, and possibly permanent eye and brain injury.

There were patriots like Monching Santos, *hacendero* [landed gentry], who were so rabid they could never be made to talk—except in defiance, hurling unhappy truth after unhappy truth at their tormentors. These received "special treatment." Held down against the violence of their own suffering, their teeth were pulled with pliers, and ice was forced into their mouths against the raw nerve ends. Monching's fingernails were pulled out, and the raw tips were tapped with a ruler edge.

Roger sat day after day, month after month, in only two positions: squaw-fashion with arms folded across his knees, in his lap, or across his breast but never dropped to the floor for balance; or with his legs drawn up, knees together and arms linked around them. Three times a day he ate a golf-ball of rice with "Manila Bay soup" of lily stems boiled in salt water, but there was a time when nothing was given to him except water for two weeks. Meanwhile comrades died, in the Fort and throughout the country.

Patag lasted one day, Allen two, Oring three.

José Patag, retired Philippine Scout, was too old to fight, and so Marking set him to collecting duck eggs. There would never be enough for one breakfast for all the fighters, but surely some for sick and convalescent ones. Because he had been a lieutenant in the army—Marking had the greatest respect for anything "real army"—he was commissioned a guerrilla captain, and at fifty-one years of age began collecting eggs. "Please, can you spare some for our boys up there?" Sometimes, because he was sickly, he would send the grandchildren: "Please, Grandpa says, Where are the eggs?"

The Japs watched, asked questions, filtered their informers through the population, and one of them had an interesting talk with sincere, kindly Patag. He even promised Patag some duck eggs.

So the Japs took Patag.

On the shore of Talim, they beat him. In a house near the shore—they walked up the street looking for a good-sized house that would have what they were looking for—they tied him to the rafters and beat him some more with a club the size of a baseball bat. The weight of the blows varied with the strength and enthusiasm of the Japs inflicting them, but the beating lasted through the day, the Japs taking turns and all being tired at the end. The people of the tiny town—his family and his friends and his thirty-second cousins—pretended not to know, not to hear. One would die, the rest would fight on.

Late in the afternoon, he was thrown into the lake. We asked when we heard, "Was he still alive?" And the answer came, "Well—not exactly." So Patag drowned in water not very deep and by morning the waves washed him ashore—"Philippine Scout Retired."

Allen lasted two days.

Allen was a *mestizo*. There are *mestizos* and *mestizos*. Like America, the Philippines is a melting pot. The tapestry of blood-blends is rich, with Malay the strong, ever-present warp and all the world's strains as the color and design of the woof. Chinese blood gives a fair, fine-textured skin. Spanish heightens the bone structure and, like Portuguese and Italian, makes for beautiful eyes; only the Hindu, called "Bombay," bequeaths a larger, deeper, more lustrous eye. German and Swiss blood is weak and usually loses to the Malay, but English and American half-breeds are strikingly occidentalized, so much so that they sometimes lack the piquant, petite charm of the oriental. Parents of mixed blend can expect and take delight in the variation among their children, especially such throwbacks as crop out.

And so came Allen in those days on Talim Island: Allen, least conspicuous of all blends, a Malay-American-negro. He was dark, chocolate brown without the bluish black undertone, well built, well educated, courteous and patriotic, physically fit as a boxer and a good one.

"I guess I can fight for two countries," he said when he reported in, "—my old man's and my old woman's." He had an appealing look. His American negro father had come with the troops in 1898, won the victory, then lost himself and it to a little Filipina.

Marking commented, "You have guts, but have you guts enough?"

"We'll find out."

Any man that quiet-spoken would know the odds. Marking, who as a rule warned men who asked for special assignments, telling what had happened to this man, what the Japs had done to that one, or describing the hardship, counting the sacrifices, percentaging the chances ("I want you to know what you're getting into," he would say), made no speech to Allen. He merely handed out the requested assignment.

Allen's work carried him into the pro-Jap Sakdal hotbeds in Laguna. From the first he did well, capturing the leader of a bandit gang, eliminating a band of extortionists. He was organizing, too, laying the ground for systematic anti-Jap endeavor and control of a shaky area. We kept tabs on him as we did on the others. Who was up and at 'em? Who was slipping? Who was going too far? Who was going too fast? Who was just riding along on the army's back? Marking was satisfied that Mestizo Allen was taking healthy jabs at the enemy, for two countries, a double lick each time. It amused and inspired us, and a discussion at the time clarified to our satisfaction the fact that Americanism is not a nationality but a code of ethics.

Then, as he slept one night, the Japs were guided to his pallet.

They tied him up. They always trussed up an outnumbered, lone soul, not merely to keep him from escaping, but because it made him more helpless, more at their mercy. They hogtied him and threw him on the ground.

Then they began on him, slowly at first.

They began with cigarette butts, matches, and candle flames, progressing to tufts of cotton soaked in gasoline which were placed on eyebrows, lips, chin, stomach, and sexual organs. Allen had curly hair, and plenty of it, thick on his chest, arms, and legs. By the time the hair was singed off, his skin, too, was badly burned. When they tired of his refusal to tell them what they wanted to know, they poured the rest of the gasoline over him and touched him off with a match.

He died without breaking, companion soul to Patag. He had never said, "I am an American"—only, "I believe in America."

Oring Reyes of Cardona, Rizal, lasted three days. An entire countryside hung upon his suffering, the whispered word of horror passing through home after home like a cold, unseen hand upon the heart.

Oring was sweet. How else describe a man who just kept on serving the cause without praise, without prompting, without even much moral support at home? Once he came through "hot" country by dressing like a farmer with the familiar *carabao* rope looped over his shoulder, to reach Marking and warn him of peril, to tell him, too, that he, Oring, and his men were already storing rice at a halfway point that the fighters would pass in their retreat. "If that is not convenient, sir," he said, "then we can bring it through to this place, but this place is not safe for you, sir."

And then the Japs caught him as he slipped in and out of their lines, doing his unglamorous duty.

Twice before, Oring had been caught and tortured. His record was in the enemy garrison. Beatings and butterfly-hangings and hunger had, from the Japs' point of view, taught him nothing. The first time they had released him. The second time he had escaped. This was his third "offense."

Now in his own town they hung him by the heels, with his head two feet from the ground. Under him they kept a low fire going, expertly, not to burn him but to bake him slowly. For three long days, they slow-roasted Oring, father of half a dozen children, major of six hundred Home Guards. He swung over the fire, his hair matted with greasy sweat and soot. His eyes, at first wide with suffering, began to dull. They were bloodshot, very bloodshot, but there was a film over them that obscured the redness.

His old mother implored the Japs to let her near him. When he was almost dead, they cut him down, tied a rope around his neck, and led him, stumbling, weaving, hardly conscious, around the *barrio* of Jalajala for all to see. His mother, too brokenhearted even to wail, stumbled after him, her scrawny old arms beseeching, her old face drawn with greater agony than his birth had ever caused her.

The Japs let her give him his last supper. The people think he recognized at least her voice, the touch of her trembling hands, because he opened his mouth obediently as he had done when she was young and he was a little tyke running around naked.

Then they lopped off his head. His mother was there.

CHAPTER 17

The tragic histories were more than Marking and the fighters could bear.

"If we have to die," they said, "let us die fighting. We left the people for the safety of the majority, but the time has come to change our tactics. If the whole Filipino nation must perish, let the conqueror pay a bitter price."

Back over the Sierra Madre into our previous stamping ground in Rizal province we filed.

We bided our time in the old Sulok camp, waiting, watching, and an event, for me of great moment, took place there. It marked the spot for me as one of particular beauty, a sylvan setting for the greatness of the human heart. For we had a distinguished visitor, and through her learned how the political wheels were turning in Manila, how a few men were risking their lives daily to keep the government alive.

Before Christmas, in the company of towering Primo Dalton, who had served recklessly in Bataan as a Philippine Army lieutenant and now as a guerrilla was making more bids for a short life, and frail, small Ruperto Batara of the large, soft, luminous dreamer's eyes, came Asunción A. Pérez and her husband Cirilo.

"Lola!" I said, calling her by the loved nickname. Proudly I introduced this great woman to Marking, and she in turn introduced Cirilo.

Marking folded her in his arms and kissed her cheek, for she was no stranger to him though this was their first meeting. "Thank you for the clothes," he said. "Thank you for the money. Thank you for your letters to me."

"Son," said Lola, "you are doing a wonderful work."

"Come meet everybody," urged Marking, his arms across her shoulders. "Everybody must know who you are."

Swiftly Primo and Ruperto warned me with their eyes, and I stepped over. "Darling, she is in too close to the Japs. If there is a leak she will have no chance."

Marking hesitated, then said to her, "Then they will only see one of the guerrilla mothers not known to anybody." To me, both plea and defiance in his face: "Nobody will know. They will only see."

Most of the men had seen anyway. Cut off from everything except the manifold activities of resistance against the enemy, they drew upon their own world for mental and emotional stimulation. Every visitor was scrutinized, and for no greater reason than human need to know.

"All right." And I said to Lola, "If you tell them how loved the fighters are by thousands of people everywhere—"

She laid her soft, veined hand upon mine. "I understand, my dear." There were tears in her eyes and tears in mine.

Thus Asunción A. Pérez, for a quarter of a century the outstanding social worker of the Philippines, whose name had been synonymous with her organization, The Associated Charities, and who under the Japs still served the poor and helpless as Director of the Bureau of Public Welfare, walked along the path and across the brook with its waterfalls and smooth, sun-and-leaf-laced pools to the drill ground where all who were not on guard duty gathered unbidden around her.

There followed the humblest and the greatest of all Lola's public addresses.

Announced Marking, "For her own safety this woman cannot be introduced—"

Sibilantly around the circle went the whisper, from fighter to fighter: "It is Mrs. Perez of the Associated Charities! It is her picture before in the newspapers!"

Marking frowned and repeated, "She is not known, remember?" And the fighters intoned: "Yes, sir. She is not known."

He continued, "She is one of the great people of the Philippines. Since October 1942, she has been helping us. Before that she was helping Colonel Yay. Before that, before the war, she was helping everybody anyway. Now she is also helping everybody, but it is us she loves very much—not so, Lola?"

"It is so, Marking."

"And so I now introduce Mrs. Asunción A. Pérez—"

He bit his lip and looked quickly for me, but I had not heard—I was deep in a whispered conference with Lola's husband, Cirilo, librarian at the Bureau of Science, chief Manila guerrilla finance officer.

"Ma'am," the fighters told me later, "she said we were heroes."

I smiled a little, for now somebody else was telling them, a somebody known to them before the war as the next Secretary of Labor. A proposed cabinet member was as good as a cabinet member any day.

"She said thousands of people loved us—" "She said a million people prayed for us and placed candles in the Church—" "She said we must be patient—" "We must keep on being good—" "Because we are heroes—"

"Ma'am, what if the Japs find out that she is our friend?"

"They will torture her first before they kill her."

There was silence, then: "Better there is no more talk upon this great event."

And I said, "Better."

Her visit and her talk were all that Marking and the fighters needed, but I was after more and pressed her, in secret conference, for full details—for facts, for her opinion, for possibilities.

"Did you read the letter Marking sent *him*?" I asked.

"It was a beautiful letter, Yay."

"We left it to you, Lola, to decide whether to give it or not."

"That letter cried for delivery. I delivered it."

"Start at the beginning."

"First tell me why there *was* such a letter."

"There had been so many reports, Lola . . . We had always believed in *him*. At least, I had. Then report after report came. One said that in Fort Santiago he had been threatened with execution. He stood tall and unafraid and told the Japs, 'All right, kill me, and give the Philippine people another hero!' There was the story from Malacañan that he alone dared to oppose the Japs' conscription of Filipinos to fight the Americans. A Jap rose and unsheathed his saber. Across the conference table, he rose to stare down at the Jap officer. The report said his eyes flashed and the Jap put his saber back into its scabbard because it would be the Jap's neck if he killed so great a Filipino whom the Jap High Command could still use. Reports like that, Lola. You can imagine how it fired the boys up here!"

"Well," said Lola, "I took the letter to Manuel Roxas. There were Japanese in his house, of course. I talked about social welfare until we were alone. Then I asked him if he remembered you. His eyes were immediately watchful. 'Wait,' he said. He walked to the porch door and went out, picking up a magazine on the swing, in order to look around the garden. He returned and went into another room, where he left the magazine. Coming back, he said, 'They are gone, but keep your voice low.' I told him then that you were with the guerrillas. 'Yes, I know.' 'She is with Marking.' He commented, 'I have heard about Marking, that he is a great leader in the resistance movement.' I then opened my purse and gave him the letter."

The letter offered Roxas (later, president of the Philippines) refuge in the hills. It stated knowledge of his courage and loyalty and assured him that far back in the jungle a hide-out would be prepared for him and veteran guerrillas would be assigned to guard and supply him with necessities.

Lola continued, "He read it, spread out on his desk. When he had finished reading, he asked me if the signature was Marking's. I assured him that it was Marking's true signature. He asked me if I had direct contact with you and Marking. I said yes. He picked up the letter and swung his chair around to read it again with his back half turned to me. It was not discourtesy. We have been friends for many years, and now he was alone in his decision. He read it through a second time, very slowly, repeating lines and phrases, I think. When he turned to me, when he looked up, his eyes were bright with tears and he could not speak."

"Wait, Lola," I said. "Marking should hear this. I'll send for him."

When he came Lola repeated the facts.

"Tell him to come right away," said Marking. "Tell him there are men all ready to bring him to us, and I will take him far back into the farthest jungle where nobody will ever find him."

"Marking," said Lola, "this is what Roxas said, 'Tell General Agustin that it is not time yet for me to escape. Tell him that for some of us the fight against the enemy is in close. Tell him that we all of us fight, but in different ways. I am old and sick. I cannot carry arms. I would be a burden. Here in another way, I fight. I did not know anybody knew it but myself.' There were tears in his eyes again, Marking."

"Tell him not to cry," said Marking. "Tell him to come."

"He cannot come," said Lola. "Not until his job is finished."

"What does he do? What Japs does he kill? It is *himself* to be killed!"

Helplessly, Lola looked at me, and I said, "He can help the men in the mountains if he stays where he is."

"How?"

"By telling us what the Japanese intend to do."

"What the Japs intend to do! They have already done it! That is why we fight! Nobody can tell me about Japs. I know everything about them—"

"Marking," I said, "Lola's time is limited. She brings you a message from Roxas, and then she must go."

"Where is it?" He held out his hand.

"The message is verbal," explained Lola. "It was too dangerous for both him and me to carry his letter."

"I wrote to *him!*"

"You are already wanted, darling," I intervened. "There are rewards posted everywhere. The Japs are fools to advertise you, but they do, and the people blow kisses at the posters. Now, you listen to Lola—"

Lola took her cue: "Roxas's usefulness to you and to the resistance movement will end when he is found out. We must take no chances. No letters. No unnecessary visits. No leaks."

Defensively, Marking said, "I have never told his name to anyone." And he turned to me. "Have I?"

"No. Listen to Lola, darling."

"Roxas tells you that he will be your adviser."

"Good," said Marking. "What is his advice?"

"Do not shoot Laurel again," said Lola.

"What! We have to! The first time was no good. There was three bullets—everywhere, in the neck, in the chest, in the exact place of the belly, where a traitor keeps his stomach. He should be dead! The Japs sewed him up, every damn hole, and they gave him transfusion—"

Lola laid her hand on his. "Marking—"

"Tell Roxas next time we shoot Laurel it will be a bery dead Laurel, bery, bery dead!"

"You are excited," said Lola.

I asked, "*Why* doesn't Roxas want Marking to order Laurel's assassination again?"

"We will assassinate him *dead,*" said Marking.

"Because," soothed Lola, "if you kill Laurel, then Roxas will be next."

"Next what?" asked Marking.

"Next puppet president. And if that happens Roxas will be more on the spot and be able to do less. The way it is, the Japs use Laurel, and so do Roxas and the loyal men behind Roxas. Another thing, Laurel has shown a change of mind—"

"Shoot him again," said Marking, "and change his mind some more."

"Seriously," said Lola, "Laurel has changed. He always was a Filipino, a good Filipino. Before the war he was convinced that the political future of the Philippines lay in a Greater East Asia. Now he knows that we will be just another Korea crushed by the same Japan. He may not love the Americans, but he does love his own people. History may show him a pitiable figure indeed, caught up by a cultural ideology, then forsaken by it. Right now, between Roxas and the Japanese, he is caught and crushed between two opposing forces."

I remembered the report that Laurel had issued an order barring all Japanese civilians from the courts because Filipino litigants had been slapped during the trials. The Jap civilians, little emperors bursting with importance under the wind of the Imperial Forces, rushed to the Japanese High Command to protest the order. Questioned by the High Command, Laurel had been adamant; and the High Command had conceded the point—because it still had use for Laurel.

Lola was still talking. "Roxas could do no better than Laurel, who now delays, distracts, gives advice that Roxas gives him to give. The Japanese will never understand the Philippine psychology. Roxas studies their plans carefully and, with other loyal leaders, maps out a counter campaign against everything they plan to do. Then they advise Laurel. Laurel knows Philippine psychology, too; he knows the significance of Roxas's advice; he knows that if he gives the advice cleverly or casually enough, the Japanese will swallow it and do exactly the thing that will warn the Filipino people, that will make them balk, that will keep them alert.

"Take the Japanese plans to conscript Filipinos no longer as labor but as soldiers. Roxas advised Laurel to make a big speech openly stating that we Filipinos must fight the Americans. That jolted the Filipinos wide-awake. They knew then the real significance of being recruited and trained to keep peace and order. In the meantime, following Roxas's advice, Laurel has been busy perfecting the plans for conscription. A headache delays him. He must go to the province on a tour of inspection. He is very ill. He recovers. He must have certain investigations made. He relapses. He recovers. He must consult with other officials. He must verify certain statistics. He is delayed by storm. He is delayed by official matters. He is delayed by family matters. It is a dangerous game that Laurel is playing. In front of the Japanese, he and Roxas disagree just enough to invite the Japanese to take Laurel's advice instead of Roxas's, and it is really Roxas's advice they take through Laurel. Laurel cannot move around too much. He is forever surrounded by the Japanese. But Roxas has connections that keep him informed of the real state of affairs, and so he puts into Laurel's mouth the words that will not only annul the endeavors of the enemy but also inform the people of the real intentions of the Japanese."

I knew in my heart how possible it was, for I had played the same game at KZRH in February 1942, before the Fall of Bataan. Jorge Vargas, secretary to Philippine President Manuel Quezon, had been brought to the station for a broadcast. Before he left he asked, in spite of all the Japs around, "What happened to Johnny Harris, Yay?" and I answered, as quietly and smilingly as if we had been talking about the weather, "He was a damn fool. I told him to be careful. They found a G-2 calling card in his desk." Vargas asked, "Where is he now?" "In Fort Santiago." The moment was over, for his Jap companions were within earshot again. He said as he stepped into the elevator, "Watch your health, Yay. The weather is undependable. There is much influenza, and it is catching." He was gone, and I was alone again in the station, though there were many about me. Six months later I told this to Marking. "Take Vargas off the list of condemned," he said.

Patiently, Lola explained the political situation in Manila to us. Pio Duran, the Japanophile lawyer who had given his children Japanese names before the war, was jockeying for favor against General Artemio Ricarte, exiled to Japan since the American occupation and returned in glory to his native land—except that the present generation had never heard of him and had to ask their grandparents. Rafael Alunan, José Yulo, Elpidio, Quirino, and scores of other political leaders were loyal but under constant surveillance. Even the brilliant Quintin Parades, once floor leader of the National Assembly, whose prewar business connections with the Japanese made him suspect, seemed to be holding out against the enemy. There was no sure way of knowing, of course. Now Benigno Aquino, former cabinet member, was the most forward of our traitors. There was terror in every home, and brother closed eyes to brother lest he discover what it would be safest for him not to know, safest for his brother, safest for the cause of the underground.

"There is tremendous greed," said Lola, "and heartbreaking treachery everywhere. The enemy have a system of espionage that traps the patriots at every turn. They send out solicitors for aid, their own solicitors, and these catch the most victims. These solicitors speak words that the desperate heart aches to hear—that the Americans have landed in Mindanao, that aid is very near, that the guerrillas need only a little help to rid the country of the enemy. These solicitors claim direct contact with MacArthur. They claim to have transmitters, and to receive and send messages. Perhaps there are some genuine contact men . . . But how do we know which is genuine and which is a Japanese agent?

Home after home has been raided by the Japanese Military Police. From the supper table, with his children around him, a father has been taken. A son waves goodbye to his mother and is not heard from again until weeks later, when they return his clothes to her from Fort Santiago—if they return anything at all. In the markets, in the throngs on the street, in restaurants, in clubs, in offices, even in schools—waking and sleeping, there are informers everywhere. What is it, Marking?"

Then she understood the tired droop of his shoulders and his bent head. "No," she said, her hand upon his, "it is nothing of which any of us need be ashamed. It is not nationality. It is human nature. This could happen in America. It was happening in Europe before the war came here. It will happen wherever there is tyranny, oppression, and a price for betrayal. And, Marking, compared to the millions who are loyal, the percentage of betrayal is very, very small. We can be proud that under such circumstances as these we still have such as you." She patted his hand tenderly. "If you were my own son, I could not be prouder of you." She felt a teardrop on her hand. Without removing it she continued, "With such as you and Roxas, we shall redeem our country. He was very moved, *very moved*, when he read your letter. It was wholly unexpected. He feels the same pride in you as I do, as all of us do. We have faith in you."

"I will order you some coffee," mumbled Marking. "It is not good coffee—"

"I would like to have some coffee, yes," said Lola. "There is one more thing I must tell you. Roxas wants you to be very, very careful. He says that the Japanese are planning another all-out campaign against you. Do not trust any amnesty. It is another trick. Your camp here is in danger—"

"Oh, always they talk, they don't come!" snorted Marking, with something to pick on again.

"The hell they don't come!" I said to Lola.

"Yay, it is your duty to advise him well."

"Lola, what Marking needs is a man twice his size to advise him."

"Patience, Yay."

"That's it," exclaimed Marking. "She has no patience, Lola. I am good to her. I am the best, best man. She cannot find another man like me. Lola, she is not beautiful! Why should I love her! But I love and love her, and everybody treats me like a general, but to her I'm just a buck private! You tell her, Lola!"

"Here, here," said Lola, laughing, "all married people have their quarrels—"

It was on the tip of my tongue to wise-crack, "We're not married."

Lola read my mind, and pursued a less touchy line, "She loves you, Marking. I know this girl. I have known her for many years. She is on top of the world, or the world is on top of her. You must consider her moods. You, too, must be patient—"

"I am the commanding officer," he said. "Let *her* be patient."

"You must both be patient." Lola's voice was firm. "Where is my coffee?"

"*She* will not order your coffee," said Marking. "I will order your coffee."

"Marking!" said Lola reprovingly.

But he knew he had an ally, or at least that she loved us equally, and he swaggered out.

"As for you," said Lola to me, "you must be the more patient."

"Yes, ma'am."

"The woman must always make the greater concession."

"Yes, ma'am."

"Yay, if anybody can spank you, I can. Remember that."

"Lola, remember the first time we met? I waltzed in and took a rose off your desk right under your nose?"

"You haven't changed."

"When the war is over, pin roses on me again."

"Yay, to think of you up here—"

"Having the time of my life—"

"It is a dangerous life. Roxas thinks the Japanese know where this camp is."

"Of course they do. They've been here before. They'll be here again." I looked at her, my admiration and fear for her safety in my eyes. "You must leave this place."

"Right away."

"It's easier to tell Marking than to make him. Look, Lola. I've kept him in the camps out of the fighting. It hasn't been easy for either of us. But he doesn't go out on raid. That much he concedes, but it's quite another thing to make him move a camp. Pride, maybe. I won't let him go to the fight, so he lets the fight come to him."

"It isn't wise."

"You tell him, sweet."

Goodbyes were being said. I kissed Lola's hand, in the age-old Philippine custom of kissing a parental hand. It embarrassed her a little, yet touched her heart, and I spoiled it mischievously by smirking,

"Filial devotion." But she knew and hugged me close to her, then turned to embrace Marking and receive his parting kiss on her cheek. And then they were gone.

In a matter of days Lola was picked up. Her escort, Primo, was taken. Her friend, Nik-Nik, sat frail in the dungeon away from the sunlight that was life to him. Her husband, Cirilo, had a thong about his head with a bullet twisted in the slack, screaming in agony. The Manila enlistment was shaken. Panic set in. Contacts were lost.

Marking looked to me in the hour of trouble as both lover and son. I comforted him, desperately in need of comfort myself. Only Lola was to live through.

CHAPTER 18

*W*e bided our time in the old Sulok camp, waiting, watching through Christmas of 1943, and it was not peace on earth nor good will to *all* men.

The Japs passed on to other areas and other helpless people. And when the pain had passed and their minds were clear again the people of Talim themselves hunted down those who had been the traitors during the zoning. Those who had hunted became the hunted.

They were delivered—alive—to the fighters.

The men looked to me. Would I insist on merciful execution for dignity's sake? Would I be cold and firm and righteous? Would I hold Marking back from brutality, preach that our boys must return to normal life not as sadists, but as heroes with clean hearts?

That one time I made exception to a rule, for my own heart was hot. "Those without mercy," I said, remembering Roger and Oring and the rest, "deserve no mercy."

Many the fists that beat them black and blue and bounced them around like basketballs. Even Nene the nurse was in it, striking a blow for one who had befriended her and been betrayed. Even the little boy-k.p. was in it, for *his* friend who had suffered. And Marking, who had wept for the loss of Deniega and Feliciano and the others, tried not to take part but sat at the table, sat questioning the one who had tricked quick, respectful, patriotic Feliciano. But when the traitor gave one wrong answer Marking vaulted over the table, touching it only with his right hand, landing on his feet like a cat, bringing his fist with all his hardwood weight behind it into the traitor's face, knocking him in a somersault against the table, to pick him up from the ground with his left hand and knock him ten feet with his right. Close around him, in and out, crowded the fighters: "Let us help you, sir! We'll do it for you, sir!"

There was no refined torture. Just fist and feet and hate. It was hate for the traitor, hate greater than the hate for the Japs, hate for the one who betrayed his own.

I had hate in me, too.

"Shall we kill them now," panted Marking, "at sunset?" "No," I advised. "Let them feel it awhile. And let those who come see them." The fighters stripped them of their clothes and stood them against trees with their wrists shackled behind the trunks. "That's what you gave the people!" "Stand up, you filthy traitor!" "That's it, *cry!* You coward!" "Mercy? Mercy? You ask for mercy? *Did you give it!* Here! *Here's some* mercy for you!" And that night, while they shivered naked against the trees in the cold gulch wind, I asked Marking a favor. "That one who violated Peggy after she was dead—may I have that one? Tomorrow morning, when we finish them, you can assign that one to me."

Peggy was the sister of Igi, the farmer who had sheltered me when I found Marking. Her face had been like a cameo. Although a Filipina, she looked more like an American girl.

The next day, the fighters drew lots. Pivet, always willing to be the executioner ("You fellows got to keep on living in this country—me, I'm going home some day"), drew one of the five. And Marking spoke. "That other is for Mammy." The fighters quickly understood why and centered their vying on the other three.

All five were herded along to dig their own graves: "C'mon, you! Make it deeper. It's your last bed. Make it soft." "T'hell with their soft bed! Make it deeper so we won't have to smell them." "Forgive you? Look. You don't know it, but you're dying easy. How'd you like what Oring got? How'd you like what Allen got?" "Yeah. We're just going to shoot you. You won't even know you're dead." "You'll just be dead forever and ever and ever." No pity.

Not even in Marking's heart, softest of all, nor in mine, continually insistent throughout the war that we remain humane. Before and after, I could preach, "Let us never sink to the level of the enemy. If we kill, we kill clean." But not that time.

Around nine in the morning, the camp assembled. The scooped-up graves, about two feet deep, were ready. The traitors, dull of eye, no longer pleaded.

"Over here, you! And you and you, here!"

"Leave that one on the far left," said Marking.

"OK, you. Over here on the left."

"Turn your backs. Who do you think you are? Men of honor?" Then, in the solemnity of the act of execution, all was quiet. "You may pray," said Marking.

They fell to their knees in prayer, little brown naked hunched people who in cowardice, ignorance, and avarice had sent too many others to their death.

"All right, you! You stand!"

A fighter touched one on the shoulder, and he stood, crumpled, had to be pulled up.

Pivet picked him off. The body fell heavy, sprawled half in, half out of its self-dug hole.

Another. He plopped on his face.

Another. He flip-flopped, breathed convulsively, and the blood gushed from his neck.

"Not in the neck," I said. "In the head. This is the end, make it quick."

"Yours next, Yay," said Marking.

My sidearm at that time was a Jap luger, called Sakai after its former Jap owner. I had not tried it out yet, so I aimed carefully. The trigger was unbelievably soft. The gun pinged; Peggy's violator sagged at the knees, slid down into a squat, swayed forward on his face, and kept on sliding until his length measured the mound of dirt he had thrown up from the hole.

"In the head, Mammy," grinned Pivet.

Then we discovered my gun had jammed after the one shot. We unloaded it by slipping out the clip, and Marking reached for it. "Cleaning will fix it up," he said.

There was one traitor left, still praying. He knelt alone, with dead or twitching bodies sprawled in and out of the ditches to his right, in front, and behind him. Marking and I had discussed him during the night. Marking had left him to the last because, technically, he had not betrayed. He had helped the Japs, had loaded one body in a *banca* upon their orders to dump it in the lake. He had been everywhere, untouched while the helpless screamed and died, but though he helped he had never quite betrayed. The people demanded his death, but in all the evidence and testimony there was no shred of proof that he himself voluntarily had given one loyal life to the enemy. He was left to the last to see what guts he had. A coward can never be trusted, but a brave man can be reformed.

"I'll take this one," said Marking.

The fighters watched, some smiling but all quiet.

Marking stepped up close behind the kneeling figure. "Aren't you through praying yet?"

There was no answer.

Marking nudged him in the small of the back with his boot. "Ready to die?"

Mutely, the doomed nodded.

"Answer me!" ordered Marking.

"Yes, sir." No distinguishable quaver.

Marking cocked his .45, fired over the fellow's head. The fellow swayed uncertainly on his knees, shook his head as if to make sure there was no hole in it, maybe it would gurgle or slosh inside like a coconut. Then, he kept on kneeling, waiting for another shot—maybe the first one had missed.

"Get up, fool!" Marking's voice was roughly kind.

"Who, sir? Me?" came the uncertain answer.

And with that the waiting fighters burst into laughter, stepped over the dead to pull him up, slapped him resoundingly on the back, shook his hand, "Congratulations!" There was no grin broader than Mapa's, though Mapa had helped to pummel them all.

Then the fellow began to whimper, and as Marking and I turned away, setting to work on a high pile of reports, rosters, and letters of inquiry, he came running and stumbling behind us to catch Marking's hand and bend over it and kiss it and to grab at mine to do the same.

"See that man there?" We pointed at Mapa, whose back was turned as he instructed his men falling in for the drill. "You go kiss him. Kiss him all over."

The fighters teased him, swatting his bare rear, "Hey, shame! Shame! No clothes, running around naked like that!" And they gave him a shirt.

"This isn't mine! It's all torn."

"Never mind! That's how you start. You're a guerrilla now."

"Oh, no! No, no!" protested the fellow, his eyes wide with fright again. "I don't want to be a guerrilla. I just want to be good. I'll never do what I did again. I promise, I promise you."

They lifted him up on the table, pouring liniment on his swollen jaw and his body, black and blue turning to purple and green. Nene massaged with strong small hands.

"*Aray* [Ouch]! How painful! Oh, how I hurt—*aray!*" And as they rubbed it in hard, laughing in gusts, the "new-life-again" groaned and whimpered louder and louder and unfolded—or just folded—in the sincerity and sympathy around him. "Oh, what a life! Now I am a guerrilla, oh, oh! Down there, put the maircuriocrome [sic—to reflect pronunciation] down there, *aray!*"

He made a fine k.p. for a while and then, sent home, a fine Home Guard.

Three days later, things began to stink.

"Why didn't you dig the holes outside the camp?" I asked. "But, ma'am, there was plenty of room here!" said the camp detail.

"Yeah. Right in the middle of the camp. Look. It's only twenty-five feet from one of the barracks. And those holes . . . how deep are they? I *told* you to dig them deep. Now you know, now you find out. And it stinks like hell."

"One of 'em keeps coming up, ma'am."

"You see! I told you to dig deep."

"I put more dirt on him, but he keeps sticking his nose out; and I smack him one with the spade, and after a while there he is again."

"Because they bloat first before they rot, and that pushes them up. You'd better dig them all up and make bigger holes and put them away proper."

"After a while they won't stink any more."

"Yeah. But they stink *now*. How many all in all, old and new?"

"Sixteen—seventeen—fifteen, I guess. But not all of them stink any more."

"Well, ma'am, what would you expect traitors to smell like? And if we put the cemetery outside the camp, the wild pigs will drag them around."

In the background Marking, watching me, said serenely, "You do it, darling." "Do it yourself." "I'll *help* you." "You will not! Ugh! Messy."

So the air was heavy, very heavy, but after a while, as the boys had said, it stopped stinking.

One day, in the stir and bustle and milling around of a full camp, Captain Joe Ano came in. Joe was one of the steadiest, one of the most faithful. If he never reported in, we knew he was still carrying on, and that Tommy, his homely, bug-eyed kid brother, was carrying on.

Dependable, Joe.

He came over and handed me a little bundle. Cloth, with a familiar, faded pattern. I unfolded it, and there were Peggy's little trinkets: a sandalwood fan, one stick broken; the cheap little chain and cross; the feather from a white parrot.

"Where did you get them, Joe?"

"And here is Deniega's watch," he said. "Please give it to the Old Man for me." His eyes were full of tears that spilled down his dark cheeks.

"Joe! What is it?"

"I'm so ashamed to you, ma'am."

My brain whirled like a roulette wheel, stopped on a number. "Joe! *Where did you get this stuff?*"

"From the house of my first cousin, ma'am. The one you killed, ma'am."

"Joe! Oh, Joe!"

His head was bowed. I pulled him nearer, took him by the shoulders. They were shaking, but there was no sound, for he was swallowing his sobs. "Joe, what can I say? I asked for the privilege. I executed him myself."

"I know, ma'am. The people told us."

"Joe, he was guilty—guilty as hell! Guilty of the worst—"

"He was my first cousin. We grew up together. We were very close, always."

"Joe, Joe!"

"I do not cry because he is dead, ma'am. I cry because *I am ashamed to you for what he did.* When I heard about it, I came to kill him myself. He is a shame to the family honor. If we the relatives could have killed him ourselves . . . But it is still the family, ma'am. You are the mother of the guerrillas. This is the family of all the families."

Then, with tears still on his face, he stepped back. I shall never forget the manliness of him as he saluted.

On his way out of the camp, he passed Marking and again saluted. Marking nodded, laid his hand on Joe's shoulder.

CHAPTER 19

It was tough on the fighters, concealing them within the camp, but we wanted to keep our return to Rizal province secret as long as possible, the quicker and better to organize the shattered city units. While our contact men floated everywhere through city and town, the fighters groused restlessly, day after day performing the camp details, and each day hoping to roll. The comradeship of the camp was good enough, but the comradeship of the trail was better.

Japs were again patrolling the foothills.

The *palay* that Lucio had piled up in great, golden piles was no more. How to eat? Marking pondered the difficult problems: to stay where we were meant long supply lines out from the towns, leading the Japs. We were low on bullets again ... Sometimes we had a peak of twenty thousand bullets; sometimes we were down to a couple of hundred. He had the alternative of dragging the fighters all the way back across the divide to Dumagat land again—a week's trip, fraught with many dangers for the cross-country runners. To keep the organization functioning, we had to stay in Rizal within a radius of ten miles. Nor could the loyal but desperately overburdened lowland towns of Morong, Cardona, Teresa, Tanay, and Binangonan covering Talim Island feed all our fighters, more than five hundred in one spot, in addition to the hundreds of convoy men, runners, and key officers from all over the country eating where they could as they went along.

Then at last Marking's orders were made ready. Cabalhin and Mapa were to base their fighters in Laguna near Santa Maria, where the rice was coming to harvest. Bernie and his unit would remain with Marking for the time being, and Pabling could proceed to Tagback behind Antipolo, both to feed his fighters and to act as distant outpost to the north from which the Jap cavalry had once come. Nothing could rattle us as the cavalry could; one thinks he can outrun a bullet, but he knows damn well he can't outrun a horse.

So down we rolled from the waterfall camp, late in the afternoon when the Japs would probably be lounging around the garrisons filling their little potbellies full of imitation beer. We serpentined along over the

Hacienda Pinugay to a yard-wide trail where the *carabao* carts had marked the way, and we rolled into the *barrio* of Lagundi and on through it to No. 1 Home Guard Officer Salvador's mango camp, where the barracks were built under the broad, thick-leaved branches and thus concealed from plane patrols. A few kilometers away was another choice spot behind Baras. The two camps formed an elliptical sphere about two miles long and half a mile wide and within an hour's walk of the Baras town. I much preferred the Baras camp because of a lazy river bend where the swimming was twenty feet from the headquarters' table.

There we settled down to work again. Until the harvest was reaped, the fighters would have to be kept quiet; otherwise there would be more fighting in the foothills than harvesting. The Japs were demanding almost more than the harvest, and most of the seasonal crops had already been gathered in, but there was still *palay* in the fields and, left in peace, the people could sneak enough of their own on the side to live through a while longer.

We kept the fighters busy in the camp at drilling and, closer to town, were able to feed them a little better. Once in a while, they got a mango each; once in a while, an egg. I had never liked eggs, but, now that I had not seen one for eight months, they were the most beautiful little miracles in special packing that Nature ever wrought. I could imagine how the fighters felt, finding eggs in the rations, for some of them hadn't seen an egg for more than a year.

The old whirling, milling, in-and-out activity of Kanumay came to life again in Lagundi. Reports were thrilling. An imaginative eye could see a whole country fighting in the only ways left. Fighters held their rifles in the hills. The tradition was not to notch the butts but never to let a rifle fall! Who sickened, who died, who fell out, who failed to come back from the raid—no matter; up from the cities and towns, down from the highland farms reached hands to catch the slipping gun and yank it to, "Atten-SHUN! Parade REST! De-PLOY!" Reserves canvassed for bullets more thoroughly than census takers for babies. "Special missions" dug into the leaves between tree roots on the quiet battlefield at Bataan, raking out the rusting, green-molded, .30-caliber shells, drying them patiently in the sun, cocking the head and shaking each shell to hear if the powder loosened, dropping the "hopefuls" into the can. They squatted there contentedly counting, "One Jap, two Japs, three Japs . . . Hey, Pepe, I got a hundred and twenty-eight Japs. How many you got?" More reserves on the job, growing a little extra, sparing a little more "for the boys up there." Long lines of convoys cutting across country, rice on their backs, none in their stomachs, toiling up the chest-bursting climbs to the mountain camps where the fighters, gaunt on gruel, pale with malaria, cleaned with coconut oil their old pitted rifles and repeated like a litany, "No surrender, no surrender, no surrender!"

Leafing through the reports of others' endeavors—the students, the laborers, the teachers, the drivers, the writers, the nurses, the stevedores, the wives and the sisters of hunted men—was enough to yank me to the typewriter again, banging off letters of praise, of advice, of encouragement. They looked to Marking, and to me, for what? It was all we could do to keep ahead of them in service and love of country. Cabalhin, Bernie, Mapa, Lucio, Salvador, Mata—these were the people's heroes, and more and more the honors were coming to us, their proud old parents.

Marking would smile at me, "Some family, we got," and I would smile back, "I don't mind growing old, this proud."

But there was heartache, too, all along the long, long way of waiting and watching for America, and fighting to hold the country down when the people grew too desperate and up when oppression beat it too low. We were losing sons, too.

A lad came in, asking for orders. Marking said, "We need more bullets. Get them." I typed out the authorization, and Marking signed it, saying, doing, hearing six other things at the same time and thinking a seventh. When Méndez left with his orders, nobody saw him go.

A day passed. A week passed. Then came a report that a young Filipino had been crucified in the Pasig garrison. The headquarters wondered pityingly, "Who?" scanned the rest of the reports, dug out maps, argued strategies, forgot an unverified story of somebody crucified—maybe a rumor, maybe anything.

It came to mind another day.

The fellow had been caught bringing through a sackful of bullets—two thousand .30s!

"Guerrilla? One of our men?" We checked the key convoy men off on our fingers. All were accounted for, including the girl, Butch. All safe, so far . . . But no non-guerrilla would be caught with one bullet, let alone the treasure trove of two thousand. It had to be a guerrilla.

At last came the story. Méndez had flown to his assignment. "Marking gave me my orders, Marking himself! And I met Cabalhin and Yay and Mapa and De la Rosa and Salvador and Lucio and all of them!" Patriotism and hero worship and a fighting heart. Méndez had a small, picked group of men. Together they had collected the bullets, one by one, a fistful at a time; from friends' friends and those friends' friends, and from among the leaves on old battlefields, they had filled a *bayong*. When Marking ordered him to get bullets, it was offhand, to give some eager lad something to do; Marking was always ordering bullets. It was the No. 1 order of the outfit. "And hurry up," he had said. So, instead of carrying it twenty or thirty miles through the fields and forests, Mendez and five fellow guerrillas whom he brought along just to share his honors with them took a chance ... They piled the *bayong* of bullets in with other *bayong*-baggage, and rode the rickety bus. With luck, they would get through—fast.

Of the six guerrillas, the Japs discovered two, for they were closest to the contraband baggage found by the sentry who, making a careless check of passengers and *bayongs*, lifted one and found it suspiciously heavy. Méndez looked around him—more than forty other passengers in the bus, four of them his buddies and a fifth arrested with him. Alone in the crowd, Méndez decided. If he took the blame, he could save the whole busload, including his men, from mass torture.

"The contraband is mine," he said.

Promptly the Japs released their second arrest, and it was he who reported on Méndez.

The Japs stretched Méndez against the wall, nailing him there by the hands. His feet, they nailed to the floor. For three days, in what had once been a schoolroom he hung as a symbol of Christ. Now and then they struck him or stood before him. The blows were nothing, probably, to his greater pain. His head drooping, he could see the boots. They meant, "Ready to talk?"

Talk what? Talk about where Marking, Cabalhin, Mapa, Bernie, Lucio, and Yay were?

"Tell us and we'll spare you."

On the third day, they dispatched him with a saber.

He had admitted ownership of the contraband, yes. It was the first thing he admitted. It was the last. Knowing other secrets, he took them with him and died as quietly as he had lived.

I can't for the life of me remember what he looked like. Neither can Marking. Cabalhin seems to remember, but he's not sure. So many in and out, so many ...

Lydia came to us. Manuel had gone to work one morning, lingering at the gate to tease and kiss Lydia goodbye as he had for ten years of happy married life. She had gone marketing. When she returned to 442 M. H. del Pilar, where their house had been an informal club to the rest of us, the yard and house were full of Japs and Jap-hired informers. She and Manuel had foreseen the possibility. "Go out to Marking and Yay," Manuel had said. Now he had been picked up at his office in the Bureau of Public Welfare. Lyd came drifting through the towns, where Lucio thought she looked like someone he had seen before. Kiko Pakiko had been courier between Lyd and me. To Kiko's house in Teresa she had gone. She was brought to us, thin as a rail, weeping.

Marking comforted her. I comforted her.

There was no comfort for her. "Manuel—Manuel—"

"Lyd," I said, "you'll get him back."

"Lyd," said Marking, "we'll have the Manila men find out where they're holding him."

"Manuel—Manuel..." wept Lyd, crying herself to sleep, waking in the night from crying in her sleep, opening her eyes to a new dawn to realize anew her loss and greet the sunrise alone through more tears.

For me, there is no woman in all this world with Lydia's courage. There is no woman I would rather have for sister. I'm lucky, having her as friend. She came to us needing comfort, and became our comfort. Valiant, keeping her sorrow deep, saving her tears for the minutes in solitude, she took heavy responsibilities on her shoulders, became Marking's only aide-de-camp, complementing our woman-writer teamwork, and none loved the fighters more than she. Fastidious, choosy, leaning to Shakespeare and classical music, Lyd brought new worlds into the lost guerrilla world—discussion, comment, sophisticated humor, intellectual stimulation, a new kind of comradeship. The men were closer to her than to me, which turned the tables for me: where before the war she had been aloof and I the roisterer, now I was pushed up out of the camaraderie and she was on a boisterous equality with the world. In the loneliness forced on me by my rank and Marking's jealousy, I envied her, and she, having what I so badly wanted and needed, frankly would not have been in my shoes for worlds, but kept me company.

"C'mere, I'll tell you a story," she would say—sure it would tickle the ribs. "Now, don't tell Marking."

That was hard. Out of loyalty to Marking, I had to keep him advised of any matter calling for his official attention. We drove a bargain, Lyd and I.

"Lyd, if it's serious and will be detrimental to the good of the work, you take it up with him, or indicate to me that I should."

"OK," said Lyd. "I won't tell you a thing."

No glamour, no authority stood between us. We were friends and fellow writers before the war; we stood shoulder to shoulder in the guerrilla.

Lagundi covered ground, as far as administrative work was concerned. Both Alora of the Cavite Saboteurs and Seneres of the Guerrilla Intelligence Division had sabotage and intelligence work going full blast. They specialized in the "war of nerves," which meant anything to baffle the Japs.

Alora ambled up. "Did you wreck those planes yet?" demanded Marking. "No, sir." "Well, what the hell are you doing down there?" "Wasting time, sir." "And you dare to say so to my face? Alora, you better be—" "Well, a ship comes in to be fixed, sir—" "Don't change the subject." "Sir, we make sabotage."

"So what?" Marking had little sympathy for sabotage. Anything short of pulling a trigger and seeing a Jap flop dead was nothing toward winning the war. He wanted action, *bang! bang!* all the time.

"Then we begin to lose the tools." No comment from Marking. "So then, more tools have to be bought or made. Then, when more tools are brought and more tools are lost and more tools are made and the Japs begin to beat up everybody—" "Then what?" "We begin to fix the ship."

"So you fix the ship after all." Marking snorted, coughed, spit.

"For a little while, sir. Then the ship catches fire—" "What? You didn't put it out, did you?" "Yes, sir." "Why, you typhoid fever—" "We put it out after a while, and then it was discovered that the tools fell overboard." "Did you throw them overboard?" "Yes, sir."

"Why, that's fine!" Marking was beginning to appreciate. "Then what happened?"

"More tools came and we have to work again." "Oh! Why didn't you throw them overboard too? Hereafter I order you to throw everything overboard." "Yes, sir. But we can't do it all the time. We have to do it between times." "What else did you do?" "We wasted time, sir. We waste time all the time."

"Yay!"

"Yes, Marking."

"Promote Alora. I guess that sabotage business is fine . . . What are you, Alora? Lieutenant colonel? . . . All right. You have a regiment, a full regiment of men? How long since you been promoted, two years? . . . All right. Make the commission for full colonel . . . Alora, you will continue carrying my orders. Also, if you don't wreck those plants like I said, you will be demoted to buck private, all the way from the top to the bottom. Those were my first orders. I never forget. While you are still going to church, I am already on my way home."

Seneres of Intelligence reported in.

"You are under arrest," said Marking. "Yes, sir. May I ask why, sir?" "No. You go stay with the k.p."

Borres fed him, made a place for him, comforted him. Seneres was a full colonel, soon to be Chief of Intelligence of the entire organization, but, as far as Marking was concerned, Seneres was in the doghouse. Forthwith he was detailed to Borres in the camp kitchen.

"Why?" I asked.

"All the time they argue in the city. All the time they tattletale here, all of them. I am sick and tired of *sumbong* here, *sumbong* there. Everybody is a tattletale. I will *sumbong* them to Borres."

"He's too valuable a man to waste time. And he's too intelligent to need that kind of discipline."

"I will see how valuable he is. I will see how intelligent he is. You just shut up. And don't you sympathize with him, either. You pity him, I'll break his neck."

So I minded my own business.

A week later, Marking called, "Seneres, come here!"

"Yes, sir." Seneres responded with alacrity.

"Report to Mammy."

I raised my eyebrows. We had scarcely touched the subject. If Marking wanted to discipline the men, that was his right and his affair. Now what? Seneres remained at attention, waiting while Marking shuffled through reports.

"Go ahead. Report to Colonel Yay."

So I said to Marking, "What are your orders, sir?" Sometimes I had difficulty in controlling my inflection on "sir."

He looked at me sharply. "You go ahead with what you said."

"Oh, the Intelligence Department!"

"Yes." Then he said to Seneres, "You are too *malambing*, too soft, too sweet. I don't like it—"

"Yes, sir." "Although you don't tattletale like the others—" "Yes, sir." "Your unit asks too much aid—aid—aid. What do you think the headquarters is—a charity?" "No, sir. It's just—" "Just what?" "My boys are so poor, sir. It is almost impossible to buy food. The Japs pay two *pesos* a day for labor, and rice costs one hundred twenty *pesos* a *ganta*, and one *ganta* is hardly enough—" "All right, I will help you—" Eagerly, "Yes, sir!" "A little bit," amended Marking.

How many the quarrels we had had over finances! Looking back, I can see that he was right. He kept his organization purely patriotic, and though his followers suffered more than necessary they were the cream of the patriot crop. I have heard of a guerrilla organization that spent 43,000,000 pesos and had an enlistment of 25,000. Marking's boast was that his 200,000 enlistment in three years spent less than the cost of one first-class American battleship, which he naively figured at two or three million. One of these days the War Department in Washington will ask about some "Liberty Bonds" Marking and I floated to feed our starving fighters, and so I am writing this book on the jump to feed the kids while I am making little rocks out of big rocks at Leavenworth. I wonder how many rocks it will take to cover a couple of million. I wonder how much money that is, in the first place.

Seneres returned to Manila to organize and direct one of the quickest and most resourceful intelligence nets the underground ever would have. Out of seventeen Manila regiments of general enlistment, he picked six hundred of the best men and women whom he trained as the Guerrilla Intelligence Division. The regiments received and sent official mail through the GID, continuing to function independently of it, and the GID itself concentrated on mapping enemy installations, aiding the escape of persons wanted by the enemy, and covering the city like a newspaper: every block a beat; every agent a reporter trained to find out who, where, why, what, which, and when, and to report to certain designated clearing stations. From such reports was compiled, daily, a general report which reached headquarters by runner. In ten hours, we could have a complete report of enemy movements within and through Manila within the past twenty-four hours. Reports carried more and more details, as the agents gained experience, until they gave not only the number of trucks in a convoy, but exactly what personnel or material was being taken where.

The GID continued to develop, pushing networks into the provinces, setting up systems of double-checking reports, training runners by relay. The veteran runners would take two new runners on each trip to teach them the way and the methods of finding the main base no matter where the Japs chased us. The "escape teams" became known as the Underground Railway, and the "cross-country couriers" as the Pony Express. Not even rumor traveled faster.

In a flurry of activity Seneres, who was a fanatic, traveled back and forth between Manila and our headquarters, working out details. I wrote letters for him until my fingers became numb. Marking financed him to the point of growing purple with indignation. Seneres drove his men, and he drove us. He trained, trained, trained the men until we pitied them, and Marking gave each of them arriving in the camp a small sum of money to buy food on the way back, saying, "Don't you give that to Seneres," but he suspected that the poor little patriots would turn it in to the GIDs common funds to train more and more men. No unit in the organization was more patriotic or more efficient, and in the strictly Home Guard enlistment only the GID ranked with the combat units in the esteem of Cabalhin, Bernie, and Mapa.

Marking further burdened the willing GID. "Mammy needs shoes." In an almost shoeless country, it found shoes. "I need binoculars." It brought him Mining Engineer Bengzon's binoculars. "Cabalhin's men need tobacco." It brought *bayongs* of musty cigars and cheap cigarettes, contributed by the members from their own slim pockets. "Bring me maps." It brought him maps. "Bring me candy." Laughingly it brought, from a pretty lady who wrote a pretty letter to accompany it, coffee, candy, and sugar. Periodically, Pedring's sister, who was the pretty lady, sent him candy. Pedring was the singing runner who brought the mail and sang for us too before taking the return run.

The GID branched into propaganda—awful propaganda. Once again Seneres was under arrest.

"What do you mean," I stormed, "turning out tripe like that! It's immature! It's stupid! 'Dear traitors, please mend your ways,' indeed! Seneres, you ought to be shot for that! Marking—"

"Shoot him, dear," said Marking.

"It isn't funny."

"I'm sad," he grinned.

"What will people think of the outfit! That we're a bunch of fools?"

Marking stopped grinning. "So," he said to squirming Seneres, "you are immature, huh? You make us look like fools, huh? That's different! Borres, Seneres is k.p. again!"

But there was too much work to be done.

"Get back to the city. Stick to news broadcasts for your propaganda, and be sure you get it straight from the radio, exactly what San Francisco says and nothing else. And be sure it's San Francisco, not Tokyo—Oh, God, oh, God, you'll get Tokyo and swear it's San Francisco!"

He was backing me up all the way. "You get Tokyo, and you'll be a buck private," he said. "You'll be a buck private in the k.p."
"Yes, sir," said Seneres.
"Here, don't forget your papers," I said.
"And don't forget what I said," added Marking.
So went the days in Lagundi.

CHAPTER 20

Suddenly there was little left to eat in the land. With hunger came another pale horseman, disease—with them both came the short tempers which almost undid us all.

Guerrillas and civilians alike clawed for food, the starving from the starving. Pride was the tail between the legs and the hand stretched out begging from the hand that clutched. He got the grain of rice who reached it first, and over and over again the Japs reached it first. Jap patrols guarded the reapers in the paddies, not from the "misguided elements" but from the very hands reaping their own self-planted seedlings. No tithe was given to the enemy; instead, the enemy took all and allowed back into the farmers' hands less than a tithe to keep them alive until the next harvest, when again from their labors and their own land only enough for survival would be granted to them.

Jap ship after ship left Manila heavy-laden, low in the water and sluggish.

For two years the Manila-Tokyo run had removed by ship and plane all that could be looted from a helpless country: scrap iron, pianos, American-made shoes and materials, fine tableware, fine hardwoods from Philippine forests—and rice. Now, more then ever, the ships carried rice. The Japs claimed to be bringing rice into the country to feed the "poor Filipinos." The GID checked up. "Sir, twenty-one ships leave the piers in Manila. Twenty ships proceed to Tokyo. One ship turns around at Olongapo and returns to Manila and the Japs publicize the rice coming to Manila from Japan. Sir, the Japs are dirty crooks."

While, of necessity, the black market soared, the people starved. In the garrisons the enemy reveled, potbellied, obese, rough and mean in their beer mugs. Two sentries argued; one shot the other and was killed in turn by the garrison commander. The people looked on, pale and impassive.

In the camp, Marking said to his men seriously, over and over again, "Do not complain of the food that does not come. We are the fish, and the people are the water. If the water dries up, the fish will die. Do not demand more from the people than they can give. Do not take the rice from the mouths of their children. The hero who has not denied himself is no hero. When the bowel pain is bad, think of after the war and the happiness that will be ours then."

Soft-spoken Onofre died. Terribly debilitated by malaria and hunger, then purged with salts to clean a bilious stomach, Onofre was too ill for self-control. In the night he devoured a green mango, more acrid than green apples. The cramps caught him, and with a gasp he writhed silently among his fellows on the bamboo-slat floor of the barracks. Long before cockcrow, Onofre's comrades folded his arms gently over his chest and pulled up over his face the threadbare, filthy floursacking that was his only blanket. The hole was dug before the water-porridge breakfast, and without ceremony the gentle hands of those who had dug the grave laid him to rest.

"Don't let them see you crying," Marking told me.

"I'll cry if I want to! That boy was so patient under hardship, so respectful.... Yesterday, I told him he'd get well—"

"The green mango, on top of the purgative, on top of the fevers, on top of malaria, killed him. Don't cry!" There was urgency in his voice, not mere impatience.

There was no time for tears.

Later, I could be cold, matter-of-fact: "Now, the rest of you who are sick and have hard heads—how many of you want green mangoes? Speak up! You won't listen to advice! Who wants to commit suicide? It hangs in the trees overhead."

That night Lyd and I talked for a while, ending to find Marking with fever mounting. Soon he, who had purged himself for loginess, was definitely sick. I sponged him and made him take the quinine and aspirin. He lay hunched in his small *kubo*, his face flushed, his eyes blearily bright. His illness delayed the moving of the camp and endangered not only the fighters but himself. Move him out, have him carried? Already night. There were too many prisoners who might make a getaway, and the light drizzle would soak him; his lungs were weak, following pleurisy.

The hours dragged toward midnight, and his fever lessened. I fell into slumber. Lyd, too, slept, for the whole camp was either sick or worn with caring for the sick. Lyd had been making the rounds three times a day, and Lagundi was a big camp, even for one round a day. Of the four hundred or more armed men, half were sick with malaria or influenza or both; a hundred were new men undergoing training, and a hundred were able fighters fatigued almost to illness themselves by carrying all guard and camp details, helping their sick friends, and fighting their own discouragement. Just counting out the limited quinine tablets took hours out of Lyd's day. We congratulated ourselves on having the quinine at all. Having it, we poured it down the fighters' throats in double doses and gave advanced cases extra amounts to hide in their *bayongs*.

I woke before dawn and reached to feel Marking's forehead and take his pulse. Almost normal, skin moist. Lyd was awake. She did not speak, nor did I, lest we disturb Marking, but I knew that ever in her lonely corner, with only palm fronds walling her off from the morning air, she was thinking of Manuel, praying for him in his cell or undergoing torture from her vivid imagination, because the night hours were worst in the Fort. Whatever Manuel suffered, his wife suffered, and in her hours alone, she kept tryst with him. She suffered for him while I suffered for her.

We lay each alone, dearest of friends, wrapped each in her thoughts but, without speech, still in communion with the other. Sometimes we might reach out to clasp hands. Usually, even that was unnecessary.

As the morning broke, damp from the night's drizzle, Lyd and I rose, she to apportion the pills and such *carabao* milk as we had, I to study reports and answer correspondence. For a week there had been threat of a Jap attack. A few days before, Jap planes had flown low over both the Baras and Lagundi camps between which we shifted back and forth, seeking to stay near the towns, yet throw the enemy off the scent.

Marking sat up, bracing himself. He was weak, and his eyes looked watery.

"How do you feel?" I asked. "All right. Coffee." "You'd better lie down, take it easy today." "Coffee." "It's coming. Lie down." He lay down.

Cabalhin came tumbling down the little incline from his own quarters, his face red, tripping over his shoestrings but recovering balance.

"Sir! Japs! At the outpost! Shall we fight or retreat, sir?" He stooped to jerk at his laces, yanked the bows in double knots.

Slowly Marking sat up again, inched along the shelf to the edge, put his feet down, and felt with them for his boots. Slowly he reached up and took his gun belt from the tree peg.

"How many Japs?"

"Plenty, sir, with cavalry. I ordered the fighters forward into deployment. Terrain here no good, sir."

Marking's condition had to be ignored in the emergency; sick or well, none could decide on his feet faster than he.

"Assemble all sick and unarmed in headquarters. Divide the able fighters between yourself, Mapa, and me. Pull in behind, but cover as long as it is wise."

"Yes, sir!"

I hurriedly folded up the blanket, stuffed it in a *bayong*; buckled my own gun belt around me; laced my shoes, jumping holes; urged Lyd to hurry, whispering, "Lyd, he's *sick!* Fever again. Look at his eyes."

Calmly Marking was motioning men on. He swayed a little, bending to take his rifle. His ammunition belt was heavy. He stood with his feet apart. His lips were dry, peeling; he breathed with effort through his mouth.

"Yay!" he said, not seeing me behind him.

"Here." A real fear was in me.

"You and Lyd stay right behind me."

He started off without looking back, and I fell in immediately behind him as was our custom on the trail. Whatever happened, I was to be within arm's reach behind him, whether we were upright or crawling.

Lyd was stuffing something into a *bayong* on a fighter's back.

"Lyd," I said, "hurry up!" I couldn't wait for her—I couldn't leave her behind.

Marking was walking steadily enough.

We reached the assembled men, the sick and the unarmed. In a separate group, a hundred fighters were in line. The rest were with Cabalhin and Mapa, between us and the outpost. What was detaining the Japs? No firing yet. Were they forming for the charge? Or creeping through the underbrush? I looked around at the low rolling hills with their stretches of short grass and brush clumps. Rotten fighting ground for guerrillas, but good enough if the fighters had been in shape.

Marking turned. "Yay, you will stay with these." He pointed to the "protected" group, the sick and unarmed that would be between Marking's unit of fighters going out ahead of us and Mapa and Cabalhin and their fighters pulling in behind us. It was the first time we should be apart. I looked at him, probing his eyes. What was it? Why? He was sick. In the tightest of pinches, who would stick by him? The men he was motioning out were mostly new recruits or trained ones not yet "baptized" by bullets. Then I saw Bernie. Bernie would be with him.

"Bernie," said Marking.

"Yes, sir."

"Stay with Mammy and Lyd."

"Yes, sir."

"Yay, whatever happens—" He caught himself and turned to Bernie again. "Bernie, I trust you . . ."

"Yes, sir."

Marking stepped into the line moving in an easterly direction. At the river, where the trail mounted out of sight, he turned to lift his hand to me, to smile.

The day before, I had told Lyd I was uneasy. "So am I," she had said. "There's something in the air. I can feel it."

Marking was out of sight. When the line had moved by it was our turn, with the weaponless and unfit, to fall in and single-file quickly along.

Before falling in, I glanced down the line at the two Jap prisoners who had claimed to be escaped Koreans, telling a pitiful tale. To Narvadez I gave the order, "The minute firing begins, kill them."

He was carrying a leather bag full of Jap war notes used to buy corn and sweet potatoes from the *kaingin* folk and salt from the town.

We moved along, Bernie, Lyd, and I, and the rest of the line fell in, serpentining behind us. We heard the drone and the typical sputtering knock of Jap planes. Into the underbrush at the side of the trail Bernie and I motioned the line ahead and behind us. The planes would spot directions for the ground troops, and they would strafe. If we could keep the recruits from scattering, the sick from lagging, the prisoners from escaping—and silence in the brush . . . The planes were low. Then everything broke at once, including the line we were trying to hold together.

Not too near us were loud bursts—bombs, and a new kind of explosion. Mortars? Rifle fire! Mapa and Cabalhin were fighting! Strafing from the air, and a plane close over our own heads, so close that we could see the pilot peering over the cockpit's edge and hear the burst of strafing against our eardrums. More explosions, still not near us, yet not far away.

Part of our line ahead and behind came in sight again. We motioned those ahead to press on, pulled up those behind us with imperative overhand strokes so that the way would be cleared for Cabalhin and Mapa and their men, hard pressed back in the camp. More bombs, nearer.

Then, as Bernie and I came into a clearing, cautiously skirting the brush beside the trail, a volley burst in the direction we were taking indicated that Marking and the men with him had run into the Jap net ahead. We distinguished the pinging of Jap guns and the boom of our .30's. But we could not tell if the .25-caliber machine-gun fire was from the Japs or from the machine rifle Marking's bodyguards were carrying—captured by Cabalhin's men in a highway raid. Or was it both Marking and the Japs?

Bernie at a low run, edged up to a slope thick with brush, bending his hulk, zigzagging.

Crouched beside a bush, I watched him. He turned, motioned us to follow through. I turned to motion the line up after me, and found only Lyd. The line had backed up. Another urgent wave from Bernie, and Lyd and I zigzagged, stumbling up the slope bent over, catching at the weeds with our hands. A burst of snipers' fire to our right brought Bernie up to his full height as he caught me by the wrist, yelled to Lyd to follow, and ran up the slope and into a ravine. As he cleared the edge for the jump down, holes appeared by magic in the earth beside his leg. A grass blade flicked. I heard little sounds—not the whine of bullets but soft thuds. One arm behind me clutched for Lyd. She tumbled into the ravine, little more than a ditch, almost on top of me. Bernie staggered at a run, turning up the ravine, loosening his hand from my wrist to pull at boulders and roots, saying low and breathless, "Mammy, hold on to my belt. Don't let go! Keep calling Lyd." Lyd was there, her precious little *tanpipi* of woven reed bumping this way and that from the thong strung across her shoulder. In the *tanpipi* was her journal.

The ravine narrowed to nothing. We had to do one of two things: stay there, or move up the hillside under cover if we could find it.

"Mammy, keep your head down," said Bernie, breathless but matter-of-fact, "It isn't safe." I said nothing because I was biting down on my teeth.

One of the boy k.p.'s from the convoyed group came tumbling along behind us, then, sighting Lyd, ran upright instead of running in a stoop. Lyd grabbed him, pushed him down, snatched the white sailor's hat off his head. "Don't you wear that cap now," said Lyd.

"We can't go to the Old Man, I'm afraid," said Bernie, adding, "I think he's safe." By Marking's orders, he was in charge. "Wait here."

Lyd and the boy and I lay quiet at the upper end of the ravine. The bombs and strafing had stopped, but snipers' fire pinged everywhere. I tore a small top-secret notebook into bits, gouging holes in the ground to poke in the shuffled pieces, tamping the holes with my knuckles, then kicking loose earth over them. To Bernie, as he left, I handed the large leather case of important records to conceal in the underbrush.

"Put it where they can't possibly find it," I said. He nodded and crawled away, lifting and pushing it before him.

Lyd wanted to hide her *tanpipi*, but there was no crevice far enough away from the tracks we had left, the scuffled ground, the broken twigs.

Bernie came back. "This way," he said.

There was a lull in the firing. We crawled up through the *cogon*.

"Lyd," I said, "*keep down!*" She was crawling on hands and knees, and the *cogon* was too short to cover her. I wished vehemently for *cogon* one mile high. Then the slope fell away and we found ourselves under a small bush all by itself on a rise between two bushless hollows that rolled away into flat valleys.

Suddenly, from where we had been, and from where we were going, at right angles to the direction Marking had taken, snipers' fire pinged simultaneously. I lay on my stomach and Lyd on her back, as flat as we could get. Where was Bernie? We were too flat to see, but we could hear the whine after each ping, and far behind us, where Cabalhin and Mapa were, there was a new outburst of rifle fire.

"This way," came Bernie's voice, low but insistent. "Lyd, Mammy! This way!" Then we saw his good face crawling toward us, we started toward him and he turned and crawled the way he had come. Back his voice floated, "Keep flat, but hurry. Don't let yourself be seen. Try not to ripple the grass."

Around the edge of the second hollow, inching toward trees and underbrush, we crawled, and because it was downward, Lyd, on her hands and knees, was in difficulties.

"Lyd, *get down!* This way," I said urgently, looking back over my shoulder, flapping my hand at my thighs flat on the ground, one knee doubled up at right angles to lever me along as my crooked elbows, flattened and thrust forward, pulled me along.

Lyd looked at me uncertainly. She was still on all fours. "I'll get dirty," she whispered, and I gritted my teeth, cursing under my breath and wanting to kick my dear friend.

Then there was a ping and a whine, and Lyd's head and chest ducked down with her rump still high. Along came another ping and whine as close over her tail as the first had been over her head. Down went her stomach and thighs.

"What do I do now?" she asked. She was down—that much she had learned the hard way, but she didn't know how to move. She pulled with her elbows. Without knee leverage, she made two inches. She was immobilized.

I showed her with my knee, shoving along, keeping flat. She got the idea and came shoving along. That difficulty solved, with Bernie's voice insistently guiding the way, I tried to make time over the twenty-five or thirty feet to a dry creek separating the *cogon* from the concealing trees.

I rolled into the creek, got to my feet, stumbled after Bernie. "Where's Lyd?"

"Here." I motioned behind me. But when I looked she wasn't there. Then Lyd came into the creek bed. No longer was she immaculate.

"Where were you? Ye gods, Lyd!"

"I went back."

"What *for?*"

"I lost Patena, but I found it." She patted the little holster strapped to her leg.

Patena was the first pistol I had worn in the outfit—the snub-nosed .32-caliber Colt that Marking had taken early in the occupation when nine Sakdals lay in ambush for him—and every fighter knew it on sight. It was a noisy little gun with a bark worse than its bite, and now I wore Sakai.

"Well," I said, "your life's worth more than your gun."

We crawled into the gloom of a wedge-shaped patch of trees. The boy k.p. huddled with us, and another, finding our trail in the grass, came plunging in. We looked hard at him, motioned him to keep very quiet; he was a Manila recruit and was scared out of his wits. He had nearly scared us out of ours.

"Wait here," said Bernie.

I lay on my back. Lyd lay on her stomach. She pointed to a dewdrop hanging from a leaf.

"Look! It has prisms."

I was in no mood for looking at dewdrops. My heart was banging in my chest, and there were needle pains through it. I could smell the damp earth and the secret, lonely odor of decaying leaves. The odor was comforting.

The boy stirred. Simultaneously we hissed him quiet. The Manila recruit shifted his leg and broke a twig as loud as a bullet to us. We frowned at him and shushed again.

Bernie was taking longer than usual.

"Lyd, do you think anything has happened to Bernie?" I asked.

Lyd hesitated, and I added, "We can go on. I know general directions around here. But we're both shortsighted—we'd walk right into the

Japs." It was the first time I ever had been without bodyguards or guides. We waited, fearing for Bernie, trying to decide what to do next.

Then from Marking's direction came the high notes of a bugle. The pounding hoofs of horses swept down the slope toward the rolling valley into which the second hollow led, past our pie-shaped hiding place. We heard the galloping and the rattling of loose rocks and the swish of the *cogon*, and then they were gone. We listened, but they were gone.

"What's that?" whispered Lyd. "What?" I whispered back. And then I knew that, being very near me, she could hear the pounding of my heart, and that it was not unlike the hoofs.

"That's me," I said. We smiled a little.

The smiles vanished as we heard the high, nasal calls of Jap troops to Jap troops closing in behind the cavalry. They shouted back and forth. We knew no Japanese. The voices came nearer.

Combing the grass, I thought. A real encirclement. Slowly, careful not to brush a twig or snap it, I drew Sakai from the holster. Lyd drew Patena. We motioned the boy and the Manila recruit not to move under any circumstances.

Footsteps came down the slope. Two Japs were talking, swishing the grass as they came. Other Japs called back and forth. Not thirty feet from us, out in the *cogon*, the Japs talked, apparently standing guard, while others combed. Then farther down, rocks rattled in the dry creek bed that ran up into our bit of trees a yard from where we lay. The footsteps came nearer, then stopped. As carefully and noiselessly as I could, I cocked Sakai.

I aimed it, rising on my elbow, at the only possible opening through which they would come, then remembered with a cold feeling in the small of my back that it had jammed after the first shot when I used it before. I should be caught after shooting once, and all the tiny bits of paper buried in the ground were still in my head and could be tortured out of me—for who knows whether he has the greatness to endure the slow, excruciating, repeated deaths? I feared capture. Quick, the decision. I turned to Lyd, for she was tougher than I and might be able to alibi her way out of it. There was a chance for her. "Lyd," I said, "tell them you were a prisoner. Tell them I had you arrested."

Lyd was looking at me. I held Sakai to my temple.

The footsteps sounded again.

"Wait," said Lyd.

The footsteps faded away.

I relaxed weakly on the ground, rested Sakai on my stomach.

Then we heard a shout about three hundred yards away. "*Preso po ako!*" [I am a prisoner!] And there was a shouting and a running of many feet and voices; then nearer, to the left instead of the right, another scream, high-pitched, then dropping to a wail and finally a sobbing rattle.

"Bayoneting, Lyd," I whispered. "That's the death scream."

Somewhere in that moment one of our fighters had died, probably a sick one, deafened by quinine, hiding in the grass and stumbled over in the combing by the Jap infantry, arms' length apart. The call of the other, declaring himself a prisoner escaped from us, had drawn the Japs combing behind us down through the *cogon* on each side of the forest wedge in which the four of us lay, and thus we were cut out of the encirclement in their haste to capture the one who had called to them.

Farther and farther away went the voices and the occasional shots. Still we lay quiet.

For four hours, the Japs had bombed and strafed, shelled and mortared and sniped, combed the grass and bayoneted. Against four hundred of us plus a score of prisoners and the weaponless, they had pitted eighteen hundred troops, a cavalry detachment, six planes, three mountain guns and, near the highway, a tank. They had encircled an area two miles long and half a mile wide, and closed in while the planes bombed and strafed and the mortars burst within an area growing smaller and smaller as they drew the net tight. They were in condition and heavily equipped; we were not.

We tensed as heavy footsteps came down the slope and into the creek bed the way we had first come. "Mammy, I'm so thirsty!"

"Bernie, we thought you'd been caught or shot!" He smiled a little; his good face was shining with sweat, and the dirt lined his neck.

"You went out the other way," said Lyd. "How'd you come back this way?"

"Long story." Bernie smiled again as he rested. He spread his fingers wide. "You know what? I had to lie in *cogon* only that thick and only about that high." His other hand measured *cogon* about eight inches high. "I was out in the open on that other side, trying to find a way out for us. And then they came down the slope, side by side in a line."

Lyd and I looked at each other. They were the ones. We had heard them.

"They were searching the bushes and the grass, poking their bayonets into the brush."

Again we looked at each other; we should not soon forget that scream.

"I flattened in the grass—"

"How did it hide you, Bernie?" I asked. "You're so big—"

"The Jap nearest me at the end of the line—They veered away, hearing all that shouting over there, and the Jap nearest me had his helmet jammed down over his ears when he came through the trees, and he had both arms up trying to get the helmet up from his eyes, and his elbows kept him from seeing me."

"You look tired," said Lyd.

Bernie smiled wryly. "I am. Let's go."

We went up through the trees to the plateau on the northeast. Bernie had found Pabling's kid brother, who had found another Manila boy. We had to call him down from the tree into which he had climbed. His face was pale as parchment. I watched Lyd digging into a *bayong* the Manila boy was carrying. She found her precious soap and flourished it at me.

We moved cautiously along, circling back to give the old camp a wide detour. There was smoke in the sky. The Japs had set fire to our barracks, *kubos*, shelters of saplings and folded coconut fronds.

Over and over again we rested, trying to keep our bearings and always keeping to the brush. Bernie drank thirstily from every stream. All of us were exhausted, even the sturdy Lyd.

We found a trail that seemed far enough back to be safe and climbed it to a pass where we could look down on the towns and get our bearings. No breakfast. No lunch. By four in the afternoon, we were beginning to feel faint. I who had general directions right had all specific directions wrong.

"This is the trail to Tanay, I think. Anyway, we're somewhere between Tanay and Baras . . ." To myself: "We're still in Rizal province. I'd rather be in Borneo."

Up and down the trails and across fields we went, Bernie scouting all the way. We crept by a farm hut from which a wisp of smoke curled up—Japs usually lay in wait all over the countryside, watching for the "scattered" like ourselves to come knocking at the door for food or water. We drank from springs and rivulets and dubiously but helplessly from mudholes; the taste of *carabao* was strong but it quenched thirst for a while.

At nightfall we found an empty hut, and in it a half-ripe jack fruit. No farmer, no wife, no kids. The raid on our camp had emptied the countryside, and the more we suspected the farm hut we had passed from which the smoke wisped up. The hut we chose stood alone in a newly plowed field far enough from trail and forest for us to see what was coming in the moonlight and make a retreat.

"It's a shame to take their jack fruit," I said, indicating that, shame or no shame, we had to eat.

"We'll leave money in the pot," said Bernie.

"Look at that moonlight!" said Lyd.

"Wait till you see it on the Kaliwa," I said.

Lyd blew at the coals, and soon the jack fruit, peeled and diced, was boiling and bubbling and bumping around the pot, tipped to cook askew because it was cracked. The aroma taunted our faintness. Into a chipped bowl and a coconut shell, she apportioned the stewed fruit; she and I dipped from one, Bernie from the other, and the rest from the clay pot. We slurped a little, with low laughter, and lounged about the hut in the contentment of those who live the moment because the hours are numbered.

A shot rang out from the direction of the trees.

Across the rough field we ran, away from the trees, away from the trail, into the underbrush to flatten out in the shadows and wait.

Nothing happened. An hour went by. Two hours. Bernie scouted the vicinity and returned. "Mammy, we had better not rest in the hut. And we had better not move around in the night. I have found a place, but it is very near the trail, and we must be quiet."

We moved through the brush, walking carefully, speaking only in undertones. Down into a dry ditch under fallen logs Bernie led us, and there we laid ourselves to rest, picking away the dead branches and sharp rocks, brushing the pebbles out from under our backs. Lyd had a towel. We spread it against the dampness of the ground, where the sun had not shone and spring water kept the earth moist. We were cold, without blankets. It was restless sleep, but we slept.

Before dawn, we were up. Again Bernie scouted the way. One by one, swiftly, we crossed the main trail and took again to the underbrush. Through thicket after thicket we pushed until we heard voices. Silently, we moved nearer.

"Baras, Mammy!" said Bernie.

Then we were still in the vicinity of the town which had fed the camp the Japs had tried to attack.

"That shot last night must have been a bullet exploding in the fire when the grass and brush caught from the burning barracks," said Bernie. "Mammy, stay here—"

"Don't go, Bernie! That's exactly what the Japs are waiting for. They always watch the towns!"

"I'll be careful."

"Send one of the boys—"

"No, Mammy. What if he was caught and tortured and brought the Japs here? The Old Man gave me my orders."

I subsided. Lyd and I were Bernie's trust. He was responsible for us. "Just be careful," I said, my heart tight with fear for him, and fear for us too.

"I'll go," said Lyd.

Bernie and I turned on her, and *she* subsided.

"I'll bring back something to eat," Bernie said to both of us. "Fine," said Lyd. "I could eat; I really could eat."

An hour passed. Then a rustling in the underbrush, and Bernie's voice, then his face as he bent to stoop through the thicket. "Mammy, Japs. Plenty of them." He handed over a *bayong* of popcorn balls cut in rectangles. "Arribas came out from the town to meet me when I sent someone to him. He thinks the Old Man is in Sampaloc. That was where Cabalhin went, he said."

"Then they're all right?" I pressed.

Doubtfully: "I think so, Mammy."

We ate. "I know where Tanay is," I said, "and Sampaloc is up in the hills between Tanay and Pililla. We could cut across country."

"We'd better get out of here," said Bernie.

We sighted a mountain I thought was just outside Tanay. All that day we walked, cutting across fields only when we had to, never taking the main trails, and being cautious on the footpaths. We lost the way. We found it again. With a guide, we could have made it in two hours. We climbed for another look at the countryside, sighting the same mountain from a different angle, and realized we were headed back the way we had come.

Late in the evening, Bernie risked approaching an occupied hut and discovered there a man who had fought in Bataan, who had been held prisoner of war and finally released. "Please," said the man, "my house is yours. Already, the womenfolk are cooking for you. Pabling always rests his men at my house. The Old Man passed here yesterday. He asked for you. He was not well, I think."

Sore of foot, picking stickers out of our palms and burrs from our hair, Lyd and I dragged into the firelit farm kitchen, sat down on a bench. An hour's haven.

The women of the house were eager to make us welcome, to give us rest. "Will you have hard rice or porridge?" one asked, and another, "We will kill our chicken." Up in the loft, another was spreading a mat and taking from the family mat rolls their own pillows.

"Imagine, Lyd, a pillow!" The hot porridge revived us. "You look tired," said Lyd. "Don't brag. Look at you." "Pabling was here yesterday. He was with Marking. When they said Marking passed, I think he did. They described his cough. He was asking if anybody had been here—women."

"A fine to-do," I said. We climbed to the loft and napped.

Lucio came, having heard by grapevine where we were. "The Old Man has been very sick. We have the doctors. We have the medicines. Last night, he was delirious, commanding the fighters and calling for you."

"Where is he?" I asked.

"We will go there now."

"Where?"

Lucio looked around. "These are good people, but it is better not to say where while the Old Man is weak. There are Japs going into the mountains every day, looking for him. *Basta* [Hurry], I will take you there."

"How about these others?" I asked, indicating the boys.

"Leave them here. You can decide when you see the Old Man."

Early in the morning Lyd and I followed him down the little footpath and onto the main trail to Tanay.

"Lucio," I said, "this is the main trail! And we're going *toward* the town."

"It's all right, ma'am. My men are guarding down below. They will warn us."

"But where is Marking?"

"In a safe place, ma'am. In the last place they will expect to find him. We take good care. Nobody knows."

My misgivings mounted as we came nearer and nearer the town. Through the graceful bamboos, I glimpsed the lake and the rice paddies and the highway. "Lucio, not here! In fifteen minutes, they could get him."

"Nobody knows, ma'am. It is where I hid during the zoning. It is the place of my father-in-law. He is a good old man."

I saw fires under the bamboo trees and fighters squatting, lying in the shade, carrying water. "Get back into the brush," I said. The fighters nearest me rose, and the one at whom I looked saluted. "Get your fires back behind something," I said. "Don't pass in the open. You can be seen from the highway." The shrew was back, scolding, nagging.

Lyd and I walked on to the farmhouse, screened by bamboos but in full sight from both Tanay and the highway. Up and down the highway Jap trucks roared, moving troops from town to town and dumping them at the trails which they climbed into the foothills in search of the guerrillas.

Bodyguards greeted me. "Ma'am, we took the best care of him."

Gil Mata said, "I brought him the news that Lucio had found you and he said, '*Sinabi mo ba masakit ako?*' [Did you tell her I am sick?]" He mimicked Marking's querulous, child-demanding-attention tone. "Ma'am, we bathed down his fever. We gave him enema. We changed his clothes to pajamas brought from the town. We cooked his porridge. And all he says is, 'Did you tell her I am sick?' Ma'am, it is *lambing, masyado naman ang matanda!*" [he's being affectionate and wants attention. The old man is too much!]

I laughed.

From the hut came Marking's voice: "Yay! Yay, you come now." He sat crosslegged on the bamboo-slat bed in pajamas, his binoculars in his hand. "Look!" he said. "They go up and down. They look for me, and they never find me. They are harassed." He laughed with small-boy mischief all over his homely face.

"Who is harassed? *Who* did you say?"

After a moment he grudgingly admitted, "We also," then took back half the admission: "A little bit."

"Marking, this is no place to be. In half an hour you could be in their hands."

"Not alive," he said, his eye on his Springfield.

"Why court death and never fight again?" I asked.

"Cabalhin is coming. I will give him most of these fighters and keep just the bodyguards. Then we can be very quiet here."

"How did Cabalhin and Mapa make out?" I asked.

"They were cut off, but broke through the south to draw the Japs that way."

Then he remembered something, fished around on the *papag*, and reached under the pillow. "Here's your jacket, darling."

I reached for the woolen shirt with the tails cut off and hemmed into a snug waistband.

"Where'd you get this?"

"I followed the Japs back in, to find you."

"Of all the stupid, reckless things!"
"I found a whole *bayong* of records, too. Good that I found them."
"Where?"
"Right on a small trail."
"Who in the world dropped them? That Manila boy! Lyd, do you remember who was carrying that *bayong* of records?"

She answered from beside the fire, where she was stirring tomatoes into a sauce, "He's gone back to Manila. Or he's still out there in the bushes."

"How many did we lose?" I asked Marking.

"The Home Guards say twelve were captured and two bayoneted near the headquarters. Maybe more. I thought they got you, too. I came here to see which garrison you were in."

"What for?"

"Then we would attack the garrison."

"How about the townspeople? You know that fighting in the town is against the policy of the organization."

"You make the policies, not me," said Marking. "Emergency is emergency."

Lyd was tasting the sauce.

"Lydia is bery, bery dirty," he said placidly. "My little sister."

She returned the compliment, "*Kuya*, my big brother."

Cabalhin checked in, his bandy legs rolling him along. "I will take the men now, sir, so your place will be less conspicuous." He grinned, and his cat-eyes closed as his curving mouth pushed his cheeks up. "Hi, Lyd! How do you like being a real guerrilla?"

"Eat," said Lyd.

"How can I eat when you are finishing it?" retorted Cabalhin. "How can I cook it if I don't taste it?"

"But you taste *all* of it."

Marking lay back. Fever again. I felt dizzy and, in alarm, took my own pulse.

"Move over," I said. "I'm going to be sick, too."

He reached over, felt my cheek, took my pulse. "Lucio, bring Dr. Artiaga!" He pulled me close beside him, threw the blanket over us. "We'll be sick together."

Lyd said, "Here, you two. Drink this soup—and no backtalk." For a moment, danger was forgotten.

CHAPTER 21

When our first fevers abated, Lucio moved the group of sixteen from his father-in-law's farmhouse some ten minutes' walk up in the hills behind it to a tiny *kubo* in a park-like mango grove. Morning and afternoon, Jap patrols climbed trails to the left and right of us, searching the farther hills. We kept very quiet, talking only in muted tones lest our voices carry.

More fevers came. Only the men needed to bring our food were allowed by Lucio to come. Marking relapsed. Lyd and I nursed him. I relapsed. She and Marking nursed me. Bernie burned with fever, although he made no complaint. Jock nursed him while Lyd brewed the broth and comforted him. Gil was sponged down to quiet his delirium, Lyd bathing him every two hours. She disliked him because he was a backbiter, but he was a fighter, too, and she a patriot; she was kinder to him because of her dislike.

Sote brooded over the machine rifle. Sammy, once again a prisoner for troublemaking, cooked. He resented Lyd's instructions, but out of his resentment friendship was born, for she had her own methods of disciplining and winning. Agaban smiled his dimpled smile and obediently went after water. Regalado was silent but ever alert. Jock pulled himself through his own sickness, not wanting Bernie to be bothered. Hour after hour, day after day, silence and sickness. And danger, which once more could not be forgotten!

Among Lucio's men bringing the small comforts of medicine, food, and an occasional magazine rolled up and tucked into the market bayong as an afterthought, was Agaton Sacramento, a Bataan boy. He and Peping Bautista, who had bullet, saber, and bayonet scars all over him, took turns in bringing loads from the town, side-stepping the Jap patrols.

Then came a runner: "Sir, Agaton caught!"

"The quiet boy here this morning?" asked Marking. "How?"

"Ledesma of the PC, sir. They arrested Agaton in the town when he returned from bringing the medicine. Sir, Colonel Lucio says you will move right away! It is not safe here. If Agaton cannot stand the torture—"

"Are they torturing him?"

"I think so, sir."

Lyd told me that Agaton had remarked on his last trip, "I feel that something is going to happen to me. I'm not afraid. I just know."

"We will wait," said Marking. But soon he decided to move back to the farmhouse among the bamboos.

He was weaker than I, and reeled on the footpath. Bernie said to Lyd, "I pity them." He himself was weak, and even she had run a temperature through two days although she stayed stubbornly on her feet.

Around the farmhouse, the bodyguards were vigilant all day, all night.

Before dawn, there was a burst of rifle fire from the direction of Baras, where Agaton had been taken. I sat bolt upright, taut and trembling. We waited, listening.

At dawn, Lucio came: "Sir, we must move."

"How is Agaton?" we asked.

"We do not know, sir, but we must go some other place. It is said that the rifle fire is only the excuse of the PC to cover the escape of Agaton, but he has not come back. Sir, I will take you to another place, somewhat away from here."

"Can you walk?" Marking asked me.

"Far enough," I said, feeling again in flight. "Can you walk?"

He refused to be carried, and stumbled on the trail, but we moved. Not far. Less than a kilometer away, very near the trail junction at Bocal for Tanay. Agaton had not come to us there. He might not know the place. If we kept out of sight and kept silent, we still had a chance.

There, whenever Lucio or Peping or Nuter came in, we asked news of Agaton. Reports conflicted. He was dead; he had escaped; he had surrendered; he was being tortured; he was leading the Japs. Always, Peping of the bullet, saber, and bayonet scars bit his lip, his eyes blank, his thoughts with the "other Bataan boy."

We waited, knowing the boy would come through if he could. In the meantime, the *kubo* near the spring was safest, for it was still near the towns while the Japs searched the farther foothills and mountains. If we could get but a short rest, we could take the offensive again when the Japs were fewer in number.

While we hesitated, we opened our eyes on June 22, 1944, to another dawn and another encirclement.

As the rice bubbled in the clay pot, many murmuring voices came to our ears. Farmers? Passers-by? Big Boy Bernie went to scout. In a few minutes he returned.

"Sir, Japs. *Fifty yards*, not more. Couldn't see all of them. They're deployed."

In the meantime Marking had stepped into the bushes for his own reasons and had sighted Japs crouching in the creek bed to the left—twenty-five yards away.

Bernie's Japs were behind us, Marking's to one side.

Hasty packing in absolute silence. Water on the fire. We left the pot with its half-cooked rice. Care in picking up the canteen, in folding and packing the meat can. We waited for orders. Soon Marking led us down the little path and pulled us into a thick tangle of bamboo and brush where we bedded down. When in doubt, don't. We were in doubt what the Japs intended to do, and so we did nothing but sink into the undergrowth, lying flat and quiet, smothering any cough or sneeze in a folded coat.

Lucio scouted back to the *kubo*. Over the wet coals, the rice had boiled down and steamed nicely. He brought it with him. "Miracle," he said. There were raw eggs and sugar lumps. We ate, urging each other with signs to take more, sharing what might be our last meal.

Then hell broke loose.

To the right, not more than another twenty-five yards above us, two pistol shots rang out. We looked at one another. That meant Japs on three sides—behind, to the left and to the right, with only bushes between them and us and not half enough bushes. One more side, and we were in for hand-to-hand fighting. The Japs never operated two by two; they maneuvered in droves. Whatever their number, there were too many for our small force and debilitated condition.

Immediately on the heels of the pistol shots, the "fourth front" became evident as a trench mortar bammed on the slope in front of us. Agaban leaped up, but Marking drew his .45 and waved him flat. Bernie and Marking looked at each other. Marking reached around to my shoulder blade and pressed me flat again as I rolled over on my stomach.

Encircled. Japs on both sides and behind us—fireworks up front. Another mortar. The slope shook. Nearer. Again Marking's imperative gesture. More mortars, in rapid succession. Rifle fire in front, behind, to the left. Voices, loud, to the left.

More mortars, in rapid succession—seven, eight, nine. Distant spitting of rifles out in front from the direction of the mortars. Then a silence worse than the noise.

During the next three hours, we momentarily expected to receive a charge from all sides, but the Japs were too close for us to crawl through without drawing all of them on us. With half of our men, including Marking, too weak to retreat, we lay in the thicket trying to interpret the Japs' plan of action.

Onésimo Soriano, certified public accountant, was lost in thought. He looked grimly handsome without his white, friendly smile. He and Lyd were the intellectuals of the group. I saw them smile at each other understandingly: the only thing for them to do was to make the most of an experience, to drink the cup to the dregs. Sammy had no intellectual activity to disturb him. With arms linked around his drawn-up legs, he fell asleep and rolled over with a snort that was quickly muffled by another's hand. At each who made the smallest noise I glowered, helping Marking.

Marking slept a little. Lyd slept. Jock dropped off, opened his mouth, and let forth a rolling grunt. Bernie crawled over and gave his leg a yank, at which he woke with two more grunts and a snort. We prayed that the Japs, whose voices we could hear now and then on the breeze, would take the sounds for a wild pig, then prayed they wouldn't.

We knew we were encircled. We knew the distances and directions.

At eleven o'clock, a bugle sounded. Less than three weeks before, a bugle had brought the cavalry charge. We braced for the worst.

Marking had been awake with his eyes closed. He rolled over, passed his eye—keen, quick—over the men available. Sometimes I could read his mind, I knew him so well.

All of us remembered Agaton. He must have broken. Now we were doomed, too: end of the trail; the last fight. There was no rancor against Agaton. Torture is torture. Days had passed since his capture. He had given us at least a head start.

We waited, tense, alert, ears pricked, and heard a few more rifle shots. Movement was sensed, rather than heard. Nothing else. By one o'clock, the birds were singing again.

Lucio, Marking, Bernie scouted in different directions; then Marking pulled the rest of us up to the right where the voices had been. There, all along the trail, were their hobnail tracks, empty cigarette boxes of thin cardboard, and flattened grass. We moved across the trail into the woods, Marking weaving as he walked.

Late in the afternoon, we clambered down a cliff by descending a giant tree, clinging, swinging, stepping from branch to branch, to a foothold in the bank, to another branch, and so down to the dam. It wasn't dangerous—farmers walked up and down the short cut as if it weren't a tree at all—but it scared me. I had to be helped. Sometimes in a pinch, I could be brave, probably because things moved so fast there was little time for fright, but the little things could make me quail. The tree was one of them.

We rested on the dam, at last, the clear green waters of the reservoir cooling our eyes.

"What were you going to do back there?" I asked Marking.

"Put the Jap machine rifle and the two Brownings back to back about fifteen feet apart, close up to the line. Then steady firing while I passed the rest of you through and pulled the machine rifle and the Brownings in behind us. Why?"

I replied, closer to him than I had ever been, "That's what I thought you had in mind."

Below Sampaloc, with the faithful Lucio and Igi grubbing for our food, we came to rest in a jungle hollow in which we built one *kubo* with three shelves to accommodate us all.

Then we heard what we had escaped.

"Sir," said Lucio, "there were almost seven hundred against the seventeen of us. They were Japs and PC both. They caught that boy, Sabu—the one who was sick, remember?—and they are torturing him. Sir, I will send rice tonight. I could not get it yet because it is impossible to enter the town. The Japs struck the mayor with the butt of the rifle and then kicked him on the ground. But there will be food tonight."

Because we could not move, and because we had survived one more danger, somehow we relaxed. We found humor and play again, the saving graces of the guerrilla.

CHAPTER 22

Lucio came in a few days later.

"Sir, it is getting worse in the towns. More and more Japs. The people say that some of them are coming backwards—that they are not from Japan but from New Guinea. They are very cruel. Sir, it is dangerous for the towns and dangerous for you here. Every day, patrols. And at night, too. We cannot get food. The Japs watch everywhere. Sir, farther back in the mountain *kaingins*—we can get *palay* there . . ."

"Try again here," said Marking, thinking of our physical condition. Obediently, filled with foreboding, Lucio left.

The hours dragged. Somehow, he kept sending up food, good food, and all of us were perking up, gaining weight, losing the gaunt, pale look. But close quarters and the inactivity were grueling. Lyd and I reviewed reports, discussed policies and reached new solutions to old problems. Marking kept check on the guards, with Bernie as his right-hand man. Sammy cooked and cooked and cooked.

Lyd kept asking me questions, necessary questions for understanding what we had done and the Japs had done before she arrived from Manila. I tried to tell her.

"How much do the people understand?" I echoed her one day.

"Well, after a couple of zonings they're too punch-drunk to do anything but kiss the rifle butt. And then this Neighborhood Association thing and all the Jap-sponsored organizations—they're all part of a system of oppression perfected in China, you know." And I meandered on while Lyd made notes in her journal.

After the Japs had zoned the towns, their propaganda began to drip into the people's poor, beaten brains. Lyd knew more about that than I, but not from the fighters' viewpoint. So I told her how oftener and oftener the people began to parrot the Japs, "It's the fault of the guerrillas. It's the fault of the guerrillas!" It was like self-hypnotism. The people began to believe that the misery of the whole world was caused by the heroic men still trying to defend their country. The bamboo army was born. The Japs gave them iron-tipped pikes, some with barbs, and instructed them to use these crude weapons on all anti-Jap elements.

Up in the hills the fighters were trying not to surrender.

There was hunger, sickness. The rains poured and the rivers rose and fell. There were skin diseases and great, bubbling, gaping ulcers. Silence. Loneliness that reached to the stars. Bickering, backbiting, quick suspicion, blind rage, hate. A yearning for home that wrenched the heart from the breast. Month after month, grubbing for sweet potatoes from the mountain clearings that were begrudged by the ignorant mountain folk, who sometimes cheated and tricked. An ear of corn was gold. Rattan core and roots from the forest, and maybe a little salt made a meal. The thinnest of gruel, cold in the bitter winds high in the mountains, cold before it could be eaten, kept some of them alive. Days of no food. Hours of no speech.

Unable to endure it, some fighters crept down to the towns—and were speared. A starving, lost population, no less miserable than the men in the hills, raised pikes against their own starved, lost defenders, and the Japs, obese on the hunger of the country, gave a handful of rice per guerrilla head. The very rice they gave to the people had been taken from the people, a handful for every truckload taken, a handful to buy away from them their own blood and their last pitiful hope. It was madness that would destroy us before we could save them.

Diminutive Cabalhin, never faint of heart, strode into Tanay town with his fighters: "Lay down your arms!"

The spears stayed up, matchsticks against rifles, and a Jap bootlicker ran to ring the bell calling the Japs from the garrison.

"Fire!"

Three dropped. Others ran.

The Jap-controlled Philippine Constabulary assembled in the street, leaving their rifles upstairs in their barracks.

"Up and bring those rifles down!"

Cabalhin's men brought seventeen rifles down. Keeping their own rifles at port-arms, they slung the new rifles on their shoulders.

"Get the mayor," he ordered.

They hunted down the collaborating mayor and left him in a pool of his own blood.

"*Mabuhay!*" [Welcome!] rang across the plaza from a dark window. "Long live the guerrillas! Long live Cabalhin! Long live Marking!"

To the PC, Cabalhin addressed a question, "Who wants to go along?" Two fell in with his men, but the rest explained, "Our families, sir—they will be held hostage." "Then stick it out, and good luck!"

On his knees in the street beside the dying and the dead, getting bloodstains on his white frock, was my Irish friend Father Cogan of the

Tanay parish. He wrote, "This is not my war, but may I speak? Mercy on these you kill! Compassion! Pity!" I wrote back, "This is every Christian's war, and the Irish aren't out of it. If they are, shame on the fighting Irish for it! Christ was a fighter, and he went forth against the Roman legions, and they called him a troublemaker. Do you lay down the cross *He* carried? Look beyond your convent walls! Stand up and fight, Father! This is a Crusade!" Father Cogan wrote again, long after, "I have seen and I have understood. God keep you safe."

Lucio came in, bringing rice and fish. "Sir, Father Cogan is very angry," he told Marking.

Lyd and I pricked our ears.

"Why?" asked Marking, pondering three pawns in a game of chess.

"Because of the Lagundi and Bocal raids, sir. He is trying to find out if it was anybody in his parish who betrayed us. He should not be asking, sir. It is dangerous for him. But he—he is very angry; his eyes are hot like fire. He is with Ildefonso Reyes, of-the-*Herald*-before, and both of them are trying to find out and tell us, sir."

Marking smiled across at Lyd and me. "You talk too much."

Lyd's journal grew thicker as the days passed, and much of it she shared with me, enriching my own new realizations.

Lucio left and came and left again. One day: "Sir, it is impossible. I cannot get more food. The towns are so packed with Japs that the people are having to find other houses. Everywhere Japs, Japs, Japs." The next day, we ate boiled green bananas.

Oftener and oftener the Japs passed the two trails in the V of which we huddled in our hollow; hollows are no good for those encircled. The Japs began to step off the trail. Each day, their patrols came closer to our hiding place.

"Pack up," said Marking.

We made *bayongs* and bundles tight.

"We must cross the trail," said Igi. "The big trail, sir."

"We will cross it then."

"Shall we start, sir?" asked Igi.

"Go ahead," said Marking, and the line began to file out. Marking, I, and then Lyd stepped in halfway along.

We had stayed in one spot too long. In a drawn out line, about thirty of us puffed on the climb out of the hollow, and our knees trembled in descending the mountain. The weight we had gained was the false fat of convalescence and brought no stamina, but we plodded obstinately along.

Marking was alert, pausing on the rises to scan the country, urging on the head of the line, peremptorily beckoning the laggards to catch up. It was afternoon. We were making time against nightfall. Bernie was heavily burdened. Onésimo, frail for a man, was carrying far more than he should. The fighters were loaded down with both *bayongs* and equipment, bringing their rifles at trail-arms, one or two at port-arms. Marking kept Sote and the machine rifle directly in front of him for instantaneous use.

No stamina. The line pulled far behind. Marking waited for them to catch up, then lost the way himself. Floro and Vásquez checked back for him. We pushed on.

We came to the big trail, crossed it hurriedly, stepped over a barbed-wire fence to catch up with the front end of the line at a farmhouse.

"Sir, the woman says the Japs were here only twenty minutes ago. The Japs took her chickens."

Lyd and I looked at the bleak, awful poverty of the scrawny mother in a faded, ragged dress with a thin baby in her arms and another clinging to her skirt. She should have fed the chickens to her kids.

Bernie, who had fallen behind to help Gil, almost stubbornly dragging, hurried across the trail.

Marking bellowed at him and the others behind him, "Damn it! Can't you keep up? The Japs were here only a while ago and you can't even stay together to protect yourselves! The hell with it! I'll leave you to take care of yourselves!"

Bernie broke into a run: "Sir, there's a Jap sentinel *down the trail* at the mango tree!"

I sat down on a half-chipped log. If firing started, I should have my neck pulled in that far. "Lyd, *sit down!*"

"Are you sure?" asked Marking. "Where are the others? Hell! Hell! *Hell!*"

As his voice ceased, from *up the trail* came the sound of Jap voices nasally chanting Jap music.

"This way, sir," said Lucio.

"That way," said the woman, trembling, clasping the child that began to whimper.

We pulled through the bushes up a creek, leaving no telltale tracks behind, and went farther into the brush. We had passed between a Jap camp and its outpost guard.

Voices came to us. A child was singing. A hen cackled. We smothered our own laughter. In whatever house was on the other side of the bushes, everything was so normal the Japs could come and go and know nothing. Our only fear was the frightened woman behind us with the whimpering child. Would she tell, or give us away just by her looks?

Igi went ahead to scout, and returned to pull us on. From the end of the line came word that the Japs were approaching. We pushed through as swiftly and silently as possible, treading on one another's heels, each pressing the back in front of him, making way for the end of the line. As darkness drew near, there was a short rest to let night cover a clearing we had to cross. Tenderly, Onésimo helped Lyd, whose shoes were coming apart. With string, then with vines, he tried to tie the soles to the uppers. Bernie comforted me, "Mammy, tired?" A gentle word, a helping hand—how truly precious they are!

We filed into the clearing lit vaguely by the moon. "Yay," said Marking, "there is cool, sweet water here. Drink, darling." Through the night we climbed.

It was Lyd's first forced march, but she trudged along without complaint. More notes for the journal were forming in her head. I whispered to her, "Don't forget the fallen moonlight. Those luminous patches are just dead leaves and logs and twigs covered with fungi. Beautiful, aren't they?" The guides fastened some of the luminous leaves to their packs to point the way they were taking. In the pitch-dark of the forest, we picked our way, groping after the luminous leaves.

On a slippery log lying at a sharp slope across a ravine we had to step carefully, holding to each other. Marking slipped, fell heavily, but slid off to drop catlike in the thick weeds below. "Are you hurt?" I asked. "No." But the fall had knocked the wind out of him. He pulled himself up the steep bank, and we groped along a clearing, bumping into stumps, turning our ankles.

Then, ahead, a hut in a cornfield and the glow of firelight gilding the doorway and eaves. It was our destination.

"Please come in," said Cruz, son-in-law of Fidel, farmer and Home Guard.

"When were the Japs here last?" asked Marking. "Never, sir." "What!" "No, sir," said Cruz. "They never found this place, not this year, not last year, not the year before. They came close, but they never came here."

"Home," I said. "Home at last."

"Here," said Marking, "sit with me in the hammock." And there was food.

CHAPTER 23

From haven through peril to haven. The world and the people in it rolled on.

There were miracles. Roger came. Roger, whom we had left to fight it out alone in the torture cells of Fort Santiago.

"Rog'!" yelled Marking.

"Rog'!" said Lyd, tears in her eyes.

"You!" I said. "At last!" He looked the same, and yet he looked different. The enormity of what he had been through and the guerrilla raid which had freed him were still upon him.

We talked, and then Marking told him we were moving. "Anderson sent word before the Lagundi raid that he wanted to see me. He will come inland from the coast for the meeting. You follow up." Roger nodded. "Rog'," continued Marking, curious, "it's awfully tight everywhere. How were you able to find me?"

"You know me, sir." There was both courage and droop-lashed cunning in his eyes.

"Well, follow up."

Anxiously, Lyd questioned Roger about Manuel. Again there was hope. She hugged her joy to her heart. For Manuel, the notes she had kept so conscientiously; for him, the pen-and-ink sketches of each camp she had seen. Her every experience she treasured in the tiny scribbling, to share with her writer husband some day.

Again the food ran low.

Lucio brought in corn, ripe avocados, a little rice, but not enough for all. Anayat shot the wild cow, and Lyd and I sliced the great hunks of meat into thin strips for smoking. We could live on jerky in emergency. "Did you ever cut up one whole cow?" I asked. "No," said Lyd, "not all at one time." We stretched our backs, brushed back untidy hair with hands on which beef blood had dried in layers.

Finally, one morning, Marking ordered, "Pack up!" Into each pack went a few avocados and little meat.

Cabalhin checked in and out, leaving more good fighters, taking the sick and unarmed we had picked up here and there. Over near Santa

Maria he had clashed with the Japs and withdrawn, and we remembered hearing a very distant crackle of rifles. "That is either Cabalhin or Mapa," Marking had said. Wherever his men, his thoughts went with them. Whenever a fight, he wanted to be in it and chafed at remaining at headquarters.

Once again we, the hunted, threaded through the *cogon*, up into the mountains toward the Dumagat country, toward a meeting with Anderson.

I drew Lyd's attention to a seat of saplings tied together near a bend in the trail. "Last year," I said. "Japs. They used to wait along the paths to catch people going in and out of the *barrio*."

Once again, we paused to bid farewell with our eyes to the sweep of forest and *cogon* and lake rolling away from Karakatmon. And then into the forest, on and up, and up and up through the gloom and coolness of the jungle peaks. No stamina. Too often we rested, losing time. Once Lyd, resting, gave a little, gasping shriek and sought frantically to pull the leeches from her ankle. Pinching tightly, she pulled, and the slimy length stretched like elastic, undislodged.

"Scrape them off with a stick," I said. Shuddering, she scraped. Off they came, and the blood spurted and dripped down her heel, thick and red and coagulating. "Don't scrape off the clots," I said. "Let the blood harden. Otherwise the bleeding won't stop."

At the top of the divide in Bangian, we found some of Salvador's fighters, a handful of miserable boys lost in Lucio's huge bark-and-*anahau* barracks, spacious enough to house sardine-fashion a couple of hundred guerrillas. Paing, leader of a tough-guy gang in Manila boydom, was stretched out with a swollen foot, unable to walk. "The throbbing," he said, "it is the throbbing, ma'am." Because they had little expected to see us, and here the Old Man and I had rolled in, there were tears. Paing turned his face away to hide them, and a younger boy sniveled.

On the ground, on beds of leaves with sacking pulled over them, lay three others—one in fever, two emaciated. Not far from them, between the two long shelves for bedding down the fighters, was a small campfire, and on it was a battered tin filled with water and leaves. The tin was lopsided on the coals. The fire flickered weakly, for the twigs were not too dry.

"Starving," said Marking. "Go and rest in the small house over there."

I sent tea in a coconut shell.

One of the three on the ground was already dead.

Our green avocados had not ripened. They were bitter, puckery, tasteless. The supply of jerky had long been exhausted. No stamina. Nothing to fall back on. After weeks of eating better than we had ever eaten in the whole two years, there was nothing to fall back on. Our hunger pangs were sharp.

A year before there had been corn; now there was no corn available. Few people had planted, and what they had planted, they needed for themselves. There was no rice. There were no Dumagats to fish and wander into the forest to bring back the persimmon-like fruits of the ebony tree and the sour rattan berries.

"Where are the Dumagats?" asked Marking.

"They are sick, sir," said a mountaineer. "Many have died." And another said, "We are all dying. There is not enough salt. We cannot buy medicine. The Japs do not allow us to sell the *almáciga*. We are cold because our old clothes are now gone. We cannot wear the G-string, for we are not as hardy as the Dumagats, and even the Dumagats are dying."

Almáciga is the resin from an evergreen tree.

"Why aren't they allowed to sell the resin?" "I don't know. Maybe the Japs want something else." "They still have rattan." "People do not buy." "Why not? Is that against the Japs too?" "People are too poor to buy. The Japs have everything, the people have nothing. Manila get poor, then the towns get poor. The towns get poor, then the *barrios* get poor. And when the *barrios* are poor the poorest of all are the little people in the mountains."

All down the river I pondered that lesson in economics. No salt, and the aborigines were dying.

The river rose, roared by, was too dangerous for continued passage. Its waters hemmed us in on one side, and the long way back on the other. All around, there was sickness and hunger and death.

The conqueror's shadow had finally reached even over the interior. What was there I planned to show Lyd? The multi-colored chips of stone in the river bed, jade and rose and blue and garnet and chartreuse—what were these against the shadow over the river people? The yellow torrent rolled over the pretty stones, hiding them from sight; pretty little stones, a gentle little people—roiling yellow waters everywhere.

Down the river, we went, risking death in the flood to escape starvation.

The purchase of a farm pig at one of the Astovesa *kaingins* brought sweet broth flowing down our throats, and there were boiled sweet potatoes, heavy within, fully satisfying in the hour.

Again, Pinagsahangan.

Still there was the wild beauty of the river country, and I turned to Lyd, only to see the pain in her eyes.

"If Manuel were here," she said, "—my dearest, with whom to share!" Then came the day: "Yay, let me go. I feel guilty, leaving you here—but I cannot stay. I must go."

"Where, Lyd?"

"I don't know. But somewhere—someone knows about Manuel—"

"Lyd, it isn't safe. And for you there is no surrender; it wouldn't bring him back; it would doom you both. Where will you go?"

"I have relatives in Laguna. Through them I can find Berting, Manuel's brother."

One morning before she left I woke to find a white ginger blossom beside my cheek and Lyd's small brown hand poised above it. The pain struck deep, stirring memories of days before the war. In the urgency and suffering and privation of guerrilla warfare, I had steeled myself against any yearning for comfort, security, or beauty. To serve, I had renounced everything, even the grieving for what had been lost. What were these hidden sorrows welling up, bringing an ache to my throat, released by the dew-sweet blossom and the friend's hand above it? Quick, the rush of tears; quicker, the need to press them back to the depths from which they had gushed.

Then Lyd was gone, rolling up the river with Cabalhin and his fighters, respected by them, escorted with gallantry.

There was work to be done, as always. It seemed to stretch ahead forever, without hope, without an ending. It was darkness before the dawn for which we had almost lost our faith.

Bernie and Onésimo were assigned to make the trip down the river and up the coast to Anderson's camp, two days from our Pinagsahangan camp.

Suddenly it all seemed pointless. For what were we suffering? An America that could not return even if she would? A cause that had never been ours except on the surface? A country in which the very people whom we fought to save turned away from us and were lost in their own agony and struck blindly at us who loved them most? How much had we accomplished, compared to the suffering we had passed? How many Japs had we killed compared with our own killed by bullets and germs and lack of vitamins?

How ridiculous, a bus-driver general and a girl-reporter chief of staff!

How fruitless the love that had bound together a great guerrilla family!

In a tidal wave of patriotism, we had accepted a leadership we had not sought, and to protect the following, because it was willing and clean of heart, we had had to spill blood.

Daily, bitter quarrels between Marking and me. Daily, squabbles among the two-score men held in our headquarters. Sullenness among the mountain people, and down the river at the bamboo grove some of the mountaineers "appointed" by the Japs in Infanta to "guard" the river passage with their bamboo spears. Everywhere, the bamboo army. We walked among them, alert against them, heavily armed, heavier of heart. The old quick smiles were less in evidence. There was a helpless grimness about them.

Sitting among the men, Marking said, "And what good are those spears against bullets?"

"None, sir," said the river man, almost surly. "America would laugh at them." No reply. "When America comes—" "What does America care for us?" muttered the skinny, sore-ridden backwoodsman. "Do the Japs love us?" countered Marking. No reply.

The river rushed by. We were alone in the wilderness, with a river rushing by. What was there left to fight? Or, rather, was there anything left with which to fight it? We couldn't even beat the hookworms eating away the fighters from within.

Bernie and Onésimo returned from Anderson filled with joy and extremely secretive. In giving their report, each interrupted the other, then urged the other to speak, and interrupted again. Their eyes shone. They were eager, quick, filled with glad secrets, hardly able to hold themselves in.

In secret conclave, with even the bodyguards forbidden, we heard for the first time of submarines and "New Guinea boys" and arms and ammunition and pamphlets and Free Philippines magazines and chocolate bars.

"Shokelet kendy! Not shokelet kendy?" demanded Marking. And there was chocolate candy for Sweet-Tooth Marking. There were "I Shall Return" cigarettes, and tiny paper kits with needles neatly arranged in red flannel folders with threads of every color.

There were toothbrushes and toothpaste and safety razors.

With the wealth in our hands, we hardly believed. We might wake up out of a dream.

Quickly into reaching hands we put the cigarettes and the sewing kits. The surliness and tension were gone from faces bright with hope, from voices breathing prayers of thanksgiving. The bamboo spears lay forgotten on the ground.

MacArthur's orders were typical—and a little musty and very fine, straight out of the Victorian era. They were also definite: no hostilities against the enemy.

"What if we are cornered? Does he expect us to surrender? To die, without fighting?"

For months, of necessity, the guerrillas had been "lying low"; but not surrendering, not quitting, was active resistance. To have their immobility ordered as such in plain words called a spade a spade, pain to the pride.

The Japs had no such orders, and up the river they came.

Marking and his men deployed on a bluff between the forks, while down on the bank, in full sight, were twice our number of Japs in perfect grouping for a massacre.

"Marking," I said, "remember the orders."

The fighters grumbled. Some deliberately reclined against trees in plain sight.

"Marking," I said, "the men are in sight of the Japs." "Aw, if the Japs fire first, it's their fault."

"Marking, it's the fault of all of you for being seen."

Smoke rose over the Kanan, upstream. The farmhouse in which we had bivouacked had been set afire by Japs patrolling up the Kanan. In moving out, the fighters had forgotten to remove and hide the notched bamboo that served as rifle rack. It was the guerrilla signature.

"Marking," I said, "you'll get them *this time*; but there are plenty more everywhere, and you'll have Jap reinforcements swarming up this river in no time."

"Let 'em come, dirty sons-of-bitches!"

"If you make this river passage hot, how will you get your arms and ammunition through to the other side? Thousands are waiting over there in Rizal for equipment, for a chance to fight."

"We can cut through the jungle. We'll make another way."

"How long will it take, through jungle? You'll lose time. There will be a day when time will mean everything."

"Oh, you God-damn woman, you shut up!"

"And if you fight now you'll be breaking your first order from MacArthur. That first order is a *test order*. They're trying to find out if you're trustworthy. They're trying to find out if you can take orders as well as give them. How do you test your own men? You give them an order first to see if they can carry it, don't you?"

"Yap, yap, yap!"

"Mind my words—"

"I won't mind anybody."

"And then, as a leader, you will have failed your fighters."

"Somebody is going to shut up, or I am going to blow somebody's top off."

"Marking, make Badidles and Gil move back behind the bushes."

"No."

"Then I will go sit with them. Maybe there's a good sniper down there."

"Oh, you son-of-a-bitch of a woman, you! Bady, you bastard, you get back before I blow your God-damn head off. You too, Gil, you hard-headed good-for-nothing. Trouble, trouble, trouble, all I got is trouble."

And so we pulled out, finding a new camp up the Kaliwa, and the people whose houses had been burned all along the lower river said, under their breath, "Cowards! Big talkers!"

In the new camp there was restlessness, a new kind of tension. Even Shep, the local dog that had fallen in with us, trotted around with an expectant, inquiring manner. "When?" each fighter asked.

Again the Manila couriers were finding the way to Marking. "Maps, sir?" they asked, smiling. "Maps for Anderson? Sir, here, we bring maps." Down the river, for we were on the north side of one ridge, came the couriers, eyes peeled for Japs, with the maps and reports for Andy. Up the river they returned, Butch the Cigar-Smokin' Gal among them, taking back the glad news to Manila. "What took you so long to get here, Butch?" we had asked. "Oh, I got scattered. The PC fired on me, and my guide was wearing white. I had to push him into a *carabao* wallow to make him not so white, and he was so frightened he almost drowned, and then I had to rescue him, and then they fired on us again. That was when I got scattered." . . .

"Sir, Japs!" "Again?" "Yes, sir. They have passed the forks and are coming *this way!*" "Many?" "Somewhat, sir." Marking buckled his belt around him, picked up his rifle. "Forward to the outpost!" To me he said, "Go farther up the mountain. Wait for me there." "Sir, the boys are already deployed at the outpost."

Came another runner from the outpost: "Sir, it is not Japs. It is New Guinea boys." "It's *what?*" "From Anderson's camp, sir."

A third runner appeared: "Sir, sir, Farretta is bringing them. They have helmets. They have jungle boots. Oh, sir! They have carbines and the grease-gun gun!"

Marking waited. A blond head in short-sleeved shirt, shorts and jungle boots pushed up the incline. It was he, the American mining engineer. "Farretta!" shouted Marking. Hubbub.

"Yay, this is—"

"My God," I said, peering around the *kubo* post from the shelf where I was perched, swinging my legs, "it's a Jap!"

Monty, the New Guinea boy, grinned, then gaped. "Are you a lady?" he asked. "Are you a Jap?" I demanded laughingly, for surely he looked like one. "No, ma'am, I'm a Filipino from America." "Strange place for Filipinos to come from. Since when?" "Oh, a long time ago, ma'am." "Why so long?" "We stopped at Australia first." "Well, welcome to your country!"

Farretta asked in a general way, "How *are* you?"

The cargo began coming up under weak but eager backs. Medicine: blessed Atabrine, blessed sulfathiazole. Undershirts and underpants, all olive-drab. We leaped for the magazines.

"Farretta," said Marking, "you have not eaten."

"Marking, I have chocolate candy." Farretta singsonged the magic words.

"Where?" Marking picked Farretta's pockets with his eyes. "Where?" We munched the chocolate bars.

Marking was eyeing Farretta's Buck Rogers grease gun with hunger in his heart.

"Mind a little target practice?"

"Go ahead," said Marking, eagerly, desirous of seeing the gun in action.

Farretta aimed at a stump across a ravine and pulled the trigger, and the stream of .45 slugs made the splinters fly. Having impishly whetted Marking's hunger, he turned and said, as if the gun were worthless, "Here, have yourself a grease gun."

Marking held himself back from leaping, but he couldn't get his hands on it fast enough.

The line was unending. More boxes, more tins, more people. "This is Melendres. This is Dagdag." We looked at the three New Guinea boys, so called because they had been trained for Signal Corps work in New Guinea. To us, they were heroes. What if they had not yet seen action? Why would they leave America, if not to give their lives for the Philippines? It was enough.

"Marking, these boxes must not get wet. They are field radios. You will be in constant contact with Andy in Tayabas. Orders from MacArthur will be relayed by radio through Andy to you."

"My goodness!" Then even more emphatically, "Jesus Christ!"

"You'll have to take care of them. You'll be held responsible for them."

"Of *course*, I'll be held responsible for them," said Marking, on his high horse again.

Farretta knew him too well to mind. "You will be responsible for them. And good luck."

"This is the good luck," said Marking, surveying all.

"And," pursued Farretta, "this is what they need: a very high place where they can look down into Manila harbor."

"That's easy."

"Montalban?"

"No. That is too close, too dangerous. I will take you to a very good place. You know me, Farretta."

Farretta nodded. "And all must be done as soon as possible." "Pack up," said Marking.

"Round up some *cargadors*." Upstream we went. The New Guinea boys were seated with important guerrilla bustle in the *bancas* along with their precious equipment, very much a part of it.

"Monty and Dagdag are the radio men," explained Farretta. "Melendres is the weather observer."

"Why?" asked Marking.

"Why what?"

"The weather."

"Oh! Well, by the clouds the observer can tell whether it's good flying weather."

"Why?"

"Well, you tell them how many ships there are in the bay—"

"Yeah."

"And you tell them what kind of clouds are floating around—"

"Yeah."

"And then you sit there and see what happens."

"What will happen? Oh! I *know!* Hey, you up there! Hurry up! We got to get through fast! All you do is take your time! What do you think this is, *pasyal?*"

Farretta said, "I can walk as fast as you can, Marking."

"You want to see it, too?" Marking laughed with excitement.

"I wouldn't miss it," said Farretta, "for the years I've spent here running around in circles."

CHAPTER 24

Good news spreads fast.

As we rolled over the divide into Rizal province, there was welcome: "Sir, my wife and I are giving you this chicken." "Sir, here is a horse for Colonel Yay." "Sir, the house over there is much bigger." "Sir, the Manila couriers are coming, according to my son who is a Home Guard." "Sir, the people in the towns are happy. They ask for the American propaganda, especially the cigarettes." "Sir, may I have a khaki undershirt? See my clothes, how torn."

Some of the fighters were wearing the drab undershirts and pants, returning ahead of MacArthur in the army glory of only the GI underwear. They were perfectly camouflaged and swaggeringly happy. Though there were not yet enough to go around, proof of America's nearing was in a new pistol belt, a new bandoleer, a jungle suit, and a helmet scattered throughout the resting throng. There was a fingering everywhere. "*Abah*," said a Home Guard, "it is *pala* made in America." And another opined, "True, it is not the made-in-Japan quality."

To all, Marking gave orders: "You will be careful. You will talk only to the most trusted. We must not be disturbed by the Japs. You must not bring them into the hills because we cannot attack them now. Also, we must not be moving every time to avoid them. You must go your ways as if nothing is happening. They must not suspect. You must not be happy. It is all understood?"

There were eager nods, excited talk.

"Oh, God," said Marking, who had recovered, from his own first excitement, "they will talk! They will tell the wife, the wife will tell the mother, the mother will tell the cousin, the cousin will tell the sweetheart, the sweetheart will tell the friend, the friend will tell all the other friends, the servants will listen to everybody and tell everybody, and then the GID will report that the Japs know all about it. My head! I always have a headache. Have you aspirin?"

In my own small woven-reed *tanpipi* were his medicines. Often we had quarreled over the double-handful assortment of pills and potions and salves in tiny tins and vials. And ever I had been adamant: "When there is no more medicine, there is no more medicine. Don't count this." And he would say, "I will give it to this farmer." "Nobody will give it to the farmer." "The man is dying." "Then he will die." "How cruel you are!" And with finality I would say, "Between you and the farmer, which do the fighters need most? If the farmer dies, it is a loss, yes. If you die, it is a greater loss. Who will lead the men to their own fulfillment and glory?" He would mutter, "Oh, you God-damn hardheaded woman!" but would not touch the small *tanpipi*, looped on a string over my shoulder.

Now into the *tanpipi* I dipped to give him his aspirin. In the big army tins were bottles containing a thousand tablets each. "How about one of those?" I asked. But he wanted it from the *tanpipi*, giving as reason, "This is mine—that is for everybody else."

The people, hearing, crowded near, hands outstretched. The tables had turned.

Marking looked at them with a flicker in his eye. He waved his arm over the fighters lounging about at rest or passing to and fro on water and kitchen details. "The fighters first," he said. "For them, who have had no roof over their heads; for them, who have slept on the ground; for them, who have hungered. True, all of us have suffered; but for the fighters first—no?"

The people, like good children, nodded obediently.

"Marking," I asked, "what are you thinking?"

"This—that once they ran from us, once they shut their doors on us."

"They had suffered too much—"

"But the fighters who suffered more never forsook the cause—nor us."

"And so?"

"There is no hate in my heart. I guess I pity them. But I *love* the fighters."

"I understand."

I did, for in my own heart was the commingling of scorn, compassion, and charity for the people, and still a tight loyalty to the fighters superimposed over the pictures of all they had suffered. Huddling in the rain, a fighter had held a broad leaf over my head; it was useless, for I was as soaked as the rest, yet the gesture was there. Gaunt, ragged men around a crackling campfire had listened to Marking's stories and mine, had told theirs. A cavalcade of brave, good men were marching by in memory, with faces among them we should not see again except in memory. Yet for the poor, uninspired, untrustworthy people we had the deepest of pity, and I realized that from them we had sprung and to them we owed the debt of our beginning—let us who touched the stars in our soaring bring back the universe to those from whom we came.

Quick to sense Marking's and my feelings, the fighters themselves were kind, even courtly, to those who came in new humility, and when there walked among them one who spoke hesitantly, in apology and explanation, they slapped his bent, ragged shoulder and shared with him their camaraderie.

We rolled down from Karakatmon into the panorama to which we twice had bidden farewell. Over the broad, green plateau of Sampaloc, through the wild guava trees with their small green balls of fruit, we rolled down into the old hide-away hollow in the V of the Sampaloc and Masanting trails.

The Japs had never found the hide-away. "Farretta," called Marking, "see! Here is your shelf! Look, the spring! And not far from here is the high place you need for the transmitter. Everything. Everything you want."

Farretta fiddled with the weather instrument. "I want this to work."

"What's wrong with it?" Two heads bent over the instrument, and Marking said, "If it doesn't work, we'll get another one." "Can't. Clear back to SWPA is too far."

"Manila isn't far."

"Do you think there's one in Manila?"

"If there is," said Marking, "I can get it." Bengzon, mining engineer, was No. 1 stand-by in Manila for all maps, binoculars, instruments, and calcium tablets. "Do you know Ernesto Bengzon?"

"H'm-m! I've heard the name."

"Well," said Marking proudly, "that's him."

"We'll try to repair this one."

"I will also order another one," said Marking. "In this war, you have to be *segurista*. Also a *suapang*. I will *suapang* Bengzon again. You tell me if you want the whole Bureau of Science, the whole Bureau of Mines, the whole University of the Philippines. *I will bring you everything except the campus*. You know, I think I will go to school again some day."

I laughed. "Farretta, that's why he leaves the campus there." But Farretta and Melendres were troubled over the instrument and consulted at intervals throughout the day.

Monty and Dagdag returned: "Sir, it is a very good place. No interference. We can pick up the Japs all around us. If they don't jam our frequencies, we're all right."

"What's 'frequency'?" asked Marking. "Many times this, many times that?" Farretta explained. "I don't like radios," said Marking. "I like automobiles and guns."

One day, two days. The September skies were overcast, and there was rain; in our hollow, we slogged through a mire of mud.

Monty said, "Good reception, sir."

Farretta said, "But we can't see Manila."

Marking said, "Never mind. The maps and reports we send to Andy tell everything."

Patiently Farretta explained, "Ships' movements, Marking. Today, maybe there are three. Tomorrow, maybe there will be fifty. Day after tomorrow, there may be none. We have to get them the day they're there."

"Pack up," said Marking.

"Not yet. Let's stay on the air, see if we can contact Andy." The hours passed, and another day. "Sir! Sir!" Dagdag and Monty were excited. "Contact, sir. Message from Andy!"

"My goodness," said Marking. "Hot damn!"

Farretta decoded the message, advising Marking of the routine details, patiently explained barriers, sound waves, interference, and powers.

"I guess I will stick to automobiles," said Marking.

"Well, this is lots of fun."

"Thank you," said Marking. "What's that noise?"

There was a distant roar, low, droning, slowly growing louder but not rising in pitch.

"Marking—" said Farretta.

"Gimme the glasses!" said Marking. Then he yelled, running out into the open, "Planes! Gimme my glasses, gimme my glasses! Who got my bernacles!"

I dumped a *bayong* upside down, scrambling for the binoculars.

Farretta laid down papers and pencil, ambled out of the patch of jungle into the open, came back when Marking dashed back.

The roar suddenly juggernauted over the hollow, swooping down from the heights, through the low-lying mist, down to the lowlands, away.

"They're different!" yelled Marking, bowling against Farretta, slamming into a tree, running backward for a better look, face parallel to the skies, half falling backward over the log bench of the mess table, staggering against others also face up and jostling one another.

Another low, insistent roar, above the clouds, then the ear deafening but low-pitched sound filling all the world with the message.

"Darling, look!"

"You're stepping all over me," I said, trying to see, too. "American planes! They gotta be! They don't look like anything before! Farretta! What are they?"

Farretta too was excited, but, in comparison to our hysterics when the realization burst full upon us, he still was calm. "They look like Navy planes," he said. "American. Some task force."

Another wave. We pounded one another's backs. Shep whined, barked sharply, quivering in the contagion of hysteria. Wave after wave. We yelled and waved and ran in circles. Wildly we urged them on, "Give them hell! Give it to 'em, give it to 'em!" Distantly we could hear rolling detonations. Between waves we leaned against trees, panting, held on to one another, said, "See? See? They're coming back!" We wiped our tears, and cried again, and laughed at one another for crying.

"Whether they came back or not, we wouldn't give up," said Marking.

Farretta nodded. "Today is not the wonder of it." His next words we have never forgotten, "The wonder, Marking, *is* how you pulled through last year. The wonder is how you kept on fighting."

Marking turned to the friend who had been more of a friend than we realized, and again there were tears. "I'm crying about the planes."

"Sure, sure," said Farretta. He blew his nose, pinching it unduly and looking into his kerchief. "It's nice to have a little civilization again."

With a lessening lump in his throat, Marking could say, "It's nice to have a friend like you, Farretta."

"Sure, sure. Call me up any time."

Down and up again we rolled through Koyambay to reach higher ground and stop at the foot of an unnamed mountain, with our eyes on the Taranka trail horseshoeing around the mountain. Marking told Farretta while I told the New Guinea boys, "This was all war zone in 1943 when the Japs encircled us at Kanumay." Farretta answered, "You forget, Marking. Schaffer and I got chased out of it."

On the way, Monty rode through a beehive. The swarm of angry bees dive-bombed the line of fighters, and there was a scattering along the trail and off the trail and around and around the hills and hollows.

At the end of the line, Rear Guard Badidles and his men deployed on a rise, puzzled by the scene of panic below. "What the hell is that?"

he asked. "If they deploy, why do they keep running around? If they retreat, why do they advance? If they advance, in which direction is the advance? If it is a Jap ambush, what kind of bullets that make no sound? And why is the Old Man laughing?" He turned to his men. "He is laughing, isn't he? And what is Colonel Yay doing to Monty, and why did Monty get down from his horse, and *where is the horse going?*"

Far down the trail, too far for Badidles's puzzled eyes to distinguish, I sought to light Monty's cigarette. His face was red and puffed, and the tears bright in his eyes. Bees crawled through his hair, curled on his ears thrusting their stingers deep, flew down his neck and buzzed about his mouth and nose. He struck the air wildly, and I, hoping the smoke would drive them away, ran to keep up with him. Not a bee in the swarm touched me.

But the lighter wouldn't work. "Oh, never mind, never mind!" Monty said, galloping off.

I came up to Farretta. "Don't slap them, don't do anything to them," I said. "Look at me. They don't bother me because I don't bother them."

In dudgeon Farretta answered, "Listen. I was minding my own business. And I got it *here!*" He jabbed his nose with an angry forefinger.

I laughed. And Marking laughed, for he too was unstung. Nobody else laughed, because everybody was as angry as the bees. "Such indignity!" I said. "Very funny," said Marking. "Where are we now?" Helplessly we burst into new laughter and were the two most unpopular people in the whole harassed crowd.

"I will organize the bees," said Marking. "They will be the front line. The snakes will be the patrol. The birds will be the couriers. The monkeys will throw coconuts—they will be the snipers. We, the guerrillas, will only mop up."

"Oh, shut up!"

"Farretta," said Marking, "here is your horse."

Farretta climbed aboard. Marking and I proceeded ahead, in fine humor. The unhurt can always afford to be happy.

Faster and faster we hiked up and down, down, down. Then from the rear came a yell and a bellow.

Marking turned. I turned.

There was Farretta, picking himself up out of the *cogon*. And there was the horse, standing patiently, almost nosing him. His arms began to move like a runaway windmill, as he stomped up and down, his face crimson in the sun. "He doesn't look so sweet," I said. "I am surprised," said Marking. "Schaffer warned us," I said.

Marking yelled, "What's the matter, Farretta?"

"The saddle broke, the saddle broke—damn, damn, DAMN!" yelled Farretta, still flailing, still stamping. Patiently stood the horse, head down, tail down, all apology.

Into hysterics went Marking and I, for America was coming back and we could laugh at anything, especially an American.

Up again we climbed, turning to scale the peak above the Taranka trail. At last: "Sir, we can see Manila from here! Look, there is Pier Seven!"

"That's right," said Marking.

Up went the miracle jungle-hammocks, for Farretta, for the New Guinea boys, for Marking, for me.

"I wish we had some for the boys."

"Yes," said Marking.

"No, sir, no, ma'am," said the boys. "We will have ours some day."

Back to the city, five days away by foot and rickety bus, went the Manila couriers, with many an injunction to be careful, with many an order to deliver. Up from the city came the key officers, the regimental commanders, Seneres, Eadie Reyes, Cordero, Baldenor. Unbelievingly they talked with Dagdag, Melendres, and Monty, and fingered the jungle hammocks and crowded around the magic of the field transmitter.

Scores carried the submarine propaganda through the towns, into Manila, and when the charts of New Guinea victories and the *Free Philippines* magazines, distributed one page to each, and the needles and soap and cigarettes were gone, hundreds more came begging, "Just one carbine bullet, sir, marked '44, please, sir." And Marking, working against time, pushing his big outfit into full speed ahead, using his head as he had never used it before, lost his temper: "Bullets are to fight with, not to show. You shut up, or else I will kick somebody."

Maps and reports began to pile up at our headquarters. One copy was given to Dagdag for evaluation.

One copy in waterproof wrapping went to Andy by cross-country courier—by the swift Juan Marquez, by the doddering but mile-covering Truadio, by the Infanta fighters who knew their neck of the woods like a book, by some of the Rizal farmers who as guerrillas had been in Tayabas as refugees or runners. Every day, a man across the

Sierras. Every day, a man in. Every day, scores out, hundreds in, a thousand out—urgent mission, urgent mission, urgent mission.

Seneres's men gave the verification in voluminous detail, for, as has been said, they were organized by zones and every zone was covered like a newspaper beat.

Eadie's work was "inside stuff," touchy jobs in close to the Japs.

What the simple agents could not get, she pieced together herself from her sources in the Jap High Command. Seneres and the GID tabulated complete reports every twenty-four hours, and not a truck nor a Jap foot soldier could enter or leave the city nor pass from one district to another but the movement was reported by courageous runners organized to run in relay and to ferret out our new camps, no matter where we moved.

When a runner was caught and bayoneted on the Mabitac trail to the south the GID called for "duplicate runners," and the two were given the same reports and maps in separate packets: one to cut through the southern towns and farms of Rizal province up into the mountains, the other to take the northern route. Some of the runners had malaria and lost time with the chills, huddling in *kubos* or in the brush beside the trails, then plodded on in fever, pressed on by the urgency of the coming Liberation.

"The city mice are pretty good," said Marking.

"The country mice are much nicer to them," I said.

It was true. The combat units began to show open respect for the Manila agents and runners, squeezing them into the crowded barracks, asking favors of them such as the delivery of a personal letter to a sister in the city; mutual obligations and gratitude knit the hill, town, and city units closer and closer together.

"What a family we have!" said Marking.

"Marking," I said, "they've mapped every enemy installation in the city. They want to know: Can they branch out into the provinces?"

"Why don't they wait until they're told? MacArthur said just Manila."

"Marking, they never wait until they're told. Here are seven maps on installations in the provinces."

"They do it. Why do they ask, Can they?"

"They need expense money."

"Aha! Tell them no."

"It's so unfair, Marking."

"It's not my money, it's the army's money."

"More money, more of what the army wants."

"I tell you what. If I see they are really starving, I will help them. They are pretty thin now. Let us see if their patriotism is more than their stomachs. I am not selfish. I am just *not a fool*."

"I have a surprise for you," I said, changing the subject. "Something Farretta gave me for you."

"Let me see it." Marking is a Filipino Missourian.

I pulled forth a small tin of deviled meat labeled "potted ham."

"Pottyham! Pottyham!" said Marking, grabbing.

"Say 'Please'!"

"Please, *please!*" and he grabbed and punched it open with a penknife.

CHAPTER 25

*L*yd came clambering up the mountain, a new person entirely, toughened, quick, reckless, all five feet two of her in the fight. She dismissed Marking with a kiss on his cheek, pulled me into a nook to rattle Laguna problems and needs at me, tried out a jungle hammock, gobbled any food within reach, and joyously greeted the New Guinea boys:

"Monty? Ah, Reinforcement No. 1!"

"This is Melendres," said Marking, "and this is Dagdag."

"One, two, three. Pretty good. Did you know what you were getting into?" She laughed and pulled me down beside her on the *cogon* grass to watch Dagdag and Monty at work, dah-de-dah-dah, with the earphones and the small jungle lights and the hooked-up wires making a very armyish picture indeed.

"Come," I said, "tell me all."

"First, these damn civilians—"

My eyebrows shot up. "Lyd! What has happened to you! Where did you learn to curse? And how come you don't defend the civilians and excoriate the fighters?"

"Shut up. It's this way. They just don't move. You want a *banca*. Maybe you get a *banca*. Everybody rides the *banca*. Some want to stop here. Some want to stop there. Some get delayed, and you have to wait for them. And all this time *you're trying to get to a certain place in the shortest time possible and you get there maybe next week*."

"Go on," I laughed.

"Shut up. I've been sending orders to Manila. I need some commissions. How do you like my bodyguard? Manuel's brother is my courier to Manila. I got to get back there. What have you been doing lately?"

"Go on."

Then she spoke quietly. "I have every reason to believe Manuel is alive. Because there is no evidence that he has been killed." There was a moment of quiet.

Lyd's last words when she left were, "The people are talking too much." And, sure enough, the people were talking.

Andy, over on the Tayabas coast line, burned a great pile of victory magazines. Marking and I could have wept, for hundreds and thousands were begging for any little proof that, truly, aid was near. We protested Andy's destruction of Allied propaganda. He was adamant, then relented and sent us a little more. A man was shot and a woman tortured for speaking of America, and when here and there an arrest brought to light the evidence the Japs clamped down with a brutality that even three years of suffering had not prepared us for. Mass torture, mass executions, mass starvation—deliberate, sadistic, deadly. We knew then why Andy had been reluctant to release any more tokens of succor.

Our own who begged, "Just to see, please, just to show one friend," we warned, "You know it is death to be caught with it. There is no excuse, no trial, only death." They answered, "But we die happy! Give, sir, give, ma'am. If not a whole page, then half a page, the half with the *date on it!*" Anything dated after the fall of Bataan was proof of submarine service, proof that America had come back and somewhere touched our shores.

Farretta fumbled with the instrument that would not work right. Melendres insisted on taking the long trek back, and carefully the instrument was wrapped against rain and river water. Farretta, too, took the long trek back, recalled by Andy for other missions.

"Pack up," said Marking. "Too many know we are here. Soon, the Japs will come."

No longer did I have to counsel caution. With precious equipment and radio personnel given into his hands as a trust, Marking's cunning quickened. The Japs came, and they left and came again.

And from mountain to mountain, back and forth, in and out, Marking pulled his forces and his mission, and he loosened up the pursestrings to feed out of a starving land duck, sweet rice cakes, and hot coffee to the New Guinea boys. While children clung to the fences around the stableyards of the Jap cavalry, children, emaciated, drooling for the sweet denied them, there was sugar for the New Guinea boys. The Japs' horses snuffed the white sugar onto the ground, and pushed the buckets over and the children dared not run the gauntlet of bullet and bayonet to eat of the sweetened earth, even had they risked the horses' hoofs, and still Marking got sugar for the New Guinea boys.

Whether Japs were patrolling or not, there was the super-caution of silence and dead fires in the camp. Only the most important officers and time-tested runners could enter. If a plane came patrolling—for the Japs, caught on the ground in September, patrolled constantly thereafter—there was a quick check-up of clothes drying, and plane or no plane, nothing might be hung in the sun.

"Put these clothes under the trees! Get them out of the open! Don't walk over there! Keep to the brush! There must be no smoke visible from afar. There must be no movement visible from the sky. Keep out of sight, and keep quiet!" Marking was ever alert. His alter ego, I was ever alert.

"Pack up," said Marking. "Too many know this camp, too." Silently we rolled, and for a titter or talk on the trail Marking or I would step aside angrily to yank the culprit out as he rolled by. Another camp. "Quiet!" "Keep out of sight!" "Watch that fire!"

"Nobody may leave the camp. Outposts alert!"

The pinpricking of men reporting, asking for orders, never ceased: "Sir, courier in from Infanta. There is a convoy from Anderson, sir. And Melendres is on his way back here." "Sir, the Japs in Manila are getting worse every day. And every day people fall dead in the streets." "Sir, the Japs say the Americans are coming, but we won't see them. They say the Americans are bringing food, but we won't be here to eat it." "Sir, here is the little girl of Colonel Yay for whom you sent." My daughter Rae, whom I had not seen for two years, smiled up at me; her chin quivered, and the tears fell. I drew her close. A moment—then the questions and the reports went on: "Sir, Melendres drowned." "Sir, the runner from Mapa is here."

"Sir, Cabalhin's courier is leaving." "Sir, Monty and Dagdag wish to tell you that the Japs seem to have direction finders. Shall they stay on the air anyway?" "Sir, the convoy from Anderson is here." The convoy men fell in line, their precious burdens still slung on their shoulders, still heavy on their backs.

Marking handed the large role of correspondence to me. Then he stood looking at the line, looking at the line.

There in the line were twenty new carbines, ten new Thompson submachine guns. The men who had carried them over the divide into Rizal were exhausted, their feet cut, some in fever from the long trip. Some were from Andy's enlistment, some from ours. This was their mission, completed. Marking cleared his throat. "Rack the guns, and fall-out the men. Give them rest and food and rice to carry with them." Slowly but hungrily, he reached for a Thompson.

I could not see his face, perched as I was at the headquarters table, banging away at the answers or marking and listing the maps and reports to be sent to Andy, but his broad back, his head bent over the Thompson in his hands, the feet-apart stance, spoke worlds! Help at last, real help. He turned to me: "Hon, now we can *fight!*"

"Pretty soon," I said.

"These are to defend the equipment. We won't defend it. We'll hide it. No more defense. Offense! No more running. No more retreating. I wish they would come now."

"Who?" I mumbled, slamming back the platen for a new paragraph.

"The Japs."

"The what! Ye Gods, Marking! One mission at a time."

"If they come, what a surprise—"

"It always surprises me. It scares the hell out of me."

"—a surprise for *them!*"

"Uh-huh, and have you noticed by the reports how many thousands of them are streaming into the Philippines from somewhere in the Southwest Pacific?"

"They are retreating."

"Yes, my love—all *over us!* It's the tidal wave rolling back. Remember what it did when it came in? Well, it'll be worse when it washes out. They won't go without giving us something to remember them by."

"I will give them something, too," said Marking, his eyes on the racked Thompsons and carbines. "Tell Andy please send us some more. More and more and more."

There was the drone of a plane. We listened. The familiar sputtering of a Jap plane distinguished it.

"Out of sight!" ordered Marking.

"Take cover!" shouted Musico.

"Keep your voice down, Musico," I said. "Especially because there's a plane, don't forget about Jap patrols."

There seemed to be more than one plane. Keeping within the farmhouse, we peered up from under the shadow of the eaves.

"Yay," called Marking to me, "look at that little one, so small, so fast!"

Two patrol planes headed south wavered as if to exchange the time of day with a zipping streak of black which looked like a very special speed-job headed in a straight south-due-north line, then curved northwest to Manila.

"Gosh!" said Marking. "Where the hell did the Japs get *that?* Do you think that's a Jap plane? God damn, it was fast."

And I agreed, "It was hell-bent for leather some place." I wandered out under the trees for an hour's rest.

Inside the headquarters, the talk went on. "Already October, maybe November," groused Marking. "Still we are waiting. *When are the Americans coming? When? When?*" His feet clumped up and down the earthen floor, pacing to and fro.

Other voices echoed his, "When?"

Marking said: "Why can't we fight now? We have the arms. We have the ammunition. I asked Andy to send more. If they keep sending us bullets, we can keep fighting."

The afternoon waned, and the heat passed. The sun left the west ablush. A cool wind rustled the leaves.

"Sir," said Musico for the hundredth time. "When are the forces coming, do you think?"

"I'm thinking, that fast plane early this afternoon means something. I'm thinking there is something happening somewhere."

Monty and Dagdag checked with Marking, chorusing: "Sir, KAZ seems to be sending us a message. That's MacArthur's station. Andy is on the air. Cabrera is on the air. But they don't answer our signal. And, sir, there's a message in the clear, and our orders are not to send in the clear, not under any circumstances."

"What's the one in the clear?"

Dagdag racked his head. "I think, sir, it says, 'South Central Luzon, stand by.'"

Marking jumped up. "That's important! Get it!"

Dagdag was flustered. "Sir, there is nothing coming through now. We will have to wait until the next hour scheduled."

Dark forms padded up the trail from the outpost, followed us into the headquarters where the small *kingki* lamp flickered.

"Sir, here are more maps. That makes almost five hundred maps, the total. Sir, *MacArthur has landed in Leyte!*" The courier panted, digging into his *bayong* for more mail, more maps, packages.

"No! Why do we not know here?" demanded Marking.

"Sir!" gasped Monty, "that must be the message we were trying to get!"

"Sir!" said Dagdag. "There is interference."

"Interference, hell! Get it!"

Mapa smiled, eyes agleam. He took his pipe from his mouth—"It is here, sir"—put it between his teeth, puffed long and sweet.

Marking sat down, jumped up, paced, sat down, stood, sat, walked a few steps, stood motionless, returned to the bench, sat, slapped the plank with the flat of his palms. "Now!" he said. "Now!"

"It's almost midnight," I said. "You better rest."

"Do you think that we should fight through to Leyte?"

"What are the orders, sir?" asked Mapa.

"How do *we* know?" spat Marking. And Monty and Dagdag kept very quiet and inconspicuous as his sharp glance shot across the table at them.

We settled down to wait, to send messages, give information. When did we roll? And the thought came again, incredibly: *MacArthur has landed on Leyte!*

Before dawn Marking was awake to another day of waiting and planning and protection. "No good," he said, "using these old camps. Better, a brand-new camp, then not so many people can visit, visit! Then only the ones supposed to come can come." Too many Home Guards, too many civilians, and recently people under suspicion had come in and out of the camp. Too many were prying into strictly U.S. Army business. He continued, "Today I will scout for a new camp."

I said nothing.

"Is that a good idea?" He nudged me with an elbow.

"OK," I said. I thought of Cote and Rae, now inseparable from us.

Cote, his twelve-year-old son, and Rae, my twelve-year-old daughter, took to guerrilla life like ducks to water. Fearing what I foresaw in Manila, I had brooded. Marking, to ease me, had had her taken out of the convent in which for more than two years she had been hidden by the nuns, and here she was now, a little girl guerrilla with regular camp chores. Cote and she were as close as brother and sister could be, and I allowed her out of sight only when he accompanied her. Cote was a fighter, carrying his own arms; I could trust him to take care of her. Both youngsters would be safer in a new camp.

Scouts dispatched by Marking reported back.

"Pack up," he said.

Waiting, waiting, more hours of waiting, and a normality that wasn't normal in between.

Up the unnamed mountain above Koyambay we climbed. On the flat top against a limestone cliff, the fighters cleared away the brush.

And one day, "Yay!" Marking yelled. Then in a lower tone: "There are two Americans coming!"

"I heard you tell everybody an hour ago."

"I did not!"

"Oh, yes, you did. You got so excited, you read the letter out loud!"

He ignored that. "Andy is sending them. They are from Australia. Truadio is bringing them. They will have more radios."

"This one has been headache enough."

"Andy says they are liaison officers from General MacArthur."

"They're all yours," I said, chewing on a piece of fresh coconut.

And the waiting went on. MacArthur on Leyte. *But where were our orders to fight!* The radio was a job, of course, but a minor one to Marking.

He wanted to *roll!*

CHAPTER 26

On November 17, Marking's birthday, an outpost guard came running. "Sir, the Americans are here!" And into the camp strolled the first genuine all-American GIs we had laid eyes on.

Did they stroll? Or did they stagger? From all over the camp, eyes focused upon them.

Said Broken-Back No. 1, Captain George Miller, "Are we here?"

Said Broken-Back No. 2, Lieutenant Brooke Stoddard, "If we aren't, I won't go another step. Oh, my *aching back!*" Mountaineers and Dumagats brought load after load to pile high.

There was a shaking of hands. The comforts of the camp were offered them.

Miller turned around slowly, craning his neck, looking at all there was to be seen, including the cliff and the patch of sky above. Stoddard, taller, heavier, gray of eye instead of blue, slumped on the first thing that looked as if it were meant for sitting purposes.

Papers were presented. Miller said, "Looks like a real camp." Stoddard said, "Gosh, I could do with a drink!" Marking jumped for a birthday bottle. "I can't drink," he said, "so I saved it for you." Actually, he had sent for it and reserved it for them.

He ordered the fighters to fall in. He would introduce his birthday present with a flourish. After all, these were liaison officers from MacArthur himself via Andy via submarine, who had come together from overseas so long ago that Miller had not seen the son with whom his wife had since presented him.

Marking said some fine words. "And now Captain Miller will speak."

Miller said some fine words.

Marking introduced the big American.

Lieutenant Stoddard said some fine words.

It was all the good old Filipino love of a program, and it brought Marking his happiest birthday ever. He had said, "We've been waiting for a long time." Miller: "We did our best to get here." Stoddard: "There's work to be done." It took half an hour to say all that.

Lyd who was there for the day said to me, "This is going to be interesting. Laguna can wait, I guess. Where's my bottle of conviviality?"

Miller and Stoddard came armed with a two-point program: to size up the Japs, and to train men for blowing bridges.

Miller was a "soft staff officer." Stoddard spoke of the Dismounted Cavalry with pride, so that everybody figured he hadn't minded losing his horse, but a guerrilla who loses his gun is just a civilian again, and so the boys liked Stoddard without understanding him.

Patiently, in simple sentences, he and Miller explained what the Allied forces wanted, "Find out exactly where the Japs are, how many, what equipment, how the guns are emplaced, what they have in transportation, where it is, what they intend to do under any given circumstances, if they expect reinforcements and from where . . ." And on and on and on.

"But we told you all that, sir," answered the unit commanders. "Go back and look again," said Miller.

"But it's not important."

"But it is important."

"But it's easy to get."

"Go get it again."

"Now?"

"Now."

Stoddard unpacked his bags and tins and gingerly placed dynamite and blasting caps far apart.

"Now," he said to his class, "this is a fuse. This is a blasting cap. This is dynamite. *Don't put the blasting cap and the dynamite together!* Don't touch anything on this table—repeat, don't touch anything on this table. Don't bite anything. Don't drop anything. *Put that cigarette out!* Don't smoke at these classes—repeat, *Don't smoke at these classes!* Now, I will show you exactly how to prepare the materials for blowing a bridge."

Lyd walked back to headquarters, notebook in hand. "How's it going?" I asked. "I'm going to blow me a bridge." She left, carrying the best pencil with her, as I discovered, hunting around for the only decent rubber eraser in camp.

"Now," said Stoddard, in the best lecture manner, "You hold this thus. Then you splice it so, whereupon you have completed the first step." He looked at the class, and the class looked at him. "Is everything understood?"

There was a murmur of "Yes, sir."

"All right," said Stoddard. "Now—" A second thought made him stop short. "Are you sure you understand everything I've been saying?"

Again a murmur of assurance.

"All right"—Again he stopped. "You tell me what I said!"

Nobody could tell him exactly what he said, and finally we heard his bellow across the clearing, "That's exactly what you must *not* do, unless you want to go up with the bridge when it blows! I will repeat." And he repeated the lecture, step by step. "Now," he said, "tell me what I said."

A few could tell him what he said. He towered over another, "Why can't you tell me what I said?"

"Oh, sir," explained someone else, "he does not speak English."

"Well, then," said Stoddard, his hands on his hips, "how can he tell me what I said?"

Nobody could tell him.

"All right. Does anybody speak Spanish? I will give the lecture in Spanish. *No hay que fumar en la clase.* [Do not smoke in class.] Repeat, *es muy peligroso fumar en la clase.* [It is very dangerous to smoke in class.] Now"—jabbing his finger at a smiling face—"what did I say?"

"I speak English, sir, not Spanish."

"How about you?" he asked another.

Others answered for the student addressed, "He is a mountain people, sir. He speaks only the dialect. He is only visiting."

"Well, who speaks Spanish around here?"

"You, sir."

"Well, I'll be a—" Stoddard stood uncertainly. "Do you understand me when I speak English? Do I speak English right? I mean, can you understand it the way I talk it?"

"Not so well, sir. You talk too fast, all one word."

"Look, we will continue this class tomorrow." He stumbled off, hand to forehead.

I followed him. "What's your trouble?"

"Well," said Stod, "I say things six times, and six times they tell me they understand what I said, and six times they didn't understand it at all."

"Why not use Lyd for an interpreter?"

"That's an idea. But look. I ask them if they understand and they say Yes—"

"They wouldn't hurt your feelings for worlds."

"You mean it would hurt my feelings if they said No, they don't understand me?"

"Well, you raised your voice a couple of times and nobody knew what upset you—"

"My God! They were smoking right over—"

"But keep your voice down—"

"Keep my voice down! When we're all gonna get blown right off the top of this mountain?"

Miller came up. "Don't mind Stod," he said. "He's having a bad time of it. He's having a baby."

Agape, for my mind functioned drop-jawed, I asked, "How?"

"His wife is going to have a baby, and Stod's sweating it out over here."

"Oh! Oh, my goodness! Oh, Stod, you poor guy!"

He groaned, his head in his hands, "I need a drink."

Miller gave him a drink.

"How about you?" I asked. "Have you had yours yet?"

"Oh, yes. I had a bad time myself, but my baby's all born."

A day or so later, Stod fainted.

"Marking," I said, "remember what I told you? Well, Stod's in a bad way, you know."

So he and Miller brought Stod through his confinement, and a week later Stod said, "Well, it's all over by now, according to her last letter. There's nothing I can do about it now."

"Even before," said Marking, "you could do what about it?"

CHAPTER 27

Miller and Stoddard were the turning point.

Marking and the two American officers were forever in a huddle, like the football hero and a couple of fussing coaches just before the big game.

"Teamwork," said Miller.

"Ya gotta have teamwork," said Stoddard.

"Don't you worry about the teamwork," said Marking. "I'll have teamwork, or I'll break somebody's head."

"When the orders to act come for you," Miller said, "you must be able to do exactly the missions you have accepted—cut communications, hit the highways and railroads, blow up bridges."

"Don't say you can," Stoddard said, "and then not do it."

"We've been doing it for three years," said Marking.

"How?" asked Miller.

"Well, for example, somebody takes down all the telephone wire and gives it to somebody else—"

"Huh?" said Stoddard.

"—and then they sell it to the Japs."

"What!" burst out Miller.

"And the Japs put it back up on the poles."

"Well, we can't have that," said Miller.

"And then somebody takes the wire down again and sells it to some other Japs, and then the Jap army buys it again."

"Let me get this straight—" said Miller.

"That's straight," said Marking, wondering how much straighter it would have to be to explain the cycle of that particular guerrilla endeavor.

"Let's begin again," said Stoddard. "You take the wires and sell them to the Jap army—"

"No!" said Marking. "You sell it to the Jap *civilians* who are making big business. Then the Jap army buys it from them to replace the telephone wires stolen off the telephone poles. Then we steal it and sell it to the Jap civilians again."

"Oh! Pretty neat. Who gets the money?"

"The people who do it. Their families got to live. Everybody doing the work gets a cut."

"How much do you get?" asked Stoddard. Then, as Marking's eyes narrowed: "I mean, the organization, for upkeep."

"We don't touch that kind of money!" The angry flush receded. "We have Liberty Bonds, and we give receipts, and we solicit aid as what the people can afford to give. The money like that from the wires is up to the ones who risk their necks to harass the enemy and to feed their children at the same time."

"Well," soothed Miller, "is it an organizational project?"

"Yes and no," said Marking. "Sometimes poor Filipino civilians get the wires first. So then it's theirs, whether they belong to our organization or not. I caught some civilians once, and they were accused as bandits because taking the wire jeopardized the lives of the people in the towns because the Japs hate anything that interferes with their plans, like taking down the wires. But when all the bandits were brought to me I recognized them as poor people from Taytay, and they explained to me. And I guess it is their right to do something against the Japs, too, especially if it will survive their children, because when children are hungry they cry, and that is very hard for the father, and he better do something quick. I guess there's nothing wrong about it. If I am in their shoes and not a leader, I guess I will get more than a little wire."

"Well," said Stoddard, "now that that is clear, where were we?"

"Missions," reminded Marking.

"Well," said Miller, "when we cut communications this time, we cut them permanently. Is that all right with you?"

"Sure. What do you want to do with the wire?"

"Huh? Oh! Well, get rid of it."

"Destroy it," said Stoddard.

"Destroy it!" expostulated Marking. "Of course not! We will hide it for after the war and put it up again for our own communications."

"That's right," said Miller. "Save it for the U.S. Army."

Stoddard grinned. "The U.S. Army said destroy it."

Said Marking emphatically, "It is a waste to destroy it. We will save it, and when they need some they will say thank you."

Stoddard laughed. Miller laughed. "Marking," they probed, "have you ever heard about carrying out orders to the letter?"

"Sure. Sometimes they don't know what they're talking about."

Through November into December, Miller and Stoddard worked. Marking had the organization; Stoddard and Miller, the equipment and specific instructions. They set up radio transmitters all over Rizal and Laguna. They carried out almost impossible orders, and sometimes they ate and sometimes they didn't, but they made only one personal demand.

"Yay," said Lyd, "he's at it again." "What's he want now?"—I was worn out, jumpy, irritated. "What he always wants." "Dear God, give it to him." "Everybody's drilling or patrolling or taking demolition courses or on details."

"Take it up with Marking. Tell him Miller *demands* a toilet." "It's not my line." "What the hell makes you think it's mine? . . . Well, all right."

Across the clearing, I could hear Stod's voice, then George's. "Stod, where did you put Mary?" "I gave it to you." "Are you sure?" "George, I'm sure."

"Lyd," I said. "They can't find Mary again. Those codes are going to end a beautiful friendship."

"It's their friendship," said Lyd.

She left. I worked. She came back.

"Sh-h-h! Look."

This was Marking's signed order:

"*Any sonumabits who removes his bowels anywhere except in the hole at which it is intended will pick it up and carry it with his own bare hands to that place because I also am very, very tired of it. I myself stepped in it last night what more Miller and Stoddard.*
                    MARCOS V. AGUSTIN, Commanding."

Stod stooped to enter the headquarters *kubo*. "Lyd, will you help me?"

"Speak," said Lyd.

"Well, it's this way. I ask one of the boys if he wants something, and he says 'Huh-uh.' So I don't give him anything, and he stands there, and pretty soon he asks me for some fuse. I tell him to bring it back after demonstrating it, and he says 'Huh-uh,' and I tell him he will bring it back because I said so, and he says 'Huh-uh' again, and I'm just too busy to take it up right then, and after a while he comes back and smiles, mind you, and gives me the fuse. Then somebody comes up and asks me if we're going to have a class, and I haven't got time right then, so I say 'Huh-uh.' They all get together at the demonstration table, and I don't pay much attention to what's going on because I'm busy, and finally one of them comes and says that everybody is ready, sir. It goes on and on, just like that."

"I will give you the secret," said Lyd. "When you say 'Huh-uh,' it means yes."

"Well," said Stod, "when you say 'Huh-uh,' it should mean 'No.'" And he shook his head slowly from side to side, saying, "Huh-uh," and looked up. "Like that. See what I mean?"

"In *your* country, maybe, but not in my country."

"That's what Marking says. I kept asking him, and I think he got tired of explaining."

"Next question," said Lyd, imps in her eyes.

Stod sat wearily, his big hands spread on his knees, his bulky shoulders hunched, his unshaven face looking worn. "Deliver me from the Philippines, huh-uh."

Miller and Stoddard were the centrifugal force in the heart of a patriotic Filipino guerrilla outfit with more individualists per square inch than they ever in their worst forebodings anticipated.

Cote, on a lone scouting tour, discovered the best observation post the outfit was ever to have—a castle-like pinnacle above the limestone cliff, and there the radio operators, Monty, Dag, Larry, and Tony and their reserve men, took turns sending and receiving the radio messages.

"Marking," said Miller, "we've got to keep an eye out for crash-landing fliers."

"Don't worry about it."

"But we've *got* to! Look at this order!"

"Well, tell MacArthur not to worry about it."

"But this is the *order!* To pick 'em up and ship 'em through."

"*Without an order*, we would do it anyway! Our kind of army doesn't need orders, every time, every time. Long time ago, while you were still sleeping, I told everybody to watch. Any flier falls down in our territory, he's our credit."

"This is what I'm trying to find out, Marking. Do you have men assigned to do exactly that—*to save American fliers, to help them out of the danger zones, to show them the way to our camps?*"

"George, there are men assigned to look after all that."

"*Who?*"

"*Everybody, of course.*" And Marking flung off.

"Don't worry about it, George," I said. "Just hope the fliers keep their feet pulled up if they fly too low. I assure you the guerrillas are anxious to carry out MacArthur's rescue orders. They want to make a good showing. Whether a flier wants to be rescued or not, the guerrillas will rescue him."

"Well," said Miller, "I hope they do, I hope they do."

A distant roar indicated another flight of Allied planes—oftener and oftener they were coming. Suddenly Marking began running back and forth and yelling for me, and that meant wave after wave.

"I'll be up at the OP," said Miller.

"Me, too," said Marking.

Wave after wave, and the distant, thundering roll of bombs formed a background of sound to the stepped-up guerrilla activity everywhere. Each day, each roll of explosion, each radio message out and each one in swept us on to the victorious conclusion.

I dropped the sheaf of letters and climbed up to the OP myself. Flak and pillars of smoke and diving bombers filled the sky over Manila. Nine, then eleven, distinct smoke pillars merged into a heavy pall over the city, and in three widely separated spots big fires could be distinguished. Binoculars picked out an enemy ship burning in the bay, another sinking.

Combat excited Marking. "When do *we* fight, when do *we* fight?" he demanded for the thousandth time.

Miller looked around at him, binoculars still trained on the city, then looked back and through the glasses. On his face was impatience with both GHQ-SWPA [General Headquarters-Southwest Pacific Area] and Marking, for every buffer state is bruised and shaken.

So I said to Marking, "Calm down. Every time the runners bring up maps and reports, and every time Miller and Stod cuss over the coding, and every time Tony and Larry and Monty tap the message through until they're cross-eyed, *that's your fight!* This outfit is the pointing finger now; those planes, America's fists."

"Blah-blah-blah!" said Marking. He demanded, "When do *we* fight? When, huh?"

"As soon as you get your orders," said Miller.

"Orders, orders. *Lie low, get information, save fliers.* Is *that* all we're going to do? Pretty soon, there'll be no more war. Pretty soon, it'll be peacetimes all the time! You better get those orders, George. You tell MacArthur what we're going to do. Tell him we better hit now."

Miller muttered, "I don't tell MacArthur—MacArthur tells me."

And by radio came messages from MacArthur to Miller, the gist of which was to keep right on doing as he was told, that he was doing splendidly.

South from Manila and its inferno a crippled plane limped through the clouds, pulling toward the Rizal mountains behind Teresa and Tanay as instructed. Rapidly it lost altitude. Then, over the placid bosom of Laguna de Bay, it wavered and crashed.

Ensign Marshall S. Hopp, suspended above the waiting waters, by his parachute, floated gently downward, and splashed not far from where the plane was sinking out of sight. He slashed at the parachute cords, treading water, but was pulled under and entangled. Kicking up, he cut again at the cords.

A *banca* slid up, paddled for dear life by our Home Guard fishermen on assignment to catch anything American that might fall from the skies. With much heaving and pulling, they got the big fellow out of the water and bore him off.

They made him lie flat in the *banca* to hide his face, which, against the green of the lake and the blue of the sky and their own chocolate-brown color flamed like a torch. They paddled on and on, firmly pressing him flat each time he lifted his head, pantomiming that he must stay exactly so. They shuddered at his rosiness, knowing that Japs on the shore would be scanning the lake with binoculars, and wondered if they should dive and scoop up some mud to cover his shockingly blond hair and his bright blue eyes. Hopp himself quaked a little inwardly: "I didn't know who my rescuers were. None of them spoke English, but their lingo wasn't Japanese, and that was the straw of comfort at which I grasped."

He heard a halloo, and chattering among the men paddling him he knew not where.

A large sailboat careened up, loosened its sails, and the fishermen paddled the *banca* lightly over the swell it made. He saw them clumsily salute Younger Soriano, who curtly nodded in acknowledgment and smiled widely at the flier, saying, "Your clothes are wet." Behind him his men smiled. Hopp's quick eyes recognized the U.S. Army Enfields, issue 1917. Younger Soriano, in charge of the guerrilla patrol, invited him to step into the sailboat.

In the sailboat, there followed the usual sidestepping. The men tacked back and forth, checked up with passing boats the position and direction of Jap movements, and sent word ahead to Cardona that a special shipment was coming through. Toward sundown, several hours after Hopp had crashed, the sailboat touched shore in a lonely spot, and a patrol of Filipino fighters escorted him along a footpath into the bushes. Some walked far ahead of him—his "advance patrol"; some were behind him—his "rear guard"; and Younger Soriano and a few more were all around him—his "bodyguards."

They hid Hopp in a small *kubo* within hearing distance of the town, where the Japs and their collaborators harangued a forced meeting of the townspeople. Among the townspeople were the fishermen who had helped Hopp. "The Americans can never come back," said the Japs. "We will never let them come back. The Filipino people must bring us any American they find." The townspeople nodded obediently, and their mayor assured the enemy that no American could return to the Philippines with impunity.

Night had fallen. Suddenly there was a rustling, a footfall. Hopp's nerves jumped, for the darkness hid the guerrillas from him and he could not see that some were "scouting the terrain" and others were at fixed stations guarding the approaches to his *kubo*. It had not occurred to the fighters to inform him, because they took it for granted that all America knew of their achievements in occupied territory. As he sat tense a voice whispered, "Food, sir. You eat now." He groped, took the object handed to him, felt its roundness, and, investigating further with his fingertips, found the contents soft, warm, and sticky. It was a bowl of rice.

There was more rustling, the footsteps fading. Around Hopp's heart there was a tightness, through it a warmth. Only he knows today what he thought and felt with the rice bowl in his hands and the knowledge that around him in the night were brave, brown men ready to die for cause, country, and one Ensign Hopp.

"You come now." He distinguished movement, sensed a group drawing in to gather him up, spreading out in a line again to lead him, guard him, and cover his passage. The night was lightening as the moon rose.

The walk across the rice fields, into the foothills, and finally up the long mountain stretch to Camp Yay above the *barrio* of Koyambay exhausted him. Instead of taking him out of his dreamy state, the night's events and the long climb under eager, triumphant escort plunged him deeper into Alice-in-Wonderland. On top of the mountain, he stepped into the clearing of headquarters camp.

"Hello," said Marking. "How are you?"

"Come on in," said Miller. "Sit down? You soft Navy guys..."

"Have a drink?" said Stoddard. "You might not get another one."

Lyd said, "Notice his manners? Straight from civilization." I said, "He looks like an Indiana farmer, a young one."

Hopp asked wonderingly, "Why don't they tell us about things like this?"

We chorused blankly, "Don't they? They sure know about us. Right now, they're hollering about where are all their precious aviators, and we keep telling them to keep their shirts on, we're doing our best."

"I mean about all *this*." His hands a little helplessly indicated the fighters, the camp, Miller and Marking, and last of all small, sturdy, grinning Lyd in her khaki coveralls with Sakai strapped to her leg.

Younger Soriano made formal report on the rescue, and Hopp told the story, in bits, from his own angle. All through his hesitant talk ran the questioning inflection, "What goes on?" His first real question of Miller and Stoddard indicated that he would appreciate knowing how the other two Americans had arrived.

"Tell him," I urged. "Tell him you got here the same way."

Miller radioed Hopp's serial number, name, and facts of rescue. "You'll get your instructions here, by return radio message."

Because the clean, grave boy appealed to Bernie, just in from the Kaliwa, and to Roger and Lyd and the fighters and me, we gave him an awkward but sincere program in his honor.

There were two bottles of *tuba*, a local wine. There was a little singing. And we told him, in halting speech, how much it meant to the Filipino people to see America's sons come flying over us, silver eagles against the sun. All that we could say to him was still too deep. First had come the Filipino radio men, recruited from America, trained in Australia, sent into the Philippines by way of New Guinea and thus become our "New Guinea boys." Next came Miller and Stoddard. And now, for a little while and a happy while, Ensign Hopp was with us. Manding did the boogie in his honor. Rae sang the guerrilla songs. We gave him a letter for his parents, knowing no better way to express ourselves. Quietly he took it, and we felt he too wanted to say more and felt as helpless as we.

As suddenly as Hopp had come, he was gone, gone across country, up and over the sierras with Bernie, forced-hiking against time, to be picked up on the Tayabas side from Andy's camp. The order had come by radio. Days after his departure, we laughed, remembering his departure.

"Is it far from here?" he had asked. "No-o-o, not too far." "Same distance as I came last night?" We looked at him incredulously: "What! Good heavens, man, you haven't even started yet! It's ten times that distance." "Well—mountains?" "The most beautiful mountains you ever saw! Leeches? Boy! A wild river? Wait till you tangle with it." "How long do you think it will take?" "Your guides could make it in five days flat, hiking from dawn to dark." "Five days isn't so bad—" "You won't make it in five days."

Miller had run his eye up and down Hopp's frame. "You boys don't get much exercise."

I said, "He'll make up for it now."

After he left, we laughed, with sympathy, for the route was a tough one, and yet not with pity, for he was having a vacation without knowing it. Bernie and his men kept him safe, fed him well, and showed him some of the most beautiful country in the Philippines—unexplored territory.

CHAPTER 28

Wings over Manila again, every day, three times a day, all day long. Frantic enemy movements in the city.

Then Marking ordered, "Pack up." "Why? This is a good camp," said Miller. "Japs." "I don't see any." "You will." "How close are they?" "Two hours, if they come through jungle."

Miller raised his eyebrows gently. He knew his orders, specifying, "Avoid any semblance of authority," and "Security of personnel will rest with the commander."

But Marking no more wanted to leave the best OP in Rizal province than he, and welcomed his reluctance to move.

"Where are the Japs?" asked Miller. "A little too near." "Where?" "At the foot of this mountain on the other side." "It's a big mountain." "About one hour from here." Miller's eyebrows raised a little: "Well, the radios—" "We'll have to be mobile again."

"Well—" "Pack up," said Marking.

The camp packed up, and Miller and Stod said, "We might as well go along."

Through Makantog, we rolled back to the shelf camp at Sulok. "I understand," said Miller, "the Japs have attacked this place twice."

"They got hurt, too," said Marking. "The retreat from here is good. We can fight, and we can withdraw."

Miller centered his attention on Mapa, Eadie, and Seneres of Intelligence. To Mapa, Marking assigned one radio set, with orders to move from town to town, staying in the foothills as near the highway as possible. To Eadie, Miller gave one "must" order: "Get the little bag that hangs around his neck, any Jap's neck. Bring along any Jap insignia you can get hold of. That's what headquarters wants, identification."

Japs began to flood in from outside the Philippines. Mapa and his men stayed close to the Jap-seething towns, and when the Japs, retreating day and night, in confusion, stepped off the bombarded highways by the thousands, he shuttled from hill to hill, changing position every few hours, day after day describing circles and figure-eights in the brush and rice paddies. He stayed on the air.

Seneres's famous GID runners and relay men, around the clock, entered and left the city, teams unknown to other teams, off a cross country through the *cogon* and forest, back again with mail to leave and more mail to take. Wherever Miller was moved, to keep him and his equipment safe, the runners found him.

Marking and Miller decided between them that the Net Control Station should be farther back, out of danger of a possible raid by the Japs. I was fast losing my grip, tired, accomplishing little, nervously irritable.

"You need a rest," said Miller.

"Colonel Yay will be in charge of the NCS," said Marking. "Rest!" I smiled ruefully at Miller. "Rest!" But I knew it would be a rest just to get away from Marking's energy.

"You can rest there, darling," he insisted. "It will be just a very small camp. You eat, you sleep, you do nothing at all except write me letters."

With a certain amount of anticipation, Lyd and I picked our men.

"Gimme Nick Cristóbal," I said. "But that's a good one," said Marking, "and I need him here." Implacably I read on, "Also Delfin, Herman, Reging, Josías—" "You don't need Josías: I need him here." "—Josías, Navarrete, Johnny—" "You absolutely cannot have Johnny." "You are lucky that I'm not taking Borres and Doy." "Take the nurses, then." "Nothing doing. We *are* going to have a small camp. Absolutely nothing but strictly essential personnel." He protested, "How about some of the useless ones here?"

"They're all yours," said Lyd, grinning.

Lyd and I filed out with some forty-five men, most of them *cargadors* carrying the equipment. Only seventeen fighters, including Marking's relatives as my bodyguards, and radio personnel numbering eleven, plus Lyd and me, were to maintain the Net Control Station.

"Watch for ambush," said Marking. "Look out at the forks of the trail."

For the first time in the history of the outfit, I was on my own to strike a new camp and hold it, and the NCS mission itself was of paramount importance.

"If she can keep that camp hidden—" said Miller.

"Oh, she can hide," Marking assured him. "She sure can hide."

For Lyd and me, it was a lark. Away from the tedious and pressure-of-work routine in the main camp, we spread our wings. A Jap plane soared up from the lowlands, skimming over the Taranka trail. We ordered the fighters into the grass. Nick and Delfin acted as advance patrol. The heavily burdened *cargadors* fell behind the rear guard, one by one lagging back, and finally we gave up struggling to pull them along. We kept ambling along contentedly, and Rae, in the new khaki overalls Marking had ordered made for her, trudged patiently between Lyd and me, the sweat running down her face.

"Tired, baby?" "No, Mother." "Have you ever walked this far in your life?" "Not up and down, Mother." "How's your Aunt Lyd making out?" Rae giggled, "Mother, she's more wet with sweat than I. She looks awful."

"How far is it?" asked Lyd. "Just Kanumay?"

"Kanumay, on the far side."

Without Marking to prod and yank the line along, we rested too often, paused on every rise to feast our eyes on the view, used the slowness of the others as excuse to linger. We made poor time, lost our way, found it again. Sunset, then dusk, found us cutting our way into the old basin, which in twenty-one months had grown over with young trees, thicket, and vines choked with *cogon*.

We threw up a tepee on the flattened *cogon*, carelessly piling more uprooted *cogon* against the tepee framework. Hot porridge and a strip of jerky beside a crackling campfire made, within the circle of firelight, a touch of home. Leaning against trees and rocks, knees drawn up, we happily planned our camp.

Delfin and Lyd worked out the details with Josías. O'Classen opened up the equipment and, early the next morning, placed it in the sun to dry. Briones and Manansala propped up their weather apparatus. On the third day, not only was the camp in shape, but Lyd had engineered bamboo lattices and I had a great tree fern placed on a terrace and two orchids tied on the lattice. Off hours in the evening, the whole camp became the Skyline Club and held open discussion with decisions by popular vote, a buck private's vote equal to that of any officer. Each evening, the next day's work was set, and so eagerly did each do his share and more that thirty pairs of hands to guard, cook, build *kubos*, cut paths, level terraces, make a latrine and keep the NCS operating were still able to weave a bulletin board and cut and bind together rustic benches. The camp was named for Lyd.

"The trouble with us," I said, "we think the war is over."

But the old camp we had left behind was the same old hurly-burly of this and that and these and those, except it was more so. Amid their troubles, they were further pestered by runners and *cargadors* between the two camps who raved over the new one and proclaimed its beauty and the freedom of decision allowed its occupants.

New Year's Eve, Camp Lyd held vigil, talking idly over the bamboo cups of thin, tasteless coffee stepped up a little by a few drops of a hoarded bottle of imitation crème de menthe. The midnight hour was already upon us, by surprise, and the spontaneity of Auld Lang Syne, crossed handshakes, and good wishes gave a further fillip.

Victor, the courier, brought us additional laughter the next morning, for grumpily and enviously Marking had written:

HELL'S CAMP
1 January 1945

To Col. Yay and the whole gang of the Seventh Heaven Camp:
Hell's Camp personnel were wishing you all a very happy and a prosperous New Year. This is all I can say.

MARCOS V. AGUSTIN, *Commanding*

Then followed personal notes, troubling Seventh Heaven: one of the new Chinese fighters, fiddling with a Tommy gun, had pulled the trigger and geysered a clipful of bullets skyward, thus routing some fifty other Chinese whom it took half the day to find and herd back into camp. Badidles and Musico pulled their guns in an argument over the manning of the outposts. Tomatoes, almost as big as golf balls, had disappeared under Marking's "very own nose" as he envisioned a touch of salad for lunch.

Then, suddenly, there was a slow, steady tightening. Miller and Stod, reading between the lines of the radio messages, began to watch and listen even more carefully, as if somewhere beyond the horizon ghosts were materializing, taking shape, coming in.

They prodded Marking continually for specific answers to radioed queries. How many Japs permanently garrisoned in Manila? How many cables were in working order, how many out of commission, since when? Where were the Japs moving? How good were their motor pools?

Tense, wound up like a spring, waiting for orders to get into the thick of it himself, Marking held himself in leash in ways familiar to me but unfathomable to George Miller. Around one of his personal letters to me was a border of typewriter soldiers, painstakingly pecked out:

"Marking," said George. Marking glowered, made no answer. "MacArthur wants to know how many Japs there are in Rizal." Marking pecked out more soldiers. "He wants to know *now*."

Scowling, Marking said, "We told him that already. We told him again, again, again, *again!*"

Patiently George, for cause and country, prodded at Marking, "He wants to know again."

"You tell him same as the last time."

"*Are* they the same in number, and in the same places?"

"Today the same. Yesterday the same. Last yesterday the same. The next tomorrow the same."

"Marking," prompted Miller, "day before yesterday is not the day after tomorrow. The forces have to know all this."

"You tell MacArthur to come here and count them himself."

"Nice soldiers." Miller craned his neck to look at the typewriter soldiers.

No answer from Marking. His grumpy silence meant, "Mind your own business."

"Well," said Miller, "I guess I'll have to tell him what you said."

It was a subtle threat.

"Go ahead." That noon Marking ate in lone state, not inviting Miller and Stoddard. After lunch, he cleaned his gun. He wandered around the camp. He made more typewriter soldiers.

Again Miller came to prod him. Said Marking, "No air drop. So tell him nothing, nothing at all. Let him guess." "I'm trying my damnedest to get the air drop, Marking, but they have lots of other things to do."

"Me, too."

Overhead, the P-38's roared, on mission along the highways. Marking leaped up, jogged across the clearing, followed the flight.

"Pretty soon, those boys won't know where to hit," said Miller. "Pretty soon, maybe they'll get shot down instead."

Wavering, Marking thought about it. Then he motioned toward his headquarters, dug out his map, and he and Miller pored over the Japs' positions. "Here," said Marking, "and here. Ten thousand in Antipolo. One thousand in New Bosoboso. Two thousand in Old Bosoboso. Two thousand in and around Teresa. One hundred, one hundred, each *barrio*. Many going to Kalinawan, no estimate yet. I dispatched men to find out about that one."

"It looks like a line from Montalban to Tanay," said Miller. "If we can just verify that line beyond a doubt—"

"That's the line. The Japs are very busy digging more trenches and tunnels and putting more ammunition everywhere. How am I going to fight that line *without any bullets?* You get that air drop, George; *you better get that air drop,* or there won't be any war in Rizal province."

"Marking, I'm just a guy named Miller. I can ask, and they can say *No.*"

"I can say *No,* too," said Marking. "You watch me say *No.*"

CHAPTER 29

Then the world began to gain true momentum all around us. For three years it had stood almost still. Soon after New Year's 1945, it began to turn a little faster—not yet to spin, but to revolve more quickly, more surely.

Miller and Stoddard decided it would be better both for the forces and for local resistance to stick closer to the Net Control Station. They dared not leave the unpredictable, hotheaded Marking behind, and so they came climbing with Marking and the inevitable string of fighters up to Camp Lyd. Commander MacWilliams, a rescued flier, the true gentleman of all time, accompanied them. Left behind at Sulok was all the rest of Hell's Camp, a conglomeration of Filipinos and Chinese, real soldiers and the rugged individualistic guerrillas, sick men and well men, visitors and camp followers, armed and unarmed, and sometimes the supply lines arrived and sometimes the ever thickening Jap swarms ran them to hell and gone.

It was easy to see that the arrivals at Camp Lyd were glad to arrive.

"H'm-m!" said Miller, looking around.

"Peacetimes," snorted Marking, but he looked around surreptitiously at the rustic beauty, the orderliness, and the satisfaction in the faces of those who had brought out of the wilderness most of its beauty and none of its trash.

"Now, *this* is a *camp*," said Stod, sticking a pin into Marking. "Welcome," we said, "welcome." And we might as well have said it to the whole countryside, for the old Sulok shelf-camp was for the third time attacked.

"There goes Hell's Camp," I said to Lyd.

"Here they come," said Lyd.

Roger and a handful of men defended the old camp in the positions from which Marking had fought in 1943 and Bernie in 1944. Now, in January 1945, the historic picture spot underwent its last lashing of enemy fire.

Standing orders had been that if the Sulok camp was attacked, the fighters and retreaters should retreat in any direction except Camp Lyd, to draw the pursuers elsewhere and leave the Net Control Station unimperiled and on the air. But from all over the retreatees straggled in. Within the day, there was a congestion of personnel, scarcity of food, and the imminence of a Jap attack on the station itself.

The equipment, the precious voice to and from MacArthur, had to be whisked out of it; nor could the retreatees be scaled off or shunted away in such immediate danger. It was better to pull farther and farther back until we could see the way clear to slip back in. To linger would bring on another three-weeks retreat, and there were less than three weeks to go, the way the Jap lines in Rizal were shaping up and the way the curt, quick, specific queries came in from GHQ night and day by radio.

Down from Kanumay we tumbled, wasting no time. In the night, because firing had been heard in the *barrio* of San Andres, we gave the *barrio* a wide berth, passing through *cogon* along the Lenatin River, pushing farther east into the interior.

Hour after hour, in the new camp, we waited for word of the promised air drop. The instructions were clear: "Three signal fires equidistant with a marker in the middle." The fliers would look for that, at the latitude and longitude to which they were ordered to drop us ammunition and food.

But when? When?

We moved the station again—and again—for safety, Marking going ahead. He had food waiting for us as we neared the latest camp, welcome food, for the country was even more barren than usual.

Lyd ate a little, then moved off by herself. I watched her, thinking, "It's on again." Joe Ano, whose cousin I had executed so long before, had faithfully checked up on Manuel, at my order and Lyd's plea, and quietly he had come to tell her that it would be better not to hope any more. So gentle were his words that she had stood a moment uncomprehending; then she had walked swiftly away among the rocks and thickets to storm out her grief. Marking and I, in turn, had held her from pounding her small fists against the jagged limestone, protecting her from blind self-injury until she sagged weakly.

I walked over to her now. "Lyd, this next camp for the NCS will probably be the last. Yours, Camp Lyd, was the first, exclusively for the NCS. Would you like to make them twin camps for remembrance? This next camp should be Camp Manuel."

One for the living, one for the dead. One for the outfit's "little sister"; one for an intelligence officer who had been the Philippines' outstanding short-story writer.

Lyd made no answer.

After the Liberation, Lyd was to kneel and touch with her small, warm hands the cold block of paving stone, miraculously unshattered in the ruins, upon which, in the months in Old Bilibid, Manuel had scratched for her his name. She was to walk, walk, question, walk, and with her whole searching being listen for a word, any word. The truck filled with black-hooded, doomed prisoners, leaning weakly against one another, sustaining one another? Yes—oh, yes—one had slipped his hood, worked it loose by rubbing cheek against shoulder, and disclosed a large, bluish black birthmark on the side of his face, which an acquaintance among the pedestrians had seen. It was a message for Lyd, to tell her which way he had gone. She was to learn that a humble gravedigger, risking his life, scattered straw about the mouth of the great pit, to ease, to give a token of comfort before the heads rolled and the torsos spurted blood. August 30, 1944. And she was, finally, to hold his skull, shriven of its evenly modeled features, its pale, clean, lemon-colored skin, its compassionate mouth, its amused eyes—and to say, "This was he."

Doomed, Manuel had chosen to die. His inquisitors during his mock trial had told him to define "democracy." His voice was resonant; his words were rich in message. He proclaimed not only what democracy was but how much more it could be!

There are no tears for Manuel, nor for Lyd, who intimately knew his greatness. There are tears only for a world which lost him.

These things were in Lyd's future when we named the camp for Manuel. They were the terrors which sucked the breath out of her lungs at night.

The churning days swept on.

Although the first false start, when Cabalhin got himself shot out of action at Santa Maria and other combat officers laid down barrages with their rifles instead of sniping, had almost finished the scant store of bullets, it was imperative that "Marking's Guerrillas" carry out missions, air drop or no air drop. They had said they could. There would be no excuses.

At our new cross-trails headquarters, two miles from the radio headquarters, Marking called in more and more fighting men. There were times when as many as five hundred fighters and supply men were in the camp, waiting for orders to roll.

Three big *kawalis* steamed with rice. Every can, large and small, was filled with thick fresh-beef soup. Fighters lay around in the shade of the coconut grove. A long line of burdened men and women filed into camp.

"Supplies," said Marking.

Two small figures in the distance came jogging toward headquarters—runners.

"Sir," said one, "report from Mapa."

"Sir," said the other, "report from Vicencio."

Marking unrolled the packet of papers, handed them one by one to Miller.

"Damn good work," said Miller.

"Of course," said Marking.

We pieced the jigsaw puzzle together. When MacArthur hit Leyte, the Japs poured down Luzon into the Bicol peninsula. Then the Forces took Mindoro to the west, and the Japs started running toward Batangas. Then the guerrillas started rumors that the landing was in Infanta, and the heavy garrison there, poised to run west to Batangas, hesitated and settled down in Infanta again. There was no new action, it seemed. The Japs kept pushing toward both the Bicol and Batangas. The Forces were to hit Lingayén, and the Japs who had rushed southward would pull northward. It was boxing against ju-jitsu, and jab after jab had worn the Japs out with running after the jabber.

Came our orders to hit, but no air drop. "We can still do a lot," said Miller. "You watch," said Marking. Long lines of fighters came rolling in, worn but jubilant. Runners came in swift succession. Fresh fighters fell in line, snappily counting off.

Suddenly Miller began to see—and hear.

"Mapa blew his bridge last night."

"Did he use that dynamite we sent?"

"Yes. With the two-hundred-and-twenty-five-pound American dud bomb his men lugged over and laid under the bridge—and they blew it to hell. The town shook like jelly. The mountain jumped."

Vicencio and more fighters checked in, hilarious, worn out. Three platoons of them fell in, counted off, fell out, swarmed around the *kawalis* and cans.

"You see?" said Marking. "They got the first line of foxholes, and American planes strafed the Jap reinforcements on the highway before they got to the fight."

"Marking, it's going swell," said Miller.

"Yeah. Mata's coming in, Badidles out. Jornación in, Bautista out. Vicencio in, Pagayunan out. We're keeping that highway hot!"

"I can see you were a good bus driver."

"George, I was the best bus driver on the line."

Miller sent out by radio the results of guerrilla activity, and Marking kept him supplied with new reports.

"The Japs repaired Mapa's bridge, and he blew it up again. Mata's men in. They hit again—truck. His men are sporting the Jap helmets and canteens." "I want one for a souvenir." "Full of bullet holes." "Now I gotta have one." "Jornación got a jitney." "Yowzah! Jap officers in it?" "Of course." "What's the condition of enemy troops now?"

Back and forth flew the runners.

"The Japs are very tired," said Marking. "Some are dying by the highway. Some ate the *carabao* that died from hauling their equipment. They move only at night now, to escape the American planes."

"How many pass in the night?" insisted Miller.

"That is impossible," answered Marking. "Does MacArthur expect us to grope among the Japs and feel each nose to count? We might be counting our own noses, trying to count theirs."

"But headquarters has to know how many are getting through."

"Tell headquarters that they pass all night, and they go very slow because they are very tired and very hungry."

"That isn't military intelligence. That's algebra."

"All right," said Marking, "You do it better without any moon. I tell you, they're not moving any more in the daytime. Next week, when the moon comes again, we won't be counting them, either. We'll be shooting them."

We were active at last!

CHAPTER 30

And in the midst of the checking in and out of the fighters, there was a loud report at the outpost. A boy came running: "Accidental shot, sir!"

They carried the wounded boy to us.

"Sir! I *have* to move! I can't lie still. I must sit up, sir."

"Fajardo," said Marking, "if you move, you'll die. You'll bleed inside."

"Mammy," groaned Fajardo. "I'm not afraid. Don't leave me."

The packings over the abdominal wound were soaked with blood, and it oozed out between Marking's fingers as he held it in place. He added another sterile packing over it, firmly, with the greatest of care, slipping the additional gauze over the bloody one under his hand.

Fajardo watched us, looking down at Marking who sat on the planking beside him, looking up at me as I held his shoulders quiet and talked to him. His arm across my lap reached up around my neck, and he pulled me down to whisper, "Mammy, please ask the Old Man to send for Josefina, the daughter of General Cailles."

I misunderstood. "Is Josefino a relative? Is he your friend?"

"Mammy, it is a girl. It is my wife."

Fajardo was "combat," and couldn't be married—it was against the rules. Home Guards could marry; fighters could not, unless they turned their rifles in and were transferred to Home Guard service.

Therefore I hesitated, and said, "The doctor is coming. Be patient. Do what the Old Man says."

"Yes, Mammy." Then, "Please, Mammy, please! I'm not afraid to die, only I am dying. Please send for her."

Roger had come to the relief of Marking, who was now digging into the surgical can.

"Fajardo, will you lie still while I talk to the Old Man?"

"Yes, Mammy."

I rose from the trestle where the young fighter, a son of Dr. Jacobo Fajardo, once director of the Bureau of Health, lay dying. Hesitantly, wondering how to say it, I walked over to Marking. He spoke to me first.

"Darling, that damn doctor... Where are the sutures? and needles?"
"In my own kit. Will you sew him up now?"

Very low, Marking said, "There's wind inside him through the wounds. That's why he always wants to move his bowels. He thinks it's his bowels. It's the wind, the air sucked in through the bullet holes."

"There's a lot of blood under the trestle."

"That's just external. It's inside him the worst is happening."

When Marking reached for the phenobarbital I knew that we were to lose another of our best fighters. My throat tightened painfully, and I bit down against rising tears. "How long will he last?" I asked.

"Four hours—but it could be ten, because he is brave." Fajardo struggled to sit up.

Marking ordered, "Lie still. All you got is a scratch, and you make nothing but hardheaded fuss."

The boy quieted.

"Marking, he asks you to send for General Cailles's daughter." He straightened, looked me full in the face, and so I said, "She's his wife."

We looked into each other's eyes, for the space of a few seconds, and all the tragedy of young

Fajardo flowed back and forth between us. We had heard about a lovely young girl who had turned down two handsome guerrilla colonels for a thin, pale guerrilla sergeant. Old Cailles, a general of the Revolution, had hidden and fed guerrillas off and on throughout the Occupation. He had a daughter named Josefina.

Marking walked out into the sunshine, motioned to a fighter and a Home Guard who had arrived earlier in the day: "Go as fast as you can to General Cailles. Tell him that one of my fighters is his son-in-law, that he is dying, that he wants to see his wife Josefina. Put the girl on a horse. Come as quickly as you can."

He walked back in, relieved Roger, touched my back as I sat in the earlier position with the boy's arm flung restlessly across my lap.

When I felt the touch I leaned down to whisper, "The Old Man has sent for Mrs. Fajardo." Fajardo opened his eyes as if very tired, and smiled faintly.

An hour passed. Again he grew restive. "I cannot stand the pain," he said. "Please let me sit. *Please.*"

Soft words were of no avail. He heaved his body, and Marking burst out, "Fajardo! You God-damn obey orders! You keep quiet! Keep quiet, you can be drilling again in one week. Keep moving, and the war will be over before you can even walk."

Roger talked, in a musical cadence. "You will be all right. A little patience, comrade. Just a little patience."

The phenobarbital began to take effect. Fajardo quieted.

At intervals Marking or I walked outside to watch the trail. At intervals, when he grew restive, we soothed or scolded to keep him quiet.

The sun began to set. The pulse beat under my fingertips skipped a beat, two beats, then raced.

Something happened to my stomach, as if the muscles tightened. I felt again with my fingertips, searching for the pulse, trying to count, trying to catch the skipping. And I looked up to find Marking's eyes upon me. Softly he walked over to us.

There was a clamminess to Fajardo's forehead, to his hands. He opened his eyes, looked blindly through Marking, Roger, and me bent over him.

"Mammy, the crucifix! I will kiss the cross."

Quickly I turned my wrist. "Against your lips, lad. It's the cross on my bracelet."

Marking's hand was under his head, and I saw the boy's lips strain against the little crucifix. Then his head lolled to one side, and Marking laid him gently back on the improvised pillow. Fajardo's pal, young Barros, threw himself across the dead boy's chest with a boy's wild cry of grief. Marking strode out into the gathering dusk, and I heard his own sobs and followed him, biting my teeth, flinging tears off my cheeks with an impatient hand.

"God damn, oh, God damn!" sobbed Marking. "That was a real fighter. That was a real boy. Three years, and how many raids, and now the Forces are here and he dies without even a fight!"

"Hold it," I said.

"Why don't they come? Why don't they come now before it's too late? *Why are they still only coming?* Oh, God, I don't want to be a guerrilla leader! I don't want to be anything! I don't want to lose my men! I just want to fight! It's all right if it's me! But my boys are so young! Oh, God, *make MacArthur come! Make him kill Yamashita!* Oh, God, let *me* kill Yamashita, let me kill *Japs, Japs, Japs!*"

Holding his arms down, making him look down at me, I said, "It wasn't Japs that killed Fajardo. It was plain damn carelessness." And I drew him back to the headquarters, where Barros and other fighters were mourning.

Barros on his knees looked up, the tears streaming down his face, "Mammy, I am the only one left now!" For lack of comforting words, I put my hand on his head, and he said, "Of the six of us who started together, *I am the only one left!*"

My grief came out in anger, as I looked around at the fighters. "OK, all of you! Fajardo was sleeping between his hours of guard duty. He was upstairs, lying on his side. And one of you who didn't know a damn thing about the Garand and had no business touching any gun but your own, took Fajardo's gun and fooled with it downstairs, and it went off and the bullet went right through his abdomen, in the right side, out the left side, and it shot his guts all to hell. He didn't have a chance. He didn't have a chance even to die in battle. One of you killed him. One of you—"

Barros said, "*I'll* kill the one who killed him—"

I caught myself up short and said, "It won't bring him back, and that would be two fighters dead, instead of one, and three when we'd have to kill Barros for murder."

Barros wept again, stormily.

Marking brought the sutures. The fighters gathered round him, bathing the body, assisting him in sewing up one small hole and one hole the size of a fist. Out of Fajardo's pack they brought a clean white shirt and striped sharkskin pants, and Barros cried again, saying, "These were his wedding clothes."

Tired, feeling sick, I walked out into the night. The *kingki* light from within fell on a boy's face, a forlorn, innocent face. More tears, I thought, as the boy stepped toward me.

"Ma'am, I didn't mean to do it."

I was too worn out for any emotion, yet pity welled up out of the weariness. It wouldn't take too much strength for one more word. That was my job, I guessed—to scold and comfort and praise and blame, and sometimes I wished I were dead.

I said, "Of course you didn't mean to do it."

"I will take any punishment, ma'am."

"That will be up to the Old Man."

The boy said, "Fajardo was also *my* friend." There were no tears on his drawn young face. He was too miserable to cry, perhaps.

"You had better rest."

"May I sit beside Fajardo tonight?"

All through the night, in the flickering *kingki* light that cast deep shadows, the boy sat beside Fajardo on the trestle-bier. He sat very near, his buttock against the dead fighter's thigh, his hand resting on the body. Fajardo was twenty years old, the boy who kept vigil, seventeen.

Marking and I together received the beautiful girl who presented herself. For once the word "maganda" had not been used in vain. Hers was a madonna face, pink and ivory, and the fluffy, wavy hair was a perfect mahogany frame to her young loveliness. The brows were dark, thick, and narrowly arched; the lashes, star-pointed with tears, were very black against the smooth skin. There was a perfect mole high on her cheek. Tremulously she tried to smile, was led to a bench by her dark, uncouth, farmers'-wife companions.

"You do it," said Marking.

"Do what?" I asked.

"Whatever people do." And he eased out of the headquarters.

So I told Josefina about her husband's last hours, what he had said, how courageously he faced death, that the only person he wanted to see was herself but he hadn't been able to last the night while the Home Guards sought her.

Captain Miller walked in from Camp Manuel, and stopped short. I introduced him to the young widow, and to her Moorishly attractive sister, as different from the young madonna as two girls could be. He spoke a few quiet words of condolence.

We walked in a group to the burial ground, a stone's throw from the headquarters. The fighters were standing in double rows on three sides, forming a square U around the grave and bier. I opened my eyes in surprise at the handiwork wrought in the night. Over Fajardo, who lay with the Philippine flag drawn over him, were bowers made of woven coconut fronds with wild flowers tied in little bouquets to the bowers. Tiny baskets and balls of woven grass and fronds swung to and fro from their woven-grass strings. And the grave, wide and very deep, had been dug under the low-hanging boughs of the *katmon* tree.

The young widow was choking with sobs.

Marking and Miller were more ill at ease than I had ever seen them.

The fighters looked from the bier to the crying girl and back to the bier and at one another and back to the bier again. They too were ill at ease.

For all of them, helpless to comfort her, I spoke. "Your husband was loved by everybody. He was one of our bravest and best. No matter what the circumstances, he died for his country. Would you want us to punish the other boy whose fault it was?"

Violently she shook her head, the halo of soft, dark brown hair like a cloud. Her face lifted from the fine linen handkerchief in her tapering fingers. She struggled to speak. I waited. She tried again, but the words were so strangled I couldn't make them out. I bent nearer. She pulled something out from under her arm—a parcel loosely wrapped in newsprint.

Her sister, who had accompanied her, stepped forward, tried to take the parcel from her.

Impatiently, defiantly, Josefina pulled it away, held it close.

To the sister I said sharply, though softly, "Let her alone."

Quickly Josefina said, "I was saving these for him," and opened the little package. There was real soap, a fine toothbrush, and a small packet of tooth powder.

"Then give them to him," I said.

Blinded by tears, she stumbled, then stopped and swayed. I held her by the elbow until she steadied herself.

"I'll do it for you," I said, and quickly she handed me the little gifts, so scarce in the countryside that I wondered how long she had been saving them or where she had managed to get them.

Into Fajardo's pockets with the help of other hands I put each article, and Josefina wept audibly, yet with a dignity that made her the more pathetic.

There was silence. A bird on the wing flicked by. The fighters shifted.

Marking looked at me, and I whispered to her that the commanding officer would speak a few words. She nodded.

Marking, usually articulate, floundered around, then began to speak intelligibly. "This boy was a guerrilla officer who fought the right way and died the right way and I guess—" He swallowed, and the muscles in his lean jaw rippled. "We will not forget him."

He indicated with a few more words that Miller, "who is from General MacArthur himself," would say a prayer.

Miller acquitted himself as one most sensitive and sympathetic to the feelings of others. In the hour of bereavement, he was the gentle voice of America when there is sorrow in a household and all the neighbors help out. The fighters joined him in the Lord's Prayer.

Then quickly it was over, as the fighters lowered Fajardo into his grave with his shoes on. Fajardo's shoes were still on because no fighter would take them from him, even in death when he had no more use for them.

We led the stumbling girl-widow back to headquarters, where Borres had hot coffee in coconut shells. She drank a little, then made her adieus. We watched while the group escorting her wound down the valley trail and out of sight.

Borres said, "Tragedy follows the 'outside' child. She was the daughter of the other woman. And Fajardo was an 'outside' son . . . If they were 'inside' children it would have been different. And, Mammy, did you see the mole on her right cheek in line with the tears?"

"Yes. It made her lovelier, I think."

"Any man who marries a girl with a mole where the tears pass will die."

Marking said, "That's right."

"What's this?" asked Miller.

I explained the superstition.

"It's no superstition," said Marking, and there was a chorus of assent from the listening fighters.

"Mammy," said Barros, Fajardo's closest friend, "I myself warned him not to marry her, that he would be doomed."

Impatiently, I brushed it aside. "An accidental shot is an accidental shot."

"He died, Mammy," said Borres, and the fighters assented.

And so I thought about it, and wrote a note to Lyd at Camp Manuel. Often in our talks together we had discussed such things, and once or twice wondered that coincidence should have such a high batting average.

Miller brought us back to reality. He spoke of the possibility, at last, of the air drop. "You've got to keep those fires ready," he reminded, and Marking assured him that three planes following the highway had veered to fly low over our cross-trails camp. The smudges had pillared up to guide them, and we had flown our flags and waved and shouted ourselves into exhaustion. Telling Miller about it lifted the gloom from the camp, and after he had left for Camp Manuel the rest of us sat about reviewing the planes that had swooped down for a good look at us and the one American flyer who had opened his cockpit to lean out, grinning and waving.

The next morning, the *katmon* tree bloomed in a profusion of full, white blossoms. From among the thick boughs came the chirping and chittering of birds. I walked over alone for a moment's communion with the boy, and noticed when I walked back that others, alone and in couples, were in their own way saying goodbye to Fajardo. It seemed odd, for Fajardo had never been "the life of the party." He had been quiet, obedient, friendly; nor was there anything particularly handsome or winsome about him. He was plain, not very articulate. Yet, of all the deaths, his was felt deepest by most of us. Was it because the end was so near that the tragedy of his not living through touched the hidden desire in us all? To fight and survive for three desperate years—and die on the eve of Liberation! To die by the bullet from one's own faithful rifle! All through the day, there was pilgrimage to his grave under the white-blooming tree. The boy whose carelessness had killed him was drawn back within the circle of fighters and comforted. But for the seventeen-year-old there were many days without comfort.

CHAPTER 31

Then, in the dawn, the Japs crawled through the grass as the moon waned and jumped the outpost guards. One boy was shot in his sleep, and the corporal of the guard, leaning over in the act of awakening him, was knocked flat and bayoneted. A third killed the Jap astride the fallen fighter, then plunged into the brush behind to circle in a frantic race against time to the main headquarters.

Marking had foreseen the attack and had kept the men alert. Bautista of Santa Maria carried the fight, with orders to draw the Japs elsewhere, while Marking and the rest pulled up toward Camp Manuel to cover the Net Control Station on retreat to Karakatmon, where Cabalhin and his bodyguards camped in the backwoods nursing Cabalhin's wounded ankle along.

The Japs' mortar fire edged away in the distance, proof that Bautista was successfully engaging them on the run, pulling them away from the station.

"If they follow up to Karakatmon," said Marking, "that's good fighting ground. All we need is more bullets, damn it."

Miller said nothing. Not even Marking realized how insistently the American liaison officer had been hammering at GHQ-SWPA for ammunition.

We filed through forest and *cogon* and were welcomed by Cabalhin with his typical elfin grin. He tried to stand and officers and enlisted men alike admonished him to sit down lest something else happen to his leg.

Up on the slope in the sunshine Marking built a camp, where once again the Signal Corps set up their paraphernalia and once again Miller and Stod tried to engineer the perfect *kubo*.

Then Marking built another camp down below on the approach to Cabalhin's camp halfway between the two. The upper camp was exclusively NCS and hospital. The middle camp remained for Cabalhin's convalescence. The lower camp was for the air drop itself, and Miller immediately transmitted to headquarters the new bearings.

Day after day passed. There was fretting and picayune quarreling.

Preparing for the orders sure to come soon, the fighters drilled more and more Home Guards from the towns. And the NCS worked through the day and half the night evaluating intelligence reports, coding and decoding, transmitting and receiving endless messages.

All day long we scanned the skies or cocked an ear for the drone of a plane, a plane for us. There was air action everywhere, especially along the highway far to the west, and sometimes a plane returning to its base passed us by and from excitement we sank back into the sweating it out. The sunlight of the great clearing was doing us good. We sweltered. From jungle pallidity we ruddied and turned good Filipino brown again. But the waiting was hard.

Miller came down the mountain. "It ought to get here at noon, Marking."

Noon passed. Afternoon passed.

"Yeah," said Marking bitterly, "by noon today."

From Lingayén, the forces were fighting their way down the Luzon plain to Manila. Steadily, surely, they were pushing southward to the city and to us.

"Well," said Miller, "maybe they're busy. I'm not running the army."

Marking hated him. Then something happened at GHQ-SWPA. MacArthur switched us to Krueger of the Sixth Army Corps.

Miller was elated. "We're going up!" Marking said, "Krueger isn't higher than MacArthur. We're going down." But Miller persisted, "Now we'll get some action."

Marking, stung over and over, believed no army promises. He pointedly ignored Miller and concerned himself with running his own guerrilla army, sending guides to bring in the supplies, stepping up the drilling orders, checking over the arms on hand.

The clearing lay hot in the sun. Walled in by forest, it was safe enough from Jap binoculars in the lowlands and to the west and north where already by the thousands the Japs were forming a defense line from Montalban to Tanay. Miller insisted on a flank of foxholes to protect the clearing from a surprise attack while the planes were dropping their load.

"What planes?" demanded Marking, "What load?"

High up on the *cogon* slope, one signal fire smoldered. Another burned weakly on the flat below the slope. The third corner of the triangle of signal fires, halfway up the slope toward the edge where most of our *kubos* were built, kept burning out. Weeds, grass, old logs were piled near all three to be used as smudges.

Drilling, cleaning rifles, counting out one pill as medical supplies, mending rags—the whole camp waited.

A plane droned in the distance. Immediately the faint wisps of smoke from the fires changed to thick pillars as the fighters leaped forward and piled the fires high with moldy sticks and green *cogon*. The drone faded out.

An hour passed.

Another plane droned closer to the clearing. Two pillars rose. The third, in the care of the Chinese unit, had died out and refused to smudge. The plane drew closer.

"Sheng!" yelled Marking. "God damn it, are all the Chinese asleep! Get that fire burning!"

The plane roared high overhead, zipped on into the east, without pause.

Anticipation turned to disappointment.

Miller and Stoddard could no longer come down to the air drop camp. Working sixteen, twenty hours a day, with operators on twenty-four-hour service, they could barely keep abreast of the flood of reports to Krueger and the queries back.

Down from Miller came a note: "No air drop today. Tomorrow maybe."

"Bullshit!" said Marking.

But to Krueger, by coded message, Miller had said, "We will stay on the air *if we can*. Ammunition needed."

A plane droned nearer. It sounded like several planes. Automatically, half-heartedly, ready hands piled on the smudge. The pillars rose, gray against the green of the forest, the clear blue of the skies, the gold of the *cogon*. The mist had cleared away. Between the snowy masses of cumulus clouds, a dark speck, then clearly two dark specks, came in a direct line toward our hidden slope clear from the air.

"They're different!" yelled Marking. "Darling, look!"

In my heart, I was hateful. I made no response. For days I had been the whipping boy, closest as always to Marking, and getting all the bitterness of his disappointment.

"Come down here where you can see!"

I did not move.

But as the planes drew nearer and began to circle, my heart lifted hopefully, then soared. For, truly, the planes were different. Unlike the silvery planes, these were dark. They seemed slow and a little clumsy. They circled out of sight, but the roar of their engines was not lost, and again they came in a lower, tighter circling, a door opened in the fat, black side of the first plane, and again unmistakably an American stood there, spread-eagled in the opening, held within by the wind of flight, grinning down on the clearing.

High on the slope, the fighters hysterically waved the American and Filipino flags. Without the need any longer for smudges, other fighters scrambled about, yanking at grass, grabbing up dead branches, frantically piling it blindly on where the fire should be as they looked up at the flyers, dumped their grass and sticks to straighten to wave wildly with both hands, grabbed again for anything to lay on the fires. Everywhere, there was wild hallooing, and for the fourth time the planes circled and we held our breath, for they were low, *too* low, and the great dead tree reached up its gaunt arms.

What if they crashed! The clearing was a ravined slope dotted with old stumps, deceptively soft from the air because of the breeze-rippled *cogon*, but under the grass, treacherously rough.

Again they circled out of sight, and on the fifth approach to the clearing, obviously using the dead tree as marker, the first plane skimmed its tip and out of the opening in its side dropped little black squares and rectangles that rapidly grew larger in their rush earthward with tadpole tails flipping and flapping, then suddenly the tails snapped, filled out, blossomed in the sun and, arrested in the fall, the boxes hung suspended and slowly floated down under the support of the shining parachutes.

"Bull's-eye!" yelled Marking.

"The other one, sir!" yelled his bodyguards.

As the second plane roared low, skimming the marker, and three more boxes dropped out, to plummet, then to stop as the parachutes bloomed and in suspension floated down swinging pendulum-fashion from their supports, there was hysteria. Fighters pounded one another on the back, Home Guards ran for the boxes settling into the grass, marked by the masses of colored silk deflating over them. There were tears, and, as I looked down where I had pressed Rae under a giant log lest she be struck by a box, she said, "Mother, *isn't it wonderful!* Here, Mamma, use my handkerchief." I had thought I was laughing. In fact, as I pressed the handkerchief to my cheeks, I *was* laughing.

From the fighters and Home Guards pushing through the hip-high *cogon*, stumbling in their eagerness, trying to run through and using their arms to divide a passage, looking a little like swimmers just learning how, came more yells.

"Sir, it is Garands!"

"Sir, it is carbines!"

From Marking: "Take them to headquarters. Do not open them there! Put them in charge of Roger!" To me, he yelled, "You watch everything there until I come."

Again came the roar of planes.

"What!" we said to one another, "More?"

From the low-flying planes there was waving. We waved back. We yelled. We tried to say thank you. But the flyers waved to clear the drop.

We saw what they meant. All over the slope, tiny figures struggled to carry the boxes up, with the parachutes, blue and yellow and red and white, rolled each in a big ball and borne separately. "Stay out of the triangle!" yelled Marking. "Clear the air drop!" But the figures were heavily loaded, and they would not drop their precious burdens.

Again the planes swooped over, and we waved to drop *anyway*.

On the third circling, when not only were there figures carrying up but other figures gathered in groups all over the slope to catch as catch can, the unloaders crossed their fingers probably and kicked their deliveries through the door. Before the boxes thudded to earth figures were already fighting through the thick grass to reach them.

"Here they come again! Get out of the way!" Figures moved five feet, ten feet, but still the clearing was not clear, for they had merely shifted within the clearing.

The flyers shrugged, dropped.

One parachute failed to open, and the long box plummeted all the way, crashed, splintered, filled the air with flying board fragments and long, dark objects.

"Kiss that one goodbye," said Stod.

"Sir! They are broken! The carbines are broken!"

"Why!" yelled Marking, almost a sob in his hoarse throat. "Why didn't it open? Why aren't they careful?"

"Can't be helped," said Miller.

The possibilities of death or crippling in the clearing brought another order: "Clear the triangle! Pull up on the slope! Get away from the blanket in the middle! Do you want to get killed!" But nobody cared much, except me for Rae—each flight over, I pushed her under the overhanging root of the log from under which she peeked out, her eyes round and shining.

Again and again the planes circled, skimmed the dead tree, kicked out three parachutes' worth each time.

"Ammunition!"
"Grenades!"
"My God, how much do they hold!"
Marking said to MacArthur's liaison officers, "George, Stod, *you did it!*"

Miller and Stoddard grinned at each other, a bit inscrutably. No air drop, and they would still be in the doghouse, but now they were fair-haired lads again. They were back in favor. They were kings in the guerrilla kingdom.

"Say," said Marking, "there wasn't supposed to be an air drop today."

"Yeah," said Miller.

"Why?"

"That's the way the army does it." Miller was both happy and rueful.

"Yeah," said Stod. "They're pretty dependable, off and on." After awhile, the planes zoomed over, higher, and nothing was disgorged from their sides.

"They're empty," said Marking, satisfaction in his face. "It's all down now."

The first plane dipped its wings. The second plane dipped. We waved them off, exhausted, not quite believing, and turned to ordering the rest of the delivery up to headquarters for distribution.

There was reverence in the unpacking of the grease-caked guns.

Parachutes were ripped, two panels to a piece, to give the fighters blankets. There was wild grabbing for the halters and cords as they were cut away, and searching through the grass for the square, canvas-covered "seats" to which the loads had been strapped or wired. Two seats, laced together, made a perfect guerrilla pack. Lyd was first to see the possibilities but the last to find a pair, for the others caught on and grabbed quicker.

"Now we fight, George," said Marking. "Not yet." "Why not?" "Shipment not complete yet. None of the things I ordered for the radio are here yet!" "Then you better ask them to drop us something to eat. The Japs chased the Home Guards all over everywhere, and there's nothing to eat." "What do the men like—rations or rice?" "The rations are for you. Rice is better for the fighters." "Well, keep the fighters here to protect the site."

And then, without rhyme or reason, rain or shine, announced and unannounced, the sky trucks, the good old C-47s, came lumbering. The novelty wore off except for novelty introduced. One air drop brought a novice at the art, and he festooned the jungle with gay parachutes caught in the treetops—red and blue, green and yellow and white patches of silk far up on the tallest trees, the burdens swinging like heavy pendulums. Each time, the second plane wavered in behind the expert first, and, no matter where he aimed, he overshot or shot short, and Truadio's men had to walk up the trees and cut the shipment loose.

Another air drop brought the faster escort planes, and the excitement on the ground seemed contagious, for suddenly three planes began cutting capers, looping the loop, side-slipping, dipping their wings, roaring low into the clearing and barely making it up over the forest walls, each outdoing the next and from their young hearts giving us on the ground a show unauthorized by any sedate GHQ-SWPA. The clumsy C-47s kept stodgily to their work while above and all around them the air show went on. In the three-ring circus of the performing planes, the sky trucks, and the guerrillas on the ground, we almost lost one of our Chinese fighters. Openmouthed, he watched the cavorting overhead, dizzy with the shine and speed and roar of it, as were the rest of us, when a shout brought him to and he looked up the other way to find a box full of Garands dropping full in his face. For all the deceptive appearance of floating, the loads landed hard. The Chinese ducked and began running; the long heavy box cleared his head by six inches, shot down past his bent back and thudded heavily into the earth, pulling the parachute after it and enveloping the running Chinese in its ballooning folds. Quick to enjoy anything, the fighters pounced upon the edges of the parachute, held them down against the Chinese fighter's escape. Inside the huge billowing, there was a frantic scramble, the course of which we could follow by the humping of the material on the ground.

Every other day, every day, finally twice a day the air drops came, and Marking called a halt. "George, we've got enough now. We ought to go fight now." "Marking, I'm just a guy named Miller. I can say stop, and they can keep right on delivering."

Air drop after air drop. "Wave those flags!" "Keep those fires going!" "Stay out of the triangle!" "Rice! Rice from Texas! From Texas!" "Rations! Ten-in-ones! That's for you, Stod!" "Get out of the way—d'ya wanna get killed?" "Don't cut that parachute! Krueger wants 'em. God bless Krueger. Real field man, Krueger. Save those parachutes for Krueger!"

The NCS tapped away, full time.

Dah-de-dah-dah, flyers! Flyers crashed! Howe, Tompkins, and Britain. Pull them out of the lake! Grab them from the rice paddies!

Save America's men! Don't let the Japs get them! God damn, oh! God damn the Japs! De-dah-de-dah-dah. Hit those highways!

Blow those bridges! Cut their damn wires! Hit, hit, hit! They're turning tail! They're crying in their foxholes! Hit and run! At last, they rolled, oh, *how they rolled!*

"Santos blew up Stod's bridge for him. He used Stod's stuff all scattered around, put it together again, and blew it up."

"De la Rosa really worked over that Santa Maria situation again. Got all but three Japs before reinforcements came. Japs crying, kept rolling their hand grenades over the trenches' edge, and the boys would just kick them back in. Lost five of our own, for fifty of theirs; we can't lose a war, fighting."

Alora came in, tail between his legs. He had done quite well, considering. Bravely he had issued forth from the mountains and into the lowlands, and bravely he had crawled through the fields to the bridge not far from a sentry post. Carefully he laid the fuse just right and tied the dynamite exactly there.

"Well, why-n-hell-didn't-you-blow-the-bridge?" bellowed Stoddard. "And don't keep telling me what I kept telling you! I want to know why didn't it go off. Repeat, Why—didn't—it—go—off?"

Humbly, helpfully, having been for three years a fine saboteur before the army came in with its new-fangled notions, Alora said, "Sir, I forgot the matches."

The air drops kept coming, and the fighters kept apportioning out the arms and ammunition, sorting the medicines, dynamite, and grenades they could not carry. Lucio was transferred from supply-scratching to combat, of which through three years he had dreamed. "But, sir, I do not know yet the manual of arms. What kind of a soldier do I make?" There was a helplessness about him, as his share of arms, ammunition, parachute material, rice rations, and "extras" was piled upon the man who had ever given and never received. He walked about the camp with his arms full, his eyes confused, asking, "Now what do I do?"

Out in the hills, the Japs flooded into the Tanay-Antipolo line. "We've got to be able to look down into what they are doing," said Miller.

"Can't," said Marking.

"With high-powered glasses?"

"Can," said Marking.

"Who can take the extra transmitter?"

Marking looked at Montano D. Nazario, former Romulo reporter, who had been a big brother to me in my cub days; but a war had swept between us, and Nazario and I eyed each other without understanding. I could not understand why he had not fought from the beginning. He could not understand why I had changed so much. Even between him and Lyd there was the gulf of appraisal and rejection.

"Nazario," said Marking, "I will give you your chance. You will be in charge."

Nazario's heavy face lighted up, and he laughed the old familiar way. "Yes, *sir!*" he said.

Back to Kanumay went Nazario, with Marking's Tarlac cousins, Nick, Johnny, Reging and Navarretto, with Truadio as guide, to peek at what the Japs were doing.

They never got near Kanumay. Already San Andrés was aswarm with Japs. Into the *barrios* behind Kanumay, by the thousands, they were pouring, and beaten on by them were hundreds of captured Filipinos loaded down with ammunition, rice, and mortar shells.

"They don't send them back to the town, sir," reported Nazario. "They just kill them, if they haven't already died of starvation."

Jornación checked in, sidestepping all the way, to get his share of the new rifles.

Mata checked in, and his men, roughest fighters of all, were riotous with the joy of new arms and grenades for all officers.

The American First Cavalry was pushing through Manila, coming out into Rizal province.

"Marking," said Miller. "It might be a good idea for you to make personal contact with the First Cavalry. We could go with just a few men." "OK." The last air drop had come and was stored except for the rifles, apportioned to Lucio's men. "Shall we go?" asked Miller. "Yep." Suddenly Marking was decided. "Assemble the camp." "Not *everybody*," said Miller. "Sure. They go, too. Do you think I will leave them here to starve? The rice is gone again. There are only the rations, and not enough for five hundred men. And this place is going to be hot with Japs, more Japs than even our new arms can handle."

A handful were left at the NCS site to guard the *bodegas* against robbery by the mountaineers. Their orders were to follow up later, but no date was set. They would wait for word from Marking. And so, for the last time, we rolled from the highlands down into the lowlands. Once again I could see the long single file serpentining up a climb, down through a valley, tiny stalwart figures with a bluebird's feather or a redbird's feather in hats and caps of every shape and color, with shredded-parachute tassels on their gun butts, trigger guards, barrel tips, and more parachute-kerchiefs at their throats, red for the fight, white for chivalry, yellow for royalty and maybe for one who might run, green for gallantry and blue for loyalty. There was sunlight on Alzate's shoulder-length curls, on Pagayunan's straight pirate-bob—for some guerrillas had sworn not to cut their hair until the Americans returned.

"Lyd?" "Yes, Yay." "Soon they'll be in the barbers' chairs." "Pity," said Lyd. "Another chapter closed," I said.

CHAPTER 32

Near the highway between Santa Maria and Tanay, we bedded down for the night, wary against crossing the open road when we could not see what lay ahead. The farmer gave us grapevine news which tallied with the more detailed intelligence reports describing the First Cavalry's drive to the Santo Tomás internment camp, the floor-by-floor fighting in the Post Office, City Hall, and Philippine General Hospital, the shelling of Intramuros and consequent leveling of the mossy walls, and the final horror of the Malate massacre in which the Japs had driven a helpless population into the bungalow-homes, set the houses afire, and machine-gunned any who tried to escape.

We rested in the *kingki*-lit farmhouse, the fighters camped outside. And then the night was gone, and in the dawn we filed swiftly across the broad highway and up into the hills of the peninsula south of Pililla. Marking waited for most of the line to pass, and his sharp eyes noted a recently loosened plank. He lifted it, found beneath a booby trap. Because we had run the length of a plank to one side, none of us had depressed the loosened board. By the freshness of the disturbed soil, it may have been laid before dawn by the last enemy troops passing during the night.

Half the line took the southwest trail; the rest the west, cutting straight across the mountains in an extremely stiff climb which was only half as far. Marking and his men reached the Quisao shore long before the rest of us who straggled in at sunset, hungry and sticky with dust and sweat.

Across the lake lay the Cardona shore line. Information declared the Americans to be there already.

Into the sunset we sailed, to be caught on the waters by dusk and then dark.

Miller said, "We'd better signal first. Front-line troops are quick on the trigger."

Marking urged him to signal.

A few lights here and there indicated someone's presence. Miller blinked his flashlight.

There was an answering blink.

Anticipation rose in us, and we were eager to dash ashore in a glad welcome. But everything was ominously quiet, and most of the town was in blackness. We neared shore, peering through the blackness. If firing started, I was tensed to roll off the thwart into the lake, whether quick-trigger Americans or a Jap ambush. The point was not to get killed.

Marking went ashore. Figures came out, sensed rather than seen. There was talk, but it was muted and indistinct to our straining ears. Lyd ached to wade ashore, and so did I, but there was still a chance of mistake or ambush. So close to victory, we were less reckless.

Someone splashed into the water to push a *banca* up against the sailboat. We stepped in, crouched down, and balanced ourselves with our hands on the boat's sides, rode the short way and jumped ashore.

"Where are they?" I asked. "The Old Man is over there," said Nazario. "And the Americans, the First Cavalry?" "They went back to Taytay. They were here today." "Why'd they go back?" "Don't know."

Lyd perched near me on a broad stone that showed up gray in the darkness.

"Hell!" I said. "Maybe they weren't here at all."

Miller decided to proceed up the shore to Pasig and report in, then wondered if it was wise to try it, for the handful of Home Guards assigned in the town to guard property declared that none could approach the First Cavalry in the night without maybe getting shot first.

Marking made his usual quick decision. For safety's sake, he would stay in Cardona and let the First Cavalry come to him.

Into a comfortable house we climbed.

The next morning, back went the sailboats to the peninsula side to bring over more fighters. Mata and his men were already in Cardona, then Morong, ahead of us. Cabalhin had not yet come through. My Rae was with Cabalhin, for he had taken her on his horse and she, delighted, had ridden gaily off. I felt no anxiety for her except ambush. For three days she was to be with the fighters, a twelve-year-old-girl on her own. I knew Cabalhin would guard her with his life. I knew that she would be rolled in the warmest blanket among them, if they slept on the ground, and that closest around her would sleep Cabalhin and the fighters charged with her safety. I who had been so long with them knew their chivalry, their goodness. I knew that as a normal mother I should worry, yet, as a guerrilla mother, I knew into whose care the splitting of the trails had given my blooming child. I slept well. I worked well. Rae would roll in when the fighters rolled in.

The First Cavalry reconnaissance patrol came through. "What?" said Lieutenant Bisson of the patrol. "No snipers?"

And Marking told him. "Mata and his men fought half the night in Morong."

Bisson consulted his map. "That accounts for it. That's one town up, isn't it?" He nodded. "Your men must be stopping the infiltration."

We offered him coffee. "Relax awhile. Mata can take care of Morong."

Bisson took the coffee, but shook his head. "Too tied up to rest. We've been coming through all the way from Leyte through Lingayén through Manila. When you get that wound up, you don't unwind without falling apart."

I studied the small, good-looking fellow. He did seem taut. It was a tautness different from guerrilla tension. It was like flint, and easy to strike sparks. It was not a tensing, then an easing, and a tension again. It was hard, as if permanently jelled for only one melting, for only one shattering. There was nothing elastic to it, nothing remediable, at least not within an hour or a week. Observing him, I began to sense strength in guerrilla elasticity, to understand why and how we had resisted so long.

What thrill to touch the dusty fenders of an armored car! What surprise to count the features of a jeep! The streets were crowded with our fighters, watching the American patrol roll through.

Came a Major Meredith, less taut but keen-eyed. He invited us to a picnic lunch farther back where he was inspecting the road for tank destroyer travel. A half-dozen casual Americans lounged about under dusty trees, themselves dustier than the trees. A package was opened, and quick as we saw what lay in it Marking and I looked up into each other's eyes.

"Bread!" said Marking.

"Sandwiches!" I said.

We ate, savoring separately, then together, the flavor of bread and the flavor of filling. So deep were the feelings evoked by fresh, white bread that, spontaneously, we "sang" for our supper, trying to tell stories that would interest the major and his men. We had no other coin, and we had lost in the mountains the ease of social graces. So we talked, jamming the minutes with a mixture of guerrilla and tourist information, not eating too much—talking to repay ten times over.

Each night, our fighters held their own in Morong, and there were deaths. They were fighting positional warfare, holding back the enemy infiltration, resting the reconnaissance men, making a stand on their own land.

Within me there was an ache for them. It seemed so unfair that from the mountain trails they should step directly into the foxholes. Too many of them needed hospitalization. Too many of them had grown instinctively hit-and-run. Too many of them should be taken into an army camp and given army training.

Old friends began to call. I heard the news.

"C. P. R. is in Manila. He wants to see you. Haven't you received his letters?"

Romulo in Manila. For a moment, Camelot stood unshattered in the sun. I could hear the Rotary Duplex pounding in my ears, thrumming faster and faster, then almost singing as the afternoon *Herald* came flipping into the rack. I could hear old Ben growling, and the telephones ringing on the city desk. Old faces and old voices and old ways for a moment were upon me, and my throat tightened.

Then I saw Marking's eyes narrow, and the old stalking stiffness was in his walk. He was arrogant, rude, harsh to the visitors. My heart cried out, "No! Don't make that mistake, Marking! Understand, darling, understand!"

But the only fear in his life had him again in its grip.

Again he was trying to drive from me everything but himself. When we were alone I tried to talk with him, to reason. He was pale with jealousy, as he had been all through the war. Whatever I said, he twisted, or roughly denied.

"Darling, look," I said, "I'm sticking with you—you know that. These people who come, they want to know you as they know me. Romulo? Perhaps it is to praise us for having fought through. Remember his note? It was addressed to 'Marking and Yay,' not just to me. Your friends and your life before the war, I have accepted. Now it is for you to accept mine. Together, our world will only be larger. We'll share it and always, in a larger world, have each other."

"Have each other!" Marking snorted. "I know you want to leave me! I know you want to go! Why don't you admit it?"

"Let's go to see the boss together."

"*You* go."

"I will come back."

"You will come back!" He gave the typical Philippine hoot of derision. "Why should you come back to a bus driver?"

"Why not? Is being a bus driver any different from being a reporter or being a farmer or being a doctor?"

"Sure it is! You don't want to be with a bus driver!"

"Marking, stop that." "You writers know so much." "It's our line, just as driving is your line." "You don't want to be married to a driver." "You get your old bus back and let's find out." "I don't have to. Women are no good. You're all the same." "What do you want me to do?" "Get out."

My head grew hot. In the old days, I would have picked up whatever was mine and gladly left, but I knew how he suffered from the thought that I might really go back to my old life without him. I knew that if I did take him at his word, proved his worst fears, there would be violence.

He eased his defiant agony by driving me away. Because I knew the reason for it, I tried to overlook it, bring him back to normality. There was enough pain in the world without hammering at each other, plunging the knife deep, twisting the blade in the wound.

I dropped reasoning and tried to remain silent, but he taunted, jeered and insulted, then shoved me roughly.

"You want to be independent again," he said. "You want to go where you want to go. You want to ignore me."

Again I tried to soothe him.

Worse came. The epithets and accusations poured forth, as before, hour after hour until he was exhausted.

Then suddenly the tempest was spent, and he humbled: "Don't leave me. Forgive me for what I do, for what I say. You might forget me, you might be ashamed of me some day. You might want somebody else."

I made no answer, for my mind was made up. At last, I could overlook no longer. Always he had promised not to repeat his jealous fits, and each time, even as the air drops had come and Liberation neared, he grew harsher and all the fighter's nature of him threw itself in force against the intangibles he could not understand and therefore feared. For three years I had tried to give him something upon which to feel secure in his heart. Tenderness, patience, little sacrifices had only endeared me the more, and as his love grew greater, so grew the insecurity. And so I knew then that I, who loved him in return, had lost, that he must undergo the thing which terrified him, for the sake of the future and the past, even if it tore us apart forever.

Early the next morning, under Borres's knowing eyes, I slipped what I wanted to take with me into the musette bag and the little canvas medical kit. To Doy, Borres said, "She is going." To Marking, he said nothing. To Marking, Doy said nothing.

As I sat by a window at the back of the house overlooking the stairway, Lyd came. "Stand by," I said.

Marking walked over to me. "I'm going to Morong to inspect the boys. Want to come along?"

"No. I don't feel too well. I'll stay here." I was glad that he was leaving the house. It would be easier to go. Through the window at the front of the house, through the open door between it and me, I could see the lake where so many times we had passed, in sailboat, in motorboat, in *banca*, side-stepping the enemy swarm hunting us down. My hands felt stiff and cold.

Marking hesitated, then left, thinking: she won't leave me. She wouldn't dare. And she will forgive me again. And so he left, bidding for forgiveness again by letting me have my way, letting me sulk it out.

Through the window I heard the reconnaissance patrol coming. There was movement in the street. The soldiers were wading through our guerrillas in the street, coming up the steps into our headquarters, leaving their motors idling. They would check up with us on action during the night.

Then I heard Marking's voice. He had returned, if he had gone at all.

It would be difficult. I steeled myself. Three years of hurt, of being his whipping boy when anything went wrong, never quite balanced by all his loving kindness, made my heart hard.

I stood and walked, stiff-kneed, toward him. "Marking, I am going to Manila."

His face lost its brown flush. His lips blackened, then paled. "Come into the other room," he said thickly.

"No, I've had enough of bullying." There was cold sweat on my palms.

Lyd asked, "Where are your things?"

I said to Rae, wide-eyed, fiercely loyal to me, "Get the musette bag and the little bag I always carry." Then I stepped through the door to pick them up myself. Marking stepped through the other door, to reach for me. I jerked away. He snatched his .45 from its holster.

At the head of the stairs, men of the First Cavalry had their heads bent over a map they were marking. Into the group I stepped. The

Americans looked up, and I said, "Will you boys stand by me? He pulled his gun on me."

"Sure," said one.

"Where is Captain Stoddard?" I asked.

"That tall guy? He was here a minute ago."

"Will you walk down the stairs with me?"

"Sure, ma'am."

I walked down the stairs and out into the street, my eyes questing for Stoddard. He was a little way off. I walked to meet him. "Stod," I said, "will you send me to Manila with these fellows?"

"Sure. What happened?"

"I can't take it anymore. I'm leaving."

"I see," said Stod.

I felt surprise within me, and my mind raced. Had so many eyes seen through into the one great difficulty between Marking and me, had they even wondered how long I could take it? I knew that none had hatred for Marking. Had others before me reached the conclusion: it won't work?

Then Marking came up the street with his son Cote. "Yay, I wouldn't hurt you—you know that."

I stayed close beside Stod. Behind Marking, down the street, the First Cavalry men waited. I said, "I'm going."

"Then take Cote with you. I give him to you."

Cote, who had ever been gallant to me, was no less loyal than my own Rae, and Cote stayed beside his father.

"I would take him, but one cannot give a child away."

Stod said, "You go over to my headquarters, Yay. Wait there for me." He walked beside me to the house in which the Signal Corps had sent up the NCS. Marking, left in the street, turned back to his own headquarters.

To the Signal Corps boys, Stod said, "Take care of Colonel Yay."

Then I was walking down the familiar street, and suddenly, without my willing them, tears came. I heard Stod's voice: "You'd better get in now. He's having one of his fits. You'd better leave right now." The armored car was drab, solid, dusty through the mist still rolling up from old storms within me. I climbed in. Lyd was there. Doy came running: "Mammy! Your gun belt!"

By that time I was unashamedly bawling. "Doy! Stick with him. You and Borres. Tell the boys goodbye. Keep fighting. I'll try to help you a little from Manila." I couldn't say more without choking, for the sobs were shaking me. Only the cold determination in me, the final resolution to leave, kept me from climbing out of the armored car and running back up the road and maybe shooting Marking down instead of leaving him, just shooting him and shooting him and shooting him, for every humiliation I had suffered. And then I understood: I was leaving to keep us from killing each other.

"Here," said Lyd, "take a swallow of this." It was an almost empty whisky bottle, handed to her by a cavalryman with a nod toward me. I took a swallow, two swallows.

"Can I just bawl?" I asked.

"You're doing fine. Gimme back that bottle." She raised it, jiggled it against the sun, then tipped it for the last swallow. "H'm-m!" she said, to nobody in particular. "Good stuff."

CHAPTER 33

At Angono, where a reconnaissance camp was in the making, the armored car stopped. From there to Manila, we would go by army truck. I heard the familiar voice of Bisson say, "Capt. Stoddard's order? OK." Then he looked up into my smeared face on the truck seat, and said, "Oh, hello!"

"Lieutenant," I said, "will you give this note to Marking?"

"That I will." He slipped it into his shirt pocket and buttoned the flap. There should be an explanation, I felt. "It's a long story."

"Sure," said Bisson, understandingly.

"The note is to keep things steady. Tell him it's from his *wife*."

"OK," said Bisson.

"May I do you a favor?"

"Sure. Get me this kind of film." He wrote his order down on a paper scrap which I buttoned into my own pocket.

Not in all Manila could I find the film to send to Bisson by Jimmy Duffy, the blarneying Irish truck driver. In the shattered turmoil of retaken Manila, there was little that I found at all, except old friends. That was all I wanted, all I needed.

At Malacanan, there was C. P. R., the old boss, known to the world as General Carlos P. Romulo. I was the lost kid come home. There were tears in his eyes and in mine, but before the filial embrace was completed the old asperity was in his voice, "Didn't you get my letters? Where were you?" And truly I was home again, ready to match him blade for blade, eager to outwit or forestall him.

The Manila units had a band for me. "Let's take it along," I said, and Lyd and I swept past the military police at the gate into the newly freed Santo Tomás internment camp, asking for Bessie Hackett, Herbert and Janet Walker, Dave Sternberg, Gene and Dot Thiele, Dave and Peggy Boguslav, and the blare of the band brought the internees to the windows and their young ones joining us.

Herbert, sixty-five years old, tall, lean, austere of mien, walked over in his wooden shoes. "You're making too much racket," he said.

"Kiss," I said. "I want a kiss."

"In all this crowd?" said Herbert, bending his cheek for my smack. "Janet!" I said. "Now I want Janet."

"She's in the hospital." To my questioning look, he assured me, "She's much better. Just kiss her. Don't jump on her and kiss her."

Lyd had him by the neck. "What will the people think?" he asked, and the little smile quirked under his nose, for he was never averse to giving people something to ponder.

We muted the band and led the way to the hospital. Only Lyd and I entered.

Janet looked up from her pillow, held wide her old arms, her young heart all in her eyes and her smiling mouth, and gathered her own, both in one hug, to her breast. And immediately, perched upon her cot, we picked up where we had left off, bragging to one who believed us.

Out of the hospital and into shanty-town, all around the old university buildings we went, and Bessie said in her pert, quick way, "All right now. Give an accounting of yourselves. What is all this you've been up to?" In the sweetness of her, in her demure, dear person, was still the loved dash of vinegar. "What are you going to do now? When was the last time you ate? I suppose you're so used to sleeping on the ground now, it would be useless to offer you a bed."

And there was Dave Sternberg, upon the crutches that I had not observed until we had been friends for a year. One day I noticed them. "Why, heavens, Dave's a cripple!" The realization sank deep. All along I had known it, yet so much had Dave to give the world and so much richness had come into my own living and thinking through him that I, the firm and the strong, had all too often leaned upon him, the infirm.

He looked pinched and tired, yet the Dave that Lyd and I had known was not essentially changed. "What do you think about independence?" he asked. "Or have you thought at all?" And, "What is being done about the mooching and thieving rampant in the city?" "Did you keep a journal?" "Have you written anything worthwhile?" "What did the guerrillas achieve in actual score, the dead against the dead?" "Do you regret the past three years?"

"God, it's good to see you again!" I said.

"You must be in trouble then."

We laughed. All the world beat a path to his door, and dropped in regularly, thereafter.

"Where's Lyd?" asked Dave. "She was here a minute ago." "She'll wander back in. You know Lyd. Lord, she's toughened." "I don't wonder, considering the company she keeps."

Home again. Home from the wars. I sat relaxed, savoring the idle banter.

Then Marking came to town, seeking me. On the trail of the band, he arrived in the internment camp.

"Yay," said Bess, "you can stay in my brother's shack. I'll bring your meals."

"What am I now?" asked Dave. "The outpost?"

Marking ordered the Guerrilla Intelligence Division, six hundred strong, to scour the city for Mammy. Mammy sat in the shanty of Allen and Florence Hackett, wondering. How well had I trained the boys? If they found me, they outfoxed their teacher. If they failed to find me, I was no fox, having failed to teach them anything in the first place. With mixed feelings I remained hidden, faithfully fed by Bess, faithfully visited by Lyd, who as faithfully made the rounds with Marking.

"You're just a headache to me," said Lyd, "both of you." Guerrillas came. "Do you want to be found, Mammy?" "No," I said.

They saw desperation and a promise of violence in my eyes, and they loved Marking too much to risk testing me.

Then Lyd came slipping into the shanty again. "Have you got a brother named Raymond?" she demanded. "Why, yes." "Very dark, hardly talks at all?" "I guess so. I haven't seen him since he was, let's see, about twelve years old." "Well, he's not twelve years old now. He looks like you, too." "Lyd, *where is he? How'd he get here?*" "The way every GI gets here. Keep your shirt on."

I waited in the shanty with Rae and the two little boys, my sons, thin, pale Junior, nine years old, and Kerty of the almond eyes, a shrill, impassioned six. Lyd had trundled by in a jeep, picked them up out of the dust, dropped them on the shanty doorstep. "They're all yours," she had said. In much the same undramatic way she ushered in my brother, simply by walking in with him following, and stepping aside so that I could see him.

For a moment, the sun-blackened figure in the worn fatigue uniform was, blankly, a stranger. Then awkwardly we embraced, eyeing each other closely as we talked, looking for the familiar traits obscured by the years and their experiences.

And finally we were at ease, and my brother Raymond Corpus, corporal in the 640th Tank Destroyer Battalion, Company B, asked me, "What's wrong with the natives?"

I winced for him and said, "Ray, you don't call Filipinos natives."

"Why not?" asked my full-Filipino, American-citizen half-brother. "Native of Colorado, native of California, native of New York, native of the Philippines. What's wrong with the natives?"

"All right, Ray. What's wrong with the natives?"

"Why, they're a bunch of God-damn moochers."

I winced again, then laughed, for here was my own GI brother, victim of the hungry, insecure hordes freed by the Liberation. "I'd have to give you the story of the whole three years past," I said.

"Don't bother," said Ray. "Tell me about yourself."

"Tell me about the folks first."

"Ma says, Come home. She says, Bring the kids with you." "Well—" I hesitated, and into my lap he tossed a wad of bills. "What's this?" I knew my brother, despite the long separation. He was no spendthrift. When we were kids, I had had to rob his bank to get anything out of him.

"Poker money," said Ray.

I laughed again, delighted to the core, for through the grammar grades and into high school Ray had carried his own pack of cards.

"Are you good at it?" I asked, counting the five hundred pesos in the wad.

"Oh, I play it close."

"What's that mean?"

"I play to win."

"You sure did," I said, counting again.

"I gotta go. I'll be back."

The children were agog with having an uncle. "Mamma," asked Rae, "are you sure that's my uncle?"

"You were named after him," I said, "and then I forgot all about him."

"Is he in the army?"

"Yes. He came through by way of Guadalcanal—remember that name? And he came in by way of Lingayén."

"He's a GI, Mother, and you're a guerrilla ... How funny!"

General Courtney Whitney dropped by the shanty, spoke to the children. "They look like bright youngsters," he said, "and well behaved." I held my breath, hoping they would keep it up.

"And so you're going home," he said.

"Yes, sir. The old folks want to send them to school."

"That's fine. You've done splendid work, young woman. Good luck to you."

He left, and the boys burst into chatter, "Ma, is that an American or a real general?" Rae argued down her brothers from the great height of superior knowledge and years, "He's both."

Again and again, Marking followed the blind trail to Santo Tomás. He talked with Dave, with Bess, Herbert, and Janet.

Dave said, "Powerful-looking man. We talked for a long time. If you're leaving, you had better leave—soon."

Bess said, "I've done nothing except tell lies ever since you got here. Now I'll never get to Heaven."

Herbert and Janet strolled over one evening, having picked their way aimlessly around the camp to escape possible observation. He smiled, "Marking is looking for you all right. He looked as if maybe we had you in our pockets." She remarked, "He didn't find a thing." He continued, "I rather like him." And I admitted, "So do I. Distance will make the heart grow fonder. The more distance, the more fond."

Three weeks later, we were in an army truck with our baggage and rolling by shattered Intramuros to the piers.

For thirty-nine days, through sweltering heat and the cold, rough weather off the California coast, we were just four more sardines on a troop transport.

Los Angeles spread out before us. A Red Cross "Gray Lady" helped us along to another Gray Lady. From hand to hand we passed, helped along the way. America, through its organized channels, gave us food, shelter, and clothing.

To the May Company we went for the children's quota of clothes. The heavy glass doors swung open to a fairyland of lights, shining cases, and shopgirls groomed like princesses. Shyly we walked among riches, conscious of our shabby clothes that had seemed so rich when they were given to us. Careful we were not to touch the fabrics with our grime-ingrained hands. Humble we were before the lovely ladies everywhere, and we took care not to brush against them.

"Clothes for boys?" I asked a saleslady.

"Second floor," she intoned. "Escalator to your left."

Escalator? Fifteen years before, I had heard of one, but had not had the experience of riding one. Then I saw what appeared a mannequin procession ceilingward, carried up from the floor on a diagonal line.

"Come along," I said to my brood.

With a little hesitation, a brave step forward, a breathless loss of balance and embarrassed recovery, we made it to a man.

Up through the floors we went, becoming veterans in ascent, ever and ever more heavily loaded with bags and boxes. There was a greed and a fear in us, as if tomorrow there would be none and today we must grab and hoard and hide our treasures.

The day drew on. Lunchtime came. Two of the salesladies who had been most gracious suddenly agreed between them that they would take us to lunch.

We seated ourselves around the table, Kerty solemnly trying to be a little gentleman. A waitress passed the menus. Suddenly Kerty shrilled, "Ma! I can't read! Ma! I can't read, I can't eat!"

My face never gets red. Instead, I perspire. "Sh!" I said, and little beads of sweat formed on my forehead and nose.

But Kerty was panicky and would not be shushed. He appealed to Rae, in great agitation, "Wae, I can't wead, I can't eat!" And by the r's that changed to w's under the stress of the moment, I knew my six-year-old was still a baby, much lost in a new land. Too many rules and too many do's and don't's, all at the same time, had given him false assumptions.

"You don't have to be able to read, Kerty. I'll order for you."

He quieted down, but until the food was before him it was plain he wasn't sure if in America the law would let him eat before he could read.

Then, at last, we arrived in Auburn, California, where for almost twenty years, in the peaceful hills covered with pear and peach trees, grapevines, cherry trees, and wild blackberry bushes, my mother and stepfather had worked and saved and now owned a postage-stamp chicken farm all their own. Auburn was the harbor toward which I had herded my helpless flock across the troubled seas. Here among a kindly people and the fruit trees of one of the most beautiful countrysides in America, I knew there would be peace and plenty for my three little ones who, because their mother had had a price on her head, had been sought for three years by the enemy to be held as hostages against my surrender.

The train rolled in, and across from the station was the Walsh Brothers' Freeman Hotel.

Freeman.

Free man.

In the mountains of the Philippines, I had fought for that, while my waifs were passed from hand to hand in the underground. It was my welcome home.

Dad, fat and flushed with health and mellowed by the years, came to meet us at the train. He bustled about, lifting our bags into the back of the coupé.

"Where's Mom?"

"She's not very well today, but she's all right."

"How all right?"

"It's not good to excite her."

Dad's hair had grayed.

"The children—they're awfully full of life."

"Well," said Dad, "your mother has worried over you and your brother."

"One GI and one guerrilla," I laughed.

"We're so happy to have you home." His face glowed, frame to the simple words. "There's the house."

I opened my eyes in surprise at the neat white frame house surrounded by oak trees. Rosebushes were heavy with blossoms. "Not *that!*"

"That's our home," said Dad proudly.

I said nothing. In my childhood we had lived in tenements, boxcars, ranch shacks, and through one severe Colorado winter somehow we had survived in a canvas tent.

The house was quiet as I walked through an empty kitchen and stepped into the dining room. "Mom," I said, "are you there?"

And then she came, stumbling a little, very shrunken and old. "My daughter," she said, "my Yay." Her work-worn hands were on my shoulders. I could feel their clutching tremble.

"Hey, it's not as bad as all that," I said.

And she started to cry. "I thought you were dead. I never expected to see you alive."

"Mom," I said, pulling her away from the old worries, "here are your grandchildren—and they're damn brats, I'm telling you."

"Don't curse in front of the children," she said.

The children came in wonderingly, looked warily around, stood waiting.

"Come here to your grandmother," said Mom.

Her blearing eyes peered at them, found the girl-child sweet, the boys full of challenge and mischief.

Dad killed and cleaned three broilers.

Mom hobbled into the kitchen and began pulling to light a variety of canned fruits and jams, a bottle of fresh milk, a loaf of bread, a dish of real butter.

"You better rest, Mother," said Dad. "I'll do it."

But Mom was in her element, however frail her body. "You know, Yay, I almost died. My heart is very bad. I can't do anything. I won't last long." She pulled out a butcher knife and set to slicing the chickens into pieces for frying. "I'm not well." She dug into a cupboard for lard. "The doctor says my heart muscle is all worn out." Out of the oven came the frying pan. "Now, do you want toast or just plain bread?"

I eyed her, doubtfully.

The next day she began assigning chores to the children. "In America, everybody works, everybody has something to do." At the table, she watched them hawk-eyed. "Drink your milk slowly so that it will digest well." An argument ensued among the children. "That is not the way for brothers and sisters to talk. They must show consideration for each other."

Between times, she lamented her illness, her weakness. But most of the time she patiently instructed her granddaughter in good housekeeping and her grandsons on the neat, dust-laying way of cleaning a floor. "Now, keep the screen door latched, and kill the flies that get in."

On the fifth day, I looked up from the typewriter as Kerty whizzed by. Then Mom hobbled through with the rice paddle in her hand. I heard a scuffle and a whack, but Kerty was tough and refused to make outcry. So clearly I heard Mom say, "Don't you think I'm too old and sick to handle you! No grandson of mine is going to grow up a heathen! Next time I tell you something, it's your grandmother you're dealing with, remember that! I'm not your mother, I'm your *grandmother*."

Dad came in, worried. "She shouldn't get excited. And the little one is too small to be punished. It isn't good, it isn't good."

"It's the best thing in the world," I said, "for both of them."

I reread the last line written and continued typing. In the next room I heard Kerty's voice, bent but not broken, "Yes, ma'am, Grandma."

Late into the night, I heard Mom swapping stories with Dad, and both of them chuckling.

CHAPTER 34

*T*he weeks went by, peaceful, healing. Then suddenly, in great batches, came APO [Army/Air Force Post Office] mail for me. First, under the letterhead of "United States Philippine Island Forces—Marking's Guerrillas," was a "pledge":

10 March 1945
Whereas, This organization, "MARKING'S GUERRILLAS," has been duly inducted into the United States Army; and
Whereas, The fully armed members of this organization will form one regular regiment according to the U.S. Army plan and strength of organization; and
Whereas, Henceforth this regiment will be known and called the "YAY REGIMENT" in honor of our beloved guerrilla mother, YAY B-67, MID, U.S. Army, Phil. Dept., who nursed us, comforted us, bawled us out, and loved us all those years we were hiding in the hills and mountains, and pulled through despite hunger and starvation, ill clad and sick most of the time;
Therefore, we, officers, noncommissioned officers, and enlisted men of this patriotic organization, *do hereby pledge ourselves with undying faith and loyalty to the cause, and that we will continue to fight side by side with our American brothers-in-arms until this war is won.*
And we bind ourselves to this solemn and sacred pledge by affixing hereunto our true signature on this document.
  MARCOS VILLA AGUSTÍN, Commanding
Leon Z. Cabalhin   Armando de La Rosa
José Mapa   Roger Moskaira
Teofilo Salvador   Lucio Penaranda
Roberto Mata   Felipe Vicencio
José Oliveros   Florencio Pérez

There were thirty-three letters from Marking alone. "Our boys are very busy in the field, and the American officers are very proud of them. Some day, you will hear much about this Yay Regiment. About me, I have reformed, and I have reformed because you don't like me anymore." "I am now courting you the hard way, darling, and hope you will forget the past and forgive me for not being so good to you, but there were lots of times that I was very, very good, remember?" "I borrowed a motorcycle and one of the soldier want to ride at my rear so I let him and told him that this is the first ride I have for three years so he must be very careful and hold on and you know what happen? Right away it go *Ptssst* and I saw the American soldier left behind flat on his behind, and I laugh like hell. He is still my good friend." "I am a new man now because I learned a very bitter lesson from you, and I sure will be careful when we meet again. It is that Irish blood in you, I guess." "I guess I will save my pay and buy us a motorcycle for our own, one jeep and one Piper Cub Plane." "We need you really because now we are motherless. You might say that we don't appreciate what you have done for us, therefore the fighting men under the Yay Regiment if granted will continue to fight to Tokyo." "Every WAC [Women's Army Corps member] I see I remember you because of the WAC wearing pants and shirt." "Sending one Jap flag captured by one of your boys here." "I am now a cold-headed fellow and some day you will be proud of me. Also, I am a full-pledged colonel and you cannot throw that in the wastebasket." "No matter where you go, I will find you. Maybe you are Yay, but I am Marking." "There are three things I most love in this world. One is love for my country. One is my love for you. One is my love for our boys." "I am looking at the moon. Even the stars are twinkling. Remember when we were in the mountains and we see the stars falling, you told me to make a wish . . . Tonight maybe a star will fall." "I cannot sleep well. There is nothing on which to put my arm and foot. These girls here are only on-again-off-again you can get them anywhere." "Do you remember Josefina the wife of Fajardo who is buried under the *katmon* tree? She is here very thin and pale and insane. It is a pity for such a beautiful girl. We are all very sorry for her." "I hope I will not become like Josefina the wife of Fajardo who was here a few days ago. True love is sometimes dangerous. I guess I have told you before that Filipinos are very serious about love, they can kill or be killed or go to jail or go crazy. You will be sorry if I go crazy." "From people I have three of your old pictures now, one when they were taking the cast from your leg, one holding your camera looking at the food on the table, one with a cigarette in your left hand. I kiss one of these pictures before I go to bed." "Give me just *one more chance*, darling. You are my only *gold braid*. Remember when it was so lonely in the mountains and you told us stories, among them about the American custom of the den? You can arrange my den in our house as you like it. I don't know yet clearly what it is even if you have explained it to me." "Just one beautiful letter is all I ask. In exchange I will answer *even a hundred letters*. Think of it." "Order just received that I with the Yay Regiment is going farther north. I and one general are going to command this important mission. Darling, if I am out of luck, then let me tell you what I have in my heart. I love you with my whole heart and soul. My spirit will be with you always."

There was a break in the letters. I wondered where Marking and the boys had gone. Over the radio, I heard about guerrillas at Ipo Dam. And suddenly, by APO mail service, came a Jap battle flag, taken at Ipo by the Yay Regiment, and several pieces of printed "evidence." The first was a newspaper clipping with the heads "IPO DAM CAPTURED INTACT—Marking's Guerrillas and 43rd Division Free Manila's Water Source—Marcos Villa Agustín's Men Close Pincers on Several Thousand Japanese Troops Prior to Final Assault":

MACARTHUR'S HEADQUARTERS, May 19.—(AP)—Ipo Dam, largest single source of Manila's water supply, was captured intact late Thursday afternoon by Filipino guerrillas and the 43rd division infantrymen, General MacArthur revealed today.

The dam was mysteriously undamaged, although the Japanese had the opportunity and demolitions sufficient to destroy it. This caused puzzled doughboys to voice that old Pacific war bromide: "You can't tell what the Jap will do except that it usually won't make sense."

A guerrilla force under Col. Marcos V. Agustin, usually called "Marking's Guerrillas," closed the pincers from the north around several thousand Japanese, but the 43rd met harder fighting in slugging the southern jaw shut and killed more than a hundred enemy troops, besides capturing six 20-mm guns.

The final assault on the dam was preceded by the biggest aerial firebomb raids in the history of this war theater, as more than 375 Thunderbolt and Lightning fighters of the 5th Airforce dropped a ton for every ten Japanese along the battle lines Wednesday and Thursday.

Capture of Ipo does not bring its water to Manila immediately, since the Japanese still hold part of the aqueduct route, but it is good news to the 900,000 people who live in the Metropolitan Water District.

The 38th division has moved toward Montalban Dam at Wawa, storming and capturing high ground 3,500 yards northwest of Mount Baytangan against heavy resistance, and killing at least 200 enemy troops in the rugged area.

Along with this I found a commendation from Major General Wing, issued at the headquarters of the 43rd Infantry Division on May 24, 1945:

To: Commanding Officer, "Marking's Guerrillas" YAY REGIMENT
1. With the capture of IPO DAM on 19 May 1945, allied forces in the Philippines culminated one of their most decisive victories.
2. The true significance of this victory does not end with the crushing of the formidable Ipo fortress, but must be evaluated in terms of the health and well-being of the tens of thousands of Filipinos and Americans in the Manila area dependent upon this source for their water supply.
3. The valiant and untiring action of "Marking's Guerrillas" Yay Regiment contributed in a large measure to the success of, and dispatch of, the Battle of IPO DAM.
4. Charged only with conducting a diversionary action to distract the enemy's attention from the main effort, Marking's Forces seized and secured strategic objectives which would otherwise have required costly and protracted action by American forces.
5. It is with great admiration and respect that I extend to all officers and men of "Marking's Guerrillas" Yay Regiment my commendation.

LEONARD F. WING
Major General, U.S. Army, Commanding

The third piece of "evidence" was a formal farewell from General Stark at Guerrilla Headquarters, Norzagaray, Bulacan:

To: All Ranks

Recent events have occurred which necessitate my being transferred from the "Marking's Guerrilla" Forces and the 43rd Division to another Division.

In leaving, I cannot express too strongly my deep appreciation and thanks for the wonderful job you have done in the capture of IPO DAM. The hardships, personal bravery and tactical leadership will never be surpassed. Truly, you have a great fighting unit and I pray that every one of you will receive the awards and recognition due you.

I am taking this opportunity to express my admiration to the officers and men of this splendid force. I hope that in the very near future we can all be together again in our future operations against the Japanese.

Goodbye for the time being and the very best of luck to each and every one of you.

A. N. STARK
Brig. Gen., U.S. Army, Commanding

Marking had gotten his fight.

CHAPTER 35

*E*xcited and happy, Marking wrote his own jumbled report to me, whom he wanted to impress most: "Yay Regiment is now *the talk of the town*. GHQ published it. *Ipo Dam* taken, then *Marking's Yay Regiment lauded,* also 'Yay Regiment Charges Across Dam Against Strong Resistance,' by H. D. Quigg, United Press Correspondent, General MacArthur's Headquarters. The *Second* Yay Regiment is also recognized by the Commander-in-Chief General MacArthur, and soon there will be the *Third* Yay Regiment and that composes a *Yay Brigade.* The Second Yay Regiment is now on the battlefront while the First Yay Regiment which fought in the Dam campaign is resting. They are given good food, show right in our resting camp, we have apples, oranges, coca cola, boxing gloves, baseball, volleyball and basketball. We have everything we need. We have our own Motor Pool and our trucks have a big sign 'Y' that means the Yay Regiment Motor Pool. The boys have good equipments, clothing and everything that the U.S. Army can give. All wounded boys and sick ones were treated in the U.S. Army Hospitals, first class treatment. I know that the U.S. Army is very busy now but not too busy to take good care of us.

"As for me, darling, this man you hate and deserted is a refine gentleman and a polish gentleman too. God, I miss you. I am still not too good in spelling. You do the writing, I will do the fighting. Shall we live unhappily apart because of those foults [sic] of mine? *Foults can be corrected.* No one ever live in this world without foult.

"You also, darling, you have foults, but I will only ignore them even if I want to break your head. Your friends are all sending their regards. I am meeting many of your friends everywhere, I tell everybody all about us in the mountains, in case they don't know. I give everybody full details, after while only I will be the one willing to marry you because of your lost reputation, and it is only fair because as you yourself said all is fair in love and war. You have wonderful friends and they laugh very much when I tell them about our adventures together. I think they are watching to see if what happens. Joe Lansang the newspaperman says it is my duty to make an honest woman out of you and then he laughs and laughs and slaps me on the back. You come back, darling, and fight with your pen and mouth and when you need help just howl for me and I'll knock the hell out of who ever you want me too. Hey, sweetheart, I'm planning to invest to buy a small Printing Press and Linotype for you so you can put up a magazine or paper, I guess you like this because that is your line."

Letter after letter. Some came in the hands of American officers on furlough from the Philippines. A hundred piled up at the chicken farm to the delight of the scandalized old people, who tittered and whispered and quoted juicy passages back and forth. Everywhere I turned, more letters assailed me. Even Mom and Dad leaned sympathetically toward Marking. Lyd wrote, "I'm not relenting, but this is as thrilling as a pulp-magazine love story. I go on record that it's love, if that's the way you like it." It was water on stone, drip-dripping away, wearing me down.

Came a fat envelope, very fat and very carefully registered. Out dropped an army check for five hundred dollars and money orders for seven hundred and fifty dollars.

Wrote Marking: "The five hundred dollars is from me the man you have so cruelly deserted. It is for your birthday because no matter how you treat me I love you very much." In a postscript he added, "You can come back any time you want now."

From the "officers, non-commissioned officers and enlisted men" under the Yay Regiment letterhead, came a laboriously composed nine-page letter explaining the "Yay Trust Love Fund." Cabalhin's hand, Bernie's hand, Nazario's hand—in a phrase here and spelling there, I recognized the literary earmarks of the key officers, who began the explanation with a phrase that made the rest of the letter completely unnecessary: "To *Mammy Yay*, Always First in Our Hearts."

Blinded with tears, I could hardly read the rest except in patches here and there:

"Your memory will never fade for you are right here in our hearts—carved for all eternity. We have missed you terribly. There were times after you left us that we were in trouble. And every time we try to solve our problems, we always asked ourselves—what would have Mammy done under the circumstances? Thus guided, thank God we came thru all right.

"The Old Man is everything to us now, father and mother of our big family, and the Old Man is trying his best and help us in everything. He has made a name for himself as a hero and a fighter, and bolstered the all-time famous organization of Marking's Guerrillas. That was for personally taking a little hill at Spoo, Mt. Quitago, incidentally the objective of the 43rd Division, their main objective. Then the Division yanked him out of the frontlines.

"He has been restless. We know you are still dearest to his heart. And you are dearest to us your sons. You are second to none. As time flies by, he realizes. The fault is his and he accepts it, as gentlemen do. And we love him the more for that. He is more levelheaded and cautious and everything he does is directed toward the fulfillment of his dreams for his boys, his sons and your sons too.

"We have another dream—to see you reunited with us again. We remember. During our three years sojourn in the rugged Sierras you have been our guiding light. You comforted and consoled us when we were low, you advised us when you found it necessary, and you bawled us out—and how!—when we did wrong. Now, in happiness, we want to share it with you. God guiding us, the path ahead will be full of roses. You will and must share it with us in spirit if not in person. Yesterday, 4th of June, for the first time we got our pay, based on U.S. Army federal pay. Everybody is happy, but we miss the ones who fell in battle and we miss you. But we know what keeps you apart from us. We understand. Out of the fullness of our hearts, Oldtimers and Newtimers alike, we have created the Yay Love or Trust Fund. You can get along without it, we guess, but that is not the point. It is the satisfaction we get knowing that we have remembered. We close now with all our love, and with the Old Marking's Guerrillas, now the famous Yay Regiment, we march on to *more victories ahead!*"

Ninety officers signed the letter. I dried my tears and examined the names. At least half of them at one time or another I had snapped at or scolded. At least a third, I had taken aside, one by one, for a heart-to-heart talk in the old miserable camps. A score I had loved more than flesh and blood, for they were such fine, strapping, honorable men. Who could have failed to take pride in them?

On the heels of their extravagant tribute came more letters from Marking, written in his impetuous, one-paragraph, both-sides-of the-page way.

"We are sending you a *brigadier general's pay*. This will be your allowance every month, *every month*. I know you want to run around. I heard a jeep there costs three hundred dollars. Get one and try and break your neck. I almost broke mine yesterday, how sorry you will be to lose a best man like me. Oh, darling, how I miss you. I admitted my foult already. Why don't you *come home?* Darling, if anybody tells you anything, yes, it is true, when you first left I didn't care what happened to me and I did on and on business with women but they come like hotcakes because of who I am and how much pay I get and now I chase them away because maybe you will come back and I don't want you to catch me and leave me again, I will die if you do.

"Yesterday we courtmarshalled Seneres for giving ammunition and petrol to the civilian without authority. While the court goes on I can see some members of the Court geegling and looking at me and when I say it I say *court must be called to order.* The members of the court are Lucio, Bernie, Roger, Cabalhin, Nicomedes Cristóbal, my cousin, as the defense counsel and Attorney Roger, my cousin, as Judge Advocate. I saw the boys passing a card and later it was turned out to be the card that you sent to Lyd and what you write there is: '*Hoy, Lyd. It's got real rocks and water and everything. We can make a last stand in the heart of Los Angeles.*' I look close and it is a restaurant and the whole front of the building is full of waterfalls and ferns. Now, after the boys handed me this card, I also read it, so I too geegle and then the whole members of the Court geegles with me and also the accused. The members of the Court say loudly, *Mammy is still the real fighter,* and I second the motion, *that's right boys,* and our Courtmarshall was all upside down and Seneres was dismissed by pardoning his guilt because its his first offence and besides he just got married. Honey, send some postcards also to our boys, they will feel better and not forgotten. *Send me one.*"

I tried to close my heart against all letters.

Came more. "Yesterday I went to see President Osmeña," wrote Marking, "about the pay of our privates which is but eighteen pesos when Osmeña promised one hundred pesos. I show him his proclamation signed by him. He answers me that he signed because he thought so and so this and that. Do you think that what I am now doing is right? Hon, I don't give a damn what will happen to me because I will fight for the right of my boys till hell and gone. I will fight also for the orphans of those that were killed before the Liberation. I will not stop till the future of these widows and their fatherless little ones is assured. I have to fight the Japs and also to fight for these people. Darling, I need you so much to help me. This is your *kind* of a fight. About politics, I just keep my temper because I say to myself that I am not a politician or I say if I lose my temper again someone will lose their teeth. So I mind my own army business which is not politics. Yes, darling, I have really reformed and I know what reformed is. I lost my right arm when you left."

And so I broke down.

I wrote light flippant letters, filled with news notes, remarks, odds and ends.

By APO return mail came Marking's protest: "Don't write about things. Write about *us*. You have already forgotten about our personal, private affair. Don't write me all about this and that. *Talk about us.* Just call me darling, even once call me honey."

So I assured him that whether I returned or not, at least I was still faithful to him, and I racked my brains for items interesting to him that would not be classified as "this and that."

On the heels of more letters came his return-mail protest again: "Don't say this that you said in your letter: *I am faithful to you because I am too damn busy to be promiscuous.* Darling, it seems to me your faithfulness is not because you love me but because of not enough time to do other things. *If you get another man in your life I hope and pray to God that something will get me then and die. I want to be dead when that time comes because I cannot suffer more.* For us Filipinos, love is a serious matter. We die for our woman."

I stopped being flippant, and his protests died down. Contentedly he wrote, "I just meet this morning Major General Chase who will be my Commanding Officer here where I am for the Division of which we were an element will move for a rest. This General says that General Krueger have spoken very well about the Yay Regiments, soon to be a brigade when the roster of the Third is approved. As for me, *I am still lonely.* Darling, I like your joke that you will get some false teeth and sink them in some fat millionaire and not let go until you shake him loose from his coin for the sake of the orphans here in the Philippines, but joke or no joke, don't joke me like that. I guess we can take care of our own orphans as biting millionaires you will get yourself sued in court."

Water on stone, the letters wore me down into nostalgia, into loneliness.

And the mail service never left me to myself.

"General Roxas brought me this afternoon to see General MacArthur," wrote Marking. "We were with the General about two hours. He shook hands with me for about *fifty seconds*. He put his left hand on my right shoulder and said, 'My boy, you have done a splendid job and done a lot for your country. I am proud of you and you deserve all the recognition that is due you. Keep up the good work. I will decorate you with the distengues service cross very soon and you deserve it.' Now, darling, after this decoration I will ask him to permit me for a leave for about a month to go there to you." My hair rose.

And among the letters was a letter from Lucio, the tip-off: "What fun, Miss Yay, to be with you in the States. The Old Man has left us for abroad, anyway it is for the good of the outfit."

Marking's last letter bore a Navy postmark instead of the usual Army postmark. In it he said, "Soon will be our third anniversary, in August. I am requesting you please to dedicate from August 7 to August 24 exclusively to the thought only of me. Please stay with your parents, resting and thinking of me, not working or going any place. This means very much to me, that in memory of our three years together and of our hardships and our happiness in the mountains, you will spend this time in one place."

Transparent.

Transparent as hell.

If that man ever gets near me again, I thought, I'll teach him another bitter lesson. I'll teach him a lesson he'll never forget. I'll marry him.

He came in all his glory, in the full uniform of an American colonel, complete with shiny eagles. He came on an army transport, by special leave of General MacArthur himself. And my heart did tricks when I saw him—not for his magnificence but because it was he.

I did marry him. We went to Mexico, where an American attorney, Roche, and a Mexican attorney, Amador, tried to untangle the legal mess of Marking's common-law marriage (five children) and my previous one (three children). Then, since time was short, we were wed by proxy. We left the two lawyers in El Paso, flipping coins to see who would be the bride and who the groom. We had our picture taken, to preserve our happiness forever.

Then, all wars ended, we started home, to build the peace.

TIMELINE OF EVENTS IN THE PHILIPPINES DURING WORLD WAR II

December 7, 1941 (December 8 across the dateline in the Philippines) Japanese attack Pearl Harbor in Hawaii and Clark Field in the Philippines.

December 8, 1941 Japanese invasion forces land in various parts of the Philippines. Filipino and American forces withdraw to Bataan and Corregidor.

December 10, 1941 The guerrilla movement or resistance movement in North Luzon begins.

December 26, 1941 General Douglas MacArthur declares Manila an "open city," and all elements of military and/or American government in the city are removed.

December 27, 1941 Japanese bomb Intramuros in Manila.

January 2, 1942 Japanese forces occupy Manila.

February 1942 Marcos "Marking" Agustín is a fugitive, hiding in Rizal Province. He founds a resistance group, the Marking Guerrillas.

February 20, 1942 President Manuel Quezon and family leave Corregidor by submarine for Australia.

March 12, 1942 General MacArthur and family escape to Australia.

April 9, 1942 General Jonathan Wainwright surrenders Filipino-American forces to General Masaharu Homma. Captured soldiers forced to march to POW camp (Bataan Death March).

May 6, 1942 President Quezon surrenders Corregidor, which marks the end of the first phase of the war in the Philippines.

April 8, 1943 A captured guerrilla brings Marking a letter from the Japanese authorities calling for his surrender and voluntary participation in the rebuilding of the Philippines.

April 18, 1943	Japanese storm Marking's camp as a response to his refusal to surrender.
October 14, 1943	Japanese puppet Philippine republic established. Jose P. Laurel appointed president by Japanese.
August 1, 1944	Death of President Quezon.
October 20, 1944	U.S. Army lands in Leyte followed by other liberation forces landings in Mindoro and Lingayen Gulf.
October 23, 1944	Philippine commonwealth reestablished with Sergio Osmeña as president.
February 7, 1945	Liberation of Manila from Japanese forces.
March 2, 1945	American paratroopers retake Corregidor.
May 2, 1945	Yay Panlilio and her children arrive in San Pedro, California.
July 4, 1945	General MacArthur declares liberation of the Philippines.
July 4, 1946	U.S. recognition of Philippine republic.

Compiled by Candice Williams
Indiana University, Bloomington

GLOSSARY

anahau — a type of palm tree
banca — boat
barrio — district, village
bayong — bag made from palm leaves
bodega — warehouse
bolo — machete
calesa — horse-drawn carriage
carabao — water buffalo
cargador — porter
cavan — container used to store rice, a measuring unit of rice
cogon — type of grass
compadre — friend (male)
dalagita — maiden, young girl
ganta — unit of measure for grain
hija — term of endearment, daughter in Spanish
jitney — (also *jeepney*) a type of jeep transport
kaingin — clearing, land used for farming
kalaw — a type of bird
kawali — frying pan
kingki — lamp, petroleum lamp
kubo — hut, shelter
lola — grandmother
maganda — beautiful

mestiza/mestizo	person of mixed racial ancestry
pala	no direct translation; indicates surprise
palay	unharvested rice
paltik	homemade gun
papag	bed
pasikat	showing off, a show
pasyal	stroll
sampaguita	small white flower
segurista	someone who does things only when certain of success
sitios	sites or districts
suapang	greedy
sumbong	complaint
talahib	coarse grass
tanpipi	(also *tampipi*) bag
tapa	salted meat
tuyo	dried fish

ABOUT THE EDITOR

Denise Cruz is an assistant professor of English and American Studies at Indiana University, Bloomington. Her current research focuses on transpacific Filipina and Filipino writers who published in the United States and the Philippines during the first half of the twentieth century.

www.ingramcontent.com/pod-product-compliance
Lightning Source LLC
Chambersburg PA
CBHW020638300426
44112CB00007B/164